Library of New Testament Studies

661

Formerly the Journal for the Study of the New Testament Supplement series

Editor
Chris Keith

Editorial Board
Dale C. Allison, Lynn H. Cohick, R. Alan Culpepper, Craig A. Evans, Jennifer Eyl, Robert Fowler, Simon J. Gathercole, Juan Hernández Jr, John S. Kloppenborg, Michael Labahn, Matthew V. Novenson, Love L. Sechrest, Robert Wall, Catrin H. Williams, Brittany E. Wilson

Reading Acts Theologically

Steve Walton

LONDON • NEW YORK • OXFORD • NEW DELHI • SYDNEY

T&T CLARK
Bloomsbury Publishing Plc
50 Bedford Square, London, WC1B 3DP, UK
1385 Broadway, New York, NY 10018, USA
29 Earlsfort Terrace, Dublin 2, Ireland

BLOOMSBURY, T&T CLARK and the T&T Clark logo are trademarks of
Bloomsbury Publishing Plc

First published in Great Britain 2022
Paperback edition published 2024

Copyright © Steve Walton, 2022

Steve Walton has asserted his right under the Copyright, Designs and
Patents Act, 1988, to be identified as Author of this work.

For legal purposes the Acknowledgements on pp. vi–vii constitute an
extension of this copyright page.

All rights reserved. No part of this publication may be reproduced or transmitted in any
form or by any means, electronic or mechanical, including photocopying,
recording, or any information storage or retrieval system, without prior
permission in writing from the publishers.

Bloomsbury Publishing Plc does not have any control over, or responsibility for, any
third-party websites referred to or in this book. All internet addresses given in this
book were correct at the time of going to press. The author and publisher regret any
inconvenience caused if addresses have changed or sites have ceased to exist, but
can accept no responsibility for any such changes.

A catalogue record for this book is available from the British Library.

Library of Congress Cataloging-in-Publication Data
Names: Walton, Steve, 1955– author.
Title: Reading Acts theologically / Steve Walton.
Description: London ; New York : T&T Clark, 2022. | Series: The library of New Testament
studies, 2513–8790 ; 661 | Includes bibliographical references and index. |
Summary: "Steve Walton collects several of his key essays into an expansive and coherent
perspective, focusing on the theological perspective of Acts while considering the book's
nature and focus, its portrait of the early Christian communities and their mission in the
culturally varied first-century world, and its major theological themes"– Provided by publisher.
Identifiers: LCCN 2021056144 (print) | LCCN 2021056145 (ebook) |
ISBN 9780567702821 (hb) | ISBN 9780567702869 | ISBN 9780567702838 (epdf) |
ISBN 9780567702852 (epub) Subjects: LCSH: Bible. Acts–Criticism, interpretation, etc. |
Bible. Acts–Theology.
Classification: LCC BS2625.52 .W355 2022 (print) | LCC BS2625.52 (ebook)
| DDC 226.6/06–dc23/eng/20211228
LC record available at https://lccn.loc.gov/2021056144
LC ebook record available at https://lccn.loc.gov/2021056145

ISBN: HB: 978-0-5677-0282-1
PB: 978-0-5677-0286-9
ePDF: 978-0-5677-0283-8
ePUB: 978-0-5677-0285-2

Series: Library of New Testament Studies, volume 661

ISSN 2513-8790

Typeset by Newgen KnowledgeWorks Pvt. Ltd., Chennai, India

To find out more about our authors and books visit www.bloomsbury.com
and sign up for our newsletters.

Contents

Acknowledgements	vi
List of Abbreviations	viii

Part I Looking at Acts

1	Reading Acts Theologically	3
2	The Acts – of God? What Is the 'Acts of the Apostles' All About?	15
3	Doing Theology Lukewise: Luke as Theologian and Storyteller	31

Part II The Believing Communities and Their World

4	Calling the Church Names: Learning about Christian Identity from Acts	45
5	Primitive Communism in Acts? Does Acts Present the Community of Goods (2:44–45; 4:32–35) as Mistaken?	63
6	A Tale of Two Perspectives? The Place of the Temple in Acts	75
7	Deciding about Deciding: Early Christian Communal Decision-Making in Acts	89
8	Trying Paul or Trying Rome? Judges and Accused in the Roman Trials of Paul in Acts	107
9	What Does 'Mission' in Acts Mean in Relation to the 'Powers That Be'?	123

Part III Theological Themes in Acts

10	Jesus, Present and/or Absent? The Presence and Presentation of Jesus as a Character in the Book of Acts	145
11	Identity and Christology: The Ascended Jesus in the Book of Acts	161
12	'The Heavens Opened': Cosmological and Theological Transformation in Luke and Acts	177
13	Turning Anthropology Right Side Up: Seeing Human Life and Existence Lukewise	191

Bibliography	211
Index of Biblical and Other Ancient Sources	231
Index of Subjects	255
Index of Names	265

Acknowledgements

The essays in this book have appeared in many different places over a period of almost twenty years as I have been working on the Word Biblical Commentary on Acts, and represent some key lines of my thinking about Acts over that substantial period of gestation. I am thankful to those who have kindly invited me to present many of these as conference or seminar papers, or commissioned them for edited collections, over that period.

I have lightly revised these essays for this book by correcting errors, bringing citation style into conformity with the *SBL Handbook of Style* (2nd ed.), spelling and grammar into line with UK English conventions, and adding details of subsequent publication of sources cited (notably, doctoral theses). Where I have cited an essay of mine which also appears in this book, I have added page details within this volume, for ease of reference.

I am grateful to Chris Keith for accepting this volume for the Library of New Testament Studies series, and to Dominic Mattos, Sarah Blake and their colleagues at Bloomsbury T&T Clark for their help and support in bringing it to publication. Diane L. Hakala did a great job in preparing the indices, for which I am very thankful.

I gratefully acknowledge permission to republish these essays here from the original publishers, as follows:

Chapter 2 "The Acts – of God? What Is the 'Acts of the Apostles' All About?" *EvQ* 80 (2008): 291–306, by kind permission of E. J. Brill.

Chapter 3 "Doing Theology Lukewise: Luke as Theologian and Storyteller" was my inaugural professorial lecture at St Mary's University, Twickenham, and has not previously been published.

Chapter 4 "Calling the Church Names: Learning about Christian Identity from Acts." *PRSt* 41 (2014): 223–41, by kind permission of the senior editor, Prof. Mikeal C. Parsons.

Chapter 5 "Primitive Communism in Acts? Does Acts Present the Community of Goods (2:44–45; 4:32–35) as Mistaken?" *EvQ* 80 (2008): 99–111, by kind permission of E. J. Brill.

Chapter 6 "A Tale of Two Perspectives? The Place of the Temple in Acts." Pages 135–49 in *Heaven on Earth: The Temple in Biblical Theology*. Edited by T. Desmond Alexander and Simon Gathercole. Carlisle/Milton Keynes: Paternoster (an imprint of Authentic Media Ltd.), 2004 (Copyright © T. D. Alexander and S. J. Gathercole), by permission of Authentic Media Ltd.

Chapter 7 "Deciding about Deciding: Early Christian Communal Decision-Making in Acts." Pages 27–49 in *Engaging Ethically in a Strange New World: A View from Down Under*. Edited by Michael Bräutigam and Gillian Asquith. Australian College of

Theology monograph series. Eugene, OR: Wipf & Stock, 2019, by kind permission of Wipf and Stock Publishers. http://www.wipfandstock.com.

Chapter 8 "Trying Paul or Trying Rome? Judges and Accused in the Roman Trials of Paul in Acts." Pages 122–41 in *Luke-Acts and Empire: Essays in Honor of Robert L. Brawley*. Edited by David Rhoads, David Esterline and Jae Won Lee. Pickwick Theological Monograph Series. Eugene, OR: Pickwick, 2010, by kind permission of Wipf and Stock Publishers. http://www.wipfandstock.com.

Chapter 9 "What Does 'Mission' in Acts Mean in Relation to the 'Powers That Be'?" *JETS* 55 (2012): 537–56, by kind permission of the editor, Prof. Dorian G. Coover-Cox.

Chapter 10 "Jesus, Present and/or Absent? The Presence and Presentation of Jesus as a Character in the Book of Acts." Pages 123–40 in *Characters and Characterization in Luke-Acts*. Edited by Frank E. Dicken and Julia A. Snyder. LNTS 548. London: Bloomsbury T&T Clark, 2016, by kind permission of Bloomsbury Publishing plc.

Chapter 11 "Identity and Christology: The Ascended Jesus in the Book of Acts." Pages 130–48 in *The Earliest Perceptions of Jesus in Context: Essays in Honour of John Nolland*. Edited by Aaron W. White, Craig A. Evans and David Wenham. LNTS 566. London: Bloomsbury T&T Clark, 2018, by kind permission of Bloomsbury Publishing plc.

Chapter 12 "'The Heavens Opened': Cosmological and Theological Transformation in Luke and Acts." Pages 60–73 in *Cosmology and New Testament Theology*. Edited by Jonathan T. Pennington and Sean M. McDonough. LNTS 355. London: T&T Clark, 2008, by kind permission of Bloomsbury Publishing plc.

Chapter 13 "Turning Anthropology Right Side Up: Seeing Human Life and Existence Lukewise." Pages 99–119 in *Anthropology and New Testament Theology*. Edited by Jason S. Maston and Benjamin E. Reynolds. LNTS 529. London: Bloomsbury T&T Clark, 2018, by kind permission of Bloomsbury Publishing plc.

September 2021

Abbreviations

Abbreviations not listed below are taken from: Billie Jean Collins, Bob Buller and John F. Kutsko, eds, *The SBL Handbook of Style for Ancient Near Eastern, Biblical and Early Christian Studies*, 2nd ed. (Atlanta, GA: SBL, 2014).

BibStL	Biblical Studies Library
BTCB	Brazos Theological Commentary on the Bible
JPTSup	*Journal of Pentecostal Theology* Supplement series
JSJSup	*Journal for the Study of Judaism in the Persian, Hellenistic, and Roman Periods* Supplement series
MisSt	*Mission Studies*
Philos. Trans. Royal Soc. A	*Philosophical Transactions of the Royal Society of London. Series A, Mathematical and Physical Sciences*
ProcC	Proclamation Commentaries
RGRW	Religions in the Graeco-Roman World

Part I

Looking at Acts

1

Reading Acts Theologically

I. What Is 'Reading Theologically'?

The book collects a number of my essays on Acts over some years under the title 'Reading Acts Theologically'. But what does that mean? In this age of methodological diversity in New Testament Studies, it is vital to identify and locate a scholar's approach to a topic, and this introductory essay aims to do that. I shall first discuss some approaches to reading the New Testament identified by their proponents as 'theological', briefly sketching those approaches, and identifying the interpretive posture they adopt towards the New Testament, and considering cautions for such approaches. I shall then note the role of a 'rule of faith' in reading Scripture theologically, before going on to apply this approach specifically to reading Acts. This chapter concludes by outlining how each of the essays in this volume attempt to read Acts theologically.[1]

I.a. Theological Reading of Scripture

In recent times a number of scholars have named their approaches to reading the Bible as 'theological reading of Scripture'.[2] Each of the three key words of this phrase is important in grasping such approaches.

To begin at the end, such scholars study *Scripture*, rather than the Bible as a collection of ancient texts. This may seem a fine distinction, but it is not. To approach these books as Scripture is to regard them as documents of a living faith community which continue to be received as authoritative, rather than merely as ancient documents of a past faith community. When Christians today read Scripture they are not reading someone else's mail, but listening to God's voice through these sacred texts addressing the one church throughout history and cultures.[3] To call the sixty-six books of the Bible 'Scripture' is

---

[1] I am grateful to Chris Tilling for reading and commenting insightfully on a draft of this essay; he should not, of course, be held responsible for the final product.
[2] For helpful introductions, see Stephen E. Fowl, *Theological Interpretation of Scripture*, Cascade Companions (Eugene, OR: Cascade, 2009); Daniel J. Treier, *Introducing Theological Interpretation of Scripture* (Nottingham: Apollos, 2008).
[3] Joel B. Green, *Practicing Theological Interpretation: Engaging Biblical Texts for Faith and Formation* (Grand Rapids, MI: Baker Academic, 2011), 17–18.

also to approach them as having a coherent overall message, a grand narrative running from creation to new creation, to which the individual authors' voices contribute distinctive perspectives and themes. To change the analogy, it is like listening to an orchestra, where different instruments bring their own pitch, tone, and sound together into a coherent whole under the baton of the conductor.

Secondly, such scholars engage in *reading*. By that, I mean that they seek to engage with these texts as each coherent and communicative. By contrast with atomistic approaches which break down books, sections, or even individual sentences and clauses, into 'tradition' and 'redaction', and regard that as having done the entire job of interpretation,[4] these readers seek the coherent overall perspective of the clause, sentence, section and book – and, indeed, the corpus of an author's work, such as Luke and Acts, or the Pauline letters. This is not to suggest that scholars adopting other approaches to reading the biblical texts do not do this; it is to say that this is a hallmark of theological reading of Scripture. If a book contains material which is in tension with other material on first blush, these approaches aim to seek and find the overall perspective within which the various kinds of material cohere. To accomplish that requires patient and persistent reading and re-reading, to find a satisfying coherence in tune with the text, and to avoid coming to over-hasty and jarring 'coherence'.[5]

Thirdly, these approaches are *theological*, in that they seek to learn about the central topics of Scripture, namely God, and God's engagement with humanity and the world.[6] These approaches focus more on the substance of Scripture than its sources, more on the teaching of Scripture than theories about its origins and editing, and more on the message of Scripture than its mode of communication. I expand on the 'more' in each of those claims below, but here it is vital to notice that these approaches are interested in what Scripture communicates, generally because the scholars reading theologically are Christian people wanting to enable today's churches to hear and respond faithfully to the message of Scripture. In academic settings, reading Scripture this way leads to critiquing the processes by which we read and 'do theology' too. That is not to say that only Christians can engage in these approaches, or that the Christians who do so engage have nothing to learn from scholars who choose other approaches or who do not share their faith (e.g. see below on historical criticism). Any sympathetic reader can read Scripture theologically: they may or may not agree with what they discover, but they will seek to listen accurately to the voice of the text.[7]

Those who have read almost any biblical scholarship over the last 250 years will recognize that these approaches differ from the historical-critical paradigm which

---

[4] For a relatively recent example in relation to Acts, see Gerd Lüdemann, *Early Christianity according to the Traditions in Acts: A Commentary* (London: SCM, 1989).

[5] For a fine brief discussion of seeking such harmony and its limits, with examples from the synoptic Gospels, see R. T. France, "Inerrancy and New Testament Exegesis," *Them* 1 (1975): 12–18, here 16–18.

[6] Cf. Joshua W. Jipp, "The Beginnings of a Theology of Luke-Acts: Divine Activity and Human Response," *JTI* 8 (2014): 23–44, arguing that theology is itself necessarily self-involving, and that a theology of Luke-Acts is certainly so.

[7] E.g. Robert C. Tannehill observes that Luke calls believers to continue to evangelize Jewish people, although, 'I would not myself advocate a Christian evangelistic mission to Jews' (*The Narrative Unity of Luke-Acts: A Literary Interpretation*, 2 vols. (Minneapolis, MN: Fortress, [1986] 1990), 2:3).

dominates that period. That paradigm is dominated by questions about the 'then' and 'there' of the biblical texts, asking what the author(s) communicates, to whom they communicate it, why they express themselves thus, what geographical, cultural, historical and social situation(s) are addressed, and so on. Such questions are important to theological readers of Scripture too, to ensure, as far as we are able, that the reading of the text proposed is in tune with the author's and first audience's engagement with the text. This rules out immediately some proposed readings of Scripture today which see (e.g.) the European Union in the book of Revelation, or justification for building a wall along the USA's southern border with Mexico to keep migrants out. '*A text cannot mean what it could never have meant for its original readers/hearers*'[8] is a pardonable overstatement, for texts can and do imply things which their authors might not have seen. However, Fee and Stuart here express an important safeguard against eisegesis in reading Scripture – we cannot expect Scripture to speak *directly* about many features of life today which did not exist in the time it was written.

Many of the skills and questions of classic historical criticism are thus important for reading Scripture theologically, for the texts are products of particular times, places, people, languages and cultural situations. These include: engagement with the Hebrew, Aramaic and Greek texts; decisions about which readings are most likely to be closest to the autograph where manuscripts and versions differ; analysis of structure, syntax and grammar; identification of the genre and 'flow' of a section or book; where possible, consideration of how the author has adapted sources (e.g. in reading the synoptic Gospels); and understanding of the social, cultural, historical and geographical settings of events, authors and first readers.[9] All these apply as far as the present state of knowledge allows; good interpreters will acknowledge the limits of that knowledge, and the provisionality of their reading of the text. The necessities of academic scholarship can push today's interpreters to make confident (sometimes over-confident) claims, for that is how scholarly careers are made (or not!). But good scholarship acknowledges degrees of confidence about our conclusions, indicating what we are more confident of, what is provisional, what is possible, and what is flying a kite.

Theological readers do not stop with the questions and issues of historical criticism. The 'more than' in theological reading is to engage with *the message understood from the texts*, read with sensitivity to language, syntax and grammar, genre, and so on. The message conveyed by individual clauses, sentences, paragraphs, sections, and books will be seen in the setting of the whole of Scripture, identifying where that message seems in tension with the message of other parts of the text. The focus will be on asking what is being communicated about God, God's action, and God's purposes for humanity and the world. The ultimate aim of theological reading is a scriptural worldview (including the lifestyle which goes with that way of seeing the world), assembled from the variety of biblical literature from different times, people, and places.

---

[8] Gordon D. Fee and Douglas K. Stuart, *How to Read the Bible for All Its Worth*, 4th ed. (Grand Rapids, MI: Zondervan, 2014), 34 (their italics).

[9] For an excellent introductory treatment of the place of these disciplines in exegesis, see Michael J. Gorman, *Elements of Biblical Exegesis: A Basic Guide for Students and Ministers*, 3rd ed. (Grand Rapids, MI: Baker Academic, 2020).

I.b. Interpretive Posture

At the heart of reading Scripture theologically stands the question of how we regard the texts we seek to interpret. Postmodernism in particular has underlined for us that there is no such things as neutrality in reading texts, for we all come with an agenda, and it is vital to be self-aware about that agenda and its potential for illuminating and hiding the text's message.[10] For some modern readers, Scripture is treated with suspicion, at least in part, as embodying ideas to which the interpreter is opposed. Often this opposition stems from perceiving such ideas as damaging to particular groups of people, such as women, people in poverty, particular ethnic groups, or those living in situations which have been or are presently under colonial domination. Theological readers have much to learn from such approaches, as they have from historical-critical approaches, but their posture towards Scripture is different, embodying a hermeneutic of consent or trust. Joel Green uses Umberto Eco's 'model reader' to express this idea, the kind of reader who engages with the text sympathetically and co-operatively.[11] A model reader will seek to understand and engage with the texts on their own terms, as far as possible. Michael Gorman observes that this is an ancient approach, rooted in the patristic period and continued in medieval and early modern times. Thus theological readers find themselves listening with care to how earlier readers, including pre-modern and pre-critical readers, have read Scripture.[12] This entails not privileging historical-critical study over other forms of reading of Scripture in which a Chrysostom or Aquinas or Calvin might engage.

I.c. Cautions

The dangers of theological reading are similar to those in these earlier readings of Scripture, principally failing to listen well enough to the text in its ancient setting, but rather seeing it only through today's cultural and historical spectacles, or the perspective of one modern culture to the exclusion of others. Allegorical readings of Scripture, much loved and practised by pre-critical interpreters such as Origen or Aquinas need to be tempered by the gains of historical criticism. To engage fruitfully with Scripture today is not to engage uncritically with older reading of Scripture, and nor is it to privilege the concerns of our time, place and culture. Careful listening to Scripture and to the setting in which we interpret Scripture are both vital to good interpretation. Karl Barth is frequently misquoted as saying that Christians should have the Bible in one hand and the newspaper in the other, suggesting that the two have equal standing. In fact, he said, 'Take your Bible and take your newspaper, and read both. But interpret newspapers from your Bible!'[13] For a theological reader such as Barth, the control in

---

[10] Anthony C. Thiselton, *New Horizons in Hermeneutics* (London: HarperCollins, 1992), 50–1; cf. the earlier, not dissimilar, perspective of Rudolf Bultmann, "Is Exegesis without Presuppositions Possible?," in *Existence and Faith: Shorter Writings of Rudolf Bultmann*, ed. Schubert M. Ogden (London: Hodder & Stoughton, 1961), 289–96, 314–15.
[11] Green, *Practicing*, 18–20; Umberto Eco, *The Role of the Reader: Explorations in the Semiotics of Text*, Advances in Semiotics (London: Hutchinson, 1981), 7–11.
[12] Gorman, *Elements*, 20–2.
[13] Eberhard Busch, ed. *Barth in Conversation: Volume 2, 1963* (Louisville, KY: Westminster John Knox, 2018), 7.

this conversation is Scripture, for Scripture is God's self-testimony and God's testimony to Christ. Certainly, the questions of the modern world, or a particular cultural setting, can and do cause readers to see things in Scripture which have not been previously noticed, but theological readers will also – and primarily – want to keep listening to Scripture for the questions and issues which are its focus: those, rather than the short-term concerns of a particular time and place, will drive theological reading.

I.d. The Role of a 'Rule of Faith'

Given that many readings of a text are possible, how do theological readers decide if a particular reading of Scripture, a scriptural book, or a section of a scriptural book, is to be welcomed and received by the believing communities? A classic answer has been to appeal to a 'rule of faith', a credal statement (or statements) which defines how Christians have understood Scripture's witness.[14] The ecumenical creeds define classic Christian understanding of Scripture by contrast with, for example, mainstream Jewish understanding of the Hebrew Bible. Christian theological readers receive the Hebrew Bible as the Old Testament Scriptures as witness to Jesus Christ, and interpret those texts in conversation with the New Testament Scriptures. The New Testament authors themselves model how to engage with the Old Testament Christologically by citing and alluding to it frequently.

How should theological readers see the relationship of a rule of faith and Scripture? The status of a rule of faith is as a summary of the teaching of Scripture, and it is always subject to revision if the teaching of Scripture is seen to be different. Thus the Church of England's Article XXI 'Of the Authority of General Councils' asserts:

> [W]hen [General Councils] be gathered together (forasmuch as they be an assembly of men, whereof all be not governed with the Spirit and Word of God), they may err, and sometimes have erred, even in things pertaining unto God. Wherefore things ordained by them as necessary to salvation have neither strength nor authority, unless it may be declared that they be taken out of holy Scripture.

The Anglican Reformers thus place human formulations of the content of Christian faith as secondary to Scripture. That said, Article VIII commends the Nicene and Apostles' Creeds on the ground that 'they may be proved by most certain warrants of Holy Scripture'. The venerable nature and widespread acceptance of these creeds gives pause to any who wish to argue that a point in them is out of tune with Scripture – but, in principle, it would be possible to challenge a credal statement on the basis that it misunderstands Scripture.[15]

For this reason a rule of faith does not provide a shortcut in scriptural interpretation which allows us to decide how to interpret a given passage, a book or the whole of

---

[14] See the nuanced and helpful discussion in Green, *Practicing*, 71–98.
[15] See Green, *Practicing*, 81–95 for a thoughtful discussion of body-soul dualism (which Green rejects) in the light of apparent tensions between human monism and the assumptions of the ecumenical creeds.

Scripture. A rule of faith is historically later than the writing of the scriptural testimony, and it would be inappropriate to 'read back' a later rule into Scripture.[16]

II. What Is 'Reading Acts Theologically'?

Given this brief sketch of reading Scripture theologically, what does it look like when we turn to reading Acts in this way? It means reading in sympathy with the text, employing what Kevin Vanhoozer, building on Augustine, calls a hermeneutic of love, a 'mutual relation of self-giving between text and reader'.[17] Such an approach entails respecting the otherness of the text, and listening as carefully and accurately as possible to its voice, and avoiding imposing readerly ways of thinking as much as can be done. To read in this way involves sympathetic engagement with the aims of Acts, the God whom Acts portrays, the divine mission which Acts describes, and the way of life to which Acts calls readers.

To read in sympathy with *the aims of Acts* involves, of course, seeking and finding those aims. I am unsure that anyone ever writes with just one purpose, and thus consider that the quest for *the* purpose of Acts (or Luke-Acts) may well be fruitless.[18] Nevertheless, Acts expresses a cluster of key ideas which invite readers into its symbolic world, particularly to do with the way the God of Israel has now revealed himself in and through Jesus and by the Spirit, and the implications this revelation has for drawing all people – gentile and Jew – into God's people. Acts 1:8 is often seen as a 'theme verse' for the book, focusing attention on the work of the Spirit, and the believing community's mission which spreads in growing circles through 'Jerusalem, Judaea, Samaria, and to the end of the earth'. That mission is incomplete at the end of Acts, for 'the end of the earth' is simply a way of saying 'everywhere' (cf. Isa 49:6).[19] On this view, Acts aims to invite and draw its readers into God's mission by educating them about God's actions and his people's responses in the earliest days of that mission.

To read in sympathy with *the God whom Acts portrays* entails readiness to listen carefully to Luke's articulation of the character of God, and the ways this God is now known in Jesus the Messiah, and by means of the Spirit's work.[20] The startling way in which Luke's characters identify Jesus as sharing the place previously occupied by YHWH, the God of Israel, alone is remarkable, and represents a major 'mutation' of the faith of Israel.[21] Notably, Jesus is the one who pours out the Spirit (2:33), whereas in

---

[16] A major frustration with Jaroslav Pelikan, *Acts*, BTCB (Grand Rapids, MI: Brazos, 2005), is that, in effect, he treats Acts as a commentary on the ecumenical creeds.
[17] Kevin J. Vanhoozer, *First Theology: God, Scripture and Hermeneutics* (Leicester: Apollos, 2002), 231; cf. Alan Jacobs, "Love," *DTIB*, 465–7.
[18] Cf. Robert Maddox, *The Purpose of Luke-Acts*, SNTW (Edinburgh: T&T Clark, 1982).
[19] In other words, I do not think that 'the end of the earth' is Rome, where Paul is at the end of the book. See discussion in my forthcoming commentary on Acts on 1:8.
[20] On God in Acts, see Ling Cheng, *The Characterisation of God in Acts: The Indirect Portrayal of an Invisible Character*, PBM (Milton Keynes: Paternoster, 2011); Christine H. Aarflot, *God (in) Acts: The Characterization of God in the Acts of the Apostles* (Eugene, OR: Pickwick, 2020).
[21] See the work of Larry Hurtado, summarized well in his Larry W. Hurtado, *Honoring the Son: Jesus in Earliest Christian Devotional Practice*, Snapshots (Bellingham, WA: Lexham, 2018). On Acts, see

second temple Jewish understanding, to do this is reserved to YHWH alone. Thus Jesus is one to whom it is appropriate to address prayer (e.g. 7:59), and can be appropriately called ὁ κύριος 'the Lord', a designation previously reserved in the context of Israelite faith for YHWH (e.g. 9:17). The Spirit in Acts bears marks of personality and being a locus of will and decision-making, too. In common with other New Testament writings, in Acts the Spirit is not addressed in prayer, but is clearly portrayed as God in action.[22] Learning from Luke about this God expands first-century Jewish understandings of God, and corrects and reshapes Graeco-Roman perceptions of their gods (not least in Lystra, 14:8–18, and Athens, 17:16–34).[23] Luke provides many of the building blocks of later Christian articulation of a doctrine of God, although it is John and Paul to whom the Fathers primarily look in developing what becomes trinitarian theology.

To read in sympathy with *God's mission in Acts* involves suspending post-Enlightenment closed-universe rationalism, and seeing how God works to bring people to trust and follow Jesus. Frequently, stories of people coming to faith in Jesus as Messiah and Lord involve 'wonders and signs', remarkable events of healing, deliverance and other ways in which God's life is manifest in mundane existence. For example, the healing of the man with a congenital disability at the temple's Beautiful Gate through Peter and John (3:1–10) leads to proclamation in the temple courts (3:11–26), followed by their arrest and a hearing before the Jewish council (4:1–22). In the midst of this story, and in response to Peter's words, many believe (4:4). Following Peter and John's return to the other believers, the community prays and calls on God as δεσπότης 'sovereign Lord' (4:24) to act both in emboldening them to speak, and in healing and signs and wonders (4:29–30). God's response leads to further proclamation (4:31), powerful testimony (4:33), and generous sharing of possessions (4:32, 34–37). The picture in Acts is that God drives the mission – it truly is *missio Dei*, as modern missiologists assert – and the believing community finds itself following the divine lead, sometimes after resistance or failure to recognize what God is doing.

To read in sympathy with *the way of life which Acts advocates* is to be ready for a scale of values very different from the modern western world. Rather than private property being considered a right to defend, it is seen as shared (e.g. 4:32), and held in trust from God for the sake of others. Hospitality for other believers is something given gladly without holding back. Persecution and suffering are to be borne for the sake of gospel mission and ministry and, indeed, are an expected part of the lives of believers (14:22; cf. 9:16). Testimony to Jesus is central to the believers' new purpose in life as Jesus-followers, including the remarkable transformation of Saul of Tarsus (9:1–2, 15, 20, 22). Saul becomes one of the greatest advocates of the faith and community he sought to destroy, and is ready to die for his fresh understanding of Judaism reshaped

---

Larry W. Hurtado, *Lord Jesus Christ: Devotion to Jesus in Earliest Christianity* (Grand Rapids, MI; Cambridge: Eerdmans, 2003), 177–216.

[22] Max Turner, *Power from on High: The Spirit in Israel's Restoration and Witness in Luke-Acts*, JPTSup 9 (Sheffield: Sheffield Academic, 1996).

[23] On this theme more widely in the New Testament, see Richard Bauckham, *God Crucified: Monotheism and Christology in the New Testament*, Didsbury Lectures 1996 (Carlisle: Paternoster, 1998).

and reordered around Jesus as Messiah and Lord (e.g. 20:22–24; 21:13). Acts articulates a new way of life which reshapes what it means to be truly human.

III. Reading Acts Theologically in This Book

The balance of this book falls into three sections. The first programmatically offers key perspectives from which the studies of particular topics are approached. The second looks at the believing communities in their world, seeking to illuminate the narrative in conversation with the social, historical and cultural settings of the stories. The third engages with key theological themes in Acts: the characterization of Jesus; the implications of Jesus's ascension for his identity in Acts; the transformed cosmology which Acts portrays; and the transformed view of being human in Luke's work.

III.a. Looking at Acts

Following this overview chapter, 'The Acts – of God? What is the "Acts of the Apostles" All About?' presents a case for Acts being a book driven by God, rather than the widespread approaches focused on the human characters in the stories, particularly in more popular level writing and speaking. Key evidence here is: verb subjects throughout the book, which show a heavy weighting towards God, Jesus and the Spirit; the prominence of terms, particularly verbs, which assume or imply divine action; the focus of attention in the speeches on who God is and how God has acted and is acting in and through Jesus and by the Spirit; and the way gospel expansion is divinely driven, rather than the result of human planning and strategy – indeed, mission frequently happens in spite of the human participants.

'Doing Theology Lukewise: Luke as Theologian and Storyteller' addresses why it is appropriate to consider Luke's twofold narrative in the Gospel and Acts as theology. Luke has been compared unfavourably with Paul, who is sometimes considered the New Testament's theologian *par excellence*; this chapter argues that such views fail to recognize ways in which theology is done narratively – that is, they mistake form for substance in 'doing theology'. Luke's theologizing is done through stories, and the crucifixion narrative (Luke 23) provides a valuable example. It is also done through characters who model (or not) what it means to live with God as known in Jesus, inviting readers to imitate or reject their traits. Luke embeds theology in speeches, as many have recognized, to the extent that a previous generation of scholars considered that the speeches were *the* place in Acts where theology exists,[24] repeating the error of mistaking form for substance. Nevertheless, the speeches do offer interpretation of who God is and how God has acted in Jesus and is now acting in the world by the Spirit and through the believing communities. Luke also does theology by patterns of action

---

[24] For examples, see Marion L. Soards, *The Speeches in Acts: Their Content, Context, and Concerns* (Louisville, KY: Westminster John Knox, 1994), 1–13, who does not himself make this claim, but is concerned to study the role of the speeches in Acts.

which echo one another, or which instantiate a pattern stated in a succinct form, such as 2:42 concerning the communal life of believers.

III.b. The Believing Communities and Their World

'Calling the Church Names: Learning about Christian Identity from Acts' addresses the self-understanding of the believing communities through Luke's presentation of names by which the assemblies are known. There is a surprisingly large number of such terms, and this chapter explores them: the brothers and sisters, disciples, assembly, the believers, the Way, and the holy ones.

'Primitive Communism in Acts? Does Acts Present the Community of Goods (2:44–45; 4:32–35) as Mistaken?' focuses on the earliest days of the Jerusalem believers and the suggestion which is sometimes made, that the believers practised an early form of communism by sharing all their possessions, and later gave up as it proved impractical. After outlining key claims made along those lines, I assess what the texts say the believers actually did, passage by passage, and conclude that there was a remarkable level of sharing of possessions in these early days, but that it did not require common ownership of everything after the manner of the Qumran community. I go on to consider what happens later in Acts, and argue that there is evidence of believers recognizing 'possessions' as held in trust from God, and this finds expression in great generosity to others in need. One delight of supervising doctoral students is that they frequently show me things which I had not seen, and Dr Fiona Robertson Gregson is one such example, for she developed this theme more widely in the New Testament, showing a fascinating series of comparisons and contrasts between early Christian and Jewish and Graeco-Roman practices in this area.[25]

It was inevitable that the believers would need to work out their relationship with the institutions of Judaism, and the temple is a key example, for it stands at the heart of the city of Jerusalem, which itself is the heart of the land given by God to Israel.

'A Tale of Two Perspectives? The Place of the Temple in Acts' explores this relationship, recognizing that there seem to be two perspectives in tension in Acts: one which sees the believers going to the temple to pray, to meet, and to proclaim the gospel, after the manner of Jesus; and another which Paul expresses in saying to the Athenian council that God 'does not live in shrines made by human hands' (17:24).

Scholars have struggled to resolve this tension – indeed, some think Luke simply records two contradictory perspectives without resolution – and this essay seeks to bring clarity to Luke's picture. I map both apparently positive views of the temple, and seemingly critical views (notably in Stephen's speech, which is a storm centre in this debate), before going on to ask about the functions of the temple in Acts in conversation with Harold W. Turner. Turner's phenomenological study of sacred places points towards the heavenly Jesus as now fulfilling the functions of such places. Further, God is at work in a wide range of locations in Acts, bringing people to engage with Jesus as

---

[25] Fiona J. Robertson Gregson, *Everything in Common? The Theology and Practice of the Sharing of Possessions in Community in the New Testament* (Eugene, OR: Pickwick, 2017).

Lord and Messiah, and is not locally present at the temple in the way at least some Jews considered him to be. The tension concerning the temple, I suggest, is best resolved by seeing Acts as depicting early Christian understanding of the temple in process of developing, rather than presenting one final, resolved position concerning the temple.

'Deciding about Deciding: Early Christian Communal Decision-Making in Acts' looks at how the early believers came to a mind on disputed issues. By contrast with the modern western world, which stresses the individual, the cultures in which the believers lived were strongly communal, and that means their decision-making was communal. Their processes contrast with the 'CEO' model, where a leader (perhaps) listens and seeks advice and then makes the decision, and with a 'democratic' system where the majority's view prevails. This essay explores a series of decision passages: the choice of Matthias (1:12–26); responding to the Sanhedrin's instruction to be silent about Jesus (4:23–31); choosing the seven to 'serve tables' (6:1–7); welcoming the now-transformed Saul of Tarsus into the Jerusalem believing community (9:26–20); the Spirit's call of Barnabas and Saul to travel (13:1–3); and Paul's team's decision to go to Macedonia (16:6–10). I then consider a large narrative decision-making arc concerning the admission of gentiles into the churches, running through Acts 10–15.

The final two essays in this section turn to consider the early Christians' relationship with the Roman empire, a much-debated issue in recent times.[26] 'Trying Paul or Trying Rome? Judges and Accused in the Roman Trials of Paul in Acts' focuses on Paul's hearings before representatives of the empire. After considering Luke's account of Jesus's trial (Luke 23), I study, successively, Paul's three appearances before Roman governors: Gallio in Corinth (Acts 18:12–17), and Felix and Festus in Caesarea Maritima (23–24 and 25–26). These four accounts offer a fairly consistent portrait of the empire's officials in relation to Jesus and Paul, favouring expediency over justice, even when they find Jesus and Paul guilty of no crime against the empire. There is a similar ambiguity here to that which I observe in Luke's broader portrait of the empire,[27] and by these stories Luke offers his readers ways to engage with the empire in their place and time.

'What Does "Mission" in Acts Mean in Relation to the "Powers That Be"?' looks at the relationship of believers and empire from a missional perspective, asking how we might characterize the way(s) in which believers engage in mission towards the political structures and powers of their day. To ask such a question requires, first, a definition of 'mission' in Acts, and I address that before studying the 'powers that be' in the book: the Roman empire, the Judaean authorities, and the question of the intermingling of political and 'religious' authority in the first century. Five case studies follow, considering: Jesus's promises to his disciples of his and the Spirit's enabling speech before the authorities (Luke 12:12; 21:14–15); Peter and John's appearance before the Sanhedrin (Acts 4:5–22); Paul and Silas's engagement with the Philippian

---

[26] See my survey of this debate, Steve Walton, "The State They Were In: Luke's View of the Roman Empire," in *Rome in the Bible and the Early Church*, ed. Peter Oakes (Carlisle: Paternoster, 2002), 1–41, reprinted: Steve Walton, "The State They Were In: Luke's View of the Roman Empire," in *Reading Acts in the Discourses of Masculinity and Politics*, ed. Eric D. Barreto, Matthew L. Skinner and Steve Walton, LNTS 559 (London: Bloomsbury T&T Clark, 2017), 75–106.

[27] Walton, "State" [2002], esp. 33–5 = Walton, "State" [2017], esp. 105–6.

magistrates (16:16–40); Paul's response to the Athenian Council of the Areopagus (17:16–34); and Paul's response to Felix (23–24).

III.c. Theological Themes in Acts

The first two studies of this section look at different aspects of Luke's Christology in Acts. 'Jesus Present and/or Absent? The Presence and Presentation of Jesus as a Character in the Book of Acts' addresses Conzelmann's claim that Jesus is an absentee following his ascension, substituted by the Spirit, and offers a rather different view. Using Alter's 'scale of means' for studying characterization, I consider Jesus's actions and appearance, the ways in which other characters speak of him, Jesus's own speech, and Luke's own comments about Jesus. This leads to considering the portrait which emerges in conversation with Richard Bauckham's 'divine identity Christology', and arguing that Acts is consistent with that kind of Christology, and that Jesus is both present in heaven and active on earth, thus sharing the characteristics of Israel's God.

'Identity and Christology: The Ascended Jesus in the Book of Acts' focuses on Jesus's ascension and its implications for his identity. Here I study the Acts narrative account of the ascension (1:9–11), and the way characters interpret Jesus's exaltation in the speeches in Acts 2–7, before turning to consider the occasions when Jesus appears or acts from heaven, appearing to Saul (9; 22; 26), healing and delivering people, and carrying out mission (26:23). I close by further relating this account to Bauckham's account of divine identity Christology.

'"The Heavens Opened": Cosmological and Theological Transformation in Luke and Acts' looks at how understanding of the world and the universe are changed by what God has done in Jesus. After a sketch of key terms for different spaces in and outside the created universe, the ascension provides a valuable way in to seeing how heaven and earth are differently related following Jesus's exaltation. Channels of communication and action between the two realms are now open in a fresh way because Jesus has pierced the barrier between them. This early Christian cosmology thus challenges other first-century cosmologies, notably a Jewish cosmology which places the temple at the centre of the world, a Roman cosmology which places the emperor at the heart of reality, and pagan cosmologies which consider the universe to be in the hands of a variety of gods who can be in conflict with each other.

Finally, 'Turning Anthropology Right Side Up: Seeing Human Life and Existence Lukewise' considers what picture of being human emerges from Luke and Acts. Luke's theme of divine reversal of human status proves a valuable perspective for studying this topic. I study here the way that sinful humanity is transformed through Peter's answer to the question at Pentecost, 'What must we do?' (2:37), and Paul's answer to the Philippian jailer's question, 'What must I do to be saved?' (16:30). This leads to considering Jesus as humanity *par excellence*, and the implications this has for human physicality being re-understood, and human community reconfigured.

2

The Acts – of God? What Is the 'Acts of the Apostles' All About?

What is Acts about?[1] This question has been posed frequently in the history of critical scholarship, not least in the last 150 years. Answers have tended to focus on questions of the *purpose* of Acts, focusing on why Luke[2] wrote his book.[3] More recently the impact of rhetorical criticism has encouraged scholars to ask what kind of effect(s) Acts is designed to produce in the beliefs and actions of its readers/hearers.[4] In this chapter we shall attempt to come at this issue from a different angle by asking what the 'topic' of Acts is, that is, we shall pay careful attention to what moves the narrative along and what Luke presents as the driving force of the story he tells.

In coming at Acts from this angle we are following a thread in recent scholarship, which is to see the New Testament, and the Bible more widely, as a collection of books about God.[5] For many who read the scholarly literature on Acts this will come

---

[1] I am grateful to the members of the Acts seminar of the British New Testament Conference, the New Testament research seminar of Aberdeen University, and the London School of Theology New Testament research seminar, especially Dr Peter Mallen, for their helpful comments on this chapter.

[2] Here we enter the usual caveat, that for the purpose of this chapter we make no assumptions about who Luke is; see Loveday Alexander, *The Preface to Luke's Gospel: Literary Convention and Social Context in Luke 1.1-4 and Acts 1.1*, SNTSMS 78 (Cambridge: Cambridge University Press, 1993), 2 n. 2.

[3] The search for a purpose for (Luke-)Acts is chronicled well in Robert Maddox, *The Purpose of Luke-Acts*, SNTW (Edinburgh: T&T Clark, 1982) and, more briefly, Todd Penner, "Madness in the Method? The Acts of the Apostles in Current Study," *CurBR* 2 (2004): 223-93, esp. 258-60; Steve Walton, "Acts: Many Questions, Many Answers," in *The Face of New Testament Studies*, ed. Scot McKnight and Grant R. Osborne (Grand Rapids, MI: Baker Academic; Leicester: Apollos, 2004), 229-50; Joel B. Green, "Acts of the Apostles," *DLNT*, 7-24, esp. 16-23. cf. also W. W. Gasque, *A History of the Criticism of the Acts of the Apostles* (Grand Rapids, MI: Eerdmans, 1975) and the standard scholarly bibliographies of Acts, Andrew J. Mattill, Jr and M. B. Mattill, *A Classified Bibliography of the Literature on the Acts*, NTTS 7 (Leiden: Brill, 1966) and W. E. Mills, *A Bibliography of the Periodical Literature on the Acts of the Apostles, 1962-84*, NovTSup 58 (Leiden: Brill, 1986). To ask the question about Acts strictly necessitates, of course, some engagement with Luke's Gospel too (e.g. the theme of God's purpose/plan is prominent in Luke as well as Acts): posing the question focused on Acts enables us to pay particular attention to this book's themes, and avoids the danger of reading Acts only through Luke, highlighted by Mikeal C. Parsons and Richard I. Pervo, *Rethinking the Unity of Luke and Acts* (Minneapolis, MN: Fortress, 1993), esp. 120.

[4] E.g. Ben Witherington, III, *The Acts of the Apostles: A Socio-Rhetorical Commentary* (Carlisle: Paternoster; Grand Rapids, MI: Eerdmans, 1998), 63–5, 68–76.

[5] E.g. Leon Morris, "The Theme of Romans," in *Apostolic History and the Gospel*, ed. W. W. Gasque and Ralph P. Martin (Exeter: Paternoster, 1970), 249-63 (arguing that God is the major topic of

as something of a surprise, since Acts has frequently been read as a book about the church, about mission, about the apostles, about Peter and Paul, about Christian-Jewish relations, and so forth. Rarely has it been seen as focused on God.[6] However, a careful reading of the book itself makes it clear that Luke presents us with the claim that God is at work in the stories (and overall story) which he tells, and that God is driving events in a particular direction. This chapter focuses on evidence for the claim that Acts is a book about God and what God is doing.[7]

Several factors together suggest that Acts is about God: the verb subjects of the book, key verbs which imply divine action, the focus of attention in the speeches, the development of the gentile mission, and Luke's use of the language of 'the word of the Lord/God.'

I. Sentence and Clause Subjects

Richard Burridge pioneered the analysis of the subjects of sentences/clauses as a tool in studying the genre of ancient documents.[8] He notes that in Graeco-Roman βίοι ('lives'), the person who is the focus of the book is also the subject of a substantial proportion of the main verbs.[9] He goes on to demonstrate that in the canonical Gospels, Jesus is the subject of a major proportion of the sentences/clauses.[10] This analysis becomes a significant plank in his overall argument that the canonical Gospels should be seen as Graeco-Roman βίοι.

Romans); Antoinette Clark Wire, "Pauline Theology as an Understanding of God: The Explicit and the Implicit" (PhD diss., Claremont Graduate School, 1974); Nils Alstrup Dahl, "The Neglected Factor in New Testament Theology," in *Jesus the Christ: The Historical Origins of Christological Doctrine*, ed. Nils Alstrup Dahl and Donald H. Juel (Minneapolis, MN: Fortress, 1991), 153–63; W. Lee Humphreys, *The Character of God in the Book of Genesis: A Narrative Appraisal* (Louisville, KY: Westminster John Knox, 2001); Marianne Meye Thompson, "'God's Voice You Have Never Heard, God's Form You Have Never Seen': The Characterization of God in the Gospel of John," *Semeia* 63 (1993): 177–204.

[6] There are, of course, exceptions, such as Robert L. Brawley, *Centering on God: Method and Message in Luke-Acts* (Louisville, KY: Westminster John Knox, 1990), esp. 111–24; Jacob Jervell, *The Theology of the Acts of the Apostles*, NT Theology (Cambridge: Cambridge University Press, 1996), esp. 18–34; John T. Squires, *The Plan of God in Luke-Acts*, SNTSMS 76 (Cambridge: Cambridge University Press, 1993); and the fine recent commentary Beverly R. Gaventa, *Acts*, ANTC (Nashville, TN: Abingdon, 2003).

[7] A fuller study is required of the nature and actions of God in Acts – that is, how Luke characterizes God in Acts – but that is beyond the scope of this chapter. Brawley, *Centering*, 111–24 and Daniel Marguerat, *The First Christian Historian: Writing the 'Acts of the Apostles'*, SNTSMS 121 (Cambridge: Cambridge University Press, 2002), 85–108 provide helpful brief studies; and now see Ling Cheng, "The Characterisation of God in Acts: With Special Reference to the Interrelationships of Characters" (PhD diss., London School of Theology/Brunel University, 2006), published as: Ling Cheng, *The Characterisation of God in Acts: The Indirect Portrayal of an Invisible Character*, PBM (Milton Keynes: Paternoster, 2011).

[8] Richard A. Burridge, *What Are the Gospels? A Comparison with Græco-Roman Biography*, SNTSMS 70 (Cambridge: Cambridge University Press, 1992), 113–17.

[9] Burridge, *What*, 134–8, 162–7, and see the pie charts in the appendix, 261–70.

[10] Burridge, *What*, 195–9, 223–5, and see the pie charts in the appendix, 271–4. Burridge estimates that Jesus is the subject of 24.4 per cent of Mark's verbs, 17.2 per cent of Matthew's, 17.9 per cent of Luke's, and 20.2 per cent of John's. He further notes that the teaching of Jesus occupies a further substantial proportion of the verbs: Mark 20.2 per cent, Matthew 42.5 per cent, Luke 36.8 per cent, and John 34 per cent.

Burridge performs his analysis on the Graeco-Roman literature mainly by using a computer analysis which identifies both the nouns found in the document under consideration, and in particular, occurrences of nouns in the nominative case (which are likely to be subjects of verbs).[11] This is clearly not a nuanced analysis (as Burridge himself notes[12]), for nominative nouns can occur in other grammatical constructions (e.g. as the complement of equative verbs, e.g. εἰμί, γίνομαι), and for numerous verbs no subject is explicitly stated. A full analysis would require examining each of the clauses of Acts by hand, as Burridge does for the canonical Gospels. Hence the results below should be regarded as preliminary, pending further detailed examination of Acts.

When we turn to Acts, the analysis is interesting. The table in Appendix A sets out the main proper nouns which are found in the book, both in any case and specifically in the nominative.[13] Unsurprisingly, Saul/Paul is found frequently, but θεός 'God' occurs more times, both in general and in the nominative case in particular. These two proper names dominate the landscape of Acts – only κύριος 'Lord' and πνεῦμα 'S/ spirit' are even remotely near them in frequency, and in the nominative case the gap is especially wide ('Saul/Paul' and 'God' are found about 7 per cent each and 'Lord' and 'Spirit' about 2 per cent each).[14]

The case for seeing God as more important than Paul for the *whole* book of Acts is supported by noticing the spread of usage within Acts. Saul/Paul does not occur until 7:58, only occurs twice in ch. 8 (vv. 1, 3), is absent between 9:24 and 11:25, and occurs once in ch. 12 (v. 25). Thus for most of the first half of the book, Saul/Paul is absent – or peripheral at most. By contrast, God is spread throughout the book.[15]

---

[11] Burridge, *What*, 114–16.
[12] Burridge, *What*, 115.
[13] Statistics cited are based on the NA[27]/UBS[4] text, and were prepared with the assistance of Accordance. There is, of course, a significant issue over *which* text of Acts we work with for this analysis – the Alexandrian or the Western, and I have sided with the majority in scholarship in regarding the Western text as secondary. For discussion, see, for example (taking the Alexandrian view) Bruce M. Metzger, *A Textual Commentary on the Greek New Testament*, 2nd ed. (Stuttgart: Deutsche Bibelgesellschaft/ United Bible Societies, 1994), 222–36; C. K. Barrett, *A Critical and Exegetical Commentary on the Acts of the Apostles*, ICC, 2 vols. (Edinburgh: T&T Clark, 1994), 1:1–29; Peter Head, "Acts and the Problem of Its Texts," in *The Book of Acts in Its Ancient Literary Setting*, ed. Bruce W. Winter and Andrew D. Clarke, BAFCS 1 (Carlisle: Paternoster; Grand Rapids, MI: Eerdmans, 1993), 415–44; and (supporting the Western text as more original) M.-É. Boismard, OP, *Le texte occidental des Actes des Apôtres*, EBib ns 40, 2nd ed. (Paris: Gabalda, 2000); Jenny Read-Heimerdinger, *The Bezan Text of Acts: A Contribution of Discourse Analysis to Textual Criticism*, JSNTSup 236 (London: Sheffield Academic, 2002); Josep Rius-Camps and Jenny Read-Heimerdinger, *The Message of Acts in Codex Bezae: A Comparison with the Alexandrian Tradition*, JSNTSup/LNTS, 4 vols. (London: T&T Clark, 2004–9).
[14] Jervell, *Theology*, 19, 21, 30–1 notes that in Acts Jesus's role and status is defined in relation to God – thus in Acts, God is never 'The God who raised Jesus from the dead' (Gal 1:1; Col 2:12), but rather Jesus is the one whom 'the God of our ancestors' raised (Acts 5:30; cf. 2:24, 32; 3:15, 26; 4:10; 10:40; 13:30, 37). One might develop this point by observing (with Brawley, *Centering*, 121–2) that God in Acts is known by his actions, notably by raising Jesus from the dead and by sending the Spirit, and not only by the preaching of the apostles.
[15] Apart from no or one occurrence being found in Acts 1, 9 and 25 – a curious phenomenon which invites further investigation. Broadly similar results in terms of the spread of usage are seen when nominative occurrences alone are isolated: then Saul/Paul is not found until 8:1 and is absent similarly to the pattern for all cases, and God is absent from Acts 1, 6, 8–9, 12, 18, 20, 24–25, 28.

When we look more widely in the NT, the sharpness of focus on God in Acts becomes clearer: in the NT generally 'God' is the commonest proper noun, forming 4.55 per cent of NT occurrences of nouns, and 4.03 per cent of NT nominative noun occurrences. In Acts the figure for occurrences of 'God' is similar to the NT in general (4.02 per cent), but the proportion of nominatives (and therefore, likely, of verb subjects) is significantly higher (6.74 per cent).

Appendix B provides statistics on the usage of θεός in the various NT books. This analysis highlights that, while the Pauline corpus undoubtedly uses 'God' proportionately markedly more than other parts of the NT,[16] we can say three things about usage in Acts. First, by comparison with other NT narrative books (i.e. the Gospels), 'God' occurs significantly more frequently, both in absolute number terms and in occurrences per thousand words of the book in question. Second, when we consider nominative uses specifically, usage in Acts (per thousand words) is at least three times as much as any other NT narrative book (John is the nearest[17]) – and, indeed, the actual number of occurrences (65) is more than the four Gospels added together (55). Third, when we measure nominative uses as a percentage of NT nominative uses, Acts emerges as having 20.70 per cent; if we compare this figure with the total length of Acts as a percentage of the NT (13.08 per cent), we can see that the nominative use of 'God' is proportionately higher than any other NT narrative book.

This statistical analysis suggests that there is a *prima facie* case for regarding 'God' as at least a highly significant subject in Acts. Further, a brief consideration of the passive indicative verbs of Acts[18] suggests that significant uses have God as the implied actor who performs the action of the verb. Examples include 'he was lifted up' (ἐπήρθη, 1:9), 'there were added' (προσετέθησαν, 2:41), 'the place in which they were gathered *was shaken* (ἐσαλεύθη) and they all *were filled* (ἐπλήσθησαν) with the Holy Spirit' (4:31), and 'your prayer *has been heard* (εἰσηκούσθη) and your alms *have been remembered* (ἐμνήσθησαν) before God' (10:31).[19]

If we further ask what other proper nouns occur most frequently, the picture expands to include κύριος 'Lord', πνεῦμα 'Spirit', πατήρ 'Father', and Ἰησοῦς 'Jesus', all key to understanding the Christian God in Acts, as well as λόγος 'word' (which is frequently accompanied by 'of God' or 'of the Lord',[20] and thus closely associated with God), υἱός 'son' (a key Christological word) and ἄγγελος 'angel' (a key divine agent). Thus persons or objects closely associated with God (to put it no stronger) take up a high proportion of the key proper nouns in Acts.

---

[16] Especially in Romans: see discussion in Morris, "Theme," esp. 250–2.
[17] And note Thompson's important observation, that God is not directly characterized in John – in the Fourth Gospel, God is only known through Jesus (e.g. John 1:18); see Thompson, "Voice," 188–94, esp. 188–9.
[18] 235 in total excluding the 20 uses of the aorist passives of ἀποκρίνομαι and δύναμαι.
[19] My initial survey identifies some 37 which *prima facie* denote divine action.
[20] Acts 4:31; 6:2, 7; 8:14, 25; 11:1; 12:24; 13:5, 7, 44, 46, 48; 15:35, 36; 16:32; 17:13; 18:11; 19:10; 20:35.

II. Terms Assuming or Implying Divine Action

A further piece of evidence needs to be added to our study at this stage, and that is Luke's understanding of divine action.[21] Notable is the use of δεῖ 'it is necessary',[22] a verb found significantly more frequently in Luke-Acts than elsewhere in the NT.[23] Luke frequently uses this word to signify that God has so organized events that they must happen this way:[24] for example, Scripture had to be fulfilled by the death of Judas (1:16); the name of Jesus is the only one given among people by which it is necessary for us to be saved (4:12, combining δεῖ with the infinitive σωθῆναι 'to be saved', whose passive voice is also suggestive of divine action); Ananias is told that the Lord will show Saul how much it is necessary for him to suffer for the Lord's name (9:16); and Paul is assured by the Lord that it is necessary for him to bear witness in Rome (23:11). This Lukan favourite term exposes his belief that God has a purpose which is being carried out through the stories which Luke tells in Acts. Cosgrove summarizes well in three affirmations: the 'divine δεῖ' (i) emphasizes that the events of the Gospel and Acts are rooted in God's plan; (ii) functions as a call to obedience and submission to this plan; (iii) guarantees God's carrying out of his plan.[25]

Wider than this, Luke strongly emphasizes the fulfilment of Scripture in what is now taking place[26] – an emphasis we shall see in considering the speeches. To provide just one example, Paul's speech in Antioch (13:16–41) uses 'fulfilment' language prominently: the Jerusalemite Jews and their leaders fulfilled (v. 27) the words of the prophets by killing Jesus; the same people carried out (v. 29) everything written about Jesus; and God is now fulfilling Scripture 'for us' in the resurrection of Jesus (v. 33).[27] The speech itself is organized as a re-telling of the story of God's dealings with Israel (vv. 17–22) to show that the sacred history leads to its climax when God brought Jesus, the Saviour of Israel (v. 23). The fourfold citation of Scripture which follows underlines

---

[21] See the valuable discussions in Squires, *Plan*: 1–3 outline the key terms used which highlight God's ordering of events; see also John T. Squires, "The Plan of God in the Acts of the Apostles," in *Witness to the Gospel: The Theology of Acts*, ed. I. Howard Marshall and David Peterson (Grand Rapids, MI: Eerdmans, 1998), 19–39; Marguerat, *Historian*, 96–103; David Peterson, "The Motif of Fulfilment and the Purpose of Luke-Acts," in *The Book of Acts in Its Ancient Literary Setting*, ed. Bruce W. Winter and Andrew D. Clarke, BAFCS 1 (Carlisle: Paternoster; Grand Rapids, MI: Eerdmans, 1993), 83–104.

[22] A fuller study would need to take account of other key terms which highlight divine action as well as the major theme of fulfilment of Scripture. Key terms include βουλή and θέλημα ('plan' or 'will'), μέλλω ('I am about to'), πληρόω, τελέω and πίμπλημι (all having a sense of 'I fulfil' – plus, of course, their compounds); see discussion in Peterson, "Motif"; Squires, *Plan*; Squires, "Plan"; Charles H. Cosgrove, "The Divine ΔΕΙ in Luke-Acts: Investigations into the Lukan Understanding of God's Providence," *NovT* 26 (1984): 168–90, here 184–5.

[23] 40 of 101 NT uses are in Luke-Acts, of which 22 are in Acts; see the careful discussion in Cosgrove, "Divine," esp. 172–84.

[24] See further Steve Walton, "Where Does the Beginning of Acts End?," in *The Unity of Luke-Acts*, ed. J. Verheyden, BETL 142 (Leuven: Peeters, 1999), 448–67, here 454 and literature cited there.

[25] Cosgrove, "Divine," 183, 189.

[26] See the very helpful discussion in Peterson, "Motif," esp. (on Acts), 94–104.

[27] See the helpful brief discussion in Luke T. Johnson, *The Acts of the Apostles*, SP 5 (Collegeville, MN: Liturgical, 1992), *ad. loc.*

this point, as Paul is presented as quoting Ps 2:7 (v. 33), Isa 55:2 (LXX 55:3; v. 34), Ps 16:10 (LXX 15:10; v. 35) and Hab 1:5 (v. 41).

Much more could be said on this point,[28] but enough has been said to show that Luke uses both specific vocabulary and the broader theme of the fulfilment of Scripture, to show that what is now happening is *God's* action for which he has prepared the way.

III. The Focus of Attention in the Speeches

We shall concentrate our discussion of this point on an examination of the speeches of Acts 3–4, but the same point could be made from almost any of the speeches in Acts. To illustrate briefly, Acts 1:16–26, spoken to a Christian audience, focuses on the fulfilment of God's purpose in Scripture (vv. 16, 20) and highlights that this was foretold by the Holy Spirit (v. 16), and the decision about who will take Judas's place is made in prayer (vv. 24–26).

Similarly, Acts 2:14–36, a speech to Jewish not-yet-believers, focuses on what God is now doing as the fulfilment of the Joel prophecy (vv. 16–21, citing Joel 2:28–32), God's attestation of Jesus in his ministry (v. 22), death and resurrection (vv. 23–24), again citing Scripture in support (vv. 25–28, 31, 34–35, citing respectively Pss 15:8–11a LXX [MT 16:8–11a]; 15:10 LXX [MT 16:10]; 109:1 LXX [MT 110:1]), and concluding with the emphatic statement, 'God has made him both Lord and Messiah' (v. 36).

Likewise, Acts 10:34–43, a speech to godfearing gentile not-yet-believers, begins with Peter's reflection that God shows no bias (v. 34), identifies Jesus's preaching as a message from God (v. 35), clarifies that the power of Jesus's ministry was a divine anointing (v. 38), asserts that God acted in raising Jesus from the dead (v. 40), states that God chose the apostles as witnesses (v. 41), and closes by identifying Jesus as the one appointed by God as judge (v. 42), and again highlights the testimony of divine witnesses – the prophets – to the centrality of Jesus (v. 43).

Again, Acts 17:22–31, a speech to outright pagans, centres on the question, 'Who is God?' This issue is raised in the narrative framework, where Paul is considered to be proclaiming a new deity, Jesus (v. 18).[29] The speech itself expounds a Judaeo-Christian view of God in engagement with the views of Stoic and Epicureans:[30] God is knowable and has revealed himself (v. 23); God is the creator and sustainer of the world and its inhabitants (vv. 24–25); God allotted places to every nation (v. 26); God wants people to seek and find him (vv. 27–28); idolatry is a misguided attempt to identify the creator with elements of his creation (v. 29); God calls people to turn from their former way of

---

[28] E.g. in considering the use of 'promise' language – ἐπαγγελία 'promise' occurs eight times in Acts (1:4; 2:33, 39; 7:17; 13:23, 32; 23:21; 26:6), always in the setting of fulfilment of God's purposes, especially in Scripture – and other key words and ideas identified by Squires, *Plan*, 1–3.

[29] Or perhaps two deities, Jesus and Anastasis. This view seems to have originated with John Chrysostom: 'they supposed *Anastasis* (the Resurrection) to be some deity, being accustomed to worship female divinities also' (*Hom. Act.* 38); so also Joseph A. Fitzmyer, *The Acts of the Apostles: A New Translation and Commentary*, AB 31 (Garden City, NY: Doubleday, 1998), 605; Johnson, *Acts*, 314; *contra* Barrett, *Acts*, 2:831; Jacob Jervell, *Die Apostelgeschichte*, 17th ed., KEK (Göttingen: Vandenhoeck & Ruprecht, 1998), 444.

[30] See the valuable brief discussion in Conrad H. Gempf, "Athens, Paul at," in *DPL*, 51–4.

life and thinking since they will face judgement at the hands of Jesus, whom God raised from the dead (vv. 30–31).

Finally in this brief survey, Acts 26:2–23, Paul's defence speech before Agrippa, centres on who rightly understands God. Paul introduces his background as a strict Pharisee, and thus a highly orthodox Jew (vv. 4–5), and argues that his trial results from his pharisaic hope in the resurrection of the dead promised by God in Scripture (vv. 6–8). He narrates his life before the Damascus Road experience to demonstrate further his fidelity to ancestral Jewish faith (vv. 9–11), before telling the story of that experience in which 'the Lord' was identified as Jesus (v. 15) – again, the key question is who God is and how God may now be known. Thus the ministry to which the exalted Jesus appoints him is to turn people to *God* (v. 18), and the vision in which this comes is stressed as being 'heavenly' (v. 19, that is, sent from the realm of God[31]) – thus Paul's whole mission derives from God.[32] So when Paul summarizes his preaching, it centres on calling Jews and gentiles to turn to *God* (v. 20), and God has helped him in this (v. 22). Moreover, all that he proclaims is supported by the testimony of Scripture, God's book (vv. 22–23).

There is thus a consistent pattern that God is the focus of the speeches, whether to believers, Jews, godfearers, outright pagans or in a forensic setting. Admittedly, this examination of the speeches is not exhaustive. Nevertheless, the evidence presented points very strongly to a focus on *God* rather than specifically on *Jesus*.

We can understand this phenomenon further by noticing a key contrast in the speeches in Acts 3–4. When Peter speaks to the people following the healing of the man with a congenital disability (3:1–10), he highlights that the healing is the action of the ancestral Jewish God (3:13), who has exalted Jesus (3:13, 15) – and the man himself and the crowd respond to the healing by praising *God* (3:8, 9). Certainly there is an emphasis on the power of the name of Jesus to heal (3:16), but it is by faith 'through him' (3:16) that the healing takes place: Jesus is the one who is the means of God healing – almost the conduit through which the healing takes place.[33]

Hence Peter's call to the people is to turn to God (v. 19), who has foretold what is now happening in Scripture (v. 18) and who will send both times of refreshing now and his Messiah in the future (v. 20).[34] The Pentateuch and the rest of Scripture[35] speak of these things (vv. 22–24) and the people are the inheritors of these divine promises

---

[31] BDAG 737 οὐράνιος.
[32] Jervell, *Apostelgeschichte*, 595 comments: 'Paul's entire effectiveness, because of which he is now arrested, can be explained by this heavenly vision. Because of it Paul has now accomplished a worldwide mission' (my translation).
[33] Jervell, *Apostelgeschichte*, 166 observes that this phrase suggests that the faith is either given or produced by Christ; he also observes (164) that in 3:13 'The Messiah Jesus plays only a passive role here' and 'The miracle which happened is portrayed in verses 11–16 as God's action through Christ' (my translations throughout this note).
[34] Here there appears to be a parallel between the two elements in each of vv. 20–21: the 'times of refreshing' (v. 20a) take place while Jesus remains in heaven (v. 20b); when he comes from heaven (v. 20b) that will be the time of universal restoration (v. 21b).
[35] I take the reference to 'the prophets … from Samuel' to be a reference not to the person of Samuel but to the book that bears his name, which is the first book in the section of the Hebrew canon known as 'the prophets' (with Jervell, *Apostelgeschichte*, 170).

and covenant (v. 25) – indeed, God's purpose in raising Jesus was to bless the people of God (v. 26).

When Peter responds to the charges of the gathering the following day (4:8–12), there is a greater attention given to Jesus – he is again the one through whose name the healing has taken place. However, Jesus's significance is that *God* has raised him from the dead (v. 10) and thus Scripture is fulfilled in what God has now done following the mistaken verdict of the Jewish court (v. 11).

The striking contrast emerges when we consider the response of the Sanhedrin, for when they discuss what to do (4:15–17), they do not mention God at all! The theocentric focus of the believers contrasts sharply with the political machinations of the Jewish leaders – and the contrast is heightened further by Peter and John's response to their warning not to speak further in the name of Jesus, for they refocus the discussion on God: it is to *God* that both believers and Jewish leaders must answer (vv. 19–20).

The narrative flow continues into the return of Peter and John to the believing community, and their reaction is to pray – and their prayer is centred on who God is and what God can do: God is δεσπότης (v. 24), the sovereign who is in control;[36] God is creator (v. 24); God spoke in Scripture (vv. 25–26); and God controls history (v. 28). Thus they pray with confidence that God will act now (vv. 29–30) – and Luke records that this is exactly what happens (v. 31).

Thus our examination of the speeches suggests that God is the central subject in speech after speech – people are called to respond to God, and they are told of what God has done and said, in Scripture, in Jesus and in God's present actions to restore and heal.

IV. Mission in Acts

There can be no doubt that the expansion of the gospel is an important theme in Acts. It is signalled by a number of key summary verses (6:7; 9:31; 12:24; 16:5; 19:20; 28:30–31) which have been seen by some as structuring the whole book.[37] For our purpose, we note how dependent the expansion is upon divine initiative throughout the book. At key moments in the story it is God who steps in and moves events on, not least in the events of Pentecost which launch the mission, for there God pours out the Spirit (2:4, 16–17, citing Joel 2:28) and thus enables the believers to proclaim God's praise in many languages (2:4–11). Peter's speech, which explains how God is acting in the event, leads to three thousand people being added to the believing community (2:41).

The healing of the man at the Beautiful Gate of the Jerusalem temple (3:1–10) is another case in point. As Luke portrays this event, it is clear that subsequent events

---

[36] '[O]ne who has legal control and authority over persons, such as subjects or slaves', BDAG 220 s.v.
[37] Notably Richard N. Longenecker, "The Acts of the Apostles," in *The Expositor's Bible Commentary*, ed. Frank E. Gaebelein, 12 vols. (Grand Rapids, MI: Zondervan, 1981), 9:207–573, here 233–4 [= Richard N. Longenecker, *Acts*, Expositor's Bible Commentary (Grand Rapids, MI: Zondervan, 1995), 29–30], building on the work of C. H. Turner, "Chronology of the New Testament," in *A Dictionary of the Bible*, ed. James Hastings, 5 vols. (Edinburgh: T&T Clark, 1898), 1:403–25, here 421.

flow from the action of God in healing this man. Peter's speech happens 'while he clung onto Peter and John' (3:11), and the healing provides the starting point for his words (3:12) – indeed, Luke chooses the verb ἀποκρίνομαι 'answer' to introduce what Peter says (3:12), thus suggesting that his speech arises from the implicit questions raised by the healing.[38] Peter's words lead to many believing, with the number rising to five thousand (4:4), and that reaction is contrasted by Luke with the negative response of the Sanhedrin who wish the believers to stop speaking in the name of Jesus (4:18). As the story moves on further, the believers' prayer leads to renewed power from God for witness (4:29–31).

The development of gospel ministry in Samaria is also greatly dependent on the power of God: Luke highlights that Philip's evangelistic effectiveness (8:6) hinged on deliverance ministry and healing (8:7) – the clause 'when they heard and saw the signs which he did' (v. 6) gives the reason for the statement of v. 6a,[39] and the two verses are linked by an explanatory γάρ 'for' (v. 7).[40] Further, the coming of the Spirit through Peter and John laying hands on the Samaritan converts is 'God's gift' (8:20). Again, the action of God is critical to the growth of the gospel.

The Ethiopian eunuch encounters Philip because of what we might call a 'divine appointment',[41] although this time God's agent in arranging the meeting is an angel (8:26). But this does not mean we should see this as any less the work of God. When the Spirit prompts Philip to go to the man's chariot (8:29), we should also see this as divine prompting. After the eunuch's baptism, Philip is removed by the Spirit to another sphere of operations (8:39),[42] in similar manner to Ezekiel being transported by the Spirit (e.g. Ezek 3:12, 14; 11:1; 37:1; 43:5).

One of the most crucial shifts in the growth of the gospel is Peter's visit to Cornelius and its consequences (10:1–11:18; 15:7–9). Here, Luke stresses the divine initiative: not only does God speak to Cornelius by an angel and give him specific information about who to find and where to find him (10:3–6, 31–32; 11:13–14), but God also gives Peter a threefold vision (10:9–16) and speaks to him by the Spirit (10:19–20; 11:12). More, for Peter has hardly started his speech ('as I began to speak', 11:15) when God sends the Spirit upon the gentile audience, evidenced by tongues-speech reminiscent of Pentecost (10:44–47; 11:15). It is this divine action which persuades 'those of the circumcision' (11:2) that *God* has acted (11:18b) – with the result that they give God praise (11:18a).

---

[38] BDAG 113 ἀποκρίνομαι §1.
[39] For this use see MHT 3:145–46; Stanley E. Porter, *Idioms of the Greek New Testament*, Biblical Languages: Greek 2, 2nd ed. (Sheffield: JSOT, 1994), 200 (although neither cite this verse as an example). This use of ἐν with articular infinitive could also be considered to be temporal (see Daniel B. Wallace, *Greek Grammar beyond the Basics: An Exegetical Syntax of the New Testament* (Grand Rapids, MI: Zondervan, 1996), 595), but the cotext seems also to require a causal element – the events are not merely coincident in timing.
[40] With Ernst Haenchen, *The Acts of the Apostles* (Oxford: Blackwell, 1971), 302 on both points.
[41] See the valuable discussion in F. Scott Spencer, *The Portrait of Philip in Acts: A Study of Roles and Relations*, JSNTSup 67 (Sheffield: JSOT, 1992), 154–8.
[42] Rudolf Pesch, *Die Apostelgeschichte*, EKKNT, 2 vols. (Zürich: Benzinger-Verlag, 1986), 1:294 sees the snatching of Philip away by the Spirit as showing that Philip did the correct thing in reaching out to a gentile and baptizing him.

Saul's Damascus Road experience, told three times by Luke (9:1–19; 22:3–21; 26:2–23), is presented as an experience of the intervention of God-in-Jesus. That it has a divine component (and is not simply focused on Jesus) can be seen by similarities with OT and Jewish theophanies,[43] as well as by noticing how Luke subsequently speaks of the experience. Ananias tells Paul that in this experience, 'the God of our ancestors has chosen you to know his will' (22:14). Paul himself says that the experience was a 'heavenly vision' (26:19), and the message he proclaims is to call people to turn to *God* (26:20), fulfilling the promises given by God to his ancestors (26:6).

When Barnabas and Saul begin their travelling ministry it is a further intervention of God which moves them out of Antioch (13:1–3). God speaks by the Holy Spirit (v. 2), most probably through a Christian prophet in the gathering who were worshipping and fasting – for other occasions when Luke uses language like 'the Holy Spirit said' (v. 2) have a prophet speaking in view (esp. Acts 21:11, but also Luke 1:67; Acts 4:25).

The rare language of God calling highlights another occasion of divine intervention in the mission. In 16:6–10 Paul and his colleagues are actively prevented by God, through the agency of the Spirit, from preaching in Asia (v. 6) or entering Bithynia (v. 7). The night vision of the Macedonian man (v. 9) is interpreted by Luke as 'having concluded that God had *called* [προσκέκληται] us to evangelise them' (v. 10). There are only four places in the NT where the καλέω 'call' word group is used in the sense of God calling people to a specific task or role (here; Acts 13:2, considered above; Rom 1:1; 1 Cor 1:1), so it is of interest that Luke highlights that they understood this vision as God calling them to a new task.[44] It may be significant that the journey to Macedonia marked the transition of the gospel into a new area of the world – Europe, in our terms – and this new step is presented as initiated by God, even to the extent of preventing the missionaries going in the wrong direction, further into Asia Minor.

IV.a. The Church Lagging behind the Divine Initiative

With these examples of God acting to initiate new phases of the mission, we may contrast the cautious, conservative nature of the believing community at times, which further highlights the divine push to take the mission onward.

Thus, in the Cornelius story, the reaction of the circumcised believers is to criticize Peter for eating with gentiles (11:2), and it takes the very full explanation of how God has managed events to persuade them otherwise.

The argument rumbles on, for the claim that circumcision and Torah observance are required for salvation is still being made vociferously (15:2–3, 5). At the resultant Jerusalem meeting Luke's characters respond by repeatedly stressing what *God* has done.[45]

---

[43] I owe this observation to my student Tim Churchill, whose published PhD thesis argues this point in full: Timothy W. R. Churchill, *Divine Initiative and the Christology of the Damascus Road Encounter* (Eugene, OR: Pickwick, 2010).

[44] See my discussion in Steve Walton, *A Call to Live: Vocation for Everyone* (London: Triangle, 1994), ch. 6.

[45] Cf. Jervell, *Theology*, 22–3; also Gaventa, *Acts*, 215–27 – her whole discussion focuses strongly on the issue that 'it is God who decides' (215).

Peter's speech focuses strongly on God who had taken the initiative (15:7–11): note 'God chose' (v. 7); 'God who knows the heart testified' (v. 8); '[God] made no distinction between us and them' (v. 9); 'why are you testing God?' (v. 10).

The meeting then hears Barnabas and Paul telling of 'all the signs and wonders which God had done among the gentiles' (v. 12).

James, in summarizing, highlights that God took the initiative in the gentile mission (v. 14, 'God *first* concerned himself about[46] taking from the gentiles a people for his name'), and cites Scripture in support (vv. 15–18, quoting Amos 9:11–12). Furthermore, these gentiles James regards as turning to *God* (v. 19). Thus the community is dragged forward, somewhat reluctantly, by the realization that God is at work and they must not resist God.

IV.b. The Growth of 'the Word'

We noted above the summary verses which track the growth of the mission. For Luke a key category in understanding the mission is that it is a mission of the word of the Lord or the word of God. Luke uses the terms 'the word of God' and 'the word of the Lord' frequently – his Gospel contains 5 uses and Acts 20 uses, from an NT total of 54 uses.[47] The genitive is likely to be plenary (i.e. to have elements of both subjective and objective genitive[48]), in that the message is both *from* God/the Lord and *about* God/the Lord.

The message which the community speaks is the word of God (4:31). Growth of the mission is growth of the word of God (12:24; 13:49), so that when new groups respond to the gospel message they are said to 'accept' the word of God (8:14 Samaria; 11:1 gentiles – Cornelius and his household).[49]

The twelve's ministry is to be focused on the word of God, so that they must not neglect it in order to serve tables (6:2), but rather must dedicate themselves to the service of 'the word' (6:4).[50] Indeed, it is following this act of delegation by the community that 'the word of God went on growing and multiplying' (6:7, using imperfect tense verbs to indicate a continuing process).

That this focus of the twelve's (and the wider apostolic group's) ministry continued can be seen from further references to the word of God/the Lord: Peter and John speak the word of the Lord in Samaria (8:25); Barnabas and Saul speak the word of God in the Cypriot synagogues (13:5) and to Sergius Paulus, the proconsul (13:7); in Antioch the city gathers to hear the word of the Lord (13:44), and Paul and Barnabas summarize

---

[46] ἐπισκέπτομαι with infinitive has this sense (BDAG 378 ἐπισκέπτομαι §3).
[47] The other significant groupings are undisputed Paulines (9), disputed Paulines (6), Revelation (7). The combination is found in the NT with 'of God' 41 times and with 'of the Lord' 13 times – Luke-Acts uses it with 'of God' 16 times and with 'of the Lord' 9 times (see listing in n. 20 above).
[48] Wallace, *Greek*, 119–21.
[49] Cf. Brawley, *Centering*, 119.
[50] Note τῇ διακονίᾳ τοῦ λόγου 'the service of the word', which echoes and contrasts with the use of the cognate verb in v. 2, διακονεῖν τραπέζαις 'to serve tables': the apostles are servants who handle the word, not tables.

their message as 'the word of God' (13:47); on their return to Antioch they continue to teach and proclaim the word of the Lord (15:35); they summarize their previous work as proclaiming the word of the Lord (15:36); in Philippi Paul and Silas speak the word of the Lord to the jailer and his family (16:32); the message preached in Beroea is identified by Luke as 'the word of God' (17:13); Paul's ministry in Corinth (18:11) and Ephesus (19:10) is centred on the word of God/the Lord.

This theme within Acts highlights a characteristic of God: the God of Acts is a communicator and a missionary – God reaches out to speak to people in his word, the gospel message, in order to introduce them to Jesus and lead them to salvation. But here we are stepping beyond the boundaries of our present study, and straying into asking about the character of God in Acts.

V. Some Implications

It seems beyond dispute that God is the key actor in Acts. To see Acts this way contrasts significantly with much of the scholarly literature until recently,[51] and is markedly different from much popular reading and preaching of Acts, which mistakenly treats the human agents in the story as most significant for the plot's development. This recognition is suggestive for at least two reasons in relation to Acts' ancient setting, which we can sketch only briefly.

First, Acts provides a focused and clear answer to the question, 'Who is God?' This question was much asked in the ancient world,[52] and the Jews were considered unusual because of their monotheism. Thus Luke could not simply announce 'God' without clarifying the nature of the god he proclaimed. Hence the stress on who God is and what God is now doing would be highly relevant to a Graeco-Roman audience. Luke's focus on God would contribute significantly to his aim to persuade his audience that the God of Israel, who had now made himself known in and through both the life, ministry, death and (supremely) resurrection of Jesus, and the work of the Spirit experienced in the believing community, was the one true God.

That said, it must be acknowledged that such readers would not find much of Luke's presentation congenial, notably his focus on the fulfilment of Scripture and his emphasis on the claim that the God who acted in Israel's history had acted in Jesus and was now acting in the life of the believing community. There are few places where the nature of God is tackled head on as a topic (the two speeches to pagans, in Lystra and Athens, are perhaps the clearest examples, Acts 14:15-17; 17:22-31).[53] This rather suggests that at least a significant part of Luke's target audience knew the Scriptures of Israel.[54]

---

[51] See n. 6.
[52] Cf. the analysis found in Cicero, *On the Nature of the Gods* (*De natura deorum*), which identifies three major positions in the Graeco-Roman world: the Stoics, the Epicureans and the Academicians (Cicero identifies his own view with the sceptical view of the latter group).
[53] I owe this observation to my student Dr Peter Mallen.
[54] So, among others, John Nolland, *Luke*, WBC 35A-C, 3 vols. (Dallas: Word, 1989-93), 1:xxxii-iii; Witherington, *Acts*, 63-5; Jervell, *Apostelgeschichte*, 89-90.

Thus, second, to write in this way would facilitate apologetic and proclamation among Jews and godfearers, who were those who knew these Scriptures. They would need no persuasion of Luke's monotheism, but they would need to be convinced that the locus of God's activity was now the community which saw Jesus as Israel's Messiah, not least because this community was now including gentiles in their midst without requiring circumcision. Such people would be well placed to grasp Luke's highlighting of the fulfilment of Scripture in Jesus and the community of his followers – and, of course, Christian hearers of Acts would find the book helpful in equipping them to engage in evangelism and apologetics among such people, as Moule judiciously comments:

> Here, then, in the Synoptic Gospels and Acts, each with its own peculiar emphasis, may be found the deposit of early Christian explanation: here are the voices of Christians explaining what led to their existence – how they themselves came to be: telling the story to themselves, that they may tell it to others, or even telling it directly to those others.[55]

In combination, this dual audience provides an audience for Acts which is wide-ranging across the Mediterranean community. Luke has written a book which communicates a 'zeal for God' both to those who have a Jewish heritage, whether as ethnic Jews or godfearers, and to those who are standing on the outside of Judaism looking in from paganism or emperor worship or the worship of any (or all!) of the gods of the Graeco-Roman world. Acts therefore fits with Bauckham's proposal that the Gospels, too, were aimed at such a wide audience.[56]

---

[55] C. F. D. Moule, *The Birth of the New Testament*, 3rd ed., BNTC (London: A. & C. Black, 1981), 133.
[56] Richard Bauckham, ed., *The Gospels for All Christians* (Edinburgh: T&T Clark; Grand Rapids, MI: Eerdmans, 1997), esp. 9–48.

VI. Appendix A: Nouns in Acts

	All nouns				Nominative nouns			
	NT	NT %	Acts	Acts %	NT	NT %	Acts	Acts %
Different words	2509		859		1229		311	
Total occurrences	28976	100.0	4156	100.0	7787	100.0	965	100.0
θεός 'God'	1317	4.6	167	4.0	314	4.0	65	6.7
Παῦλος, Σαούλ, Σαῦλος 'Paul, Saul'	182	0.6	152	3.7	87	1.1	63	6.5
κύριος 'Lord'	717	2.5	107	2.6	183	2.4	24	2.5
πνεῦμα 'spirit'	379	1.3	70	1.7	102	1.3	22	2.3
πατήρ 'father'	413	1.4	35	0.8	134	1.7	11	1.1
Ἰησοῦς 'Jesus'	917	3.2	69	1.7	462	5.9	10	1.0
λόγος 'word'	330	1.1	65	1.6	78	1.0	10	1.0
Ἰωάννης 'John'	135	0.5	24	0.6	54	0.7	10	1.0
Βαρναβᾶς 'Barnabas'	28	0.1	23	0.6	10	0.1	8	0.8
Other nouns	24558	84.8	3444	82.9	6363	81.7	742	76.9
ἀνήρ 'man'	216	0.8	100	2.4	114	1.5	58	6.0
Πέτρος 'Peter'	156	0.5	56	1.4	100	1.3	37	3.8
ἀδελφός 'brother'	343	1.2	57	1.4	188	2.4	26	2.7
ἄνθρωπος 'person'	550	1.9	46	1.1	150	1.9	14	1.5
ἄγγελος 'angel'	175	0.6	21	0.5	70	0.9	11	1.1
υἱός 'son'	377	1.3	21	0.5	194	2.5	10	1.0
ὄχλος 'crowd'	175	0.6	22	0.5	74	1.0	6	0.6
γυνή 'woman'	215	0.7	19	0.5	88	1.1	4	0.4
Χριστός 'Messiah'	472	1.6	14	0.3	76	1.0	3	0.3

VII. Appendix B: Uses of θεός 'God' in the New Testament

NT book	Total words in book	Uses in any case				Nominative uses		
		Times	Times per 1000 words in book	NT % of uses	Book as NT %	Times	Times per 1000 words in book	NT % of uses
Matt	21259	51	2.40	3.87	13.34	9	0.42	2.87
Mark	13090	49	3.74	3.72	8.21	12	0.92	3.82
Luke	22433	122	5.44	9.26	14.07	15	0.67	4.78
John	18207	83	4.56	6.30	11.42	19	1.04	6.05
Acts	20845	167	8.01	12.68	13.08	65	3.12	20.70
Rom	8278	153	18.48	11.62	5.19	32	3.87	10.19
1 Cor	8127	106	13.04	8.05	5.10	33	4.06	10.51
2 Cor	5193	79	15.21	6.00	3.26	20	3.85	6.37
Gal	2655	31	11.68	2.35	1.67	8	3.01	2.55
Eph	2788	31	11.12	2.35	1.75	6	2.15	1.91
Phil	1914	23	12.02	1.75	1.20	8	4.18	2.55
Col	1833	21	11.46	1.59	1.15	2	1.09	0.64
1 Thess	1715	36	20.99	2.73	1.08	7	4.08	2.23
2 Thess	944	18	19.07	1.37	0.59	5	5.3	1.59
1 Tim	1862	22	11.82	1.67	1.17	2	1.07	0.64
2 Tim	1445	13	9.00	0.99	0.91	2	1.38	0.64
Titus	775	13	16.77	0.99	0.49	1	1.29	0.32
Phlm	386	2	5.18	0.15	0.24	0	0	0.00
Heb	5691	68	11.95	5.16	3.57	24	4.22	7.64
Jas	2077	16	7.70	1.21	1.30	4	1.93	1.27
1 Pet	1953	39	19.97	2.96	1.23	5	2.56	1.59
2 Pet	1243	7	5.63	0.53	0.78	1	0.8	0.32
1 John	2494	62	24.86	4.71	1.56	13	5.21	4.14
2 John	278	2	7.19	0.15	0.17	0	0	0.00

Appendix B (continued)

NT book	Uses in any case					Nominative uses		
	Total words in book	Times	Times per 1000 words in book	NT % of uses	Book as NT %	Times	Times per 1000 words in book	NT % of uses
3 John	254	3	11.81	0.23	0.16	0	0	0.00
Jude	535	4	7.48	0.30	0.34	0	0	0.00
Rev	11117	96	8.64	7.29	6.97	21	1.89	6.69
Total	159391	1317				314		

3

Doing Theology Lukewise: Luke as Theologian and Storyteller[1]

I. Introduction

I am a theologian who happens to be a New Testament scholar, and a person of Christian faith. I thus live and work at the intersection of church and academy, and seek to contribute to both places in my scholarship and theologizing. This chapter aims to do exactly that: I shall look at how theology is done through the lens of the way that Luke does it.

Luke is the author of his Gospel and the book of Acts – around 25 per cent of the New Testament – and yet he does not get the attention that study of the historical Jesus, or Paul, or John do. There has always been a stream in scholarship which has engaged with Luke, but often simply to compare him unfavourably with Paul, or to suggest that Luke has misunderstood or misrepresents Paul in Acts.[2] Instead, I shall shine the spotlight on Luke's two books in order to see how he 'does theology'.

II. What Is Theology and Who Is a Theologian?

To ask that question requires a prior question: what is theology, and who is a theologian? In other words, what are we looking for in Luke and Acts, and does Luke qualify as a 'theologian'?

The terms 'theology' and 'theologian' go back a long way, before the rise of Christianity. 'Theology' derives from the Greek θεολογία, which roughly means 'God words', 'an account of, or discourse about, gods or God'.[3] The cognate θεολόγος 'theologian' was used for poets such as Hesiod and Orpheus (by Aristotle), of cosmologists (again, by Aristotle), and of diviners and prophets.[4] In each case, it was their writing or speech

---

[1] This chapter was originally presented as my professorial inaugural lecture at St Mary's University, Twickenham on 15 May 2017.
[2] See especially the key essay, Phillip Vielhauer, "On the Paulinism of Acts," in *Studies in Luke-Acts*, ed. Leander E. Keck and J. L. Martyn (London: SPCK, 1968), 33–50.
[3] David F. Wright, "Theology," in *New Dictionary of Theology*, ed. Sinclair B. Ferguson, David F. Wright and J. I. Packer (Leicester: Inter-Varsity Press, 1988), 680–1, quoting 680.
[4] See LSJ θεολόγος §1.

about the gods which was in view. Philo of Alexandria, a Hellenistic Jew of the first century BC, called Moses 'the theologian' (*Moses* 2.115; *Rewards* 53), but none of the books of the Greek Old or New Testament use either θεολογία or θεολόγος. The nearest is that two eleventh-century manuscripts of the book of Revelation have running headers, 'The revelation to John the theologian (τοῦ θεολόγου)'.[5] It is only with the apologists of the second and third centuries that Christian usage appears, and 'theology' comes to mean Christian teaching, specifically about God.

Allen Brent discusses the attribution of 'theologian' to John of Revelation and shows that θεολόγος described a role in a pagan cult for gods such as Artemis or for deified emperors.[6] A θεολόγος in such contexts was one who told stories through drama and music: it could be used of a director and choreographer, and sometimes a choir director too. The θεολόγος pronounced a eulogy for the emperor, and perhaps took the role of the emperor in drama. John, argues Brent, would have appeared to those who knew such usage as one of the same kind, for Revelation offers a large-scale dramatic presentation of history with the exalted Jesus at its centre, and includes hymns and celebration.

This certainly offers a model of 'doing theology' which Luke would have appreciated, for it is narrative-based. This contrasts with the way 'theology' is often (mis-)portrayed today, as a dry, rational, purely intellectual exercise. This may be rooted in the way Augustine spoke of theology as 'reasoning or discussion concerning the Deity' (*City of God* 8.1), restricting it to discussion of God himself; it is rare within the Fathers to find 'theology' used for a wider range of Christian belief and practice. The medieval Scholastics stressed clear, analytical thinking about God and his ways in engagement with philosophical and cultural traditions, and this could – and did – lead to theology being in hock to philosophy, and as appearing abstract and irrelevant.

However, the Christian tradition is richer than this. The New Testament authors sought and lived a wholehearted and rounded response to God in Christ, and made no separation between doctrine or theology (on the one hand) and spirituality or Christian living and practice (on the other). While the Fathers may have formally separated the two, they were clear that both were crucial to the Christian community's life – and that the best theologians qualified as such by their godliness of life as well as their intellectual apprehension of the gospel.[7] In the Gospels, Jesus's saying that people are to love God 'with heart and soul and mind and strength' (Mark 12:30) comes to mind as exemplifying this: if we characterize 'theology' as loving God with the mind, it should not be separated from the application of all human powers – heart, soul and strength – to the life of discipleship to which the Lord calls believers. The working definition of theology from my St Mary's University colleague Dr Anthony Towey, 'thoughtful conversation about God',[8] is heading in this direction, for to speak about God is necessarily to involve yourself and your life in the conversation. More fully we

---

[5] The minuscules 525 and 1006.
[6] Allen Brent, "John as *Theologos*: The Imperial Mysteries and the Apocalypse," *JSNT* 22 (2000): 87–102.
[7] See Hans Urs von Balthasar, *Explorations in Theology*, 4 vols. (San Francisco, CA: Ignatius, 1989), 1:181–86; John Paul II, Apostolic Letter *Novo Millennio Ineunte* §27. (I owe these references to my St Mary's University colleague Prof. Stephen Bullivant.)
[8] Anthony Towey, *An Introduction to Christian Theology* (London: Bloomsbury, 2013), 3–14, esp. 3–4.

might say that full-orbed theology is 'speaking about God in order to evoke a response of faith, love and obedience'.

In this light, I shall look at Luke's double-work for the ways in which Luke communicates through narrative about God, and about what it means to live with and for God as known through Christ and by the Spirit. I shall look at this from four angles, each with an example: how Luke does theology through stories, through characters, through speeches, and through patterns.

III. Luke Does Theology through Stories

Making narrative is central to human existence, as Edward Branigan notes:

> Narrative has existed in every known human society. Like metaphor, it seems to be everywhere … Making narrative is a strategy for making our world of experiences and desires intelligible. It is a fundamental way of organising data.[9]

So it is no surprise that one of the early Christians' ways of communicating their faith, of 'doing theology', with both insiders and outsiders, was by storytelling. The four Gospels and Acts show this in action by exploiting the power of story. Scholars have long recognized that Luke uses techniques similar to those in other ancient narratives, whether history or fiction.[10] While the narrative techniques involved in writing fiction and history may have been similar, this does not mean that ancient authors did not differentiate between the two. Luke sets out his stall at the beginning of his Gospel thus:

> 1 Since many have undertaken to set down an orderly account of the events that have been fulfilled among us, 2 just as they were handed on to us by those who from the beginning were eyewitnesses and servants of the word, 3 I too decided, after investigating everything carefully from the very first, to write an orderly account for you, most excellent Theophilus, 4 so that you may know the truth concerning the things about which you have been instructed. (Luke 1:1–4 NRSV)

Luke draws attention to his investigation of the stories he tells, including eyewitness testimony (v. 2), previous writers (v. 1), and his own research (v. 3), all of which he has assembled in an 'orderly' manner (v. 3) in order to persuade Theophilus that what he has been taught is true (v. 4). Luke is not attempting to write 'objective' history – in

---

[9] Edward Branigan, *Narrative Comprehension and Film*, Sightlines (London: Routledge, 1992), 1. (I owe the reference to my student Dr Peter Mansell.)
[10] Loveday Alexander, "Fact, Fiction and the Genre of Acts," *NTS* 44 (1998): 380–99 discusses ancient authors' uses of fact and fiction and how they were distinguished, and concludes that Acts is different from both. It 'implies and creates the presumption of a shared religious experience' (399). Richard Pervo makes the error of assuming that features in Acts which parallel those in Greek novels necessarily imply that Acts is fictional in Richard I. Pervo, *Profit with Delight* (Philadelphia, PA: Fortress, 1987).

any case, an illusory goal, as scholars increasingly recognize – but narrative which will communicate and convince.

III.a. The Death of Jesus (Luke 23)

As an example, let us consider Luke's account of the death of Jesus (Luke 23). It is frequently asserted that Luke has no 'atonement theology', that is, that he has no understanding of what the death of Jesus achieves.[11] My usual reaction to this is to wonder whether such people have read Luke 23, for in this chapter Luke tells the big story of the death of Jesus using a series of mini-stories about particular people or groups in a way which communicates the significance of the events.

Predicted by Jesus First, notice that Luke prepares for the crucifixion narrative by predictions from Jesus: Luke 9:31 ('he spoke about his *exodus*, which he was to fulfil at Jerusalem'), 51 (he set his face to go to Jerusalem); 12:50 (Jesus has a baptism with which he will be baptized); 13:32-33 (a prophet must be killed in Jerusalem); and 17:25 (Jesus must endure suffering and be rejected). Second, it is notable that Luke uses Scripture to interpret the passion narrative: 18:31-33 (everything written must be fulfilled); 20:17 (Ps 118:22); 22:37 (Isa 53:12); 24:26-27 (Moses and all the prophets), 44 (everything in the law, the prophets and the Psalms), 46 (it is written). So when we read Luke 23, we should read it with these passages in mind.

Jesus's innocence A major feature of Luke 23 is the stress on the innocence of Jesus, which is identified eight times: three times by Pilate (vv. 4, 14, 22), and also by Herod (v. 15), the criminal on the cross (v. 41), the centurion (v. 47), the people (v. 48), and Joseph of Arimathea (v. 51). Luke makes clear that Jesus does not deserve his fate.

Not only this, but the careful reader of Luke knows that the charges brought against Jesus (v. 2) are false, although *they are true of the Jewish leaders* who bring these charges. Jesus is charged with subverting the nation – whereas the Jewish leaders are doing this by treating God's plan to use Israel to bless the world (e.g. Gen 12:3), which Luke has signalled (e.g. 2:32), as divine favouritism and bias towards Israel and against the gentiles. Remember that a devout Jewish man could daily thank God that he had not been born a gentile.[12]

Second, Jesus is charged with forbidding tribute to Caesar, a twisting of Jesus's answer to the question about whether it was lawful to pay tribute to Caesar (Luke 20:21-26). Jesus's answer made clear that Caesar had a subordinate jurisdiction under God, for they should give to Caesar what belonged to him. However, the Jewish leadership in fact accept the jurisdiction of Caesar, even to the extent of carrying the coin with its blasphemous slogan 'Tiberius Caesar son of the divine Augustus, Pontfiex maximus'.[13] By going to Pilate, they accept Roman jurisdiction and act as if Israel were merely another secular state; they negotiate politically rather than rely on Israel's God.

---

[11] E.g. Hans Conzelmann, *The Theology of St Luke*, trans. Geoffrey Buswell (London: Faber & Faber, 1960), 199-201 (with other references cited by Conzelmann, 201).

[12] b. Menaḥ. 43b.

[13] H. StJ. Hart, "The Coin of 'Render unto Caesar …' (A Note on Some Aspects of Mark 12:13-17; Matt. 22:15-22; Luke 20:20-26)," in *Jesus and the Politics of His Day*, ed. Ernst Bammel and C. F. D. Moule (Cambridge: Cambridge University Press, 1984), 241-8.

Third, they claim that Jesus self-identifies as a king, and thus, by implication, opposes Caesar. Jesus was indeed a king, as Israel's Messiah, but not the kind of king they suggested – he was not there to lead an uprising against the Romans. By contrast, and deeply ironically, the Jewish leaders (effectively) surrender YHWH's claim to be Israel's king by collaborating with the Romans.

All three charges are untrue of Jesus, but reflect Israel's tragic failure to be the people of God they were called to be. Jesus in his death is being charged with things of which he is innocent – but the Jewish leaders, and by extension the nation, are guilty of exactly those things. Jesus dies bearing the sin and failure of the nation who had turned their backs on God's purposes for them. Jesus obediently and lovingly does what Israel should have done, so that Israel can be forgiven and renewed.

Barabbas Next, consider Barabbas. We meet him as the man the Jewish leaders want to have released instead of Jesus (vv. 18–19). Luke says plainly that he is a murderer and insurrectionist (v. 25). He is certainly guilty. So notice how Luke beautifully juxtaposes Barabbas and Jesus: 'He released the man they asked for, the one who had been put in prison for insurrection and murder, and he handed Jesus over as they wished' (v. 25). The guilty Barabbas goes free and the innocent Jesus dies in his place. An amazing exchange takes place. Luke may not use the explicit language of Jesus dying in the place of sinful humanity which Paul does, but this exchange of the guilty Barabbas and the innocent Jesus could not say more clearly that Jesus dies for others. Jesus, the Father's true and innocent son dies, while guilty Barabbas – whose name ironically means 'son of the father' – is freed.

The two criminals To speak of Barabbas leads to the two criminals crucified alongside Jesus (vv. 39–43). One reacts by railing against Jesus (v. 39). He wants proof. He wants Jesus to perform a miracle and show himself to be great by great acts. He wants a Messiah who will save him from death. The second thief is different. He recognizes the justice of his situation and the injustice of Jesus's situation (vv. 40–41) and has a flash of insight. Instead of asking for Jesus to save him *from* death, he asks Jesus to save him *through* death. He asks Jesus to remember him when he comes as king in the future (v. 42), and gets far more than he could dream: Jesus promises that the man will be with him *today* in Paradise. Jesus in his death is opening the door of Paradise to repentant sinners like the thief.

The darkness The darkness which falls at noon is part of Luke's portrait of Jesus's death (vv. 44–45). Darkness in Scripture symbolizes God's absence – hence a feature of the new Jerusalem is that there is *no night* (Rev 21:25). As Jesus is crucified, the sun's light fails. So awful is this time when Jesus takes the sin of the world upon himself that even nature turns its back on him.

The temple curtain 'and the curtain of the temple was torn in two' (v. 45b). The temple was in sections, with growing limitations as to who could enter each section. Furthest out was the court of the gentiles, where non-Jews could come and pray. This was the area Jesus cleared of the money changers and sellers, who were preventing its use for that intended purpose (Luke 19:45–46). Then there was the court of the women, where Jewish women could pray. Jewish men could go on into the court of Israel, and from there could observe (but not enter) the court of the priests, where sacrifice was offered by priests with the assistance of the Levites. Within the court of the priests was the Holy Place, which contained the incense altar – again a place for only the priests. The Holy of Holies was inside the Holy Place: it was a cubic room into which only the high priest went, and only once a year, on the Day of Atonement, to offer the sacrifice for that day. The Holy of Holies was separated from the Holy Place by a curtain thick as a human hand, to protect the people – even the priests – from the holy presence of God. Were God to break out of the Holy of Holies, devout Jews expected that God would consume the people with his holiness – indeed, when the high priest entered annually, he had bells on the bottom of his long robe, so that those outside could know that he was still alive, and a rope attached to his leg, so that if he was killed by God, those outside could drag him out without having to enter the Holy of Holies themselves.[14] So when this curtain was torn in two, the danger was gone: it was now possible for people to mingle with God and not be consumed. The evidence of Acts is that God had abandoned the Holy of Holies and gone out into the world to meet people there.[15] How could this be possible? Only if the danger of human sin had been dealt with, for that was why God's presence was such a threat, in the way that extreme radioactivity threatens human life. Through Jesus's death, as he commends himself into God's hands (v. 46), the way is open. In Acts, the places where God meets people are all over – in the streets, in homes, even in the Diaspora (and note how Stephen's speech in Acts 7 criticizes the tendency to confine God's presence to the temple).[16]

Simon of Cyrene When a condemned criminal was led out for crucifixion, he was surrounded by four Roman soldiers in a square, with a fifth walking in front carrying a placard with the charge written on it. For Jesus this read 'the king of the Jews' and was written in the three main languages: Latin, Greek and Aramaic (v. 38; cf. John 19:19–20). The prisoner would be carrying the *patibulum*, the crossbeam: the whole cross would be far too heavy to bear. It seems Jesus was too weak to carry even this, and Simon felt the tap of a Roman spear on his shoulder, meaning that he must serve the Romans – here by carrying the crossbeam behind Jesus. Simon may well have become a believer, for Mark tells us he had two sons, Alexander and Rufus – the latter may be named in Rom 16:13.[17] Simon models the cross-bearing about which Jesus has twice spoken in Luke (9:23; 14:27), portraying the Christian life as following in the steps of the humiliated Jesus. Luke signals that there is no true version of the Christian way which misses this: the route to glory is through humiliation and suffering – God has no alternative, including for his own son.

I could go on, but this is sufficient to show that this is a very rich telling of the crucifixion which shows us Luke theologizing about the death of Jesus in narrative

---

[14] Bells: Exod 28:33–35; rope/chain: 'Rabbi Yitzchak said, A chain was tied to the feet of the High Priest, when he entered the Holy of Holies, so that if he dies there they will take him out, since it is forbidden to enter there.' Zohar Emor 34: Yom Kippur §251.

[15] Raymond E. Brown, *The Death of the Messiah*, 2 vols., ABRL (London: Geoffrey Chapman, 1994), 2:1101–2.

[16] More fully, see Steve Walton, "A Tale of Two Perspectives? The Temple in Acts," in *Heaven on Earth: The Temple in Biblical Theology*, ed. T. Desmond Alexander and Simon J. Gathercole (Carlisle: Paternoster, 2004), 135–49, esp. 138–43 [in this volume 76–87, esp. 78–82].

[17] Robert Jewett, *Romans*, Hermeneia (Minneapolis, MN: Fortress, 2007), 969.

mode. Time fails me to show how this story develops in Acts – simply note that central to the early believers' meetings is the meal focused on remembering Jesus's death (e.g. Acts 2:42, 26; 20:7, 11).[18]

IV. Luke Does Theology through Characters

Our second example of how Luke does theology is that Luke's presentation of characters portrays theology believed and lived. We have already seen this in a measure in characters in the story of Jesus's death. It is widely recognized that characters drive the plot of a story – and that the plot finds expression through characters.[19] Given that Luke's story is a story of God's engagement with humanity through Jesus and the Spirit, both human and divine characters are significant to his theologizing.[20]

Characterization can be *direct*, by the author *telling* about a character or group, such as Luke's description of Elizabeth and Zechariah: 'Both of them were righteous before God, living blamelessly according to all the commandments and regulations of the Lord' (Luke 1:6) – these are definitely the good guys! Characterization can be *indirect*, by the author *showing* the character of a person or group through their words and actions, such as the way the synagogue leader criticizes Jesus for healing on the sabbath and is then himself criticized by the most reliable of characters, Jesus, with the result that Jesus's opponents are shamed and the crowd rejoices (Luke 13:14–17).[21]

Narrative critics notice three different kinds of characters in stories.[22] Some are 'flat' characters, and have a small number of predictable traits, such as the Jewish leaders who oppose Jesus in Luke's Gospel.[23] Some are 'stock' characters, who have only one trait and are there only to move the story along, such as the widow who gives her two small coins to the temple (Luke 21:1–4). Some, the most interesting, are 'round'

---

[18] See especially discussion of 2:46 in my forthcoming commentary on Acts, in conversation with Ulrich Wendel, *Gemeinde in Kraft: Das Gemeindeverständnis in den Summarien der Apostelgeschichte*, NTDH 20 (Neukirchen-Vluyn: Neukirchener, 1998), 183–6.

[19] E.g. Mark Allan Powell, *What Is Narrative Criticism?* (London: SPCK, 1993), 51.

[20] Cf. Steve Walton, "The Acts – of God? What Is the 'Acts of the Apostles' All About?," *EvQ* 80 (2008): 291–306 [in this volume 15–30].

[21] On characterization in Luke-Acts, see now Frank Dicken and Julia A. Snyder, eds, *Characters and Characterization in Luke-Acts*, LNTS 548 (London: Bloomsbury T&T Clark, 2016). On characterization more broadly, see Cornelis Bennema, "Character Reconstruction in the New Testament (1): The Theory," *ExpTim* 127 (2016): 365–74; Cornelis Bennema, "Character Reconstruction in the New Testament (2): The Practice," *ExpTim* 127 (2016): 417–29 or, more fully, Cornelis Bennema, *A Theory of Character in New Testament Narrative* (Minneapolis, MN: Fortress, 2014).

[22] The terms vary between critics, but the central ideas are common.

[23] *Telling*: 16:14 (they are lovers of money); 7:30 (they refuse John's baptism and thus reject the purpose of God for themselves); 18:9 (they trust in themselves to be righteous and despise others). *Showing*: 11:40 (they are foolish – Jesus speaking); 11:42 (they lack love for God and concern for justice – Jesus speaking); 11:52 (they have the key of knowledge but do not use it – Jesus speaking); 7:40–47 (Jesus tells Simon the Pharisee a parable to contrast the forgiven woman's state and his real state – he is not a forgiven person).

characters with a variety of (potentially conflicting) traits – the disciples in Luke are such a group character, as we shall see.

To assess what the narrator is saying about a character involves considering the reaction the writer seeks from the readers to that character. This is where we see the message, the theology, which Luke is communicating. Is the narrative inviting *empathy*, identifying strongly with the character, perhaps because readers see their own likeness in the character or because they aspire to be like them? The message here is to imitate the strengths of these characters. Or is the narrative inviting the less intense *sympathy*, still identifying with the character, and frequently signalled by a positive view of that character by a reliable character with whom the readers empathize – in Luke, Jesus's positive attitude to the woman who washes his feet with her tears is such an example (7:36–50, esp. 44–50). The message here is to be like the woman in her devotion to Jesus and generosity to him and his work. Or is the narrative inviting *antipathy*, alienation from or disdain for a character, such as Judas (see Luke 6:16; 22:3, 47–48; Acts 1:16–20)? The message here is to avoid this way of living.

As a fuller example, consider Jesus's disciples. They are called to be with Jesus after he has prayed specifically about this (Luke 6:12–16), and yet they are of little faith (8:25), illustrated by their inability to cast out a demon (9:40). Nevertheless, they are blessed by seeing what they see (10:23), and recognize their need to learn to pray (11:1). However, they fall asleep rather than praying with Jesus in Gethsemane (22:40, 45–46). After the resurrection, Jesus opens their minds to understand Scripture (24:27, 32, 45), and renews their commitment with the promise of the Spirit (24:44–53).

As the story continues in Acts, the promised Spirit comes (Acts 2:1–4), and they are never the same again. There is a beautiful contrast between their failure to pray in Gethsemane and the believers' reactions when under pressure. Thus, when Peter and John report to the believers after being forbidden by the Sanhedrin to speak in the name of Jesus, the believers' first response is to pray (4:23–30), to which God responds by empowering them further by the Spirit to speak the gospel message boldly (4:31). Further, when Peter is imprisoned by Herod Agrippa with a view to execution, the believers' response is to pray (12:5), and the outcome is his release (12:6–11). The story is comical, of course, because the praying believers cannot quite believe that it *is* Peter when he comes knocking at the house where they are praying – it must be his angel, they tell Rhoda the maid (12:15). Happily, they are persuaded, for Peter keeps knocking until they let him in (12:16) – but they are clearly not yet fully transformed as far as trusting God to answer prayer goes!

The characterization of the disciples in these stories, which is rich and 'round', invites readers who are believers to identify with them, recognizing both that they aspire to follow Jesus and that, like the disciples, they fail to live up to those aspirations consistently. Nevertheless, such believing readers can be encouraged that failure is not final – the Lord's recommissioning of them after his resurrection (Luke 24:44–49; Acts 1:6–8) and the (repeated) coming of the Spirit (Acts 2:1–4; 4:8, 31; 6:5, 10; 8:17, 29, 39; 9:17; etc.) show that God-in-Christ responds with forgiveness, generosity and grace to those whose lives face towards God.

V. Luke Does Theology through Speeches

Ancient authors, including historians, used dialogue and monologue liberally to communicate their story, although in ways which were 'in tune' with the character(s) speaking.[24] As with speeches in biblical books, they are invariably too short to have been the actual speech delivered – they are necessarily the author's *précis* of the speech, often in the author's own language and style. It would be an anachronism to think that this labels the speeches necessarily as fiction, invented by the author solely for the purpose of forwarding his (for it is usually 'his') agenda – not least because authors can present speeches on opposite sides of a question.[25] The ancient expectation was that the author would present speeches with *faithfulness* to the reported historical event and the speaker.[26] Indeed, the historian Polybius inveighs against his opponent Timaeus for inventing speeches (12.25).

When we turn to Luke and Acts, it is the speeches of Luke's reliable characters (as narrative critics say) we should consider, for these characters are Luke's heroes, those whose deeds and words Luke stands behind – or perhaps we should say, especially in the case of God, whose deeds and words stand behind Luke. These speeches seek to persuade, as ancient oratory normally did; they offer models for imitation or warnings of ways to avoid.

As an example, consider Paul's teaching to the Ephesian elders (Acts 20:18–35). This is the only passage in the New Testament which calls the same group of people both ἐπίσκοποι (overseers or bishops) and πρεσβύτεροι (elders or presbyters). However, Luke is more interested here in the *exercise* of leadership than its form or organization; I have argued elsewhere that this speech focuses on four themes: the faithful fulfilment of ministry; suffering; wealth and work; and the death of Jesus.[27] Not only that, there are extensive parallels of not just the four themes, but also the vocabulary, in Jesus's farewell to his disciples (Luke 22:14–38). Let me give just a few examples – for a full treatment, see my book, *Leadership and Lifestyle*.[28] *Faithful fulfilment of ministry* is seen in Paul's emphasis on his humble service: he served the Lord with all humility (v. 19); Jesus, similarly, says, 'I am among you as one who serves' (vv. 26, 27). Humble service is not characteristic of leadership in the first-century Graeco-Roman world, as Jesus highlights by contrasting his service with the world's rulers who want to lord it over others. *Suffering* is a feature of Paul's ministry, particularly his trials from the Jewish

---

[24] See Conrad H. Gempf, "Public Speaking and Published Accounts," in *The Book of Acts in Its Ancient Literary Setting*, ed. Bruce W. Winter and Andrew D. Clarke, BAFCS 1 (Carlisle: Paternoster, 1993), 259–303.

[25] E.g. Thucydides 3.37–40 presents a speech of Cleon, followed by a counter-speech of Diodotus 3.42–48, followed by the author's comment that 'opinions had been maintained with equal force' (3.49). (I owe the references to Gempf, "Speaking," 280; see his discussion there.) In Acts, note the speeches of non-believers, such as Gamaliel (5:34–39), the town clerk of Ephesus (19:35–40), and Tertullus (24:2–8); more fully, see Osvaldo Padilla, *The Speeches of Outsiders in Acts: Poetics, Theology and Historiography*, SNTSMS 145 (Cambridge: Cambridge University Press, 2008).

[26] Gempf, "Speaking."

[27] Steve Walton, *Leadership and Lifestyle: The Portrait of Paul in the Miletus Speech and 1 Thessalonians*, SNTSMS 108 (Cambridge: Cambridge University Press, 2000), 84–93.

[28] Especially 100–18.

people (v. 19), and his expectation of future suffering (vv. 23, 24); Jesus, too, can speak of his 'trial' (as in Acts 20:19, πειρασμός, a rare word in Acts), and of his forthcoming suffering (v. 15). *Work and wealth* are key themes in the closing part of Paul's speech, where he shows how he has modelled proper handling of money and wealth, and urges the elders to do the same in order to provide for those in need (vv. 33–35); Jesus speaks in a different vein – for it is a different situation – to call on his disciples to act wisely with their money (vv. 35–38). Finally, *the death of Jesus* is a relatively rare, but significant theme in both speeches: Paul speaks of God obtaining the church 'through the death of his own' (v. 28);[29] and Jesus institutes the eucharist, a meal to remember his giving of his body and blood for them (vv. 19–20).[30]

This looks like Lukan design to portray a model of leadership which Jesus embodies and then teaches to his disciples, and which Paul also embodies and then teaches to some from the next generation. Luke paints a picture of Christian leadership for his readers' education and imitation.

VI. Luke Does Theology through Patterns

The previous example leads into my final observation, that Luke uses *patterning* to communicate theological themes and emphases. He can use techniques of foreshadowing a topic before picking it up later, or echoing a theme from elsewhere in his double-work, or artistic patterning.[31]

As an example, consider the use of a 'programmatic' statement followed later by repetition of the elements of that statement in narrative. Luke's model of communal life for believing communities is a good example. Acts 2:42 offers this description of the early Jerusalem believing community:

> They were devoting themselves to the apostles' teaching and the fellowship, the breaking of bread, and the prayers. (my translation)

Here are four elements of their life together: the apostles' teaching, fellowship (shared life and sharing of possessions)w, breaking bread, and the prayers. Each is illustrated and developed in the immediately following verses, 43-47:[32]

> 43 Fear kept coming on everyone, and many wonders and signs were taking place through the apostles. 44 All who had come to believe were together and the used to hold everything in common; 45 they used to sell their possessions and belongings and distribute the proceeds to all, as anyone had need. 46 Day by day, spending much time together in the temple and breaking bread in homes, they shared food with joy and

---

[29] On the text and translation, see Walton, *Leadership*, 94–8.
[30] I take Luke 20:19b–20 to be original; see Walton, *Leadership*, 137–40; I. Howard Marshall, *Last Supper and Lord's Supper* (Exeter: Paternoster, 1980).
[31] For example, see David Wenham and Steve Walton, *Exploring the New Testament, vol. 1: A Guide to the Gospels and Acts*, 3rd ed. (London: SPCK, 2021), 316–19.
[32] My translation. For what follows, see more detail in my forthcoming commentary on Acts, *ad loc.*

singleness of heart, 47 praising God and having favour with the whole people. Every day the Lord added to their group those who were being saved. (my translation)

The apostles who teach do wonders and signs (v. 43) which bear witness to the truth of their teaching, and with the teaching lead to the numerical growth of the community (v. 47). The believers' 'fellowship' is explained by their shared life – they were 'together' (ἐπὶ τὸ αὐτό, v. 44a) – and sharing of possessions in order to help those in need (vv. 44b–45).[33] Provision for the needy would be a further powerful testimony to the Jerusalemites, and a further factor in the community's growth (v. 47). 'The breaking of bread' is repeated and expanded to include meals in both the temple courts and homes (v. 46). The referent of the phrase is debated; in my view, it most probably includes both the specific eucharistic action of breaking bread in remembrance of the Lord's death and the shared meals they ate.[34] '*The* prayers' includes their participation in temple worship (v. 46a) and their praise of God (v. 47a).

There is debate whether these four-fold activities are a pattern for the life of believing communities,[35] or (as Joachim Jeremias proposes) the actual sequence of each weekly community meeting.[36] The actual descriptions of community meetings in the rest of the book of Acts speak against Jeremias – they do not follow the sequence of teaching, sharing, breaking bread, and prayer found in 2:42. However, and this is where the 'patterning' idea helps, the four elements *are* regularly present when the believing communities meet. Let me illustrate with one of Luke's fuller descriptions of a Christian meeting, in Troas (20:6):

7 On the first day of the week, when we met to break bread, Paul was instructing them; since he intended to leave the next day, he continued speaking until midnight. 8 There were many lamps in the room upstairs where we were meeting. 9 A young man named Eutychus, who was sitting in the window, began to sink into a deep sleep while Paul talked still longer. Overcome by sleep, he fell to the ground three floors below and was picked up dead. 10 But Paul went down, and bending over him took him in his arms, and said, 'Do not be alarmed, for his life is in him.' 11 Then Paul went upstairs, and after he had broken bread and eaten, he continued to converse with them until dawn; then he left. 12 Meanwhile they had taken the boy away alive and were not a little comforted. (Acts 20:7–12, my translation)

Notice the elements from 2:42. Teaching comes at beginning and end: Paul is instructing, even up to midnight (v. 7), and continues to speak with them until dawn (v. 11b). Poor old Eutychus – whose name, ironically, means 'Lucky'! – falls asleep during Paul's discourse (v. 9). That, of course, leads to the 'wonder and sign' of Eutychus being

---

[33] See Fiona J. Robertson Gregson, *Everything in Common? The Theology and Practice of the Sharing of Possessions in Community in the New Testament* (Eugene, OR: Pickwick, 2017), 46–50.
[34] See my forthcoming commentary, *ad loc.*
[35] E.g. Marshall, *Supper*, 127.
[36] Joachim Jeremias, *The Eucharistic Words of Jesus* (London: SCM, 1966), 118–21.

raised from the dead (v. 10). Their purpose is 'to break bread' (v. 7) and a specific part of the meeting is designated as such (v. 11), indicating both a thanksgiving focused on the cross and celebrated with bread broken, and a meal, where doubtless there was sharing of food together. Prayer may be understood as part of Paul's action which leads to Eutychus's revival (v. 10). Although corporate prayer is not explicitly mentioned in this story, Paul's regular practice on saying farewell to his communities was to pray with them on the beach before boarding ship (20:36; 21:5-6) – so we may reasonably assume that Paul prayed with this community. Certainly this is not a 'tidy' echo of the four elements from 2:42, but it is reasonable to see them all present in one form or another, and a wider study of the Christian meetings in Acts confirms this.[37]

VII. Conclusion: Luke as Theologian and Storyteller

We have looked at four ways in which Luke tells stories with theological intent. He writes to communicate and persuade; he wants Theophilus to be convinced of 'the truth concerning the things which you have been taught' (Luke 1:4, my translation). Central to Luke's persuasive intent is to invite response to the identity of Jesus alongside the Father, and the powerful effects of his ministry, death, resurrection and sending of the Spirit. Luke uses narrative to convey these key truths through careful storytelling (as we saw with Luke's account of the cross), through characters (as we saw through Luke's portrait of Jesus's disciples), through speeches (as we saw in Paul and Jesus teaching on leadership), and through patterns (as we saw through Luke's portrait of the early Christian communities). Luke is a skilled and nuanced storyteller, who 'does theology' by this means. He deserves to stand alongside the great theologians of the New Testament, such as Paul and John, and those of any age. He calls and invites believers today to learn from his example, and to tell and re-tell both the Christian story of Jesus, the Christian stories of his church throughout the ages, and the Christian story of the lives of believers today throughout the world – he calls us to do theology Lukewise.[38]

---

[37] The Revd Sheila Pite helped me recognize this in her MA essay on the theme which I supervised at St John's College, Nottingham.

[38] I am indebted to my student Dr Peter Mallen for the coinage 'Lukewise'; see Peter Mallen, *The Reading and Transformation of Isaiah in Luke-Acts*, LNTS 367 (London: T&T Clark, 2008), 159.

Part II

The Believing Communities and Their World

4

Calling the Church Names: Learning about Christian Identity from Acts

The question, 'What is the church?' is perennial among students of the New Testament. Paul Minear earlier produced a fine study of *Images of the Church in the New Testament* which mapped 96 different analogies used for the church by the New Testament authors – although, rather curiously, without discussing 'church' as a term in its own right.[1] There are several recent studies of the church in Acts, including two from a narrative-critical perspective,[2] as well as wider studies of how the earliest Christians conceived their corporate identity.[3]

The questions arising from these studies, and from reading Acts itself, are live questions for churches in the West today as they engage with being 'church' in a postmodern age suspicious of traditional institutions – and as they come to terms with being a minority in world Christianity. We shall not, of course, be possible to face many of these questions, so we shall consider some of the complexities of the issues before identifying the contribution this chapter makes.

I. Complexities of This Area

The study of the church in Acts is complicated by several levels of issues. For example, scholars have discussed the sources of Acts,[4] and there can be little doubt that

---

[1] Paul S. Minear, *Images of the Church in the New Testament* (London: Lutterworth, 1961). On Acts specifically, see Henry J. Cadbury, "Names for Christians in Acts," in *The Beginnings of Christianity, Part I: The Acts of the Apostles*, ed. F. J. Foakes Jackson and K. Lake, 5 vols. (London: Macmillan, 1933), 375–92; Joseph A. Fitzmyer, "The Designations of Christians in Acts and Their Significance," in *Unité et diversité dans l'Église*, ed. Pontifical Biblical Commission, Teologia e filosofia 15 (Vatican City: Libreria Editrice Vaticana, 1989), 223–36.

[2] Richard P. Thompson, *Keeping the Church in Its Place: The Church as Narrative Character in Acts* (London: T&T Clark, 2006); Graham H. Twelftree, *People of the Spirit: Exploring Luke's View of the Church* (London: SPCK, 2009).

[3] Notably Kevin N. Giles, *What on Earth Is the Church? A Biblical and Theological Enquiry* (London: SPCK, 1995); Paul R. Trebilco, *Self-designations and Group Identity in the New Testament* (Cambridge: Cambridge University Press, 2012). Trebilco's fine work has been a considerable help and inspiration to me in research and writing this chapter.

[4] E.g., recently, Joseph A. Fitzmyer, *The Acts of the Apostles: A New Translation and Commentary*, AB 31 (Garden City, NY: Doubleday, 1998), 80–9, including helpful bibliography of earlier work.

Luke[5] used sources, most probably some written and some oral. However, all work on sources in Acts is conjectural, for we lack any of Luke's extant sources, and thus to seek the ecclesiology of each of these conjectured sources would be to pursue something on which there is likely to be little scholarly agreement, and thus little profit for the wider question, 'What is the church?' Perhaps it is partly this difficulty which leads both Thompsons to address the issue by reading the final form of Acts.[6]

A further approach to our question, then, is through the portrait of the church in the final form of Acts.[7] This is certainly much more accessible to us, but raises a further issue: is there a consistent view of the church in Acts or is there variety? It is intrinsically likely that there will be variety among the believing communities portrayed by Luke, for the period he describes is extensive in both time and geography. Further, we might ask whether Luke, writing later, has imposed one view (of his own time) on his sources. In times when 'early catholic' was a widely-used category in New Testament scholarship, Luke was frequently identified as such, along with the author of the Pastorals.[8] While discussion has moved on, and the category of 'early catholicism' has largely fallen into disuse, the question of Luke's unification, or otherwise, of his material continues to be significant, not least because scholars are asking about his rhetoric – that is, how and of what he seeks to persuade his readers. I argue elsewhere that, in the developing narrative of Acts, Luke presents a Christian understanding of the Jerusalem temple which is also in process of developing,[9] and I suggest below that the same might be true of Luke's presentation of a Christian understanding of the believing community.

II. Calling the Church Names

The name by which a person or a group is known often encapsulates an understanding of their identity. The 'Methodists' in Oxford were so-called by others because of

---

[5] I use the traditional 'Luke' to designate the author of Acts to indicate the common authorship of the Third Gospel and Acts without necessarily implying any particular identification of the historical author of Acts

[6] Alan J. Thompson, *One Lord, One People: The Unity of the Church in Acts in Its Literary Setting*, LNTS 359 (London: T&T Clark, 2008), 17; Thompson, *Church*, 2–3.

[7] I here sidestep the question of the text of Acts, for which there is (notoriously) a bifurcation of the textual tradition into the Alexandrian and 'Western' traditions. My working hypothesis is that the Alexandrian tradition is closer to the original. For discussion, see Peter M. Head, "Acts and the Problem of Its Texts," in *The Book of Acts in Its Ancient Literary Setting*, ed. Bruce W. Winter and Andrew D. Clarke, BAFCS 1 (Carlisle: Paternoster, 1993), 415–44; William A. Strange, *The Problem of the Text of Acts*, SNTSMS 71 (Cambridge: Cambridge University Press, 1992); Josep Rius-Camps and Jenny Read-Heimerdinger, *The Message of Acts in Codex Bezae: A Comparison with the Alexandrian Tradition*, 4 vols., JSNTSup/LNTS 257, 302, 365, 415 (London: T&T Clark, 2004–9).

[8] See, e.g., Ernst Käsemann, "The Disciples of John the Baptist in Ephesus," in *Essays on New Testament Themes*, ed. Ernst Käsemann, SBT 41 (London: SCM, 1964), 136–48, here 145. For critique, see C. K. Barrett, "Apollos and the Twelve Disciples of Ephesus," in *The New Testament Age*, ed. William C. Weinrich, 2 vols. (Macon, GA: Mercer University Press, 1984), 1:29–39, esp. 35–6.

[9] Steve Walton, "A Tale of Two Perspectives? The Temple in Acts," in *Heaven on Earth: The Temple in Biblical Theology*, ed. T. Desmond Alexander and Simon J. Gathercole (Carlisle: Paternoster, 2004), 135–49 [in this volume 76–87].

their perceived methodical approach to the spiritual life.[10] A 'Sim' in Cambridge at a certain period was one who was a disciple of the Revd Charles Simeon, for many years vicar of Holy Trinity, Church there – this, too, was an outsider's term, and not complimentary.[11] The first-century Zealots were so-called because of their zeal for the Jewish law – Josephus claims this is an insider's term, although it is hard to be sure; it certainly was used by insiders for the group.[12]

The focus of this chapter is on the names which the group(s) of Jesus-believers call themselves in Acts, that is, self-designations. These give us a window into how these groups understood their identity, at least in Luke's eyes and, I shall argue, in the eyes of the earliest believers themselves. This delimitation excludes 'outsider' designations, notably the term 'Christian' (Acts 11:26): such terms certainly contribute to our understanding of the early Jesus-believers' identity, but they are not our focus here.

Six principal terms are used in this way, some more frequently than others, and each contributes to a portrait of the community from an insider perspective.[13] The terms are (in order of frequency, from most to least): οἱ ἀδελφοί 'the brothers and sisters', μαθηταί 'disciples', 'the believers', ἐκκλησία 'assembly', ἡ ὁδός 'the way', and οἱ ἅγιοι 'the holy ones'.

III. Οἱ ἀδελφοί 'The Brothers and Sisters'

The commonest self-designation of all is οἱ ἀδελφοί, a term which Trebilco rightly judges to be 'inclusive', that is, to include both women and men.[14] This term most probably stems from biblical usage, where אח is used not only by Israelites for immediate blood-relatives, but also for Israelites who are not blood-relatives.[15] The LXX translators generally use ἀδελφός in these passages.[16] However, it is also used in the Graeco-Roman world in a similar, metaphorical sense, including for fellow-members of an association.[17]

---

[10] W. R. Ward, "Wesley, John," in *The Blackwell Dictionary of Evangelical Biography 1730–1860*, ed. D. M. Lewis, 2 vols. (Oxford: Blackwell, 1995), 1171–3, here 1171.
[11] H. C. G. Moule, *Charles Simeon* (London: IVF, 1948), 60.
[12] Josephus, *J.W.* 7.8.1 §§267–70; cf. Martin Hengel, *The Zealots: Investigations into the Jewish Freedom Movement in the Period from Herod I until 70 AD*, 2nd ed. (Edinburgh: T&T Clark, 1989), 59–75.
[13] We might also add two uses of λαός 'people' which include gentiles, Acts 15:14; 18:10 (with Nils Alstrup Dahl, "'A People for His Name,'" *NTS* 4 (1958): 319–27; Jacques Dupont, "Note sur le 'Peuple de Dieu' dans les Actes des Apôtres," in *Unité et diversité dans l'Église*, ed. Pontifical Biblical Commission, Teologia e filosofia 15 (Vatican City: Libreria Editrice Vaticana, 1989), 209–22, here 212–13; *contra* Fitzmyer, "Designations," 236). Other uses of this term in Acts refer to the people of Israel (e.g. 7:17; 26:17, 23; 28:17); cf. Jacob Jervell, *The Theology of the Acts of the Apostles*, NT Theology (Cambridge: Cambridge University Press, 1996), 23–5. William Horbury notes that this represents an appropriation of a biblical term for Israel by the believing community ("Septuagintal and New Testament Conceptions of the Church," in *A Vision for the Church: Studies in Early Christian Ecclesiology in Honour of J. P. M. Sweet*, ed. Markus Bockmuehl and Michael B. Thompson (Edinburgh: T&T Clark, 1997), 1–17, here 8–11).
[14] Trebilco, *Self-designations*, 24–5. His evidence is drawn from Paul; similar passages in Acts include 3:17; 11:1; 15:1, 3, 32, 33, 36, 40.
[15] E.g. Exod 2:11; 4:18; Num 20:3; Judg 20:28.
[16] Trebilco, *Self-designations*, 17 n. 8.
[17] Trebilco, *Self-designations*, 17–18.

Luke's use is not only for Jesus-believers, but can be for blood-relatives,[18] or by Jesus-believing and non-Jesus-believing Jews who address other Jews, including in the context of evangelism or Christian explanation.[19] However, it is the use of 'the brothers (and sisters)' for Jesus-believers without further explanation that is striking. This term can designate a group, such as Judas and Silas's encouraging τοὺς ἀδελφούς (15:32) or the Judeans who taught τοὺς ἀδελφούς that they needed to be circumcised (15:1) – and the latter must be a reference to gentile believers. Similarly, the Jerusalem meeting addresses its letter 'to the brothers and sisters (τοῖς ... ἀδελφοῖς) drawn from the gentiles in Antioch, Syria and Cilicia' (15:23). Trebilco acutely observes that 15:23 represents a shift in usage, for in Acts 13–14, gentile believers are never referred to as ἀδελφοί, but as μαθηταί 'disciples' or ἐκκλησία 'assembly'.[20] The Jerusalem meeting is a watershed in Luke's story of the Jesus-believers; here is an example of development in the church's self-perception reflected in its name-calling which does not exclude continuing use of ἀδελφοί by believing Jews to and for other Jews.[21] Luke's story, written some time after the events, is not artificially 'tidied up' to reflect the later partings of ways between Jesus-believers and non-Jesus-believing Jews.

This 'fictive kinship' language is very striking, and it probably stems from Jesus's own diction.[22] Notably, in Mark 3:31–35, Jesus uses family language, contrasting blood-relations with those who do God's will: 'Whoever does the will of God is my brother and sister (ἀδελφός μου καὶ ἀδελφή) and mother'. This language signals the Jesus-believers' perception that they are bound together as a divinely-formed family, and that that family is in continuity with the family of Israel. The call elsewhere in the New Testament to love the brothers and sisters is an ethical implication of this perception,[23] a call which finds expression in Acts in the community's shared life.[24]

So here is language which fits well into the earliest community's life, language which would come naturally out of the Jewish matrix of the earliest believers. It is also language which re-uses terminology for Israel used by Jewish people of this period, and thus portrays the believing communities as both a sub-set of Judaism (in the earliest days) and (at a later date, when gentiles become believers) also as claiming to inherit Israel's privileged position as God's people.

IV. μαθηταί 'Disciples'

This term is used almost exclusively for Jesus-believers in Acts and is widespread.[25] It is used in the Gospels and Acts alone in the New Testament, although there is a

---

[18] E.g. Acts 1:14; 7:13; 12:2.
[19] E.g. Acts 2:29, 37; 3:17; 7:2; 13:15; 22:1; 23:1, 5; 28:17, 21.
[20] μαθηταί: 13:52; 14:20, 22, 28; ἐκκλησία: 13:1; 14:23, 27 (Trebilco, *Self-designations*, 52).
[21] So also Trebilco, *Self-designations*, 52–3.
[22] Trebilco, *Self-designations*, 39–42. Note especially his discussion of Matt 8:21–22.
[23] E.g. Rom 14:15; Gal 5:13; 1 John 2:10; 3:10, 16–17; 4:20–21.
[24] E.g. Acts 2:42–47; 4:32–35; 5:12–16. See discussion in Steve Walton, "Primitive Communism in Acts? Does Acts Present the Community of Goods (2:44–45; 4:32–35) as Mistaken?," *EvQ* 80 (2008): 99–111 [in this volume 63–73].
[25] It is found 27 times in Acts. The main possible use for non-Christians is 19:1, where the 'disciples' may well be those of John (cf. 19:3).

small number of uses in the Apostolic Fathers.[26] Luke's usage is in continuity with the pre-resurrection ministry of Jesus, for 'disciples' is used in the Third Gospel for the close followers of Jesus who travelled with him (Luke 6:13), a group wider than the Twelve (Luke 6:17; 7:11). The term 'his disciples' can also be used for the Twelve, as appears to be the case in Luke 8:22, where 'he got into a boat with his disciples (καὶ οἱ μαθηταὶ αὐτοῦ)', or in the story of the feeding of the five thousand, where 'the disciples' organize the crowd and distribute the food (Luke 9:14, 16). Being Jesus's disciple involves an itinerant life with Jesus, a wholehearted commitment which comes above family loyalties (Luke 14:26 – a shocking saying in first-century Palestine), a readiness to suffer (Luke 14:27), and a freedom from possessions which bespeaks dependence on God's loving provision (Luke 14:33; 12:22).

The term μαθητής is not univocal in the ancient world, although its broad meaning of 'learner, pupil, disciple' is clear.[27] It is used in the Graeco-Roman world for those learning a teaching or a trade, and could be used for those who held a particular stance or worldview or who came from a particular culture.[28] By the first century AD the more specific sense of following a master (usually a master teacher) predominates.[29] Interestingly, μαθητής itself is rare in the Greek OT (only at 1 Chron 25:8), the Greek Pseudepigrapha, Philo and Josephus, and the Hebrew equivalent *talmîd* is absent from the Dead Sea Scrolls – although in each case the *idea* of following as a disciple is present.[30] It is widely used in the Gospels, for Jesus's disciple-group[31] as well as for John's disciples[32] and the disciples of the Pharisees.[33]

Trebilco makes a cogent case that Jesus himself used the Aramaic word for 'disciple', *talmîdā*, and its plural *talmîdayyā'*.[34] He observes that μαθητής is multiply attested in the Gospel tradition, found in the triple tradition, Q, and John independently.[35] Thus to suggest (as Fitzmyer does[36]) that μαθητής was introduced into the Gospel tradition from Graeco-Roman diction in place of 'one who follows'[37] or similar is unlikely,

---

[26] Trebilco, *Self-designations*, 242–5.
[27] BDAG 609 s.v.
[28] E.g. Plato, *Protagoras* 343A ζηλωταὶ καὶ ἐρασταὶ καὶ *μαθηταὶ* ἦσαν τῆς Λακεδαιμονίων παιδείας '[they] were enthusiasts, lovers and *disciples* of Spartan culture' [LCL] (Trebilco, *Self-designations*, 209–10).
[29] For references, see Trebilco, *Self-designations*, 210.
[30] Trebilco, *Self-designations*, 210–12 gives examples.
[31] Note particularly Matt 5:17–48, where Jesus presents a righteousness which fulfills the prophets and demonstrates that he understands Scripture rightly. This passage portrays Jesus as rabbi/teacher and his disciples being instructed in how to read Scripture.
[32] E.g. Matt 9:14; 11:2; Mark 2:18; 6:29; Luke 7:18; 11:1; John 1:35, 37; 3:25; 4:1; cf. the 'disciples' of Acts 19:1, 3, who appear to be John's disciples.
[33] Mark 2:18; Matt 22:16. It is likely they were simply Pharisees: compare Matt 9:14 and Mark 2:18. Contrast Josephus, *Ant.* 13.10.15 §§288–90, where Hyrcanus is said to be a disciple of the Pharisees, which does appear to be in the sense of one who follows their teachings (with Trebilco, *Self-designations*, 212 n. 40).
[34] Trebilco, *Self-designations*, 220–3.
[35] E.g. *Triple tradition:* Mark 14:14; 2:23; 9:18 and parallels; Q: Luke 6:40; Matt 10:24–25; *John* 4:31; 9:2; 11:8.
[36] Fitzmyer, *Acts*, 346 (mis-cited as Joseph A. Fitzmyer, *To Advance the Gospel: New Testament Studies*, 2nd ed., Biblical Resource series (Grand Rapids, MI: Eerdmans, 1998), 346 in Trebilco, *Self-designations*, 221 n. 88).
[37] Expressed using various forms of ἀκολουθέω.

for it requires that each of these Gospel sources introduced the term independently. Fitzmyer's proposal also fails to explain the absence of μαθητής in the rest of the New Testament. It is further unlikely that the term was used in the earliest churches for Jesus-believers and yet is completely absent from the New Testament outside the Gospels and Acts (although the Johannine usage – depending on when John is dated – suggests that its use continued at least into later in the first century). Here is a strong argument from double dissimilarity for the use of the term by Jesus himself. Thus (Trebilco argues) it is likely that Jesus himself used *talmidā* for his followers (distinctively among his contemporaries, it appears from our sources). It disappeared from use in Greek-speaking churches because Jesus had given it the very specific sense of one who travels with and learns from Jesus, breaks ties with family and work, and faces suffering in consequence, and this was not how the term could be used after the resurrection of Jesus in two ways. First, the vast majority of Jesus-believers were rooted in a particular place and, secondly, the form of 'following' Jesus changed in the light of his exaltation, for the relationship was no longer that of learner to teacher, but included a distinctive constellation of devotional practices, including prayer to and worship of the exalted Jesus.[38] ' "Adherence" to the risen Jesus was simply conceived of differently after the resurrection'.[39]

So what of use in Acts? The predominant use is plural,[40] echoing use in Luke's Gospel (and the other Gospels[41]), and this alone suggests that discipleship was understood as a corporate enterprise. It is used of the group of Jesus-believers in a place, including Jerusalem, Damascus, Joppa, Syrian Antioch, Pisidian Antioch, Lystra, Galatia and Phrygia, Achaia, Ephesus, Tyre, and Caesarea.[42] The puzzle is why, if Jesus-believers over such a wide area were known as 'disciples', Paul and other New Testament writers never use the term. Trebilco observes that we never see μαθητής used in the mouth of a character in Acts, but only in the narrator's voice (other than 15:10), and he thus proposes that this is a Lukan term which was not used by the Jesus-believers themselves. Rather, he suggests, we should see Luke's use of μαθητής in Acts to signal continuity with Jesus's disciple-band (for readers of the Third Gospel would have had their understanding of the term shaped by usage there).[43] This makes Luke's use of μαθηταί for gentile believers particularly noteworthy.[44] While we noticed above that Luke reserves 'brothers and sisters' for gentile believers until the Jerusalem meeting in Acts 15, his use of μαθηταί for gentile believers is striking, for a careful reader of the Third Gospel will recognize that gentile believers are being put in the same category

---

[38] Larry W. Hurtado, *Lord Jesus Christ: Devotion to Jesus in Earliest Christianity* (Grand Rapids, MI; Cambridge: Eerdmans, 2003).
[39] Trebilco, *Self-designations*, 230; cf. Fitzmyer, "Designations," 228–9.
[40] The exceptions are 9:1 (of Ananias), 26 (of Saul); 16:1 (of Timothy); and 21:16 (of Mnason), each concerning named individuals. The feminine form μαθήτρια is also found once (9:36), concerning Dorcas, another named individual.
[41] Trebilco, *Self-designations*, 224–5.
[42] 6:1–2, 7; 9:1, 10, 19, 26, 38; 11:26, 29; 14:20–22, 28; 18:23, 27; 19:9, 30; 20:1, 30; 21:4, 16 (*twice*).
[43] Trebilco, *Self-designations*, 226–7.
[44] 11:26, 29; 14:22, 28 (of the mixed Jew-gentile congregation in Syrian Antioch); 14:20 (Lystra), 21 (Derbe).

as the Twelve and the wider group of Jewish disciples who travelled with Jesus. This prepares for gentile believers to be called 'brothers and sisters' from Acts 15 onwards.

'Disciples' occurs in Acts in contexts of suffering, notably in 14:22, 'they strengthened the souls of the disciples and encouraged them to continue in the faith, saying, "It is through many persecutions that we must enter the kingdom of God." This exhortation comes hot on the heels of Paul being attacked and stoned in Lystra (14:19–20). Similarly, 19:9 presents 'the disciples' as being spoken of badly in the synagogue in Ephesus, leading Paul to separate from the synagogue. Suffering is, of course, a wider theme in Acts than purely associated with 'disciples',[45] but its use provides an interesting point of continuity with the Third Gospel's teaching on discipleship.

The uses of 'the disciples' in Acts show us the process of definition of the Jesus-believers taking place. The term is used by Jesus a semitic setting in Palestine for his group of itinerant followers, and defined closely by Jesus's own call and teaching of disciples. The growth of the believing community after the resurrection makes it less appropriate as a term, because it has connotations which are both insufficiently strong for the view of Jesus the believers now hold, and much too sharply defined for the form which Jesus-following now takes. Luke himself uses the term to broaden its sense to include Jesus-believers who do not fit the classic itinerant mould, but who share the same commitment to follow Jesus, even through suffering, and the same readiness to learn, grow and develop in their discipleship.

V. ἐκκλησία 'Assembly'

ἐκκλησία is found frequently in Acts (23 times – more than any other New Testament book). It is found in the Greek OT and Graeco-Roman writings. Its general meaning is 'assembly'.[46]

In the Greek OT it denotes the 'assembly of Israel' (ἐκκλησία Ισραηλ), when the people of Israel were summoned together.[47] It could denote the assembly of Israelite men to go to war.[48] Muraoka thinks that it can denote a *place* of assembly, citing Jdt 6:16, 21,[49] but in this passage ἐκκλησία seems to denote an assembly of *people*. The cognate verb ἐκκλησιάζω 'assemble', not found in the New Testament, is used for the activity of assembling.[50] Generally, the noun and verb in LXX translate קהל,[51] the standard Hebrew term for an assembly, particularly the assembly of Israel.[52] The noun

---

[45] See the work of my student Brian Tabb, 'Suffering and Worldview: A Comparative Study of Acts, Fourth Maccabees, and Seneca' (PhD thesis: London School of Theology/Middlesex University, 2013), published as: Brian J. Tabb, *Suffering in Ancient Worldview: Luke, Seneca and 4 Maccabees in Dialogue*, LNTS 569 (London: Bloomsbury T&T Clark, 2017).
[46] LSJ 509 s.v.
[47] E.g. Deut 4:10; 9:10; 18:16; 23:1, 2, 3, 8; 31:30; 1 Kgs 8:14, 22, 55, 65; 1 Chron 13:2, 4; 28:2, 8; 29:1, 10, 20; Ezra 10:1, 8, 12, 14.
[48] E.g. Judg 20:2; 21:5, 8.
[49] *GELS* 209 s.v. §1.b.
[50] E.g. Lev 8:3; Num 20:8; Deut 4:10.
[51] The exception is Est 4:16.
[52] קהל is translated in other ways, but ἐκκλησία is the large majority translation (73/123 uses).

can be found with a qualifying genitive to signal its relationship to God, such as 'of YHWH' (יהוה LXX κυρίου);[53] 'of the people of God' (קהל עם האלהים LXX τοῦ λαοῦ τοῦ θεοῦ);[54] 'of God' (האלהים LXX θεοῦ);[55] and 'of the Most High' (LXX ὑψίστου).[56] קהל is found frequently in the post-exodus wilderness passages,[57] and in return from exile and post-exilic contexts,[58] which suggests that it can be used for an 'ideal Israel'; if so, a further dimension is added to early Christian usage.

The Dead Sea Scrolls use קהל for the community's assembly,[59] as well as assemblies of their opponents.[60] The Qumran community refers to itself as קהל on occasion.[61] This usage shows that קהל was current at least in some circles in Palestine at the time of Jesus.

The Graeco-Roman world knew ἐκκλησία as a city's citizen-assembly (Acts 19:39),[62] a denotation found in Acts 19:32, 40, where the town clerk politely calls the riot in Ephesus ἐκκλησία. George van Kooten argues that this denotation is the basis of Paul's expression ἡ ἐκκλησία τοῦ θεοῦ 'the assembly of God', chosen to contrast the believing assemblies with the civic assemblies of the Greek cities.[63] Richard Horsley thus suggests that Paul is adapting a term from LXX's description of Israel, which also denoted city assemblies in the Greek world, and thus '[Paul] was building an international political-religious movement … Paul's ἐκκλησίαι are thus local communities of *an alternative society to the Roman imperial order*'.[64] We may readily agree that the term ἐκκλησία in Greek cities would bring the citizen-assembly to mind,[65] while remaining agnostic about the origins of the believers' use of the term for their assemblies. Van Kooten wishes to argue that Paul self-consciously used ἐκκλησία because it was well-known among Greek and Roman readers, and seeks to draw parallels between Paul's usage and known features of the Greek ἐκκλησίαι:[66] (i) both were places of instruction;

---

[53] E.g. Deut 23:2, 3, 4 [twice], 9; 1 Chron 28:8; George H. van Kooten, "Ἐκκλησία τοῦ θεοῦ: The 'Church of God' and the Civic Assemblies (ἐκκλησίαι) of the Greek Cities in the Roman Empire: A Response to Paul Trebilco and Richard A. Horsley," NTS 58 (2012): 522–48, here 527, notes that the expression ἐκκλησία κυρίου is never found in the New Testament as part of his argument that that phrase is unlikely to be the model for the New Testament expression ἐκκλησία τοῦ θεοῦ.

[54] Judg 20:2.

[55] Neh 13:1; van Kooten, "Church," 527 observes that ἡ ἐκκλησία τοῦ θεοῦ is found 11 times in the Paulines and once in Acts, but only here in LXX, and thus suggests it is unlikely that the New Testament expression is based on LXX usage. This may be so, although it is not impossible that a New Testament author might light on one particular LXX use of a term which s/he could utilize as a specifically *Christian* expression.

[56] Sir 24:2.

[57] E.g. Exod 35:1; Lev 4:13, 14, 21; 8:3, 4; 16:17, 33; plus Num (21 uses); Deut (14 uses).

[58] E.g. Jer 31:8; 44:14; 50:9; Ezek (17 uses); Mic 2:5; Ezra 2:64; 10:1, 8, 12, 14; Neh 8:2, 17; 13:1.

[59] E.g. CD 11.22; 12.6; 1QSa 2.4.

[60] E.g. 1QM 11.16; 14.5; 1QH 10.30.

[61] E.g. CD 7.17.

[62] LSJ 509 s.v. §I.1.

[63] van Kooten, "Church," esp. 527.

[64] Richard A. Horsley, "Introduction to Building an Alternative Society," in *Paul and Empire: Religion and Power in Roman Imperial Society*, ed. Richard A. Horsley (Harrisburg: Trinity Press International, 1997), 206–14, quoting 209 (my italics).

[65] E.g. Wayne A. Meeks, *The First Urban Christians: The Social World of the Apostle Paul* (New Haven, CT: Yale University Press, 1983), 108.

[66] van Kooten, "Church," 539–47.

(ii) both were places of factions and divisions (iii) both valued rational discussion, and Paul opposes the presence of 'mania' in the Corinthian assemblies (note 1 Cor 14:23); (iv) both had meetings which were in principle open to the public; (v) both sought to prevent women present from speaking.

This is not a strong set of parallels: (i) the instruction was not the focus of the city-assembly, but rather the decision-making based under the information given as 'instruction', whereas in the believing assembly the instruction was designed to inform the individual and corporate lives of believers; (ii) Paul hardly thinks that factions and division are a good thing which is to be encouraged in Corinth; (iii) although Paul puts limits on speaking in tongues (a non-rational activity) in Corinth, he does not forbid it entirely – indeed, he wants the whole community to be able to speak in tongues (1 Cor 14:5) – rather, his concern is for the community to be built up, which requires good order (1 Cor 14:26–33a); (iv) there is no evidence that the believing assemblies were intentionally open to the public, especially if they were held in private houses;[67] (v) there is evidence that women could and did pray (which would necessarily be aloud in the ancient world) and prophesy in the Corinthian assembly: to read 1 Cor 14:33b–35 in isolation from 1 Cor 11:3–15, esp. vv. 5, 13 (as van Kooten seems to do) is to mis-read the letter as a whole.[68] There is nothing here which would necessarily lead to the conclusion that Paul himself used ἐκκλησία deliberately to echo and challenge the use of the term for the citizen-assembly, although (we note again) such a parallel would be likely to be heard by Greeks and Romans.

Returning to New Testament narrative, as is well-known, Matthew alone among the Evangelists uses ἐκκλησία (16:18; 18:17), so Luke's abundant use of the term in Acts comes rather out of the blue. Luke uses it for Israel (Acts 7:38) as well as for the citizen-assembly of Ephesus (19:32, 39, 40), but his predominant use is for the believing communities.

Luke's first use is for the Jerusalem congregations in Acts 5:11: 'and great fear came upon the whole assembly (ἐφ' ὅλην τὴν ἐκκλησίαν)'.[69] He regularly uses the term for local assemblies in specific places: Antioch (11:26; 13:1; 14:27; 15:3), Lystra and Iconium (14:23, κατ' ἐκκλησίαν 'in each church', a distributive use[70]), Syria and Cilicia (15:41), Ephesus (20:17), and more generally (16:5). 14:27, συναγαγόντες τὴν ἐκκλησίαν 'having called the assembly together', may suggest a sense of ἐκκλησία as 'the *assembled* body of Christians',[71] but it might equally well refer to the community of people who form the assembly, as it clearly does in 8:3.[72]

---

[67] Although see Edward Adams, *The Earliest Christian Meeting Places: Almost Exclusively Houses?*, LNTS 450 (London: T&T Clark, 2013), who suggests there may sometimes have been outdoor meetings, including in the garden of a house belonging to a believer.
[68] Cf. Horbury, "Conceptions," 4–5, showing that the believing communities involved both women and men contributing.
[69] Cf. 8:1, 3; 11:22; 12:1, 5; 15:4, 22; 18:22.
[70] Kevin N. Giles, "Luke's Use of the Term ἐκκλησία with Special Reference to Acts 20:28 and 9:31," NTS 31 (1985): 135–42, here 135–6.
[71] So C. K. Barrett, *A Critical and Exegetical Commentary on the Acts of the Apostles*, 2 vols., ICC (Edinburgh: T&T Clark, 1994, 1998), 1:691; Trebilco, *Self-designations*, 181 agrees.
[72] Trebilco, *Self-designations*, 181 cites 20:17 as having this sense too.

Two uses suggest a use for a believing body wider than the local assembly: 9:31 and 20:28.[73] In 9:31 we face an interesting textual variant: should we read 'The ... assembly (Ἡ ... ἐκκλησία) throughout the whole of Judaea and Galilee and Samaria' (with singular verbs following) or 'the ... assemblies (αἱ ... ἐκκλησίαι)' (with plural verbs following)? The manuscript support for the singular form is much stronger.[74] It is also unlikely that the change was made from plural to singular to signal the unity of the assemblies (considered as one assembly), for no such variants occur for the plural uses in 15:41 and 16:5.[75] Barrett proposes that the singular refers to a single assembly covering a large area.[76] Bruce, similarly, considers that the 'assembly' here is 'the original Jerusalem church, now in dispersion'.[77] However, the geographical spread considered is rather wide, and it seems unlikely that the assemblies of Samaria would be considered to be part of 'the original Jerusalem church'.[78] It thus seems that this may be Luke's first use of ἐκκλησία for the believing community in a wider geographical area, seen as one entity – and this is a usage unique in the New Testament.[79] This is not yet the *ecclesia catholica* ('universal church'), considered as one assembly in the whole world, but it is a step along the way to that usage.[80]

20:28 is rather different. Here, Paul's exhortation to the Ephesian elders calls on them 'to shepherd the assembly of God (τὴν ἐκκλησίαν τοῦ θεοῦ), which he obtained through the blood of his own'. There are significant issues of text and interpretation in this verse too,[81] but no variation concerning the singular τὴν ἐκκλησίαν is extant in the manuscript tradition. There is an echo of Ps 73:1–2a LXX [MT 74:1–2a] here:[82]

> Why did you cast us off, O God, to the end; why are you angry with the sheep [πρόβατα] of your pasture? Remember your assembly [τῆς συναγωγῆς σου], which you obtained [ἐκτήσω] from the beginning. (my translation)

Although the word for 'assembly' in the Psalm is συναγωγή rather than ἐκκλησία, it is nevertheless singular, and the uses of πρόβατα 'sheep' and κτάομαι 'obtain' are

---

[73] Cf. Fitzmyer, "Designations," 232, 236.
[74] 𝔓74 ℵ A B C (Ψ) 33. 81. 323. 453. 945. 1175. 1739 vg (syp) co; PsDion vs. E L 614. 1241. 1505 M it syh bomss. Bruce M. Metzger, *A Textual Commentary on the Greek New Testament*, 2nd ed. (Stuttgart: Deutsche Bibelgesellschaft/United Bible Societies, 1994), 322–3 regards this range and age of support as 'superior'. Giles, "Use," 140 overstates his case in claiming that 'the plural readings are well supported textually'.
[75] Cf. Barrett, *Acts*, 1:474–75.
[76] Barrett, *Acts*, 1:475.
[77] F. F. Bruce, *The Acts of the Apostles*, 3rd ed. (Leicester: Apollos, 1990), 245; similarly, Giles, "Use," 139; contrast Richard I. Pervo, *Acts*, Hermeneia (Minneapolis, MN: Fortress, 2009), 248.
[78] With David P. Seccombe, "Luke's Vision for the Church," in *A Vision for the Church: Studies in Early Christian Ecclesiology in Honour of J. P. M. Sweet*, ed. Markus Bockmuehl and Michael B. Thompson (Edinburgh: T&T Clark, 1997), 45–63, here 56.
[79] As noted by Giles, "Use," 138.
[80] Trebilco, *Self-designations*, 181 n. 108 allows that 'ἐκκλησία may also have a wider meaning in 9:31'.
[81] For discussion, see Steve Walton, *Leadership and Lifestyle: The Portrait of Paul in the Miletus Speech and 1 Thessalonians*, SNTSMS 108 (Cambridge: Cambridge University Press, 2000), 94–9.
[82] See discussion in Murray J. Harris, *Jesus as God: The New Testament Use of Theos in Reference to Jesus* (Grand Rapids, MI: Baker, 1992), 135.

strongly echoed in Acts 20:28. The Psalm speaks of God acting to rescue his own people, considered as *one* assembly or congregation. Likewise in 20:28, the believers throughout the world are encompassed in the term ἐκκλησία, 'the worldwide company of the redeemed, *ecclesia catholica*'.[83]

By contrast, Giles argues that this use is non-Lukan and thus contributes nothing to a Lukan view of the church. He offers in evidence: (i) it is unique in Acts in referring to 'the assembly *of God* (τοῦ θεοῦ)'; (ii) it is unique in Acts in implying that the assembly is brought into existence by God, rather than by the human decision to meet together; (iii) the redemptive death of Christ is said to be for the community, presenting ideas of 'communal salvation and substitutionary atonement' which Giles considers un-Lukan.[84] Giles considers that this expression stems either from Pauline tradition available to Luke or is a Lukan creation, based on his knowledge of Pauline diction.[85]

This seems rather too sweeping to my eye. I rather wonder if this is not another case of Luke presenting the process of Christian self-understanding developing without putting that process into a tidy form.[86] We have seen that 9:31 can be understood as a step along the way to a view of the church as universal; could not 20:28 be the point where this step is made? And if the universal church view can be seen in Paul as early as Gal 1:13 and 1 Cor 15:9, where Paul says he persecuted 'the church of God (τὴν ἐκκλησίαν τοῦ θεοῦ)', in the singular in both verses,[87] why is it unlikely that Luke sometimes wrote (and thought) this way too?

To sum up on this designation, it is clearly used by the community(ies) for themselves. Stephen's use for the assembly of Israel (7:38), and its regular use in the LXX in this way, implies that the believing community is in continuity with Israel. 'Though the Church was undoubtedly new in form, Luke contends that properly understood is it an ancient foundation.'[88] Horbury helpfully suggests that ἐκκλησία is easier for the believers to appropriate than λαός 'people', which has 'strongly national associations', whereas ἐκκλησία is not universally used for Israel's assembly (as we saw above, συναγωγή was used too) and can refer to gatherings other than Israel's assembly.[89] Luke's use of ἐκκλησία for the believing assemblies from 8:1 onwards reflects his wider understanding of the believing community as the restored and renewed Israel.

However, the fact that ἐκκλησία is not used until 5:11 for the believing community may suggest that Luke is avoiding using a term known in his day as dividing Christians from Jews.[90] Again, this may be a signal that we are seeing the process of development going on within Luke's story, whether put there consciously by Luke or simply his inheritance from his source material. Thus ἐκκλησία may not be a term used in the

---

[83] Barrett, *Acts*, 1:lxxxviii.
[84] Giles, "Use," 136.
[85] Giles, "Use," 136–7.
[86] With Fitzmyer, "Designations," 231.
[87] Cf. also Phil 3:6.
[88] Seccombe, "Luke's Vision," 56.
[89] Horbury, "Conceptions," 13.
[90] Seccombe, "Luke's Vision," 48.

earliest days after Pentecost, but a term used a little later in a Greek-speaking setting as a Christian equivalent of קהל.[91]

VI. 'The Believers'

The way in to the community of the Messiah was by believing, as aorist uses of πιστεύω in the sense 'came to believe' suggest, notably in Acts 16:31, where the aorist imperative is used for Paul and Silas's exhortation to the Philippian jailer 'believe (πίστευσον) in the Lord Jesus and you and your household will be saved'.[92] Thus it is no surprise that 'the believers', in the form of a participle of πιστεύω (mostly – but not exclusively – articular), occurs a dozen times in Acts.[93] The participle can be present,[94] aorist,[95] or perfect.[96] The perfect is of particular interest, designating people who had come to believe and continued to believe.

Πιστεύω has the sense of trusting, being confident in or about something or someone, and hence, believing, having or exercising faith.[97] Classical Greek usage can pertain to trusting a god or an oracle from a god, although this use is not widespread.[98] In the Hellenistic period such usage increases in frequency.[99]

The form found in Acts, an articular participle, is found seven times in LXX, usually with the sense 'one who trusts in'.[100] Of these seven, it is rare in the books paralleled in the Hebrew Bible, only found twice (Prov 30:1; Isa 28:16). Similar uses can be found in Josephus,[101] Philo,[102] and pseudepigraphical writings.[103]

Thus other Jews of the first century were probably familiar with this terminology, and it is possible that 'the believers' is an expression from the earliest days of the church.[104] Because the designation was used by other Jews, the three places where Luke adds an object to the participle are significant in signalling who was being trusted. In 10:43 it is 'in him' (εἰς αὐτόν) – in the context (10:39–42) a reference to Jesus. In 22:19,

---

[91] For a thoughtful discussion of why ἐκκλησία specifically was used, see Trebilco, *Self-designations*, 183–98; cf. I. Howard Marshall, "New Wine in Old Wineskins: V. The Biblical Use of the Word Ekklēsia," *ExpTim* 84 (1973): 359–64.

[92] Cf. 4:4; 8:12, 13; 9:42; 11:17, 21 (where it parallels ἐπέστρεψεν ἐπὶ τὸν κύριον '[they] turned to the Lord); 13:12, 48; 14:1; 15:7; 17:12, 34; 18:8; 19:2. Daniel B. Wallace, *Greek Grammar beyond the Basics: An Exegetical Syntax of the New Testament* (Grand Rapids, MI: Zondervan, 1996), 621 n. 22 suggests that the force of the present as denoting continuing faith (rather than the inceptive force of the aorist) is a major reason that the present participle is commoner in the articular participle construction.

[93] Articular: 2:44; 4:32; 10:43; 11:21; 13:39; 18:27; 19:18; 21:20, 25; 22:19. Inarticular: 5:14; 15:5 (with τινες).

[94] 2:44; 5:14; 10:43; 13:39; 15:5; 22:19.

[95] 4:32; 11:21.

[96] 18:27; 19:18; 21:20, 25.

[97] LSJ 1407–8 s.v.

[98] For references, see *EDNT* 3:92 s.v.; BDAG 816–18 s.v.

[99] *TDNT* 6:179–82.

[100] Notably Isa 28:16 (believing in the divinely-laid cornerstone); Sir 32:24 (faith in the torah).

[101] *Ant.* 20:48; *C. Ap.* 2:160; *J.W.* 2:187.

[102] *Heir* 90, 101, 14; *Rewards* 28.

[103] T.Dan 5:13.

[104] See Trebilco's cogent case for the usage being pre-Pauline (*Self-designations*, 90–9).

it is 'in you' (ἐπὶ σέ) – again a reference to Jesus, as Saul addresses Jesus on the road to Damascus. In 16:15 the adjective πιστός 'faithful' is used with 'the Lord' (τῷ κυρίῳ) as object. These uses make clear the distinctiveness of *Christian* faith, trust in Jesus, the Lord.

It is highly unlikely, in the light of the wider use in Jewish circles, that 'the believers' was a designation used by outsiders for the Christian communities. The uses without an object are of real significance, then, in pointing to 'in house' language for the community, who used 'the believers' as a semi-technical term. It is also of interest, then, that Luke can write of 'Jewish believers' (21:20), 'gentile believers' (21:25) or believers who were Pharisees (15:5). Trebilco plausibly proposes that the term 'believers' in these passages (by contrast with the qualifiers, 'Jewish', 'gentile', and Pharisees) indicates the uniting factor amidst the real differences of ethnicity and party-loyalty within Judaism. Hence the expression 'all who believe' (πάντες οἱ πιστεύοντες or similar) indicates their unity.[105] 'The designation 'the believers' is clearly an 'instrument of unity' for Luke'.[106] Moreover 'all who believe(d)' and similar expressions come in contexts of the shared life of the community(ies): in 2:44, they share possessions; and in 4:32, they are united in one heart and life and share possessions.

This usage is not a complete innovation in Acts, for Luke uses believing language in his Gospel. In the parable of the sower, Luke has redacted Mark to add in explicit references to faith.[107] The contrast of Elizabeth, who believes what is said to her (Luke 1:45), and Zechariah, who does not (Luke 1:20), is one of Luke's uses of male-female pairs to make a point both positively and negatively. After the resurrection, Cleopas and his companion are upbraided for being 'slow to believe' what the prophets said (Luke 24:25). Here is clear evidence of Luke writing in a way that helps his (probably) Christian readers to make connections with their own faith and experience. Nevertheless, this is not likely to be a Lukan innovation, for the widespread Pauline use of 'faith' language implies that it is highly probable that 'the believers' was a term used in the Pauline churches, at the very least[108] – and it is likely that it did not originate there.[109]

In sum, 'the believers' is not a form found in Graeco-Roman religious language, but it is found – although not commonly – among Jewish writings prior to the New Testament. Its use in Acts, along with its widespread use elsewhere in the New Testament, especially by Paul, signals a key 'boundary marker' of the Christian community. Its use without an object implies that it was an insider designation. The fact that present and perfect (rather than aorist) participles predominate suggests that the ongoing aspect of faith and trust in Jesus the Messiah was considered highly significant for members of the community.

---

[105] 2:44; 10:43; 13:39; 21:20–25.
[106] Trebilco, *Self-designations*, 105.
[107] Luke 8:12 (cf. Mark 4:15), 13 (cf. Mark 4:16–17).
[108] See Trebilco, *Self-designations*, 72–90.
[109] See n. 106.

VII. Ἡ ὁδός 'The Way'

This intriguing designation sounds, on first blush, as if it might be more at home among philosophers than believers. However, 'the way' is a term found at Qumran,[110] indicating the community's strict observance of the torah (1QS 8.12–15).[111] It may also be helpful to consider the Jewish idea of *halakah*, the teaching on lifestyle which was seen as a development of the torah, as an influence on this choice of term.[112]

The use at Qumran is strongly influenced by seeing the life of the community as an embodiment of Isa 40:3: 'A voice cries out: "In the wilderness prepare the way of the LORD (LXX τὴν ὁδὸν κυρίου), make straight in the desert a highway for our God."' This text is quoted in 1QS 8.11–15 to justify the community living in the desert, and there preparing the Lord's way, a 'way' which the community understands to be the study of torah.[113] George Brooke rightly sees the Qumran interpretation of Isa 40:3 as living in a literal 'desert'.[114] 'The way' is also used in CD 1.8–13, where the community's origins are described, again speaking of study of and following torah as 'the way of his [God's] heart'. Bauckham observes:

> It is clear that Isa 40:3, and the understanding of 'the way' mentioned there as a reference to the community's practice of the Law and thus to its distinctive lifestyle, has been highly influential for the community. Its study of the Law was the preparation of the way, its practice of the Law its walking on the way.[115]

The Qumran community uses 'the way' in other ways too, not only for the community, but also for their lifestyle of torah study and observance. People who do not follow this lifestyle have 'departed from the way' (CD 1.13).

This usage should not necessarily be seen as the source for the believers' use of the term[116] – the temptation to parallelomania needs resisting here![117] The Qumran use certainly shows that at least one group of Jewish people in the first century were using 'the way' in what an 'absolute' form as a self-designation, but it need not follow that the believers drew their use from the Qumran use. Indeed, the Acts uses are different from the Qumran ones.[118]

---

[110] E.g. CD 1.13; 2.6; 20.18; 1QS 9.17, 18; 10.21; 11.13.
[111] Joseph A. Fitzmyer, *Essays on the Semitic Background of the New Testament* (London: Geoffrey Chapman, 1971), 282.
[112] Barrett, *Acts*, 1:448.
[113] Cf. also 1QS 9.17–21.
[114] George J. Brooke, "Isaiah 40:3 and the Wilderness Community," in *New Qumran Texts and Studies: Proceedings of the First Meeting of the International Organization for Qumran Studies, Paris, 1992*, ed. George J. Brooke and Florentino García Martínez, STDJ 15 (Leiden: Brill, 1994), 117–32, esp. 117–29.
[115] Richard Bauckham, "The Early Jerusalem Church, Qumran, and the Essenes," in *The Dead Sea Scrolls as Background to Postbiblical Judaism and Early Christianity: Papers from an International Conference at St Andrews in 2001*, ed. James R. Davila, STDJ 46 (Leiden: Brill, 2003), 63–89, 63–89, 77.
[116] As suggested in Fitzmyer, "Designations," 229–30.
[117] Cf. the justly famous article, Samuel Sandmel, "Parallelomania," *JBL* 81 (1962): 1–13.
[118] For what follows, see Trebilco, *Self-designations*, 256–7.

First, the Qumran uses refer to a strict interpretation of torah, whereas the believers did not see their 'way' thus. Secondly, there is no trace in Acts of the dualism seen at Qumran in the use of 'the way'. Thirdly, the desert at Qumran is seen as a place to *prepare* the Lord's way, not the way itself, whereas in Acts the 'way' is *present* and offers salvation *now*. Fourthly, the use at Qumran is more varied than in Acts. Fifthly, the Qumran uses, while significantly influenced by Isa 40:3, also draw on other biblical passages, whereas the (Luke-)Acts uses seem to depend on Isa 40:3 alone.

ἡ ὁδός 'the way' is used for the Christian 'way' in the context of opposition, and is a term which Luke places on the lips of outsiders.[119] The use in 9:2 particular suggests that this is a self-designation for the believing community: '[Saul] asked ... for letters to the synagogues at Damascus, so that if he found any who *belonged to the Way* (τῆς ὁδοῦ ὄντας), men or women, he might bring them bound to Jerusalem' (NRSV).

Similarly, Paul, when speaking to Felix, implies that 'the way' is a self-designation by contrast with the opponents' designation of the believers as 'a sect' (αἵρεσις, 24:14). There is certainly no suggestion by Luke that this is an outsider-coined term; the absolute use, 'the way', suggests that it was shorthand, in-group language.

Trebilco argues that the uses of 'the way' in Mark and Q, which pre-date Luke's uses (on the commonest view of synoptic origins), indicate that Luke did not coin this phrase.[120] Further, the slim use of this term (eight times in Acts) does not suggest that Luke regards this as a major designation of the community: were he seeking to make a strong point using 'the way', we might expect more uses.[121] It is found only in Palestine (9:2; 22:4; 24:14, 22) and Ephesus (18:25–26; 19:9, 23),[122] rather than being widespread across the believing communities of the Mediterranean basin.

18:25–26 include two distinctive, qualified uses, 'the way of the Lord' (v. 25) and 'the way of God' (v. 26), concerning Apollos's knowledge of and instruction in 'the way' by Priscilla and Aquila. These collocations on their own were ambiguous, for they could denote 'the way of YHWH', although that Apollos spoke 'the things concerning Jesus' (v. 25) clarifies that the *Christian* way is meant here (and thus that Apollos was already a believer[123]). The collocations echo Isa 40:3, which we have seen quoted in Luke 3:3–5, and thus further underline the believers' self-perception as the fulfilment of Isaianic hopes for a restored Israel.

'The way' is used by Luke for what we might call a movement (9:2; 22:4).[124] The work of preparing the way of the Lord had been done by John the baptizer (hence Luke

---

[119] Acts 9:2; 19:9, 23; 22:4; 24:14, 22.
[120] Trebilco, *Self-designations*, 259–61.
[121] Trebilco, *Self-designations*, 261.
[122] John 14:6 is a clear echo of Isa 40:3 and probably links with the wider Isaianic theme of 'the way of YHWH' (see discussion in David M. Ball, *'I Am' in John's Gospel: Literary Function, Background and Theological Implications*, JSNTSup 124 (Sheffield: Sheffield Academic, 1996), 232–40). Dr Ball suggests orally to me that the frequently-proposed connection of John with Ephesus may be a partial explanation of the Ephesian references in Acts.
[123] With Barrett, *Acts*, 2:887–89; Fitzmyer, *Acts*, 638–9; Eckhard J. Schnabel, *Acts*, ZECNT 5 (Grand Rapids, MI: Zondervan, 2012), 784–6.
[124] This compares interestingly with some OT usage which focuses on an individual as walking God's way (in spite of NRSV, which for reasons of gender inclusion, translates using plurals, e.g. Pss 1:1–2 (where walking in the God's way is delighting in YHWH's law); 2:12 (the 'righteous way'); 119.

quotes Isa 40:3–5 in introducing John, Luke 3:2–5), and Jesus himself was the Lord whose way John prepared.[125] Thus believers walked in the way, following Jesus.

As with our other terms, 'the way' belongs within a Jewish matrix, and further signals that the believing community saw itself as the inheritor of Israel's mantle, the restored people of God, who were experienced the restoration promised in the prophets of the exile, especially Isaiah 40–55.

VIII. Οἱ ἅγιοι 'The Holy Ones'

Finally, in our discussion of terms used as self-designations for believers in Acts, we come to οἱ ἅγιοι 'the holy ones'.[126] This adjective is not very common among Graeco-Roman writers.[127] LXX usage is relatively rare.[128] Second Temple Jewish writers again use the term relatively rarely, but when they do use 'the holy ones' it designates people in eschatological settings, notably in 1 *En.* 92–105 (the Epistle of Enoch) and 37–71 (the Similitudes of Enoch). In 1 *En.* 100:5 the holy ones are guarded by holy angels, which implies that there the holy ones are humans.[129] In the Similitudes, uses are similar (e.g. 43:4; 51:2).[130] The Qumran community saw itself as cohabiting with angelic beings and living in the eschatological era; thus, in the Dead Sea Scrolls, 'the holy ones' is used for such angelic beings.[131] There is arguably no clear case of this phrase used for humans in the Qumran literature.[132] In sum, prior to the New Testament, 'the holy ones' rarely designates humans, and when it does, it generally occurs in eschatological contexts.

Thus the widespread Christian use of 'the holy ones' (not least in Paul) reflects the believers' understanding that history had changed with the death, resurrection and exaltation of Jesus, and they now live in the age to come. 'The holy ones' as a self-designation signals an inaugurated eschatology: it is highly unlikely that outsiders would use such a term of the believing community, for it could imply a recognition of the believers' claim about the epoch-changing role of Jesus.

In Acts there are four uses of the articular plural adjective (9:13, 32, 41; 26:10) and two uses of the articular substantival plural participle of ἁγιάζω ('sanctify, make holy', 20:32; 26:18, both interestingly perfect). All of the uses are plural (as they are in

---

[125] Bauckham, "Early," 76 notes that Isa 40–55 was highly influential on the earliest Christians' self-understanding; cf. the work of my student Peter Mallen, *The Reading and Transformation of Isaiah in Luke-Acts*, LNTS 367 (London: T&T Clark, 2008).

[126] This is commonly translated 'the saints', a term I prefer to avoid because of the unhelpful baggage 'saint' carries in today's world and church.

[127] BDAG 10 s.v.; LSJ 9 s.v.

[128] In MT, it is found only in Ps 34:10 [EVV 34:9] for humans, and in Dan 7:18, 21, 22, 25, 27; 8:24 for celestial beings (with John J. Collins, *Daniel*, Hermeneia (Minneapolis, MN: Fortress, 1993), 312–19). In LXX it is also found in Exod 15:11 (although inarticular); Pss 73:3; 82:4; Wis 18:9.

[129] With Trebilco, *Self-designations*, 125.

[130] Cf. 39:1, 4–5; 41:2; 47:2, 4; 48:7, 9 50:1; 58:3, 5; 61:8, 10; 61:12; 62:8; 65:12; 69:13; 71:4.

[131] E.g. 1QSa 2.8–9; 1QM 1.16; 10.9–11; 12.1, 7–8.

[132] See the valuable discussions in Collins, *Daniel*, 314–16; John J. Collins, "Saints of the Most High," in *Dictionary of Deities and Demons in the Bible*, ed. K. van der Toorn, Bob Becking and Pieter Willem van der Horst, 2nd ed. (Leiden: Brill; Grand Rapids, MI; Cambridge: Eerdmans, 1999), 720–2.

Paul[133]), signalling that this term denotes a community: there is no singular 'holy one' in Acts (or elsewhere in the NT).

These uses are found in or concerning Palestinian settings, except for Paul's words to the Ephesian elders (20:32). There is a cluster of uses concerning Peter's travels within Palestine in Acts 9, and this may suggest that Luke is using a source which is aware, and/or is himself aware, that it is a term most at home in Palestinian soil. Like the use of rare Christological terms in Acts 3:13–15,[134] we may well here be seeing a term which is used in a Palestinian context and which needs clarification and interpretation for gentiles – notable here is that these uses are almost all concerning Jewish believers.[135]

Trebilco makes an interesting suggestion concerning why 'the holy ones' was chosen out of all the possible terms which could be used in eschatological contexts, namely that the association of 'the holy ones' with the son of man figure in Dan 7:13–14 led to this.[136] Without entering the debate on the meaning of 'the son of man' in relation to Jesus (on which the literature is vast!), we may note that Dan 7:13, 18, 22, 25, 27 interpret the son of man as representing and in some sense embodying 'the holy ones of the Most High'.[137] Thus if the earliest Christians knew Jesus as 'the son of man', and heard this phrase from Dan 7 being used by Jesus in eschatological contexts, it would only be a short step after the resurrection of Jesus ('the great turning point'[138]) to understand themselves, as the Messiah's people, to be the 'holy ones' of Dan 7. We may further notice that 1 Cor 6:2 seems to echo the picture in Dan 7: 'the holy ones (οἱ ἅγιοι) will judge the world'.[139] If this connection with Dan 7 is right (and it seems highly plausible), we have further indication that the earliest believers saw themselves as the restored Israel, living in the new age inaugurated by the Messiah.

IX. Conclusion

The cluster of terms we have studied seems to have originated and to make most sense as having Jewish origins. Given that the early believers were all Jewish, and that the origins of Christianity were Jewish, this is hardly surprising. What is significant here is that this cluster of uses chimes in with Luke's signals that the Christian community should be understood as the restored Israel, a theme which has received renewed

---

[133] Technically, the adjective is singular in Phil 4:21, but Ἀσπάσασθε πάντα ἅγιον 'Greet *every* holy one' is hardly a real exception.
[134] '[God's] servant', 'the holy and righteous one', and 'the author of life'.
[135] The exception is 20:32, where the use of the participle may reflect Pauline usage (so Trebilco, *Self-designations*, 139–40, citing 1 Cor 1:2; Rom 15:16; 1 Cor 6:11; 7:14; 1 Thess 5:23; Eph 5:26; 1 Tim 4:5; 2 Tim 2:21).
[136] For what follows, see Trebilco, *Self-designations*, 143–6; cf. 'Originally, at least, [holy ones] had probably an eschatological rather than an ethical significance' (Cadbury, "Names," 381).
[137] Ernest Lucas, *Daniel*, AOTC 20 (Leicester: Apollos, 2002), 191–2; Maurice Casey, *Son of Man: The Interpretation and Influence of Daniel 7* (London: SPCK, 1979), 24–5, 39–40 (and the intervening discussion); *contra* John Goldingay, *Daniel*, WBC 30 (Dallas: Word, 1989), 176–8; Collins, *Daniel*, 319.
[138] '[L]e grand tournant' (Dupont, "Note," 222).
[139] Cf. Matt 19:28; Luke 22:28–30.

prominence in recent scholarship on Luke-Acts.[140] It is not simply a naïve taking over of Israel language, however, for the Jesus-believing community's self understanding may be summarized as Israel *reinterpreted and reunderstood* through the lens of Jesus as Messiah.[141]

These uses also, notably 'the holy ones', signal that the older view of Lukan eschatology (that Luke is coming to terms with the failure of parousia hope[142]) is oversimple: if this term does come from the earliest days of the believing community (as seems likely), then it is at least compatible with an inaugurated eschatology which can still look to the End to come.

Finally, we may also note that Luke does not appear to have imposed one, uniform view of ecclesiology through these terms. While there is a strong Jewish restorationist flavour to them, their distribution and use rather suggests that, in Acts, we are seeing some of the development in early Christian self-understanding happening before our eyes.

---

[140] See Richard Bauckham, "The Restoration of Israel in Luke-Acts," in *Restoration: Old Testament, Jewish and Christian Perspectives*, ed. James M. Scott, JSJSup 72 (Leiden: Brill, 2001), 435–87; Alan J. Thompson, *The Acts of the Risen Lord Jesus: Luke's Account of God's Unfolding Plan*, NSBT 27 (Nottingham: Apollos, 2011), 103–24; Göran Lennartsson, *Refreshing and Restoration: Two Eschatological Motifs in Acts 3:19-21* (Lund: Lund University, Centre for Theology and Religious Studies, 2007); Michael E. Fuller, *The Restoration of Israel: Israel's Re-gathering and the Fate of the Nations in Early Jewish Literature and Luke-Acts*, BZNW 138 (Berlin: de Gruyter, 2006); David Ravens, *Luke and the Restoration of Israel*, JSNTSup 119 (Sheffield: Sheffield Academic, 1995).

[141] Horbury, "Conceptions," 14–15 rightly stresses that the congregation of believers is regularly connected in the New Testament, including in Acts, with Jesus as Israel's Messiah.

[142] Notably in Hans Conzelmann, *The Theology of St Luke*, trans. Geoffrey Buswell (London: Faber & Faber, 1960).

5

Primitive Communism in Acts? Does Acts Present the Community of Goods (2:44–45; 4:32–35) as Mistaken?[1]

I. Setting the Scene

How should we understand the passages in Acts 2:44–45; 4:32–35 which speak of some form of sharing of possessions among the earliest believers?[2] This chapter seeks to assess the view that the author of Acts[3] presents this practice as mistaken, since sharing of possessions seems to disappear from view in the remainder of Acts. I shall not be considering the different, but also interesting, question of whether such a sharing of possessions ever took place,[4] although I hope my discussion may shed some light on that question too. Nor shall I be seeking to answer the very large, wider question of the role of wealth and poverty in Luke-Acts, although again, I hope I shall contribute to such discussion.[5]

---

[1] This is a revised version of a paper presented to the Tyndale Fellowship New Testament Study Group in July 2006 and the London School of Theology New Testament research seminar in September 2006. I am grateful to the participants on both occasions for their helpful comments, and also particularly to Dr Brian Capper, who kindly read and commented graciously and helpfully on an earlier version.

[2] For a helpful survey of the views of some key figures from Chrysostom to the twentieth century, see Daniel B. McGee, "Sharing Possessions: A Study in Biblical Ethics. Selected Interpretations of Acts 2:43-47 and 4:32-37, Patristic Times to Present," in *With Steadfast Purpose: Essays on Acts in Honor of Henry Jackson Flanders, Jr.*, ed. Naymond H. Keathley (Waco, TX: Baylor University Press, 1990), 163–78. Gerd Theissen, "Urchristlicher Liebeskommunismus: Zum 'Sitz im Leben' des Topos ἅπαντα κοινά," in *Texts and Contexts: Biblical Texts in Their Textual and Situational Contexts: Essays in Honor of Lars Hartman*, ed. Tord Fornberg and David Hellholm (Oslo: Scandinavian University Press, 1995), 689–712, 689–92, provides a convenient summary of nineteenth- and twentieth-century German scholarship.

[3] I shall refer to the author as 'Luke' henceforward, without necessarily assuming him to be Paul's travel companion of that name.

[4] See the judicious discussion of Brian J. Capper, "Community of Goods in the Early Jerusalem Church," *ANRW* II/26.2 (1995): 1730–74, which makes a solid case for the historicity of such a sharing on the grounds of parallel practices among the Essenes – although note that I shall differ from Capper in the extent to which the early believers' practices were the same as those of the Essenes.

[5] For a valuable survey, see Thomas E. Phillips, "Reading Recent Readings of Issues of Wealth and Poverty in Luke and Acts," *CurBR* 1 (2003): 231–69; for a helpful discussion from an anthropological perspective, see Louise J. Lawrence, *Reading with Anthropology: Exhibiting Aspects of New Testament Religion* (Bletchley: Paternoster, 2005), 152–71.

What are the grounds for arguing that Luke views the sharing of possessions as mistaken, and therefore as something which he *describes* rather than *pre*scribes for the church of his day?

First and foremost, scholars suggest that there is a tension – not to say a contradiction – between the various accounts of the earliest believers' sharing of possessions. Thus Holtzmann argues[6] that 2:44–45 and 4:32–35 present a community with 'all things common' who sold their belongings and gave them into a common fund, thus practising a form of communism. However, he then notes that the examples given of Barnabas (4:36–37) and Ananias and Sapphira (5:1–11) both suggest that the sale of property and donation of the proceeds were voluntary. In particular, 5:4, where Peter asserts that Ananias's property belonged to him before the sale and that the proceeds belonged to him after the sale, show that there was no genuine common ownership. 6:1–6 further shows, asserts Holtzmann, that the earliest believers were far from well organized in their provision for needy people, and thus undermines any suggestion that there was a genuine common ownership. Thus the picture painted in 2:44–45; 4:32–35 is 'idealized', which is a polite way of saying 'made up'.

Second, it is suggested that the size of the pot of shared possessions gradually shrank to virtually nothing under the weight of the needs of widows and other economically unproductive people, and thus that the community had to abandon their bold experiment in communism.[7] As evidence for this, references to the poverty of the Jerusalem church are cited, notably Acts 11:27–30 (concerning the famine during Claudius's time); 24:17 (where Paul states that he came to Jerusalem to bring many offerings for his own nation, thus [it is argued] suggesting that there was a 'chronic' ongoing state of shortage[8]) and Gal 2:10 (where Paul says that he was asked to 'remember the poor').[9]

Third, had all of the earliest believers sold all of their lands and houses, they would have lacked anywhere to meet, not to say live![10] But 12:12 shows the believers meeting in Mary's home, a home which was large enough for such a gathering and had a front porch (12:13),[11] further underlining its size. This feature further suggests that the portrait in 2:44–45; 4:32–35 is unrealistic and idealized.

Fourth, Capper claims that the move from a Jewish context to a Hellenistic setting, which he detects in 6:1–6, was what led to a move away from common ownership.[12]

---

[6] H. J. Holtzmann, "Die Gütergemeinschaft der Apostelgeschichte," in *Strassburger Abhandlungen zur Philosophie. Eduard Zeller zu seinem siebenzigsten Geburtstag* (Tübingen: Akad. Verlagsbuchhandlung, 1884), 27–60 (cited by Capper, "Community," 1731).

[7] Everett F. Harrison, *Acts: The Expanding Church* (Chicago: Moody, 1975), 67, 90.

[8] The gifts mentioned are usually identified with the Pauline 'collection', cf. Rom 15:26, although note the recent cogent argument that this is not so in David J. Downs, "Paul's Collection and the Book of Acts Revisited," *NTS* 52 (2006): 50–70.

[9] Harrison, *Acts*, 90; Capper, "Community," 1774.

[10] Gerhard Krodel, *Acts*, ACNT (Minneapolis, MN: Augsburg, 1986), 117.

[11] τὴν θύραν τοῦ πυλῶνος 'the door of the porch' (12:13) suggests quite a large house (BDAG 897 πυλών §1), cf. Josephus, *J.W.* 5.5.3 §202 writing of temple gateways which each had two doors.

[12] Capper, "Community," 1766–71. In correspondence, Dr Capper suggests that the period where common ownership was practised may have been a matter of months or even weeks (depending on the chronology adopted for the early chapters of Acts). He notes two possible points which might

He sees the 'Hellenists' as a 'fringe group' of Greek speaking Jews who did not practise common ownership, and for whose widows there was no daily provision like that of the 'Hebrews'. Capper thus considers the appointment of the seven to 'serve tables' as being the appointment of leaders for the Hellenists, one of whose first tasks was to be to work out an arrangement for care for their widows which fitted into their cultural setting. In response the Hellenists established a looser kind of community life, notably in not having common ownership – and it was this model which spread into the churches planted in the Diaspora.

Fifth, as part of the common scholarly reconstruction that the earliest communities lived with a lively imminent expectation of the *parousia*, scholars frequently consider that there could have been a brief period of sharing of possessions such as that portrayed in 2:44–45; 4:32–35. However, this practice would have faded as impractical once believers realized that the *parousia* would not be happening any time soon.[13]

More than that, Krodel argues that the presence of Galilean disciples would necessitate some form of economic sharing, since they had left their trades behind in Galilee and would need support in the daily necessities of life.[14] Thus, in Krodel's view, the gifts of Barnabas and Ananias and Sapphira were exceptional and unusual, and not a precedent for any future action.

These arguments do not form a coherent overall position – indeed, some of them are mutually contradictory – but they illustrate the combination of historical incredulity and a hermeneutic of suspicion being applied to this feature of Acts. So what is to be made of this? In what follows I shall consider, first, the key passages in 2:44–45 and 4:32–35 with the allied stories of 5:1–11 and 6:1–6, to see what Luke affirms about the earliest believers' practice concerning sharing of possessions. Second, and much more briefly, I shall then consider how the theme of possessions develops in the remainder of Acts by focusing on two key themes: the place of almsgiving (9:36; 11:28–30; 12:25), and Paul's practice of self-support (20:33–35).

In what follows, I propose to doubt both parts of the reconstruction that I am considering. I shall argue both that Luke does not present the earliest communities as practising common ownership, and that the later churches' practice of almsgiving and care for the poor is consistent with the earliest believers' practice in Jerusalem.

---

have marked the introduction of a category of believers who did not practise common ownership: (i) the incident with Ananias and Sapphira (Acts 5:1-11), which he believes would give potential new converts pause about joining common ownership; or (ii) Acts 5:12-14a, where people are unwilling to join 'them', which Capper takes to refer the 'inner circle' which practised common ownership, although believers continue to be added to the Lord, and Capper takes these to be the new category of non-common-ownership believers (on Acts 5:12-14a, Capper is following Daniel R. Schwartz, "Non-joining Sympathisers (Acts 5.13-14)," *Bib* 64 (1983): 550–5, esp. 75–6). See more fully Brian J. Capper, "'With the Oldest Monks ...' Light from Essene History on the Career of the Beloved Disciple?," *JTS* ns 49 (1998): 1–55, here 42–7.

[13] Krodel, *Acts (ACNT)*, 118; C. K. Barrett, *A Critical and Exegetical Commentary on the Acts of the Apostles*, 2 vols., ICC (Edinburgh: T&T Clark, 1994, 1998), 1:168.

[14] Capper, "Community," 118.

II. What Did the Earliest Believers Actually Do?

We shall first consider the key passages in the early part of Acts in turn: 2:44–45 and 4:32–35; 4:36–5:11; and 6:1–6.

II.a. Acts 2:44–45; 4:32–35[15]

2[44] All the believers were together and they used to hold everything in common; [45] They used to sell possessions and belongings and distribute the proceeds to all as each was having need.

4[32] The heart and soul of the multitude of those who believed was one, and not even one used to say that any of their possessions was their own, but all things were shared by them. [33] With great power the apostles regularly gave their testimony to the resurrection of the Lord Jesus, and great grace was upon them all. [34] For there was no-one in need among them; for those who were owners of fields or houses used to sell them and bring the proceeds of the sales [35] and lay them at the apostles' feet, and they were distributed to each one, as they had need.

The use of imperfect verbs throughout 2:44–45 and 4:32–35 (all of the indicative verbs are imperfects) is usually taken as indicating that these are summary statements indicating the habitual practices of the earliest believers.[16] Our reading of these two passages turns on a series of exegetical decisions about key words and phrases.

First, what form of togetherness is implied by ἐπὶ τὸ αὐτό (2:44), usually translated 'together'? Bruce speculates that they formed themselves into a synagogue of messianic believers.[17] Taylor similarly suggests that this expression parallels the semi-technical use of the Hebrew equivalent יחד or יחדו (*yhd* or *yhdw*) as a label for the community in the Dead Sea Scrolls, notably 1QS 5.2, and thus might be rendered 'all the believers *belonged to the community*'.[18] While both Bruce and Taylor may be going beyond the evidence,[19] there is certainly a form of shared living implied in these and the surrounding verses (2:42–47), a form which includes shared learning, shared meals and hospitality, shared prayer, and regular, daily, gatherings in homes and the temple to facilitate this shared living (v. 46). Other uses of this favourite Lukan expression suggest shared living as the focus of this specific phrase,[20] and thus point us to the

---

[15] Translations are my own.
[16] E.g. Barrett, *Acts*, 1:169.
[17] F. F. Bruce, *The Acts of the Apostles*, 3rd ed. (Leicester: Apollos, 1990), 132.
[18] Justin Taylor, SM, "The Community of Goods among the First Christians and among the Essenes," in *Historical Perspectives: From the Hasmoneans to Bar Kokhba in Light of the Dead Sea Scrolls*, ed. David Goodblatt, Avital Pinnick and Daniel R. Schwartz, Studies on the Texts of the Desert of Judah 37 (Leiden: Brill, 2001), 147–61, here 148; so also Capper, "Community," 1738–9; Max Wilcox, *The Semitisms of Acts* (Oxford: Clarendon, 1965), 93–9.
[19] For critique of the arguments of Capper and Wilcox (n. 18), see Richard Bauckham, "The Early Jerusalem Church, Qumran, and the Essenes," in *The Dead Sea Scrolls as Background to Postbiblical Judaism and Early Christianity: Papers from an International Conference at St Andrews in 2001*, ed. James R. Davila, STDJ 46 (Leiden: Brill, 2003), 63–89, here 85–8.
[20] Luke 17:35; Acts 1:14; 2:47; 4:26; it is found elsewhere in the NT only at Matt 22:34; 1 Cor 7:5; 11:20; 14:23.

likelihood that this phrase prepares for the fuller description of their meetings in v. 46, both all together in the temple and in smaller groups in homes.[21]

Second, a central phrase for our discussion is εἶχον ἅπαντα κοινά 'they used to hold all things common' (2:44). As is widely recognized, this phrase echoes key phrases from Graeco-Roman writings concerning the ideal community, notably Plato and Seneca,[22] as does the parallel expression in 4:32, ἦν αὐτοῖς ἅπαντα κοινά 'all things were common to them'. The Greek ideals did not preclude private ownership, however, since (e.g.) the Cynic Epistles include a letter purportedly to Plato saying, 'And if you need anything that is yours, write us, for my possessions, Plato, are by all rights yours, even as they were Socrates'.[23] It was a matter of possessions being held loosely, so that friends might ask for them as they needed help. Thus it is entirely compatible for Luke to write of people selling their property and the proceeds being distributed to those in need (2:45; 4:34–35) alongside references to private homes where the believers met (e.g. 2:46, κατ' οἶκον; 12:12). Indeed, it seems likely that these references imply that believers did not sell their own houses, but other properties which belonged to them.[24]

This key phrase 'they used to hold all things common' may be elucidated further by reflection on the earlier part of 4:32, Τοῦ δὲ πλήθους τῶν πιστευσάντων ἦν καρδία καὶ ψυχὴ μία, καὶ οὐδὲ εἷς τι τῶν ὑπαρχόντων αὐτῷ ἔλεγεν ἴδιον εἶναι, 'The heart and soul of the multitude of those who believed was one, and not even one used to say that any of their possessions was their own'. As Taylor notes,[25] the picture found here is of a continuing 'private ownership' of property, denoted by τῶν ὑπαρχόντων αὐτῷ 'the things which belonged to him', combined with a radical willingness to share one's goods with others in need. Verse 34 sharpens the focus of the picture, for it explains the mechanism by which the provision for needy people happened, with γάρ introducing an explanation of how it was that 'great grace was upon them all' (v. 33). This construction parallels the epexegetical use of καί in 2:45, which introduces an

---

[21] In v. 46 ὁμοθυμαδόν indicates their meeting all together in the temple, by contrast with their smaller group meetings in homes; see discussion in Steve Walton, "Ὁμοθυμαδόν in Acts: Co-location, Common Action or 'Of One Heart and Mind'?," in *The New Testament in Its First Century Setting: Essays on Context and Background in Honour of B. W. Winter on His 65th Birthday*, ed. P. J. Williams, Andrew D. Clarke, Peter M. Head and David Instone-Brewer (Grand Rapids, MI; Cambridge: Eerdmans, 2004), 89–105, esp. 99.

[22] Note especially Seneca, *Epistles* 90.38; Plato, *Republic* 420C–422D; 462B–464A; *Laws* 679B–C; 684C–D; 744B–746C; 757C; *Critias* 110C–D. For a full listing of parallels, see Charles H. Talbert, *Reading Acts: A Literary and Theological Commentary on the Acts of the Apostles*, revised ed. (Macon, GA: Smyth & Helwys, 2005), 48–9.

[23] Socratics 26.2 'To Plato', translation from Abraham J. Malherbe, *The Cynic Epistles: A Study Edition*, SBLSBS 12 (Missoula, MT: Scholars, 1977), 281. [By 'anything that is yours' the author implies that 'what's mine is yours', as the rest of the sentence goes on to show.] Cf. Cicero, *De Officiis* 1.16 §51: 'Nature has produced for the common use of man is to be maintained, with the understanding that, while everything assigned as private property by the statutes and by civil law shall be so held as prescribed by those same laws, everything else shall be regarded in the light indicated by the Greek proverb: "Amongst friends all things in common (*amicorum esse communia omnia*)"' (LCL).

[24] Andreas Lindemann, "The Beginnings of Christian Life in Jerusalem according to the Summaries in the Acts of the Apostles (Acts 2:42-47; 4:32-37; 5:12-16)," in *Common Life in the Early Church: Essays Honoring Graydon F. Snyder*, ed. Julian V. Hills (Harrisburg, PA: Trinity Press International, 1998), 202–18, here 211 n. 46.

[25] Taylor, "Community of Goods," 152.

explanation that the theme of 2:44 was carried out by means of people selling property and possessions.

What lies behind the assertion made in v. 32? Again, Greek ideals have been seen as echoed here, notably the oneness of heart and soul which was a feature of friendship. Aristotle cites two proverbs with approval in expounding his understanding of friendship: 'Friends are one soul' and 'Everything belonging to friends is common' (*Nicomachean Ethics* 9.8.2). Diogenes Laertius cites Aristotle as saying that friends were 'one soul dwelling in two bodies' (*Lives* 5.20). Plutarch similarly says that friends 'who, though existing separately in bodies, forcibly unite and fuse their souls together' (*Dialogue on Love* 21.9 = *Moralia* 767E; my translation). There may well be an echo of such ideals in Acts 4:32, and Luke may thus be asserting that the primitive Christian community realized all the highest hopes for human community of the Graeco-Roman world.

But the biblical background to the common life of the earliest believers ought not to be neglected either, and a third key phrase points us clearly to Scripture as a resource which Luke draws on here. οὐδὲ γὰρ ἐνδεής τις ἦν ἐν αὐτοῖς 'for there was not a needy person among them' (4:34) echoes Deut 15:4. This verse in Deuteronomy comes in the midst of laws on the remission of debts every seven years – laws which may never have been enacted – and asserts that the regular redistribution of property implied by these laws would not cause poverty or deprivation, 'for there will be no poor among you (for the LORD will bless you in the land which the LORD your God gives you for an inheritance to possess)' (NRSV). The LXX rendering is closely echoed by Luke here, using ἐνδεής ('needy'), an NT *hapax legomenon* found in Deut 15:4 LXX: ὅτι οὐκ ἔσται ἐν σοὶ ἐνδεής 'because there will not be among you *a needy person*'.

More than that, the language of the community being 'one heart and soul' (4:32) which we noted as paralleled in Graeco-Roman authors, also has biblical parallels. Unity of heart and soul in the knowledge of God and the pursuit of godliness is a theme running through Deuteronomy, not least in the *Shema* (6:5), where Israel is exhorted to love YHWH with heart, soul and strength. The prophets similarly point to a time when humans will have singleness of heart (e.g. Jer 32:29; Ezek 11:19), which means complete devotion to YHWH and his concerns and ideals.

Thus Luke presents the messianic community in Jerusalem as fulfilling the hopes and ideals embodied in the Torah for a community life in which no one was poor or in need. There are, of course, Graeco-Roman writers who envisage such a state of affairs too. Seneca writes of ancient times when 'you could not find a single pauper' (*Epistles* 90.38). My point here is simply that Luke's portrait of the earliest believers is not only an echo of Greek ideals, but also of biblical ones.

Luke is clear, of course, that this community life flows from the pentecostal outpouring of the Spirit, for 2:44–45 follows hot on the heels of the promise of the Spirit to those who believe (2:38), and 4:32–35 follows on the description of a fresh filling with the Spirit in response to prayer (4:31).[26] It is notable that Jer 32 and Ezek 11

---

[26] Lawrence, *Reading*, 163–5 notes the thoughtful work of Douglas Davies, arguing that the Spirit acts as a divine gift which functions as a 'boundary marker' for the new community, 'linking believers to their origins in Jesus and his resurrection' (164).

are both passages which hint at God's intervention to bring about the radical change to human attitudes and actions which they cannot accomplish unaided.[27] Thus divine power is behind the early believers' ability to hold their possessions lightly, and this background suggests that a broader biblical theology of stewardship may underlie our two passages in Acts 2:44–45; 4:32–35.

For the biblical authors, 'the earth is the LORD's and everything in it' (Ps 24:1) and thus humans hold it in trust from God as those who image him (Gen 1:26–28), rather as statues – that is, *images* – of the emperor populated the Roman empire to mark his claim upon it. Accordingly, property and money are held in trust on behalf of their divine owner: the forgiving of debts every seven years, as well as the radical Jubilee legislation, were signals of limits on the 'rights' (if we may use such a term in relation to biblical thought) of private property under the sovereign rule of YHWH.

If such an understanding underlies these key passages, then we may have a way to hold together both the radical provision for believers in need and the evidence of continuing ownership of property by individuals. But that is to run ahead of ourselves, for we need first to consider one particular reading of these passages which arises out of the examples of Barnabas, and Ananias and Sapphira, and that is Brian Capper's proposal that the Essene community provides the model of a two-stage membership which explains the way in which possessions were shared.

II.b. Acts 4:36–5:11

Capper's proposal hinges on his reading of 5:4 in the light of his suggestion, noted above,[28] that behind the key phrase ἐπὶ τὸ αὐτό (2:44) stood a Semitic expression meaning 'together', an expression which had a semi-technical sense in Essene writings for the community. Building on this suggestion, Capper argues that the natural reading of Peter's explanation to Ananias in 5:4 is that Ananias is not yet a full member of the community and thus that he is not obliged to contribute all of his goods to the common fund.

Capper is reflecting on the two stage membership of the Qumran community, which consisted in a novitiate of one year, following which property and possessions were handed over to the community bursar and the prospective member became a postulant. However, at this stage possessions were not merged with the common fund or spent, but a record was kept of them (1QS 6.19–20). After a further year, the postulant could become a full member of the community, and at this stage his property was merged fully into the communal property (1QS 6.21–22). This community of goods was what marked out the community from outsiders (1QS 9.8–9). Thus, severe penalties were enacted on those who lied about property: they were excluded from the common meal for a year and their rations were reduced by 25 per cent (1QS 6.24–25).

---

[27] Were I N. T. Wright, I would also be noticing that they come in 'return from exile' contexts; see N. T. Wright, *Jesus and the Victory of God*, Christian Origins & the Question of God 2 (London: SPCK, 1996), esp. (e.g.) 126–7, 203–4, 209.

[28] See n. 18.

Capper proposes that Peter's explanation in 5:4 reflects these two stages: Ananias and Sapphira were in full possession of their property before it was sold and of the proceeds after the sale. After laying the money at the apostles' feet, Capper suggests, it remained Ananias and Sapphira's property, for they were not yet full members of the community, by analogy with the 'novitiate' at Qumran. In other words, Peter's assertion, 'after it was sold, was it not in your power?' identifies that at the point of laying the proceeds at the apostles' feet Ananias and Sapphira were beginning the second phase of membership, which involved surrender of their property to the community, but not yet merging of their property into the common fund. Thus to lie about this was to incur punishment, by analogy with the penalties for lying about property at entry into the Qumran community.[29] However, for the earliest believers, such lying was lying to God, understood to be identified with his representative, Peter.

This is an attractive and interesting proposal, which has the merit of locating the events of the early chapters of Acts within a Jewish matrix. Thus Capper argues, cogently it seems to me, that there is a strong case for some form of sharing possessions among the earliest Christians being historical, since there is evidence of other Jewish groups practising some form of shared possessions in this period in Palestine.[30]

However, it seems doubtful that the parallels he proposes are exact, and thus doubtful that the earliest Christians practised a 'common fund' analogous with that at Qumran. The key weakness in Capper's view is that the assertion of Peter in 5:4 *prima facie* is that *prior to handing over the money* to the apostles, the proceeds of the sale were Ananias and Sapphira's to dispose of as they wished, rather than that this was so *after* they handed the money over. While Peter's question οὐχὶ μένον σοὶ ἔμενεν καὶ πραθὲν ἐν τῇ σῇ ἐξουσίᾳ ὑπῆρχεν; is not straightforward to translate, its general thrust seems clear enough, giving the sense, 'Surely it is the case that,[31] while it remained yours, it was at your disposal, and that after it was sold, it was still in your authority?' Capper attempts to evade the apparent thrust of this verse (which he notes is translated in similar ways in all the modern English versions[32]) by arguing that the expression ἐν τῇ σῇ ἐξουσίᾳ 'in your authority' is equivalent to a Semitic phrase 'in your hand', based on Hebrew NT translations having used this phrase, and that the Hebrew expression involved might have been used at Qumran for the situation of a postulant's funds following their completing the one year novitiate.[33] This argument seems to be stretching the point considerably and to be building hypothesis on hypothesis in an unpersuasive way.

---

[29] In particular, Capper argues that Luke's choice of νοσφίζω in Acts 5:3 has the sense 'pilfer, embezzle' (Brian J. Capper, "The Interpretation of Acts 5.4," *JSNT* 19 (1983): 117–31, here 123); but see the entries of BDAG 679 s.v. and LSJ s.v., neither of which suggest this sense for Acts 5:3. For a full and helpful discussion of the echo of the same verb from Josh 7:1, see Hyung Dae Park, "Finding חרם? A Study of Luke-Acts in the Light of חרם" (PhD diss., London School of Theology/Brunel University, 2005), 186–204; published version: Hyung Dae Park, *Finding Herem? A Study of Luke-Acts in the Light of Herem*, LNTS 357 (London: T&T Clark, 2007), 132–8.
[30] So also Taylor, "Community of Goods," 155.
[31] Taking οὐχί as implying the answer 'Yes' to the rhetorical question.
[32] Capper, "Community," 1751.
[33] Brian J. Capper, "'In der Hand des Ananias': Erwägungen zu 1QS 6:20 und der urchristlichen Gütergemeinschaft," *RevQ* 12 (1986): 223–36.

Further, there appears to have been variety of practice among Essenes outside Qumran, as Capper acknowledges.[34] The Damascus Document provides evidence of Essene communities which did not practise a compulsory sharing of possessions, but which did have a common fund for provision for widows and orphans; for example, CD 14.13 asserts that for each member of the community, at least two days' income each month should be given to the 'Guardian and the Judges' to provide for those in need. Philo[35] and Josephus[36] similarly record evidence of such Essene communities. These looser communities seem a likelier analogy for the situation of the earliest Christians than a fully residential community such as that at Qumran. If Capper and others are right in postulating an Essene quarter in Jerusalem near to the likely site of the Upper Room,[37] then the likelihood increases of such a nearby community's practices being a more relevant analogy than the isolated community at Qumran.[38]

II.c. Acts 6:1-6

So what should we make of the 'daily distribution' (6:1)? It is hard to see that this contributes much to our understanding of the sharing of possessions among the earliest Christians in Jerusalem – the focus here seems, rather, to be on the distribution of food to those in need. Later rabbinic literature attests a synagogue-based distribution to those in need, and Jeremias argues that a similar system obtained before AD 70.[39] Seccombe argues cogently against Jeremias, noting that the presence of beggars in the Gospels and Acts is a key argument against any widespread system of synagogue-based poor relief.[40]

However, as Capper notes,[41] Philo records the behaviour of the Essenes at their evening gathering each day:

> [10] Accordingly, each of these men, who differ so widely in their respective employments, when they have received their wages give them up to one person who is appointed as the universal steward and general manager; and he, when he has received the money, immediately goes and purchases what is necessary and furnishes them with food in abundance, and all other things of which the life of

---

[34] Capper, "Community," 1760.
[35] *Every Good Man is Free* 76-7, 85-7; *Hypothetica* 11.4-13.
[36] *Ant.* 18.1.5. §§20-2; *J.W.* 2.8.3-4 §§122-7.
[37] Capper, "Community," 1752-9; see Brian J. Capper, "The Palestinian Cultural Context of Earliest Christian Community of Goods," in *The Book of Acts in its Palestinian Setting*, ed. Richard Bauckham, BAFCS 4 (Carlisle: Paternoster, 1995), 323-56, esp. 341-50; Rainer Riesner, "Synagogues in Jerusalem," in *The Book of Acts in its Palestinian Setting*, ed. Richard Bauckham, BAFCS 4 (Carlisle: Paternoster, 1995), 179-211, esp. 190-2 (with helpful further references).
[38] Although proximity need not imply direct influence, as Bauckham argues by noting that key designations of the earliest Christians were not used in the same way as at Qumran. He considers 'the way', 'the holy ones/the saints', 'the church of God' and 'the community' (Bauckham, "Early," 75-89).
[39] Joachim Jeremias, *Jerusalem in the Time of Jesus* (London: SCM, 1969), 131-4.
[40] David P. Seccombe, "Was There Organised Charity in Jerusalem before the Christians?," *JTS* ns 29 (1978): 140-3.
[41] Capper, "Community," 1764.

mankind stands in need. [11] And those who live together and eat at the same table are day after day contented with the same things, being lovers of frugality and moderation, and averse to all sumptuousness and extravagance as a disease of both mind and body. (Hypothetica 1:10–11)[42]

The daily nature of this feature of life may provide a useful parallel, Capper argues, to the 'daily distribution' of the early Christians. We may agree that this provides a possible analogy, particularly in relation to the looser Essene communities which existed around Palestine,[43] while at the same time denying Capper's wider case for a Qumran-like community of goods among the earliest believers.

II.d. Summary

In sum, I have argued that the life of the earliest believers in Jerusalem was marked by a remarkable level of economic sharing which fell short, however, of the common ownership found at Qumran. They grasped, I suggest, the theological keynote of God's ownership of all things, and thus held their possessions lightly as in trust from God, being ready to give them or to realize their value in response to needs among the poorer members of the believing communities.[44] The Essenes provide a partial parallel to the life of this community, as do the aspirations of Graeco-Roman writers such as Plato, Aristotle and Seneca.

III. And Later in Acts …

The limits of this chapter forbid a full study of the role of possessions in the rest of Acts, but two features suggest that a similar understanding of God's ownership of all things and believers holding possessions in trust, to be placed at the disposal of those in need, underlies later practice.

First, almsgiving was a key feature of the life of the believers, inherited from their Jewish origins. Dorcas is commended for her generosity, which seems to have featured making clothes for widows in particular (9:36, 39). The Antiochene believers gathered financial help for believers in Judaea during the Claudian famine (11:28–30) – a gift which would reflect the aggravated conditions of need caused during a famine,[45]

---

[42] Here in Yonge's translation.
[43] Cf. Jeremias, *Jerusalem*, 131.
[44] Cf. Eckhard J. Schnabel, *Early Christian Mission*, 2 vols. (Downers Grove, IL: InterVarsity Press, 2004), 1:413, arguing (in dependence on Wendel) that 'Luke presents a pragmatic ethic of possessions that places the needs of the poor in the center', rather than 'a world-denying "love-communism"' which rejects private property as a concept.
[45] Cf. Josephus, *Ant.* 20.2.5 §51, describing Queen Helena purchasing corn from Egypt and figs from Cyprus for the general population of Jerusalem during the same famine. Jeremias, *Jerusalem*, 123 estimates (on the basis of Josephus, *Ant.* 14.2.2 §28) that the price of wheat went up sixteenfold during the famine of 64 BC, and notes that Josephus, *Ant.* 3.5.3 §320 records that during the Claudian famine, the price of wheat was about thirteen times the usual. See also Ze'ev Safrai, *The Economy of Roman Palestine* (London: Routledge, 1994), 223.

but also a gift going to believers in the city of Jerusalem, a city in a parlous financial position as a result of a series of disasters over the previous 150 years[46] and containing large numbers of poorer people.[47] In addition, the building of the Herodian temple was in process, absorbing vast amount of money. The commendation of Dorcas and the gift from Antioch to Jerusalem both present people ready to give from what they had to meet others' needs.

Second, Paul's practice according to Acts was not to be dependent on people financially in the towns and cities where he proclaimed the gospel; rather he is presented as providing for himself and his companions by working (20:34; 18:3) – work expressed using κοπιῶντας (20:35), a verb denoting tiring, physical labour.[48] He is, moreover, a man free of the desire for others' money or high quality clothing (20:33). But most significantly, the principle behind his self-support is that he might have a surplus to support 'the weak' (τῶν ἀσθενούντων, 20:35), a phrase which likely connotes some form of physical weakness which would prevent those affected working for their own living.[49] As an example of such charitable support, we might think of the men whose hairdressing expenses Paul pays (21:23–24, 26). This practice Luke's Paul commends to the Ephesian elders – a theme, as I have argued elsewhere, thoroughly in tune with the Paul of 1 Thessalonians.[50]

IV. Conclusion

In sum, then, in asking 'Does Acts present the community of goods as mistaken?', I suggest that we are looking at a 'Have you stopped beating your wife?' question. By this I mean that we are presented with a question whose premises we should doubt. We should doubt that Luke believes that the earliest believers in Jerusalem practised common ownership of all of their possessions *and* we should doubt that the theme of sharing possessions vanishes from the rest of the book. Whether or not Luke knew the Pauline letters, he would have approved of Paul's expression of the theological basis of such economic action for those in need:

> I do not mean that there should be relief for others and pressure on you, but it is a question of a fair balance between your present abundance and their need, so that their abundance may be for your need, in order that there may be a fair balance. As it is written, 'The one who had much did not have too much, and the one who had little did not have too little.' (2 Cor 8:13–15, NRSV)

---

[46] Jeremias, *Jerusalem*, 140–4 notes the series of impoverishing disasters impacting on Jerusalem during the period from 169 BC to AD 70.
[47] The Jewish religious duty to give to the needy likely drew people with disabilities or others unable to support themselves financially to the city, to beg from those who came to the Temple (cf. Acts 3:2; John 13:29). For discussion and further references, see Jeremias, *Jerusalem*, 116–19, 128–30, 138.
[48] BDAG 558 κοπιάω §2.
[49] For discussion, see Steve Walton, *Leadership and Lifestyle: The Portrait of Paul in the Miletus Speech and 1 Thessalonians*, SNTSMS 108 (Cambridge: Cambridge University Press, 2000), 170–2.
[50] Walton, *Leadership*, 167–72.

6

A Tale of Two Perspectives? The Place of the Temple in Acts

'Things take time.' This slogan of those who have studied the management of change aptly summarizes the development of early Christian thought and praxis in relation to the Jerusalem temple in Acts. Luke portrays the earliest Christians as going to the temple to pray (Acts 2:46[1]), but also presents Paul as stating that God 'does not live in shrines made by human hands' (17:24). Is Luke consistent in Acts? Can these strands be held together within a wider view?

The aim of this chapter is to examine these questions by, first, carefully examining Luke's usage of temple language in its various contexts, highlighting both positive and negative views, and then by attempting to place these texts within a wider Lukan framework in order to see how they might hold together. The first of these tasks will necessitate a sustained engagement with Stephen's speech, which has been a storm centre in scholarship on this question. Finally, we shall reflect very briefly on the place of Acts' view of the temple in wider biblical theology.

I. Naming the Temple

In Acts there are four main terms used for the Jerusalem temple and other temples: 'temple' (ἱερόν), 'shrine' (ναός), 'house' (οἶκος) and 'this [holy] place'.[2]

While Luke uses 'shrine' (ναός) in his Gospel for the central shrine or sanctuary of the Jerusalem temple (Luke 1:9, 21–22), he never uses this word in relation to the Jerusalem temple in Acts – presumably partly, at least, because he has no occasion to describe events taking place in the shrine. Rather, 'shrine' is a generic term used in Paul's Athens speech of places where God does not live (17:24), and in describing the silversmiths' models of the temple of Artemis (19:24, 27). Thus this term may have negative connotations in relation to the central shrine of the Jerusalem temple, for that

---

[1] References henceforward in this paper are to Acts unless stated otherwise.
[2] Cf. Discussion (of these names and other issues concerning the temple) in Peter M. Head, "The Temple in Luke's Gospel," in *Heaven on Earth: The Temple in Biblical Theology*, ed. T. Desmond Alexander and Simon J. Gathercole (Carlisle: Paternoster, 2004), 101–19, coming to (unsurprisingly) similar conclusions.

is also called a ναός, and the tearing of the curtain in front of it may denote that God has departed (Luke 23:45).³

When Luke is narrating, he commonly writes simply of 'the temple' (τὸ ἱερόν, e.g. 2:46; 3:1). Similarly, his Christian characters speak of the temple this way (e.g. 22:17; 24:12, 18; 25:8; 26:21) or occasionally as a 'house' (7:47).⁴ Both of these terms appear to be neutral and descriptive, rather than carrying a lot of theological freight.

The final description, 'this [holy] place' is found only on the lips of non-Christian Jews in Acts (6:13-14; 21:28), and always in an accusation against Christians – in 6:13-14 against Stephen and in 21:28 against Paul.⁵ The fact that no Christian speaker ever uses this phrase rather suggests that Luke does not believe in the holiness of the temple thus asserted.

II. Positive Views of the Temple

A number of features point to a positive view of the temple on Luke's part.

First, *the early Christians go there to pray*. This is habitual, for they do it 'daily' (καθ' ἡμέραν, 2:46). It can be at the time of sacrifice: 3:1 specifies that Peter and John were going into the temple 'at the hour of prayer, the ninth [hour]' (ἐπὶ τὴν ὥραν τῆς προσευχῆς τὴν ἐνάτην), which was the time of the prayers associated with the afternoon sacrifice.⁶ While Luke does not specify explicitly that they go to pray, it does look as though he presents the apostles acting as devout Jews who live near enough to the temple to take part in its services.⁷

---

³ See the careful discussion in Raymond E. Brown, *The Death of the Messiah*, 2 vols., ABRL (London: Geoffrey Chapman, 1994), 2:1098-18, esp. 1101-2.

⁴ This appellation gives rise to discussion whether the Pentecost event took place in the temple courts, since the location is called 'the *house* where they were sitting' (τὸν οἶκον οὗ ἦσαν καθήμενοι, 2:2); cf. 7:47; Josephus, *Ant.* 8:65 (= 8.3.2), both using οἶκος for the temple. C. K. Barrett, *A Critical and Exegetical Commentary on the Acts of the Apostles*, 2 vols., ICC (Edinburgh: T&T Clark, 1994, 1998), 1:114 is open to that possibility, *contra* Ernst Haenchen, *The Acts of the Apostles*, trans. R. McL. Wilson (Oxford: Blackwell, 1971), 168 n. 1. However, the posture of sitting is unlikely in the temple courts, and it is hard to believe that Luke, who is in many respects very focused on the temple, would miss the opportunity to highlight the coming of the Spirit being in the temple if he understood that to be the case.

⁵ 7:6-7 has Stephen quote Gen 15:13-14 adding the words 'and they will serve me in this place' (λατρεύσουσίν μοι ἐν τῷ τόπῳ τούτῳ), but the 'place' is the promised land in general, not the temple.

⁶ Dan 9:21; Jdt 9:1; Josephus, *Ant.* 14:65 (= 14.4.3); also cited by Jacob Jervell, *Die Apostelgeschichte*, 17th ed., KEK (Göttingen: Vandenhoeck & Ruprecht, 1998), 199 n. 311; F. F. Bruce, *The Book of Acts*, revised ed., NICNT (Grand Rapids, MI: Eerdmans, 1988), 77; Hans Conzelmann, *Acts of the Apostles*, trans. James Limburg, A. Thomas Kraabel and Donald H. Juel, Hermeneia (Philadelphia, PA: Fortress, 1987), 25.

⁷ In agreement with C. K. Barrett, "Attitudes to the Temple in the Acts of the Apostles," in *Templum Amicitiae*, ed. William Horbury, JSNTSup 48 (Sheffield: JSOT, 1991), 345-67, 347-8. Roger Stronstad, *The Prophethood of All Believers: A Study in Luke's Charismatic Theology*, JPTSup 16 (Sheffield: Sheffield Academic, 1999), 73-4 speculates that in 4:23 the phrase πρὸς τοὺς ἰδίους means Peter and John returned to a group of disciples numbering thousands on the temple mount, *contra* Joseph A. Fitzmyer, *The Acts of the Apostles: A New Translation and Commentary*, AB 31 (Garden City, NY: Doubleday, 1998), 307 (and many others).

At a later date Paul also goes to the temple to pray in order to rebut the charge that he teaches Jewish people to disregard the Mosaic law (21:21) – a charge that was a (perhaps understandable) misunderstanding of Paul's insistence that gentiles need not keep torah. The rite in which he takes part involves offering sacrifice – indeed, the provision of a sin offering (Num 6:13–20, esp. vv. 14, 16) – and Paul agrees both to take part himself and to cover the hairdressing expenses of the others involved (21:24), thus demonstrating that he is an observant Jew. In response to charges that he has profaned the temple by bringing in Greeks (21:28; 24:6), Paul is anxious to make clear that he has acted entirely properly in the temple (24:12, 18; 25:8). Rather, he asserts, the reason he was arrested was because of his declaration that gentiles could enter the people of God (26:19–21) – the real issue is following the lead of Jesus, not the temple in itself.

Second, *the early Christians preach in the temple courts*. Following the healing of the man with a congenital disability[8] (3:2) at the Beautiful Gate of the temple, Peter preaches in Solomon's Portico (3:11–26), which Luke presents as an habitual meeting place of the earliest Christians (5:12) – in line with the common practice in the ancient world of meeting in the open air (cf. 17:17).[9] Not only this, but the apostles are specifically commanded by an angel to preach in the temple courts on their release from prison by the angel (5:20). The use of the imperfect tense 'they were teaching' (ἐδίδασκον, 5:21) suggests an ongoing activity, especially if it is seen as ingressive, marking the start of an activity which continued for some time (= 'they began teaching').[10] 5:42 goes on to make it clear that this public preaching in the temple courts took place daily, in combination with daily meetings in the homes of the Jerusalem-based believers.

Third, *God acts to reveal himself in the temple*. This is evident in the healing of the man at the Beautiful Gate (3:1–10), and also in Paul's later account of his vision, while praying in the temple, of Jesus calling him to ministry and mission among the gentiles (22:17–21). Whilst (as we shall see) God is not limited to the temple as a locus of revelation, neither does he regard the temple as an exclusion zone for revelatory activity. More, it is precisely at the heart of the Jewish faith that Paul receives his call to include the gentiles in the renewed people of God.[11]

III. Critical Views of the Temple?

There is wide scholarly agreement on the positive material about the temple in Acts, but considerable disagreement on the apparently more critical passages, and two in particular: Stephen's speech (esp. 7:48–50) and Paul's comments in Athens (esp. 17:24).

---

[8] This terminology is used in agreement with Kerry H. Wynn, "Disability in Biblical Translation," *BT* 52 (2001): 402–14, esp. 406.
[9] So also Barrett, "Attitudes," 349.
[10] Daniel B. Wallace, *Greek Grammar beyond the Basics: An Exegetical Syntax of the New Testament* (Grand Rapids, MI: Zondervan, 1996), 544–5.
[11] David Peterson, *Engaging with God: A Biblical Theology of Worship* (Leicester: Apollos, 1992), 138 sees the preaching of the earliest Christians as part of God's activity of revelation.

III.a. Stephen's Speech

Stephen's speech results from an accusation that he speaks against the temple and the torah and claims that Jesus will destroy the temple and replace the torah (6:13-14). Luke makes it clear that he considers these accusations mischievous, for members of the Hellenistic Synagogue of the Freedmen have stirred people up to make these accusations (6:11), but nevertheless there is a charge to be answered.

Within the speech itself Stephen does not criticize the torah; his main thrust is to parallel the ancient people's rejection of Moses with the contemporary people's rejection of Jesus, the prophet-like-Moses (note 7:35, 37).[12] The crucial question from our perspective is how he regards the temple, and there are broadly two streams within scholarship on this question: one sees Stephen as attacking the temple, even regarding building it having been a mistake; the other sees Stephen's focus as on God's transcendence over the temple and all earthly 'shrines'.[13]

Those who believe that Stephen sees the temple negatively focus on five main points within the Stephen stories.

First, they note the criticisms of Stephen (6:11, 13-14) and observe that Luke has not included in his Gospel the claims which Mark records, that Jesus will destroy/replace the temple (Mark 14:57-58; 15:29). Thus Stephen is the one, within Luke's narrative, who presents the temple as bound for destruction.[14]

However, it is clear that Luke presents these accusations as scurrilous. Luke calls what they say 'false testimony' (6:13) and presents the synagogue members instigating some to accuse Stephen in this way (6:11).[15] The charges presented are in fact charges about Stephen's teaching about Jesus, and Stephen answers them not by a careful defence speech – for the charges are manifestly false[16] – but by going on the offensive and presenting his own positive testimony to Jesus. Careful reading of Luke also reveals that Jesus predicts the destruction of the temple there as clearly as in Mark's account (e.g. Luke 21:5-6).

Second, while v. 44 notes God's initiative in beginning the tent of meeting, and v. 46 sees David's desire to find a 'tent' (σκήνωμα) for God positively, v. 47 has no such note of divine approval for Solomon's building of the temple.[17] More than that, David's actions, according to Simon and Haenchen,[18] are in relation to finding a proper place

---

[12] See the insightful discussion of Luke T. Johnson, *The Acts of the Apostles*, SP 5 (Collegeville, MN: Liturgical, 1992), 135-8.

[13] Dennis D. Sylva, "The Meaning and Function of Acts 7:46-50," *JBL* 106 (1987): 261-75; 261 n. 4 identifies three groups and provides useful documentation of sources.

[14] See Barrett, "Attitudes," 350-1; Harold W. Turner, *From Temple to Meeting House: The Phenomenology and Theology of Places of Worship*, Religion & Society 16 (The Hague/New York: Mouton, 1979), 116-17.

[15] So Francis D. Weinert, "Luke, Stephen and the Temple in Luke-Acts," *BTB* 17 (1987): 88-90, here 89.

[16] Ben Witherington, III, *The Acts of the Apostles: A Socio-Rhetorical Commentary* (Carlisle: Paternoster, 1998), 256-7.

[17] John J. Kilgallen, *The Stephen Speech: A Literary and Redactional Study of Acts 7,2-53*, AnBib 67 (Rome: Biblical Institute Press, 1976), 89.

[18] Marcel Simon, *St Stephen and the Hellenists in the Primitive Church: The Haskell Lectures 1956* (London: Longmans, Green, 1958), 51; Haenchen, *Acts*, 285.

in Jerusalem for the tent of meeting, since v. 46 alludes to Ps 131:5 LXX (MT 132:5),[19] and the Psalm itself refers to the taking of the ark to Jerusalem (2 Sam 6:17).

On the latter point, however, Sylva notes[20] that this is Luke's only use of 'tent' (σκήνωμα), and it is used in the LXX with reference to both temple[21] and tent.[22] This observation means that it is not possible to draw the clear conclusion that Stephen speaks of David locating the tent, rather than seeking a place for a temple. More than that, Ps 132 contains positive reference to God's choice of Zion (vv. 13-17) and is linked to the dedication of the temple by the use of vv. 8-10 in the conclusion of the prayer at the temple's dedication in 2 Chr 6:41-42,[23] so that this link cannot be used to claim that v. 46 is implicitly anti-temple.

Third, the use of adversatives often translated 'but' in vv. 47 (δέ) and 48 (ἀλλά) is held to suggest a contrast is being drawn which in each case presents Solomon's action in building the temple negatively. Solomon is being presented as bad and David, who 'finds favour' with God, as good. Barrett argues that the only alternative is to take Luke as meaning that Solomon having built a house for God must be understood in the light of the principle found in vv. 48-50.[24]

However, δέ (v. 47) is hardly a strong adversative: it frequently has the sense of a consecutive connective, meaning 'and'.[25] Further, the use of ἀλλά (v. 48), whilst certainly suggesting a contrast, need not suggest the contrast which Barrett proposes, nor his rejected alternative. Rather, it is more likely to have a concessive sense, 'though' or 'yet': 'Solomon built a house for him, *though* the Most High does not dwell in hand-made things' (vv. 47-48a, my rendering).[26] The statement about Solomon cannot be assumed to be negative, for it is a simple statement which contains nothing explicitly critical.

Fourth, vv. 49-50 indicate the divine displeasure with the temple, for the temple 'betrays the real meaning of God'[27] by suggesting that he can inhabit a temple. The use of 'hand made' (χειροποίητος, v. 48) suggests a number of contrasts, all negative. Simon observes that the word order in v. 48 might suggest a translation: 'It is not the Most High who dwells in temples made with hands', thus highlighting that it is *idols* who dwell in such temples.[28] Further, 'hand made' in LXX usage standardly connotes idolatry,[29] and

---

[19] Verse 46 has a difficult textual variant; some manuscripts read ' a tent for the *house* of Jacob' (σκήνωμα τῷ οἴκῳ Ἰακώβ) and others 'a tent for the *God* of Jacob' (σκήνωμα τῷ θεῷ Ἰακώβ). The manuscripts are fairly evenly divided, although 'house' is supported by a combination of Alexandrian and Western manuscripts. Decisive is the fact that 'house' is the more difficult reading and that 'God' appears to betray the influence of Ps 131:5 LXX; thus, 'house' is more likely original. See Bruce M. Metzger, *A Textual Commentary on the Greek New Testament*, 2nd ed. (Stuttgart: Deutsche Bibelgesellschaft/ United Bible Societies, 1994), 308-9.
[20] Sylva, "Meaning," 264.
[21] Pss 14:1 (MT 15:1); 45:5 (MT 46:5); 73:7 (MT 74:7).
[22] 1 Kgs 2:28; 8:4.
[23] Artur Weiser, *The Psalms: A Commentary*, OTL (London: SCM, 1962), 779, *contra* Leslie C. Allen, *Psalms 101-150*, WBC 21 (Waco, TX: Word, 1983), 207, although Allen concedes that 'The psalm ... demands ... a temple setting.'
[24] Barrett, "Attitudes," 352 n. 21.
[25] BDAG 213; Sylva, "Meaning," 264-5.
[26] Weinert, "Luke, Stephen," 90; Witherington, *Acts*, 273.
[27] Kilgallen, *Stephen Speech*, 91; R. A. Cole, *The New Temple*, Tyndale Monograph series (London: Tyndale Press, 1950), 44.
[28] Simon, *St Stephen*, 54.
[29] Lev 26:1, 30; Jdt 8:18; Wis 14:8; Isa 2:18; 10:11; 16:12; 19:1; 21:9; 31:7; 46:6; Dan 5:4, 23.

is here (v. 50) contrasted with God's hand, which makes all things.[30] Scharlemann also claims that being 'hand made' is a feature of the golden calf of Exod 32 (v. 41).[31]

However, it is clear that being 'hand made' is not in itself a weakness, for the tent of meeting was (presumably) made by human hands – a fact which strongly suggests that the contrast being drawn is not between the tent and the temple.[32] Rather, as we shall go on to argue, the issue is where God may be considered to dwell.

Finally, it is agreed that there is an allusion to the story of 2 Sam 7, where David seeks Nathan's counsel over building a house for the Lord (vv. 1–2). In both Hebrew and LXX texts there is considerable play on the words for 'house' (Hebrew בית Greek οἶκος) throughout this chapter. After initially advising him to pursue the idea (v. 3), Nathan is then told by God that David must not do this (vv. 4–10). Rather, God will build a house – that is, a dynasty – for David (vv. 11–16). A son from David's house will be the one to build a house for God (v. 13). Simon sees the allusion to this story as suggesting that God is declining to have a house built for him, and that, in Stephen's view, Solomon is therefore transgressing God's will in building a house for him.[33]

This need not follow, of course: the building of the temple in 2 Sam 7 has about it the same kind of ambivalence as the development of kingship within Israel,[34] and reflects a wider OT caution about seeing YHWH as localized in a particular place. This caution is reflected in other Jewish critiques of the temple, such as Jeremiah's repeated 'temple sermon' (Jer 7, 26), or the view of the Qumran community that they themselves formed the true temple, replacing the polluted and discredited Herodian temple.[35] And, what is more, God does say that David's heir will build the temple (2 Sam 7:13), which suggests that it is at least not a wholly bad idea.

The alternative, more persuasive, view sees the key emphasis in relation to the temple as on God's transcendence and presence. A number of arguments show that this reading of the text makes most sense in context; for the sake of brevity, we confine ourselves to two major and two minor observations.[36]

First, Solomon's prayer at the dedication of the temple (1 Kgs 8:15–53, esp. v. 27) recognizes the transcendence of God in very similar terms to Acts 7:48–50 and Isa 66:1–2 (quoted in Acts 7:49–50).[37] Stephen is critical of the view that God may be

---

[30] Kilgallen, *Stephen Speech*, 90; Barrett, *Acts*, 1:373.
[31] Martin H. Scharlemann, *Stephen: A Singular Saint*, AnBib 34 (Rome: Pontifical Biblical Institute, 1968), 106, 119.
[32] Witherington, *Acts*, 262; Craig C. Hill, *Hellenists and Hebrews: Reappraising Division within the Earliest Church* (Minneapolis, MN: Fortress, 1992), 79.
[33] Simon, *St Stephen*, 52–3.
[34] Gordon McConville, "Jerusalem in the Old Testament," in *Jerusalem Past and Present in the Purposes of God*, ed. P. W. L. Walker (Cambridge: Tyndale House, 1992), 21–51, here 28–9.
[35] A. F. J. Klijn, "Stephen's Speech – Acts VII. 2-53," *NTS* 4 (1957): 25–31, here 28–31; William Horbury, "New Wine in Old Wine-Skins: IX. The Temple," *ExpTim* 86 (1974): 36–42, here 38; Bertil Gärtner, *The Temple and the Community in Qumran and the New Testament: A Comparative Study in the Temple Symbolism of the Qumran Texts and the New Testament*, SNTSMS 1 (Cambridge: Cambridge University Press, 1965), 22–30.
[36] 1QS 5.4–7; 8.4–7, 8–10; 9.3–6. See more fully Sylva, "Meaning."
[37] Weinert, "Luke, Stephen," 89; Eric Franklin, *Christ the Lord: A Study in the Purpose and Theology of Luke-Acts* (London: SPCK, 1975), 106; J. Bradley Chance, *Jerusalem, the Temple and the New Age in Luke-Acts* (Macon, GA: Mercer University Press, 1978), 40.

confined to a temple, that he 'dwells' (κατοικεῖ) there,[38] but this does not mean that he believes that God cannot be encountered in a temple: 'the issue is not "tent" versus "house" but rather true and false thinking about God's presence'.[39]

A careful reading of 7:48 underlines this point, for neither 'tent' (σκήνωμα) nor 'house' (οἶκος) are mentioned in this verse: it is simply that the Most High does not dwell in hand made *things* – a principle with which any right-thinking first-century Jew would agree. At most this verse resists the idea that God is to be localized.[40] The quotation from Isa 66:1-2 in vv. 49-50 strengthens this point further, for the context in Isaiah is positive about the temple (notice Isa 66:6, which presents God as speaking from the temple);[41] it simply resists the idea that God is limited to that location – it is not his 'resting place' (Isa 66:1). If, as is very frequently the case in the NT, an OT quotation or allusion brings with it the whole context in the OT, this quotation in Stephen's speech should not be seen as criticizing the temple.

Second, Sylva observes four elements which are found in both 1 Kgs 8:14-30 and Acts 7:46-50 in the same sequence,[42] a parallelism which strongly suggests that similar theological points are in view. In each case the elements are:

(i) David's desire to find a place for God 1 Kgs 8:17; Acts 7:46;
(ii) an immediately following statement that Solomon will build the temple 1 Kgs 8:17-21; Acts 7:47;
(iii) the question whether God will dwell with humans on earth 1 Kgs 8:27a; Acts 7:48;
(iv) an assertion of God's transcendence of the temple by reference to God's relation to the heavens, the earth and a house 1 Kgs 8:27b; Acts 7:49-50 (quoting Isa 66:1-2).

This close parallel invites us to see the same theological perspective in both passages, a perspective that combines belief in God's transcendence and the appropriateness for Solomon's day of a temple.

The first minor observation is that, throughout Stephen's speech, YHWH is referred to as 'God' (ὁ θεός),[43] except in v. 48, where God is 'the Most High' (ὁ ὕψιστος), a title that stresses precisely his transcendence, and thus underlines the thrust of the sentence as denying that God can be localized. The emphatic forward position of this title in its clause highlights the point further.[44]

---

[38] I. Howard Marshall, "Church and Temple in the New Testament," *TynBul* 40 (1989): 203-22, here 209.
[39] Witherington, *Acts*, 263; so also Peterson, *Engaging*, 141.
[40] Hill, *Hellenists*, 74.
[41] T. C. G. Thornton, "Stephen's Use of Isaiah LXVI,1," *JTS* ns 25 (1974): 432-4 notes a midrash on Isa 66:1 which may have roots in the first century, in which the author interprets Isa 66:1 to mean that the temple is not to be seen as a guarantee of safety, for God can send someone to destroy it.
[42] Sylva, "Meaning," 266-7.
[43] 7:2, 6, 7, 9, 17, 20, 25, 32, 35, 37, 42, 45, 46, 56.
[44] Barrett, *Acts*, 1:373; Barrett, "Attitudes," 352.

The second minor observation is that there may be a polemical edge to the use of 'hand made' (χειροποίητος) in Stephen's speech, for by its use Stephen may be claiming that the temple has in fact become an idol for the Jewish people,[45] in similar manner to Jeremiah's dire warnings about leaning on the temple for safety in the face of foreign military might (e.g. Jer 7:1–15).

Overall, then, the material in Stephen's speech related to the temple should be seen as highlighting the transcendence of God over against the universal human temptation to localize the deity, and specifically against the common Jewish belief that YHWH was locally present in the temple in a way that was not regularly or predictably true of other locations on earth.[46]

III.b. Paul's Athens Speech

To listen to Luke's report of Paul speaking in Athens is to hear much of Stephen's theology, as we have understood it, transposed into a pagan key in order to communicate with Paul's hearers there. 17:24 certainly echoes the sentiments, and some of the precise words, of 7:48-50,[47] but in relation to pagan shrines, for Paul uses 'shrines' (ναοῖς), a word never used of the Jerusalem temple in Acts,[48] but used for the 'shrines' of Artemis in 19:24. Much of the Athens speech is standard Jewish polemic against pagan idolatry, using ideas (but not usually language) from the OT critique of idols,[49] and the differences in emphasis and presentation relate to the different target audience.

IV. Where Are We Now?

Thus far, then, we have seen much in Acts which seems at least not against the temple *per se*, but rather critiques a view of the temple as the primary locus of YHWH's presence. We have also seen positive signs of the earliest Christians' use of the temple for prayer and preaching, and God's use of the temple as a venue for his activity. In what follows we shall attempt to put the specific references to the temple into a wider framework in

---

[45] So Peter W. L. Walker, *Jesus and the Holy City: New Testament Perspectives on Jerusalem* (Grand Rapids, MI/Cambridge: Eerdmans, 1996), 66–7.

[46] Cf. Matt 23:21; Sir 36:18–19; Josephus, *Ant.* 3:215–218 (= 3.8.9), the latter speaking of God 'assisting' at the sacred ceremonies in the temple. See further E. P. Sanders, *Judaism: Practice and Belief 63 BCE-66 CE* (London: SCM, 1992), 70–1. Certainly Jews believed that YHWH could manifest himself outside the temple, but they strongly believed that he resided there and could be encountered there in particular, whereas appearances elsewhere could not be counted on.

[47] 'He does not dwell in hand made things' (χειροποιήτοις κατοικεῖ) is echoed precisely, but in 17:24 'shrines' (ναοῖς) is added; the subject of the verb is 'the Most High' (ὁ ὕψιστος) in 7:48 and 'he who is Lord over heaven and earth' (οὗτος οὐρανοῦ καὶ γῆς ὑπάρχων κύριος) in 17:24.

[48] See above, 75–6.

[49] James D. G. Dunn, *The Acts of the Apostles*, EC (London: Epworth, 1996), 230–1; Marion L. Soards, *The Speeches in Acts: Their Content, Context, and Concerns* (Louisville, KY: Westminster John Knox, 1994), 97–8; Conrad H. Gempf, "Athens, Paul at," in *Dictionary of Paul and His Letters*, ed. Gerald F. Hawthorne, Ralph P. Martin and Daniel G. Reid (Downers Grove, IL: InterVarsity Press, 1993), 51–4; Bertil Gärtner, *The Areopagus Speech and Natural Revelation* (Uppsala: Gleerup, 1955); *contra* Martin Dibelius, *Studies in the Acts of the Apostles* (London: SCM, 1956), 36–77.

order to seek Luke's own perspective. Two key elements are important: seeing Jesus as performing the functions which the temple was designed to perform, and noticing the locations where God acts in the apostolic mission.

V. Jesus as the True Temple?

In his fascinating study *From Temple to Meeting House*, Harold W. Turner proposes a fourfold phenomenological characterization of the functions of a sacred place.[50] First, a sacred place functions as a *centre* which provides orientation and focus to the society which it serves, offering a dependable anchor amidst the changes and vagaries of life. Thus, for example, the Jerusalem temple was described as the navel of the earth.

Second, a sacred place functions as a *meeting point*, where God (or the gods) and humanity engage with each other. It is a place where God reveals himself and communicates with people, and where people go to commune with God. In the case of the Jerusalem temple, the sacrificial system was centred on the temple and provided daily atonement for sin, as well as being a focus for teaching which would enable faithful Jews to engage with YHWH.

Third, a sacred place is a *microcosm of the heavenly world*, a place which shares most fully on earth the characteristics of the other realm. It mirrors or models the heavenly regions. This finds expression in the shape and design of the building(s), as in the perfect cubical symmetry of the holy of holies, as well as in the design for the temple being seen as God's handiwork.

Fourth, a sacred place is a place of *immanent-transcendent presence*, both the location of the presence of the gods on earth, and at the same time a sign of their presence throughout the world. Hence the Jerusalem temple was seen as the 'house of God', where God was specially thought to dwell.[51] The gradations of holiness within the temple complex – which permitted only certain persons to progress into certain areas, climaxing in the high priest alone being allowed into the holy of holies, and that only on one day each year – highlighted the particular presence of God in that inner shrine. More than that, the absence of images in the Jerusalem temple showed the transcendence of YHWH who dwelt there,[52] and the remote nature of temple worship, being in the main conducted by the priests and Levites on behalf of the people, emphasized further YHWH's inaccessibility and transcendence.[53]

When we examine the Acts accounts of the life of the earliest Christians, it is striking that each of Turner's four functions of sacred places is actually performed by God, and in particular by Jesus and/or the Spirit.[54]

---

[50] Turner, *Temple*, 18–42; he applies it to the Jerusalem temple on 54–67.
[51] See n. 47 above.
[52] Turner, *Temple*, 41.
[53] Turner, *Temple*, 42.
[54] This approach, via Turner's four functions, avoids the criticisms of Chance, *Jerusalem*, 41–5 that, in order to demonstrate that Jesus supersedes the temple, there need to be specific Acts texts transferring technical temple *language* to Jesus.

First, rather than the temple being the focus of their prayers, providing a centre and point of orientation, the earliest Christians pray in many different locations,[55] but always focused on Jesus. More, his 'name' is the authority and power of their work.[56] He provides the 'centre' which they lean upon.

Second, rather than the temple being the meeting point of heaven and earth, it is the person of Jesus who provides the means by which God and humanity are brought together:[57] through him forgiveness of sins is available (2:38; 3:19); by his work 'times of refreshing' come from the Lord (3:20); his is the only effective saving name among humanity (4:12) – and hence water baptism is in his name (2:38; 8:16; 19:5; 22:16); as Lord of all he brings peace between God and humankind (10:38); and through his grace Jews and gentiles alike are saved (15:11; 16:31). He takes over this function of the temple and extends it to gentiles, who were not permitted into the majority of the temple complex, as well as to women and Jewish laymen, who were not allowed into the places of sacrifice within the temple.

Third, rather than the temple being a microcosm of the heavenly realm, Christians now experience the life of the heavenly realm – at least in part – because of Jesus. Hence they experience 'times of refreshing' (3:20) and healing (e.g. 4:10; 9:34), and they experience the Spirit's transforming work, making them into the people they are called to be. For example: 1:8 has them experiencing 'power' by the Spirit to do God's will; 2:16–21 interprets the pentecostal gift as fulfilling the eschatological promise of Joel; 7:55–56 has Stephen by the Spirit seeing into heaven, where Jesus stands at God's right hand; and 20:22 presents Paul as ready to face suffering because he is 'captive to the Spirit'.[58]

Further, angels, the inhabitants of the heavenly realm, appear in the story of the church in Acts (e.g. 5:19; 8:26; 10:7, 22; 11:13; 12:7–11; 27:23). Not only that, but 6:15 shows Stephen's face shining like an angel's as a result of his being filled with the Spirit, grace and faith (6:3, 5, 8, 10)[59] – and this is a preparation for his entry into heaven itself (7:59–60).

Fourth, Jesus and the Spirit convey the immanent-transcendent presence of God, which is not understood as localized. Transcendence is clear from the departure of Jesus in the cloud (1:9), echoing the presentation of the son of man figure to the

---

[55] E.g. 1:13–14; 4:24–30; 7:59.
[56] Steve Walton, "Where Does the Beginning of Acts End?," in *The Unity of Luke-Acts*, ed. J. Verheyden, BETL 142 (Leuven: Peeters, 1999), 448–67, here 459; cf. John A. Ziesler, "The Name of Jesus in the Acts of the Apostles," *JSNT* 2 (1979): 28–41; Jacob Jervell, *The Theology of the Acts of the Apostles*, NT Theology (Cambridge: Cambridge University Press, 1996), 33–4; Franklin, *Christ*, 102.
[57] Cf. John Calvin, *Commentaries on the Minor Prophets, vol. 3: Jonah, Micah, Nahum* (Edinburgh: Calvin Translation Society, 1847), 277–8 (on Micah 4:7): 'Mount Zion then is now different from what it was formerly; for wherever the doctrine of the Gospel is preached, there is God really worshipped, there sacrifices are offered; in a word, there the spiritual temple exists.'
[58] See further Max Turner, *Power from on High: The Spirit in Israel's Restoration and Witness in Luke-Acts*, JPTSup 9 (Sheffield: Sheffield Academic, 1996), 404–27, esp. 415–18.
[59] Crispin H. T. Fletcher-Louis, *Luke-Acts: Angels, Christology and Soteriology*, WUNT II/94 (Tübingen: Mohr Siebeck, 1997), 96–8.

Ancient of Days (Dan 7:13). The martyr Stephen sees Jesus as this son of man at the right hand of God, in a position of power and authority (7:55-56).

Immediate presence is experienced by the Spirit, who comes upon the early church and indwells them, both collectively (e.g. 2:4, 16-21, 38; 4:31) and individually (e.g. 4:8; 6:3, 5; 8:15, 17). The Spirit directs the mission of the church, providing guidance to individuals and groups (e.g. 8:29, 39; 10:19; 11:12, 28; 13:2, 4; 16:6-7; 19:21;[60] 20:22). And this presence is found, as we shall see, in a wide variety of locations.

VI. Where God Acts[61]

Throughout the book of Acts God acts outside the temple and, indeed, outside the land of which the temple is the focus. 1:8 sets the agenda, echoing Isa 32:15[62] and 49:6, seeing the apostolic mission as beginning with the renewal of Israel and extending to the whole world;[63] the remainder of the book charts the progress of that mission in Jerusalem (1:1-5:42), Judaea and Samaria (6:1-11:18), and to the end of the earth (11:19-28:31).

Throughout the book, the Spirit breaks barriers in order to enable people to come to God. Linguistic barriers are overcome in the miracle of Pentecost (2:5-11). Ethnic barriers begin to be overcome in Philip's mission to Samaria and the apostles' visit to pray for the Spirit to come upon the converts (8:4-25),[64] and of course continue in the gradual and increasing inclusion of gentiles in the church. The Ethiopian eunuch, who has been to worship in Jerusalem (8:27) – although he would be excluded from full participation in temple worship because of his castration (Deut 23:1) – finds admission to full membership in the people of God through Philip's ministry (8:26-39).

God, often acting by the agency of the Spirit, brings people to himself in a variety of settings, whether the eunuch in the desert (8:26-39), an unclean gentile household in Joppa (10:1-48), Saul of Tarsus well outside Jerusalem (9:1-19),[65] or many areas outside the land (Paul's mission makes this clear).

---

[60] See discussion in Steve Walton, *Leadership and Lifestyle: The Portrait of Paul in the Miletus Speech and 1 Thessalonians*, SNTSMS 108 (Cambridge: Cambridge University Press, 2000), 88, arguing that the reference of ἐν τῷ πνεύματι is to the Holy Spirit.
[61] What follows draws extensively on the work of my student, Dr Dee Dyas, in "Where is God in Luke-Acts?" (unpublished).
[62] See Turner, *Power*, 301-2, 345.
[63] This is the likeliest meaning of the phrase 'to the end of the earth' (ἕως ἐσχάτου τῆς γῆς, 1:8, echoed in 13:47) in the light of LXX usage (see Isa 8:9; 14:22; 48:20; 49:6; 62:11; Jer 10:13; 35:16 [MT 28:16]; 39:32 [MT 32:32]; 45:8 [MT 38:8]; 1 Macc 3:9. See brief discussion in David Wenham and Steve Walton, *Exploring the New Testament, vol. 1: A Guide to the Gospels and Acts*, 3rd ed. (London: SPCK, 2021), 317.
[64] R. J. McKelvey, *The New Temple: The Church in the New Testament*, Oxford Theological Monographs (London: Oxford University Press, 1969), 88 notes that the admission of Samaritans to the believing community without mention of their worshipping at the Jerusalem temple immediately downgrades the importance of the temple, for Samaritans worshipped at a different temple, at Gerizim.
[65] Note 22:3, which shows that Luke understands Saul to have spent most of his life in the city.

In the latter case, God directs the mission to these new areas: Barnabas and Saul are sent from Antioch in response to the Spirit's call (13:1–3), and Paul is called by God to Macedonia (16:9, 13) – both passages contain rare examples of 'call' language used for God's call to specific tasks,[66] which thus underlines that they are doing this not at their own behest but at the impulse of God. Further, Paul's arrival in Rome does not represent the arrival of the gospel message there, for Christians come from the city to meet him (28:14–15) – God has got there before Paul!

A further dimension of this expansion is that God acts in homes and on the streets, and not simply in 'sacred places'. Certainly healing can come at the temple gate (3:1–10), but it can also come on the streets of the city (5:15) or in a home (9:39–41; 20:9–12) – God's presence and activity is not tied to the temple. Similarly, the believers meet in homes to pray (e.g. 2:46; 12:12; 20:7–8), or even on the beach (20:36–38), and the Spirit comes in homes (e.g. 10:44).

We can expand this point by noticing that the vocabulary of 'worship' is used by Luke, in common with other NT writers, for what Christians do with their whole lives, rather than being confined to what they do when they meet together.[67] For example, Paul can describe his apostolic mission and ministry using λατρεύω (24:14; 27:23).

Thus there is a clear stream of evidence in Acts that God's activities are not confined to the temple, the land or any other form of sacred place.[68] Because of the death, resurrection and exaltation of Jesus, the world itself is now being repossessed by God. The OT texts which saw the nations coming to Zion (e.g. Zech 8:20–23) are now being redirected, as the apostolic gospel goes out from Zion to the nations.[69]

VII. Is Acts Consistent?

Barrett's conclusion from the evidence of Acts is that Luke is not consistent, although he concedes that the same apparent inconsistency is there in Luke's treatment of the Jewish people (and wants to treat Luke's view of the temple as part of this wider question).[70] But is Luke so inconsistent? We have seen reason to argue that the view (which Barrett holds) that Stephen is opposed to the temple *per se* is mistaken, and have argued that Luke presents a wider understanding of God's transcendence within which the temple fits – a view with which few first-century Jews would have argued, at least in principle. We have also seen that the broader work of God which Luke narrates

---

[66] The only other clear NT examples are Rom 1:1 and 1 Cor 1:1, which both refer to Paul's call to be an apostle. See further Steve Walton, *A Call to Live: Vocation for Everyone* (London: Triangle, 1994), esp. ch. 2.

[67] See the seminal article, I. Howard Marshall, "How Far Did the Early Christians *Worship* God?," *Chm* 99 (1985): 216–29.

[68] For a similar conclusion based on Luke and Acts, see Nicholas H. Taylor, "Luke-Acts and the Temple," in *The Unity of Luke-Acts*, ed. J. Verheyden, BETL 142 (Leuven: Peeters/Leuven University, 1999), 709–21, here 719–20.

[69] Cf. Paul's adaptation of Isa 59:20–21 in Rom 11:26–27, changing the coming deliverer's role from 'for the sake of Zion' to 'out of Zion'.

[70] Barrett, "Attitudes," 366–7.

deconstructs any notion of sacred space that is narrower than the world, for that world is the arena of God's saving activity. But Luke's presentation is not so explicit or clear-cut as the way in which other NT writers use 'temple' language for the Christian community, even if it is accepted that James's quotation from Amos 9:11–12 in Acts 15:16–17 hints in this direction.[71]

This collection of conclusions suggests that in Acts we are seeing the process of change going on before our eyes.[72] The stories in Acts represent, as it were, the cusp of the change from a localized view of God dwelling in the temple to what we might call a universalized view, in which God is available, and reveals himself, anywhere and everywhere. Luke says implicitly what Paul or Hebrews or 1 Peter or John or Revelation say explicitly, but does not express their view outright because he is concerned to describe faithfully the historical process of development. Luke is not imposing his own, later view on the material, but is presenting the period as carefully as he can in order to enable his readers to see where the Christian faith has come from (Luke 1:1–4) and how a Jew-plus-gentile church has come into being from the followers of a Jewish Messiah.

Thus Luke's presentation runs alongside the view of the other NT writers we mentioned, showing how the implications of the resurrection and exaltation of Jesus were gradually worked out and understood. Luke belongs with a salvation-historical development scheme in the sense that he engages us, his readers, in the process of development, and lets us in on the moments when new insights begin to take hold. He thus invites Christian readers not to buy into every perspective on the temple which he offers, for some of them are 'works in progress' rather than the end of the development process.[73]

Luke's own perspective seems to be expressed most clearly by the insistence on the transcendence of God (7:48–50; 17:24), for this characteristic of God enables the church to be the church, crossing barriers and moving into new territory at the prompting of the Spirit – often, it must be said, after the believers' initial resistance to or hesitation about what God is doing. Within such an overarching view the early Christians' readiness to continue to pray, or even offer sacrifice, in the temple should give no cause to accuse Luke of inconsistency – they are learning what it means to live in the light of the coming of the Messiah, who fulfils all that the temple pointed towards, and who sees the whole of creation as his temple in which he is to be worshipped and served.

---

[71] Cf. the valuable discussion of Mark L. Strauss, *The Davidic Messiah in Luke-Acts: The Promise and its Fulfillment in Lukan Christology*, JSNTSup 110 (Sheffield: Sheffield Academic, 1995), 185–92, surveying four views and concluding that the rebuilt tent of David is about the restoration of the Davidic *dynasty* through Jesus's life, death and resurrection, rather than a reference to a people, whether Jewish or mixed Jewish and gentile. The parallel with 4QFlor 1.12, which also quotes Amos 9:11, is significant; there 'the fallen tent of David is he who shall arise to save Israel' – that is, an individual messianic figure is seen as the fulfilment of Amos 9:11, thus showing that such a view was current in first-century Judaism.

[72] Cf. McKelvey, *New Temple*, 85: 'One may say, therefore, that the apparent devotion of the first Christians to the temple of Jerusalem was a transitional phenomenon' (by 'the first Christians' he refers to the period described in Acts 2).

[73] This parallels the debate about how far Acts is descriptive and how far it is prescriptive in its material; for valuable introductory discussions, see I. Howard Marshall, *The Acts of the Apostles*, NT Guides (Sheffield: JSOT, 1992), 101–5; Gordon D. Fee and Douglas K. Stuart, *How to Read the Bible for All its Worth*, 4th ed. (Grand Rapids, MI: Zondervan, 2014), 112–31.

7

Deciding about Deciding: Early Christian Communal Decision-Making in Acts

Rachel Dolezal is a woman in the USA who caused – and causes – great controversy because of her self-identification as a black woman. She was elected president of the Spokane chapter of the National Association for the Advancement of Colored People in 2014, and this led in June 2015 to a major controversy after she was asked whether her parents were African American in a press interview, and walked out rather than answer. It turned out that her parents were both white, and her parents later said that she had 'disguise[d] herself' as African American.[1] When photographed at age eighteen, her skin was pale and freckled, and she was unquestionably white; now her skin is significantly darker. When pressed on this, Dolezal said that she considered herself to be black. In a TV interview in November 2015, she acknowledged that she was born white, but said, 'I acknowledge that I was biologically born white to white parents, but I identify as black.'[2] More recently, in a February 2017 interview with the UK newspaper *The Guardian*, she said that racial identity 'wasn't even biological to begin with. *It was always a social construct.*'[3]

I am telling you Dolezal's story not to comment on the rights or wrongs of it, but to illustrate a key feature of the postmodern world in which we westerners live. People wish to self-identify on the basis of how they see themselves, and identity is seen as an 'inner' quality of a person, rather than something seen because of their external features, body characteristics or family origins. This view locates identity in the private, individual sphere rather than the public sphere, and represents an historical shift from how people predominantly have been seen and understood. In some ways it could be liberating, for it gives people the opportunity not to be defined by their family or their

---

[1] Polly Mosendz, "Family Accuses NAACP Leader Rachel Dolezal of Falsely Portraying Herself as Black," *Newsweek*, 12 June 2015. http://www.newsweek.com/family-accuses-naacp-leader-rachel-dolezal-falsely-portraying-herself-black-342511, accessed August 2017.

[2] Sam Frizell, "Rachel Dolezal: I was Born White," *Time*, 3 November 2015, http://time.com/4096959/rachel-dolezal-white/, accessed August 2017.

[3] Decca Aitkenhead, "Rachel Dolezal: 'I'm not Going to Stoop and Apologise and Grovel,'" *The Guardian*, 25 February 2017 (my italics). https://www.theguardian.com/us-news/2017/feb/25/rachel-dolezal-not-going-stoop-apologise-grovel, accessed August 2017.

family's past. The point to notice here is not whether it is particularly good or bad, but that it is a symptom of this wider movement concerning human identity.

Some years ago, I asked a Kenyan student whom I taught in Nottingham what major differences he noticed between British culture and his native culture in Kenya, and his response was fascinating. He said that Kenyans think of themselves as 'we' first, whereas (white) British people think of themselves as 'I' first. I think that's an accurate observation, at least about British people. This individualization affects many, many areas of modern western culture, and it particularly affects our decision-making. We want the freedom to make decisions and to (as we say) 'think for ourselves' – indeed, our education systems encourage such individual thinking and reflection. This has an impact on church culture, where the predominant way that Protestants, and increasingly Catholics too,[4] make decisions about the church they will join – or leave – is about how 'at home' they feel there. People have adopted a consumerist, 'shopping mall' attitude, that of all the options around, at this period of their life they want to self-identify as Pentecostal or Anglican or Vineyard, etc. – or even, that they want to identify with a particular local church within a wider grouping because it has a particular theological and cultural flavour. The key thing to notice is that this is an *individual* choice or, at most, a nuclear family choice.

Such an approach to decision-making is historically unusual, and does not reflect the culture of the ancient texts found in the Bible. In particular, when we engage with the book of Acts, a book which perhaps more than any other New Testament book shows us how the earliest believers went about their decision-making on major and minor topics, we encounter a different culture and a different approach to decision-making. That is the approach I shall explore in this essay.

We shall look at this through first noticing the communal nature of the believing community in Acts, and then through studying some specific examples of decision-making. We shall notice some common features to these decision-making processes, and then look in more detail at the major decision about the terms on which non-Jewish people were to be allowed to participate as members of the believing community.

I. The Importance of the Communal in Acts

In line with their Jewish heritage, the earliest believers acted and lived communally. We can see this particularly in the early chapters of Acts, where Luke sketches key features of their shared life, notably in 2:42–47:

> [42] They were devoting themselves to the apostles' teaching and the fellowship, the breaking of bread, and the prayers. [43] Fear kept coming on everyone, and many wonders and signs were taking place through the apostles. [44] All those who had come

---

[4] For example, consider the phenomenon of the growth of the traditional Latin mass among young people in the West, e.g. Eric J. Lyman, "Latin Mass Resurgent 50 years after Vatican II," *USA Today*, 13 March 2015; online: https://eu.usatoday.com/story/news/world/2015/03/12/catholicism-latin-mass-resurgence/70214976/, accessed August 2018.

to believe[c] were together and they used to hold everything as common; [45] they used to sell their possessions and belongings and distribute the proceeds to all, as anyone had need.[46] Day by day, spending much time together in the temple and breaking bread in homes, they shared food with joy and singleness of heart,[47] praising God and having favour with the whole people. Every day the Lord was adding to their group those being saved.[5]

Throughout this section, the verbs are plural, denoting the shared life of the community. Indeed, the community are 'the fellowship' (κοινωνία, v. 42), which involved daily meetings and a commitment to sharing material resources. This sharing is not unnatural within middle Eastern culture, but Luke presents it in terms which echo the highest aspirations of both Jewish Scripture and Graeco-Roman writings (vv. 44–45 with 4:32–35).[6] The believers included diaspora Jews who remained in Jerusalem after Pentecost (2:9–11), Galilean disciples and apostles, and urban Jerusalemites, both wealthy and poor. This diversity highlights a contrast with Graeco-Roman approaches to sharing possessions, for those were limited to those of equal (normally high) social status – here the needs of believers in poverty are met through their wealthier sisters and brothers.

Specifically, the shared meals happened in public and private (as we would say). Verse 46 portrays their shared meals as taking place both in homes and in the temple. Notice the way that two participial clauses 'spending much time together' (προσκαρτεροῦντες ὁμοθυμαδὸν ἐν τῷ ἱερῷ) and 'breaking bread in homes' (κλῶντές ... κατ' οἶκον ἄρτον) are dependent on the same main verb 'they shared food' (μετελάμβανον τροφῆς). Thus some of their meals took place in public space, probably in Solomon's Portico, a part of the temple complex which was covered and where they met (Acts 5:12) – perhaps in imitation of Jesus's own practice of teaching in the temple.

Two more passages in the early part of Acts underline this common life. 4:32–35 reiterates and develops the earlier portrait, and in particular, v. 34 echoes Deut 15:4–5:

> there was no-one in need among them (Acts 4:34)
>
> There will, however, *be no one in need among you*, because the LORD is sure to bless you in the land that the LORD your God is giving you as a possession to occupy, if only you will obey the LORD your God by diligently observing this entire commandment that I command you today. (Deut 15:4–5, my italics)

Luke portrays the life of the early community as fulfilling hopes for the shared life of Israel. In this respect the believers resembled the Essene communities dotted around Palestine who met evening by evening and pooled the money they had gained from working that day in order to buy food, which they then ate together (Philo, *Hypoth.* 1.10–11). However, by contrast with the strictness of the residential Essene community

---

[5] My translation, as are other translations from the NT in this chapter.
[6] See Steve Walton, "Primitive Communism in Acts? Does Acts Present the Community of Goods (2:44-45; 4:32-35) as Mistaken?," *EvQ* 80 (2008): 99–111, here 103–5 [in this volume 63–73, here 67–9].

at Qumran, the pooling of goods among the believers was not compulsory – people gave as they were able.[7] Note, however, that 'community' was not a vague thing, but highly practical. 4:32–35 prepares for the following two passages, where Barnabas is pictured as positive example of sharing (4:36–37), and Ananias and Sapphira, who lie about what they are giving to the community, are a negative example (5:1–11). A further summary follows (5:12–16) which repeats the message of shared meetings in the temple area (v. 12b), and focuses on the 'signs and wonders' happening through the apostles.

Not only this, but even when a dispute happens, it is as *a result of their shared community life*. The argument about the care for widows in 6:1–6 could not have happened had the Hebrew and Hellenistic believers never met together, for they would not have known of the practices of each other's groups. Their disagreement suggests that the two language-groups met as one, at least some of the time (most likely in the larger meetings in the temple courts), and that when teaching was given, interpretation was provided for those who could not understand the language used.

To read these passages is naturally to be provoked to ask what happened later in the life of the believing community, since such immediate economic sharing did not continue. Luke himself goes on, however, to describe other forms of economic sharing among believers, including between communities of believers.[8] The Antiochene believers sent aid to the Jerusalem believers at time of famine (11:27–30). Dorcas is commended as one who contributed by making clothes for widows (9:36, 39). Paul provides for himself and his companions through his physical work (20:34; 18:3). Paul asserts that he does not desire others' goods (20:33), but rather seeks to support the weak (20:35), a practice which he presents to the Ephesian elders for their imitation. As an example, Paul pays the hairdressing expenses of a group of Jewish believers who take a vow (21:23–24, 26). This variety of forms of economic sharing as expressions of response to the gospel is in tune with Paul's own teaching in 2 Cor 8–9, where his call for generous giving is rooted in God's generous giving in Christ (8:9), and his invitation to the Corinthians is that their surplus should provide for others in need (8:13–14). In sum, it seems that the principle that believers should be ready to share economically with their sisters and brothers in need underlay a 'mixed economy' of expressions of that principle.

So what about Paul? We tend to think of him as the great individualist, the great 'lone ranger' among the apostles. But is that an accurate portrait? Notice two features which suggest otherwise.

First, Paul regularly has co-workers travelling with him who provide a 'support group', and are part of his mission team.[9] For example, when he leaves Antioch for the first time, Barnabas goes with him – indeed at this point, Barnabas seems to take the lead, for he is named first (13:2). We also learn that John Mark also goes with them and

---

[7] See my discussion in Walton, "Communism," 106–8 [in this volume 69–71].
[8] More fully, see my student Fiona Gregson's work: Fiona J. Robertson Gregson, *Everything in Common? The Theology and Practice of the Sharing of Possessions in Community in the New Testament* (Eugene, OR: Pickwick, 2017), ch. 3.
[9] See the helpful brief article, E. E. Ellis, "Coworkers, Paul and His," in *DPL* 183–9.

acts as their assistant (13:5), although at some point he abandons them and returns home (15:38). When Paul wants to set out to visit the churches he has planted on that first trip, his first instinct is to take a companion, Barnabas, but when they cannot agree over taking John Mark, Paul takes Silas (15:36–40). Paul later adds Timothy to the team in Lystra (16:1–4), and he is part of the group which plants the church in Thessalonica (1 Thess 1:1).[10] Throughout Paul's travels from here the group is plural, either described as 'they' (e.g. 16:6–8) or 'we' (e.g. 16:10–18).[11]

Not only is Paul a team-worker, but his travelling ministry and mission is based on his relationship with the community in Antioch. It is they who, directed by the Holy Spirit, send him and Barnabas out (13:1–3), after this duo have served in what appears to be the leadership team of that community (13:1). It is to Antioch that Barnabas and Saul return after their travels and report back on what God has been doing through them (14:26–27), and they stay for some time with the community there (14:28) before being appointed by the Antioch community to go to Jerusalem in response to debate with the circumcision group (15:1–2). After the Jerusalem meeting, they return to Antioch (15:30), where they stay for 'some days' (τινας ἡμέρας, 15:36).

II. Examples of Communal Decision-Making

Not only did the early believers live and act communally, they also made their decision that way. Let us consider some examples.

II.a The Choice of Matthias 1:15–26

Here we meet the community at a time of transition. They are waiting, following the command of Jesus, for the coming of the Spirit, and as they wait they pray together in unity – notice again the stress on their shared life[12] (v. 14). The loss of Judas, who betrayed Jesus and subsequently died, requires attention, and Peter leads the community in reflecting and acting. Peter reads Pss 68:26 LXX (MT 69:25) and 108:8 LXX (MT 109:8) as speaking of Judas's betrayal; both come from psalms of lament in a situation where a godly person suffers at the hand of ungodly people, and Ps 108 LXX was understood by early Christians to speak of Jesus's unjust suffering.[13] Here, Peter interprets them as applicable to Judas who is an ungodly man *par excellence* who betrayed Jesus into the hands of other ungodly people. The story of Judas's gruesome death (vv. 18–19) is laid alongside these verses (v. 20) to draw the conclusion that Judas

---

[10] Interestingly, Timothy is not named in Acts as part of that team (17:1, 4, 5, 10).
[11] For a discussion of the possible meanings of the plurals, see Stanley E. Porter, "The 'We' Passages," in *The Book of Acts in Its Graeco-Roman Setting*, ed. David W. J. Gill and Conrad H. Gempf, BAFCS 2 (Carlisle: Paternoster, 1994), 545–74.
[12] See discussion of the key term ὁμοθυμαδόν in Steve Walton, "Ὁμοθυμαδόν in Acts: Co-location, Common Action or 'Of One Heart and Mind'?," in *The New Testament in its First Century Setting: Essays on Context and Background in Honour of B. W. Winter on His 65th Birthday*, ed. P. J. Williams, Andrew D. Clarke, Peter M. Head and David Instone-Brewer (Grand Rapids, MI; Cambridge: Eerdmans, 2004), 89–105, here 101.
[13] E.g. Matt 27:34, 48; Mark 15:23, 36; Luke 23:36; John 2:17; 15:25; 19:29; Rom 15:3.

ust be replaced by another (vv. 21–22). The replacement will restore the number of twelve, a key development of the early community, because Luke stresses that Israel is being restored and renewed[14] – hence the need for twelve, to symbolize the twelve tribes.

Having laid the situation out and interpreted it by reading Scripture, Peter offers a person specification for the one they need (vv. 21–22), the decision is placed in two sets of hands. First, the community – the 120 people (v. 15) – identify two men who could do the job: Barsabbas Justus and Matthias. Human assessment and work goes into the appointment. Secondly, the final decision is placed into God's hands as they pray for wisdom (vv. 24–25) and cast lots (v. 26). Some think that the casting of lots was mistaken, and point to the lack of casting lots after Pentecost, when the Spirit has come upon the whole believing community – and even speculate that they should have waited, for Paul was the one who should have been the twelfth apostle.[15] That seems unlikely, however, given the stress on the restoration of Israel in the early chapters of Acts. Casting lots removes all human interference in the choice and places the decision in God's hands (Prov 16:33) – it was not understood as random in the way in which westerners see it today, whether in Jewish or Graeco-Roman society. Paul himself, of course, lacked the qualification of having been with Jesus from the beginning through to the resurrection, so he would not have been eligible in any case.[16]

This decision, in other words, is a combination of human and divine, and the human part is a corporate part – it is not the apostles, or Peter alone, who select the candidates, but 'they', that is the community.

II.b. Rejecting the Sanhedrin's Requirement of Silence 4:23–31

As a second example, consider the community's response to the Sanhedrin's instruction to Peter and John that they should not speak further in the name of Jesus (4:18). Peter and John report back on what has happened (v. 23).[17] The group then engage with the situation in unity (ὁμοθυμαδόν again, v. 24) and pray together – Luke portrays a united prayer in one voice, as 'those who heard' address God. Their prayer builds on the promise of Jesus, that 'you will be my witnesses' (1:8), and offers a reading of Ps 2:1–2 as a lens through which they interpret their present and recent experience (vv. 25–28). Shockingly, they identify the opponents of God in the psalm with the present Jewish leadership as well as the Romans, whereas in the psalm it is the pagan nations who oppose God's people (v. 27).

It is the *community* who call on God to 'pay attention to their threats', using language which is used elsewhere for God's care for creation and for his people.[18] It

---

[14] Cf. 1:6–8; 3:21. See the fine discussion in Richard Bauckham, "The Restoration of Israel in Luke-Acts," in *Restoration: Old Testament, Jewish and Christian Perspectives*, ed. James M. Scott, JSJSup 72 (Leiden: Brill, 2001), 435–87.
[15] E.g. Rudolf Stier, *The Words of the Apostles*, 2nd ed. (Edinburgh: T&T Clark, 1869), 12–15.
[16] Note 1 Cor 15:3–5, where he says that he received resurrection stories from others.
[17] It is not completely clear whether τοὺς ἰδίους (v. 23) indicates the apostolic band or the wider believing community; either way, the situation is presented to a group for response.
[18] Job 22:12; Pss 34:17 (MT 35:17); 112:6 (MT 113:6); 137:6 (MT 138:6); 2 Macc 8:2.

has the force of the American idiom, 'take care of', which means 'deal with' – such as, 'Let me take care of that bill.' They have come to a mind through reading Scripture together concerning what God's purpose is, and now they ask God to enable them to keep speaking[19] the message of Jesus boldly. As with the choice of Matthias, placing the situation into God's hands results in a divine response – the place is shaken (v. 31), after the manner of rushing wind at Pentecost (2:2), and the Spirit re-fills them so that they do speak boldly.

II.c. Choosing the Seven 6:1-7

As we noted earlier, the dispute over the care of widows in 6:1–7 is evidence of the nature of the shared life of the believers in Jerusalem, for the two language-groups among the believers (Hellenists and Hebrews) must have been sufficiently involved with one another for them to know what was happening. It is striking that the twelve's response is not to decide what to do by themselves, but they call a community meeting to resolve the situation (v. 2). Potentially, this is a massive group, since the believing community may now be over 5000 (4:4), so the meeting would have needed to take place somewhere public, such as the temple courts – there is no handling of their dirty washing in private for the early believers!

As with replacing Judas, the apostles offer leadership by proposing a solution, that the community chooses seven to oversee this matter. Notably, they use the same vocabulary for the role of the seven, 'to *serve* tables' (διακονεῖν τραπέζαις, v. 2), as they do for their own apostolic role 'the *service* of the word' (τῇ διακονίᾳ τοῦ λόγου, v. 4), so this is not setting up a hierarchy of importance which would suggest that the apostles' work is more important than that of the seven – they are all 'serving'.

The community responds in two ways: by affirming the proposed solution, and by nominating seven candidates for the role of overseeing the provision for the widows (v. 5). At least one, Stephen, is from the Greek-speaking group whose widows are being neglected, for he engages with a Greek-speaking synagogue later on (6:8–10); others have Greek names and thus may be 'Hellenists' too. The seven are then commissioned and prayed for in their role, and it is notable here that it is not simply the apostles who prayed and laid hands on them, in spite of what most English versions say. Rather, the Greek is most naturally read as portraying the whole group laying hands on and praying for the seven.[20] Thus the decision is made and executed by the community, a process which reflects the universal gift of the Spirit to the community (2:17, 38; cf. Num 11:29).

Again, we see God's hand in this event, for the summary in v. 7 makes clear that the community continues to grow as the word spreads, even among priests. God works with and through the decision-making of the community – well-fed widows would demonstrate the reality of the impact of the gospel and the gift of the Spirit among Jews, who would be horrified if needy people like widows were neglected.[21]

---

[19] This is the probable force of the present infinitive λαλεῖν (v. 29).
[20] See my forthcoming commentary in the Word Biblical Commentary, on this passage.
[21] See the fine discussion in Nigel Biggar, "Showing the Gospel in Social Praxis," *Anvil* 8 (1991): 7–18.

II.d. Welcoming Saul of Tarsus in Jerusalem 9:26–30

When Saul of Tarsus meets the exalted Jesus on the road to Damascus, he is welcomed by the believing community as he immediately begins proclaiming this Jesus (9:19b–21). Presumably Ananias spoke of the reality of Saul's transformation from persecutor to believer, as Ananias himself had heard the Lord speak about this, and had been the one who baptized Saul and prayed for his healing from temporary blindness (9:10–18).

Things become trickier when Saul goes to Jerusalem for the first time since his encounter with Jesus, for the community there are, understandably, cautious of him (v. 26). Here Barnabas plays a key role, for he shares testimony with the apostles about the reality of Saul's faith and meeting with the Lord, and his preaching of Jesus in Damascus (v. 27). This is a fascinating case of testimony changing how a community thinks, and it is noteworthy that Barnabas's testimony is expressed from Saul's point of view (v. 27). The result is that the community accepts Saul as a genuine believer and supports him (vv. 28–29a), and then arranges for him to leave for safety in Tarsus when there is a threat to his life (vv. 29b–30). The community's decision-making here is focused in the acceptance of Saul by the apostolic group on the basis of Barnabas's testimony. Further, yet again, God's action goes with community decision, for Saul not only speaks boldly in Jesus's name – a mark of the Spirit's work in him (v. 28; cf. 4:30–31) – but speaks with other Greek-speaking Jews about the Lord (v. 29a).

II.e. The Spirit Calling Barnabas and Saul from Antioch 13:1–3

We meet Saul with Barnabas again in (Syrian) Antioch, working among the believing community there. Barnabas brings Saul there to work with him among the first Jew-gentile community (11:25–26), and they seem to have been there for some years by the time of the events in Acts 13. By then, they are part of a multi-cultural, multi-aged, and multi-ethnic five-person leadership team (v. 1) in the community there. As the group[22] are worshipping the Lord and fasting, the Spirit speaks to them (v. 2), probably through one of those identified as a prophet (v. 1), for 'the Holy Spirit said' is echoed in Agabus's words later (21:11).

The community then take their time in responding to this prophetic announcement. The wording 'Then, after they fasted and prayed' (v. 3) suggests that a further time of fasting and praying took place before the decision that this was indeed the voice of the Spirit, and thus that they should send Barnabas and Saul out. It is not hard to see why such discernment was necessary, for the community was potentially losing two of its five key leaders, and they would want to be as sure as possible that this was God's purpose. Not only that, but we know from Paul's writings that the proper response to a prophet speaking was for the community to discern what was the voice of God from what the prophet said (e.g. 1 Cor 14:29; 1 Thess 5:20–21).[23] Prophecy here does not

---

[22] It is not completely clear whether αὐτῶν (v. 1) refers to the five names in v. 1 or the wider Antioch community; either way, the experience which follows is a group experience and decision.

[23] See the very helpful discussion, highlighting the role of human discernment in understanding what God says, in John B. F. Miller, *Convinced That God Had Called Us: Dreams, Visions, and the Perception of God's Will in Luke-Acts*, BibInt 85 (Leiden: Brill, 2007). On the role of discernment in

give infallible access to God's mind – it requires human engagement, and corporate engagement at that, to discern what God is saying.

II.f. Going to Macedonia 16:6–10

One of the most puzzling and interesting incidents in Acts is the decision to go to Macedonia from Asia in Acts 16. For the only time in the Greek Old or New Testaments, the Spirit 'hinders' (κωλύω, v. 6), and thus acts negatively to prevent Paul and his companions going to certain places. Luke is not specific about the means by which the Spirit hinders them from preaching in Asia (v. 6) or entering Bithynia (v. 7), but he is explicit that the Spirit engages directly with them in this process. Perhaps this is a further example of prophecy at work.

A rare example of specific divine guidance follows in the vision which Paul has at night of the Macedonian man[24] calling for help (v. 9). The man is beseeching or exhorting them (παρακαλῶν), rather than giving a clear command (contrast 10:5–6, where Cornelius is instructed by the angel to send for Peter), although this verb is in some tension with the imperative 'help!' (βοήθησον). The one who appears to Paul is human, rather than a divine character or agent, by contrast with most visions in Luke-Acts, where God or the Lord is the speaker or the Spirit or an angel.[25] Nevertheless, this vision is critical to events and facilitates a significant plot transition.[26]

It is Paul and his companions who respond to the vision – another example of corporate discernment and decision-making. Luke makes this clear by shifting from third person singular 'he saw' (εἶδεν, v. 10) to first person plural 'we began seeking' (ἐζητήσαμεν, v. 10). Luke's explanation of the ground for the decision is given in the following causal participial clause 'since we were convinced that God had called us to evangelize them' (συμβιβάζοντες ὅτι προσκέκληται ἡμᾶς ὁ θεὸς εὐαγγελίσασθαι αὐτούς). The participle is plural, indicating that the decision that this was God's call was made by the group, not by Paul alone. Interestingly, there is no specific mention of God speaking to them, by contrast with 'the Holy Spirit said' (13:2) and 'the Lord spoke to Paul in a vision' (18:9–10). The group have to interpret Paul's experience of the dream in order to discern the next step they must take.

It is worth noticing what happens next, for after such a remarkable experience, which stands out because it is unusual, the mission in Macedonia is somewhat 'underwhelming'.[27] Certainly there are positive results, for Lydia becomes a believer (16:13–15), but there are the problems with the girl with the Pythian spirit (16:16–18) which result in Paul and Silas finding themselves in prison (16:19–24). There is no specified divine action to free them, neither miracle nor escape, by contrast with Peter (12:3–11), and there is no mention of God or an angel causing the earthquake. Indeed,

---

relation to prophecy specifically, see Wayne A. Grudem, *The Gift of Prophecy in the New Testament and Today* (Eastbourne: Kingsway, 1988), 74–9.

[24] Some wonder how Paul knew that the man was Macedonian: the phrase 'come to Macedonia' (διαβὰς εἰς Μακεδονίαν, v. 9) seems a clear indication of this.

[25] E.g. Acts 10:3; Luke 1:11.

[26] Miller, *Convinced*, 98.

[27] Miller, *Convinced*, 107.

they do not take the opportunity the earthquake provides to escape from jail, but stay put (16:25–28). The jailer and his family come to faith in Jesus (16:29–34), but Paul and Silas have to leave Philippi (16:40).

None of these events necessarily means that Paul and his companions got their interpretation of Paul's vision wrong. Indeed, if they were right, that suggests that getting God's will right does not automatically mean that things will be successful; this story rather suggests the reverse, that if the guidance seems remarkable and (relatively) clear, that may mean that things are going to be difficult.

II.g. Key Factors Involved

Looking over these examples, we can see four factors involved in the decision-making processes, all of which are conducted corporately. All four are not involved in every story, but they occur sufficiently consistently to see a pattern.

First, the believers trust God and are dependent on God. This finds expression in various ways: casting lots; prayer for God to act; interpreting Scripture, heard as God's voice; divine speech by the Spirit and by God; and dreams and visions which convey God's purposes.

However, secondly, each of these 'divine' activities requires interpretation – they are not self-explanatory, but need the believing community to reflect and study in order to discern God's purposes. That discernment happens as they engage together in considering how to respond. For sure, it involves turning to God, as the Antiochene church does in further fasting and prayer (13:3), but there is real human involvement in this process in collaboration with God.

Thirdly, testimony to what God is doing is important, whether telling the story of recent events to show why a decision needs taking (as Peter does before the choice of Matthias), or speaking on behalf of one who is regarded with suspicion (as Barnabas does for Saul in Jerusalem), or (as we shall see) telling the story of God's action in the beginnings of the mission to gentiles.

Fourthly, human leadership has a role in offering a path forward to the community, but is never carried out in a dictatorial or authoritarian manner. Even before the coming of the Spirit on the whole community at Pentecost, it is the group who nominate the two potential apostles from whom Matthias is chosen by lot (1:23) in response to a proposal by Peter (1:21–22). After Pentecost, there is a clear role for the apostles in shaping a response to circumstances, but it is never done in isolation from the community. Thus, in choosing the seven, the community gathers at the apostles' invitation (6:2), and responds to the apostles' proposal (6:3) by choosing the seven (6:5) and commissioning them (6:6). Similarly, Paul (as team leader) tells his companions about the vision he has received, and the group then draws conclusions about God's purposes (16:10).

As we turn now to our major case study, the path to the inclusion of gentiles in the believing community, we shall see these features repeated with some fresh features and factors as they together discern what God is doing.

III. The Inclusion of Gentiles

The story of Acts moves gradually from insiders to Judaism becoming believers towards rank outsiders being included in the community. After Pentecost, the healing of the man with a congenital disability at the temple marks the inclusion of one whose disability would have excluded him from temple worship (3:1–10) – and that is why his first action on being healed is to run and jump praising God and to enter the temple (3:8–9). Philip, as part of the group driven out of Jerusalem because of the persecution after Stephen's death (8:1, 4), goes to the half-breed Samaritans whom the Jews consider to be heretics and outsiders, and Samaritans are included in the gospel community with the approval of the Spirit, who comes on the believing Samaritans at the prayer of Peter and John (8:5–25). A further step occurs when Philip meets the Ethiopian eunuch (8:26–40), a meeting arranged carefully through an angel directing Philip (8:26). The eunuch has a deeply ambiguous status and had desired to worship in Jerusalem (8:27), but almost certainly had not been able to do so because he was castrated.[28] Nevertheless, he is seeking God, as his reading of Isaiah and his questions demonstrate (8:30–34), and through Philip he is baptized (8:36, 38). If the eunuch was a gentile, as seems most likely, Luke makes no major point about this – it is a later story which Luke presents as the turning-point in God's present actions.

This turning-point happens through a further 'divine appointment', this time arranged at the behest of an angel on one side, and a vision accompanied by a voice on the other. This is the story of Peter's encounter with Cornelius and his household, an encounter which is told three times in Acts, which highlights its significance (10:1–48; 11:1–18; 15:7–11).[29]

III.a. Peter Going to Cornelius 10:1–48

The first telling of the story, in 10:1–48, is from an external narrator's perspective. The story focuses separately on Cornelius (vv. 1–8) and Peter (vv. 9–23) until they are together in Cornelius's house (vv. 24–48). As the story develops, we the same combination that we have seen elsewhere, of divine action and human interpretation, and the human interpretation is a corporate process.

The divine initiative is clear, for an angel appears to the godly centurion Cornelius and instructs him to send for Peter (vv. 3–6). The angel instructs Cornelius what to do, but this would nevertheless require Cornelius to reflect and decide that he was not crazy, but had heard a genuine divine instruction. As a centurion in the occupying Roman army, however sympathetic he was to Jewish beliefs, he would not wish to appear foolish and gullible. He sends a *group* to Peter – two servants and a soldier whom he knows to be 'devout' (εὐσεβής, v. 8) – and briefs the group about what has happened, thus trusting them to discern and respond appropriately to what they encounter in Joppa.

---

[28] Deut 23:1; Joachim Jeremias, *Jerusalem in the Time of Jesus* (London: SCM, 1969), 343–4.
[29] See Ronald D. Witherup, SS, "Cornelius Over and Over and Over Again: 'Functional Redundancy' in the Acts of the Apostles," *JSNT* 49 (1993): 45–66.

Peter's experience is similarly dramatic, for he has a baffling three-times-repeated vision of animals on a sheet which he is told to 'Kill and eat' (v. 13). Good Jew that he is, he knows that he must discriminate among animals and can only eat those permitted by the torah (v. 14). At this point, Peter is simply puzzled (v. 17a), but his puzzlement will be resolved at a later point. He is told more directly by the Spirit to go with the visitors who are just arriving (vv. 19–20), and responds – and without that divine speech he surely would not have shown hospitality to pagans (v. 23).

When Peter travels to Caesarea to visit Cornelius, he takes a group with him from the community in Joppa (v. 23b). Finally, when he meets Cornelius, the penny drops and he understands the vision of the animals on the sheet – it is not about animals but about people. He is not to 'call anyone impure or unclean' (v. 28) and he (perhaps a little disingenuously) tells Cornelius that he came 'without objection'. The scene broadens out as Peter and the Joppa believers meet Cornelius' household, potentially quite a large group, and Cornelius tells his side of the story. Now we hear the encounter with the angel filtered through Cornelius (vv. 30–33), and this edited version adds Cornelius' conclusion that he and his household want to hear what 'you have been instructed to say by the Lord' (v. 33). Cornelius thus draws a conclusion from his vision, and invites Peter to share that conclusion.

Peter recognizes and agrees with Cornelius's interpretation of Cornelius's vision, and draws his own, quite remarkable, further conclusion, that God will accept people who fear him from every nation (vv. 34–35). In terms of the story of Acts, we see here a discernment process going on between these two men which leads to Peter telling the gospel message in terms familiar from the earlier evangelistic speeches in Acts (vv. 35–43). At this point, Peter is interrupted by the outpouring of the Holy Spirit on the household (v. 44), evidenced by the gentiles speaking in tongues and praying God (v. 46). The group who came with Peter are astonished, but they draw the conclusion from these phenomena that this is the Spirit (vv. 45–46; note γάρ 'for' introducing the ground for their interpretation). In agreement with the group's assessment, Peter draws the further conclusion that these people should be baptized, since they are clearly marked by the Spirit as members of the community (v. 47).

As in other stories, the discernment process here is a corporate one, even including someone who, at the outset of the story, is not yet a believer. The story itself is as much about the conversion of Peter – the transformation of his mindset – as the conversion of Cornelius and his household, for Peter grows in understanding as he engages in discernment with others: the group Cornelius sends, the believers who travel from Joppa with him, and with Cornelius himself as he gives testimony to Peter.

III.b. Debate and Discernment in Jerusalem 11:1–18

On his return to Jerusalem, Peter faces challenges from Jewish believers over his acceptance of hospitality from uncircumcised men (v. 3). The challenge is over shared meals, for a key distinctive behaviour of Jewish people was to keep the food laws of the torah. This meant that they were very cautious over what they ate: there is evidence of kosher meat stalls in the Corinthian meat market.[30] Such specialist stalls and shops would ensure both that the meat had been killed and hung according to Jewish practice and that it could not have been polluted by being offered in idol temples. Hence Jewish people did not eat with gentiles, since the meat they would be offered in a gentile home would almost certainly be both non-kosher and tainted with idolatry.

Now we hear the story again, but this time filtered through Peter. This time we hear little of what happened with Cornelius, even though Peter knows Cornelius's story – for to persuade his audience in Jerusalem, Peter must convince them that it is the God of Israel who sent him to Cornelius and who has now accepted Cornelius. So Peter's speech focuses on the vision, and the way his thinking has been transformed by God's action. His reference to Cornelius is not by name – he is simply 'the man' (v. 12) – and he says very little of the angel's appearance to Cornelius, but only reports (some of) what the angel said, with an added clause, indicating that Cornelius knew that he and his household 'will be saved' through Peter's message (v. 14). Peter makes it clear that a devout group ('these six brothers', v. 12) accompanied him, thus invoking their testimony to what took place – this was the group, recall, who concluded that God had acted in accepting the gentiles (10:45-46). Peter then tells the story of the Spirit's coming and interprets it through the promise of Jesus (v. 16; cf. 1:5), and blames God for what has happened: 'Who was I that I could hinder God?' (v. 17). This testimony tips the balance for the critics, and they (perhaps a little reluctantly) concede that 'even' (καί) the gentiles have been given repentance and life by God (v. 18).

The corporate process is very significant here in persuading the sceptics in Jerusalem that the acceptance of these gentiles is truly God's work. In response to their questions, themselves part of the corporate discernment process, it requires a number of contributions to swing the decision: Peter's testimony, the (implicit) testimony of the six brothers, and the *interpretation* of events as being the action of God because they resemble their own experience at Pentecost. The latter implies that at least some of the doubting group were members of the original 120. Peter does not simply dictate what happens, however eminent he is considered to be, and however much God has clearly worked in and through him in the past growth and development of the community: it requires a corporate engagement with what is going on to be confident in discerning that God is doing.

III.c. Sending Barnabas to Antioch from Jerusalem 11:19-26

Luke now picks up from the scattering of the believers through persecution from 8:1, 4 to explain what happens. Thus, it is likely that these events are happening around the same time as Peter's visit to Cornelius: the gradual inclusion of gentiles in the believing community is not entirely dependent on one event.

The thing to notice here is that the scattered believers arrive in Syrian Antioch and start to talk 'also to Greeks' (v. 20) – not Greek-speaking Jews, as in Jerusalem (6:1), but

---

[30] Bruce W. Winter, *After Paul Left Corinth: The Influence of Secular Ethics and Social Change* (Cambridge; Grand Rapids, MI: Eerdmans, 2001), 293–5.

outright gentiles.³¹ The result is that a substantial number of gentiles become believers (v. 21), and this raises a similar issue to the conversion of Cornelius: is this a genuine work of God?

The Jerusalem community's response to this news is to reflect, and to send Barnabas as a delegate to see what is going on (v. 22). Barnabas goes, not on his own initiative, but to advise the community in Jerusalem, which is still led by the apostles (note 8:1) – we might think of Jerusalem as functioning at this point as a 'mother church'. The outcome is that Barnabas recognizes that God is at work in his grace, and then takes the initiative to fetch Saul from Tarsus – he knows Saul from his earlier visit to Jerusalem (9:26–30) – and he and Saul teach the church in Antioch (vv. 25–26).

The decision-making about this new step of speaking to Greeks about Jesus is again a corporate process. The community in Jerusalem take responsibility for assessing what is happening, and send Barnabas as their representative to investigate. They clearly trust Barnabas's judgement of the new situation – and that trust is vindicated as the community in Antioch grows to the point where they can send financial help to the Jerusalem believers during a famine (11:27–30).

III.d. The Jerusalem Meeting 15:1–35

The drawing in of gentiles continues through Barnabas and Saul's mission, initiated, as we saw, by the Spirit speaking to the community gathering in Antioch (13:1–3). Barnabas and Saul develop a pattern which will be the pattern of Paul's own ministry in later days: their first port of call in a new place is the Jewish synagogues (13:5), but they are also ready and willing to speak about Jesus with gentiles when opportunities arise, as they do on Cyprus when the proconsul Sergius Paulus summons Paul to speak with him (13:7–12). More than that, when the synagogue community is divided – as frequently happens – they deliberately go to gentiles and speak of Jesus. This is their experience in Pisidian Antioch (13:14–52). The proclamation of Jesus divides the synagogue, particularly because word spreads in the city and many gentiles come to hear Paul speak (13:44–45), and this provokes a zealous anti-gentile reaction among some of the Jews. At this point Paul and Barnabas make what can be misunderstood to be an absolute change of direction, towards gentiles and away from Jews (13:46), and they interpret present events through the lens of Scripture in making this decision, quoting Isa 49:6 (13:47). However, it is not an absolute change of direction, for when Paul and Barnabas arrive in Iconium, the next city they visit, the first place they go is the synagogue (14:1), with similar results to Antioch – the Jewish community is divided; some join Paul and Barnabas, and others revile them and plot to stone them to death (14:2–5). This pattern continues as Paul and Barnabas travel through Phrygia and southern Galatia, and they eventually return to Syrian Antioch, their 'sending church', and report 'all that God had done, and that he had opened a door of faith to the gentiles' (14:27).

---

³¹ The word used is Ἑλληνιστής in both 6:1 (where it is clearly speaking about Greek-speaking Jews) and 11:20 (where the contrast with μόνον Ἰουδαίοις 'only to Jews' in v. 19 makes it clear that non-Jewish Greek-speakers are intended).

However, not all the believers are happy about this development, and the issue which appeared in 11:1 after Peter's visit to Cornelius returns – on what basis can gentiles be members of the believing communities? I think it is likely that Paul writes Galatians around this time,[32] as he hears of the issue and responds in this most polemical letter to clarify his view, that gentiles do not need to be circumcised and keep the law in order to be believers – exactly the same issue which is raised in Acts 15:1. Paul and Barnabas engage in debate with the Judaean Jewish believers who want gentile believers to be circumcised and keep the law, and the result is that the Antiochene community send them as delegates to discuss with the Jerusalem apostles and elders what to do (15:2b–4). Here we see the most critical decision the early believers face. It is not about whether gentiles can be accepted by God – all Jews believed that was possible already, providing they took the yoke of the law and were circumcised (if men) or went through a ritual bath (if women). The debate was about whether gentile believers had to take the yoke of the law to be followers of Jesus, or whether God accepted them without that commitment, and thus whether Jewish and gentile believers could be recognized as part of one community of God's people purely on the basis of faith in Jesus.

The meeting in Jerusalem was an extended affair: there had been 'much debate' (15:7) before Peter stood to speak. Peter's speech is strongly focused on God and what God is doing, echoing and alluding to his experience with Cornelius: almost all the main verbs have God as subject, and the critical question is, 'Why are you trying to test God?' (v. 10). This chimes in with the testimony which Paul and Barnabas had given on their arrival in the city of 'all that God had done with them' (v. 4), a testimony which is now repeated in the larger gathering (v. 12).

James – probably the brother of Jesus – exercises a role of leadership by proposing a solution to the gathering. He interprets contemporary events through Scripture, drawing particularly on Amos 9:11–12 (and snippets of other OT passages[33]). He sees the restoration of Israel through the founding and growth of the believing community as so far in train that Amos's expectation that the 'tent of David' would be rebuilt has been fulfilled. This means, according to Amos, that the time has come in which gentiles may 'seek the Lord' (v. 17) – a common eschatological expectation among second temple Jews.[34] The surprising thing was that this means the age to come *has already arrived* in and through the life, death, resurrection and exaltation of Jesus and the giving of the Spirit. James interprets events with this passage of Scripture to mean that

---

[32] The issue is debated; the clinching argument is that, had the Jerusalem meeting happened before Paul wrote Galatians, why would Paul not cite the ruling from the apostles and elders in Jerusalem? For discussion of the issues involved, see Richard N. Longenecker, *Galatians*, WBC 41 (Dallas, TX: Word, 1990), lxxii–lxxxiii.

[33] See valuable discussion in Richard Bauckham, "James and the Jerusalem Church," in *The Book of Acts in its Palestinian Setting*, ed. Richard Bauckham, BAFCS 4 (Carlisle: Paternoster, 1995), 415–80 esp. 453–8; Richard Bauckham, "James and the Gentiles (Acts 15.13-21)," in *History, Literature, and Society in the Book of Acts*, ed. Ben Witherington, III (Cambridge: Cambridge University Press, 1996), 154–84, here esp. 155–70.

[34] For the range of views, see the helpful discussion in Michael E. Fuller, *The Restoration of Israel: Israel's Re-gathering and the Fate of the Nations in Early Jewish Literature and Luke-Acts*, BZNW 138 (Berlin: de Gruyter, 2006), 102–96.

it is not necessary for such gentiles to undergo circumcision and keep the law (v. 19). He is emphatic about this being his own view of the situation: '*I myself* (ἐγώ) judge ...'

James's proposal, and its relationship to the text of the letter, is much debated in scholarship, and we do not have space to discuss the various understandings of it here[35] – the key thing to notice for our purpose is that James does not make a ruling; he makes a proposal as to what 'we' should do (vv. 19, 20). The apostles' and elders' response is to endorse and embrace this proposal: 'it has seemed good to the Holy Spirit and to us' (v. 28) they write to the gentile communities who sought their advice through Paul and Barnabas. Not only that, but the 'whole assembly' (ὅλῃ τῇ ἐκκλησίᾳ, v. 22) agrees to send delegates to share the decision with, and they stress in the letter which they send with these delegates their unity in deciding to act in this way (ὁμοθυμαδόν, v. 25). Notice that this must mean that those who initially argued that gentile believers must keep the law and be circumcised must have agreed with this decision, a remarkable change of view. Luke describes no steamrollering of those who disagreed – the process was sufficiently careful that a wide range of contributions were heard (we have only three reported in Luke's account); notice again that they debated for a long time (v. 7).

This was a critical moment in the life of the earliest believers, for it decided whether the believing communities were to continue to be an exclusive or inclusive community, whether they were (in effect) to be a new party within Judaism alongside others, such as the Sadducees, Pharisees and Essenes, or to embrace the purpose of God that through Abraham's descendants all the children of the earth would be blessed (Gen 12:1–3).

III.e. Lessons from This Process

In conclusion, let us sketch some features of this decision-making process which are striking and which have implications for how churches today take their decisions.

First, and perhaps most important of all, there is a focus on God which is combined with a real openness to God. Instead of deciding in advance what God wants, they enter into conversation knowing what they presently think, but willing to engage fully with those with whom they disagree. They look for God's activity and actions in the stories they hear, and seek to discern God's purposes.

Secondly, they read contemporary events through the lens of Scripture, and interpret Scripture in the light of the remarkable events of the coming of Jesus, his death, resurrection and exaltation, and the coming of the Spirit. We saw the believers doing this in reading Ps 2:1–2 when they pray in response to the Sanhedrin's instruction to stop speaking in Jesus's name (4:24–30). We saw James drawing on Amos 9:11–12 in assessing the terms on which gentiles were to be included in the community (15:13–18). This does not seem an arbitrary approach to Scripture which finds individual phrases or clauses which support a point irrespective of their context, but an in-depth engagement with Scripture's overall flow and a careful reading of texts in context. As C. H. Dodd taught us, so often when the NT authors cite a snippet or a verse of

---

[35] Helpful discussion in Bauckham, "Jerusalem Church," 460–7.

Scripture, we need to look at the whole context in the OT to hear the full message which is being invoked in the NT.[36]

Thirdly, they are ready to listen to testimony and to weigh that testimony in the light of Scripture and the purposes of God revealed there. The Jerusalem Jewish believers listen with care to Peter and draw the conclusion that God really has – to their surprise – accepted the gentile Cornelius and his household (11:18). The apostles and elders listen to Paul and Barnabas speaking about their experience of gentiles coming to faith (15:12), and also to Peter, who combines testimony with a focus on God (15:7-11) – 'all that God had done' is a theme phrase for this whole process (14:27; 15:4, 12; cf. Luke 8:39).

Fourthly and finally, the process is corporate, open and unhurried. The sequence of passages we have studied probably covers a period of some years, and the Jerusalem meeting itself was lengthy – long enough for different voices to be heard, and long enough for real reflection and change of mind to take place. The process was not held in secret: for sure, there was a clear role for leaders in the meeting, and for James in particular in proposing a solution to the presenting issue; but the decision was not settled in smoke-filled rooms with only a select group present and others excluded – as well as being corporate, there was (as we would now say) real transparency about the decision-making process.

---

[36] C. H. Dodd, *According to the Scriptures: The Sub-structure of New Testament Theology* (London: Nisbet, 1952), with useful summary on 126–7.

8

Trying Paul or Trying Rome? Judges and Accused in the Roman Trials of Paul in Acts

It has frequently been remarked that the trial(s) of Jesus in the Fourth Gospel 'turn the tables' on Jesus's judges: rather than Jesus himself being on trial, it turns out to be others who are on trial. Thus, Pilate, the Jewish leadership, and even the world, stand under the judgement of God in the trial of Jesus.[1] Andrew Lincoln observes:

> In his witness to the truth, Jesus becomes the judge, and both 'the Jews' and Pilate are judged by their response to Jesus. Thus the Roman trial becomes the vehicle for the irony that the apparent judge and the apparent accusers are in reality being judged by the apparent accused. Indeed, one could just as easily entitle the episode 'The Trial of Pilate and the Jews before Jesus' as 'The Trial of Jesus before Pilate'.[2]

This chapter seeks to ask whether a similar turning of the tables is taking place in the three Roman trials of Paul in Acts; that is, we shall consider Luke's narrative to see how the Roman empire and its official representatives appear in their handling of Paul. In light of the widely-recognized parallelism of Jesus and Paul in Luke and Acts,[3] our approach will be to look first at the Roman trial of Jesus in Luke's Gospel, to see whether features there might suggest a similar trial of the empire and its spokesmen. We shall then turn to consider the trials of Paul before the proconsul Gallio in Corinth, and before the governors Festus and Felix in Caesarea, before closing with some brief reflections on how the presentation of the empire in these three trials sits with Luke's wider engagement with imperial ideology and issues.

---

[1] See Andrew T. Lincoln, *Truth on Trial: The Lawsuit Motif in the Fourth Gospel* (Peabody, MA: Hendrickson, 2000), 123–38 with further references. More broadly, A. E. Harvey, *Jesus on Trial: A Study in the Fourth Gospel* (London: SPCK, 1976) and Allison A. Trites, *The New Testament Concept of Witness*, SNTSMS 31 (Cambridge: Cambridge University Press, 1977), 78–124 see the whole of the Fourth Gospel as presenting a 'cosmic trial' scene, an insight developed in Lincoln's work.

[2] Lincoln, *Truth*, 137.

[3] See Steve Walton, *Leadership and Lifestyle: The Portrait of Paul in the Miletus Speech and 1 Thessalonians*, SNTSMS 108 (Cambridge: Cambridge University Press, 2000), 34–7 and literature cited there.

Our approach will be to focus on the narrative presentation of the empire and its representatives, in tune with the fine work of this volume's honouree.[4] To take such an approach is not in conflict with careful consideration of the historical context: rather, it necessitates placing the text in its proper historical context, so that (as far as possible) we are seeing features which a first-century reader might see.[5]

I. The Trial of Jesus in Luke (Luke 23)

A number of features of the Roman trial of Jesus are pertinent to our theme.

First, Luke's portrait of Jesus throughout his arrest and trial is of one who is in sublime control of events and of himself,[6] stemming from his commitment to do the Father's will in Gethsemane (22:42). Indeed, Jesus heals one man who comes to arrest him after his disciple has cut off the man's ear (22:50–51). The same sense of control is evident in the trial before Pilate. Jesus answers Pilate almost monosyllabically (23:3), and does not answer Herod, from whom Pilate has sought advice (23:9). When Jesus does speak, *after* the trial, it is to bring words of judgement on Jerusalem (23:28–31) and of assurance to the penitent thief (23:43).[7]

Luke has prepared for this portrait of control by assuring his readers that Jesus's suffering and death are the Father's will, announced in advance by Jesus (13:33–35; 18:31–33) and in Scripture (e.g. 24:27, 44), thus ironically redefining messianic expectation to include suffering.[8]

Second, the three accusations against Jesus (23:2) are false. By handing over Jesus to the gentile Pilate to deal with, the chief priests are admitting that they cannot deal with him as they would like to do – they are the ones 'perverting the nation' by implicitly accepting pagan rule.[9] Further, Jesus earlier refused the dilemma offered to him as to whether the Jews should pay taxes to Caesar or not in a brilliantly ambiguous answer (20:25). Most ironically of all, in Luke's Gospel up to now Jesus never himself explicitly

---

[4] The essay was first published in a *Festschrift* in honour of Robert L. Brawley.
[5] Mark Allan Powell, *What Is Narrative Criticism?* (London: SPCK, 1993), 96–8.
[6] Walter Moberly, "Proclaiming Christ Crucified: Some Reflections on the Use and Abuse of the Gospels," *Anvil* 5 (1988): 31–52, esp. 36–9.
[7] According to some manuscripts, Jesus also speaks in v. 34a to ask God's forgiveness on those crucifying him, and if these words were original they would add to the sense of Jesus's control. However, an impressive array of our most ancient manuscripts including $\mathfrak{P}^{75}$ ℵ¹ B D* W Θ omits the words. NA²⁷ includes the passage in its main text, albeit in double square brackets, on the rather romantic basis that the phrase 'bears self-evident tokens of its dominical origin' (Bruce M. Metzger, *A Textual Commentary on the Greek New Testament*, 2nd ed. (Stuttgart: Deutsche Bibelgesellschaft/United Bible Societies, 1994), 154). Luke T. Johnson, *The Gospel of Luke*, SP 3 (Collegeville, MN: Liturgical, 1992), 376 argues for its inclusion on thematic grounds. More fully in defence of inclusion, see Joel B. Green, *The Death of Jesus: Tradition and Interpretation in the Passion Narrative*, WUNT II/33 (Tübingen: J. C. B. Mohr (Paul Siebeck), 1988), 91–2 and Raymond E. Brown, *The Death of the Messiah*, 2 vols., ABRL (London: Geoffrey Chapman, 1994), 2:975–81.
[8] Robert L. Brawley, *Centering on God: Method and Message in Luke-Acts* (Louisville, KY: Westminster John Knox, 1990), 51.
[9] The point is made more sharply in John 19:15, where the chief priests claim to have 'no king but Caesar'.

claims to be Messiah – when that title is offered to him by others, he offers an alternative title or deflects the question (9:20–21; 22:67–69). Of course, Luke wants his readers to believe that Jesus is Messiah, for it is announced by the angels to the shepherds (2:11), and Jesus's *deeds* imply messianic claims,[10] but Luke does not present Jesus *speaking* of himself as Messiah before his resurrection (note Acts 2:36).[11]

Third, Jesus is declared innocent at least six times[12] in the trial and crucifixion narrative. Three times Pilate asserts his innocence (23:4, 14, 22), and Herod agrees (23:15). The penitent thief recognizes Jesus has 'done nothing wrong' (23:41) and the centurion declares him innocent (23:47). And yet Jesus is condemned by Pilate to crucifixion – strikingly, Luke is the only evangelist to record Pilate giving sentence (23:24; the verb ἐπέκρινεν is used technically for giving a formal judgement[13]).

Pilate appears to want to dismiss the case against Jesus quickly, so that his first verdict of Jesus's innocence follows the most cursory of interrogations (23:3–4).[14] Walaskay justly observes that a Roman reader would have been very surprised at such a hasty ruling without due process.[15] Pilate seeks advice from Herod on learning that Jesus is a Galilean (23:6–7). He further attempts to give a ruling, but is shouted down (23:13–18[16]). He twice proposes a beating (23:16, 22), presumably the lighter *fustigatio* which functioned as an informal warning,[17] but cannot persuade the Jewish leaders to accept his proposal. As events develop, he finally accedes to persistent pressure from the chief priests, leaders and people (23:1–2, 5, 10, 18, 21, 23) and hands over an innocent man to death. Not only that, but Pilate hands over a recognized insurrectionist and murderer, Barabbas, to the people in response to their demands (23:18, 25). The irony of this exchange is underlined by the meaning of Barabbas's name, 'son of the father', for Jesus has been recognized as God's son at key points in Luke's narrative (1:32, 35; 3:22; 4:41; 8:28; 9:35) and on two occasions even self-identifies this way (10:22; 22:70[18]).

---

[10] E.g. Luke 7:18–23; 19:37–38, 45–46.
[11] See the judicious discussion of Richard N. Longenecker, *The Christology of Early Jewish Christianity*, SBT 2/17 (London: SCM, 1970), 72–4.
[12] Perhaps eight if the women's mourning (23:27) is an implicit recognition that Jesus does not deserve to die, and the people's mourning following Jesus's death (23:48) are included – the former may anticipate the latter (Joel B. Green, *The Gospel of Luke*, NICNT (Grand Rapids, MI; Cambridge: Eerdmans, 1997), 815).
[13] An NT *hapax legomenon*; see 2 Macc 4:47; 3 Macc 4:2; MM 240; LSJ 641; Helen K. Bond, *Pontius Pilate in History and Interpretation*, SNTSMS 100 (Cambridge: Cambridge University Press, 1998), 158. Luke's use of this term suggests that Walaskay is mistaken in thinking that Luke presents the Roman trial as incomplete (Paul W. Walaskay, *And So We Came to Rome*, SNTSMS 49 (Cambridge: Cambridge University Press, 1983), 44).
[14] By contrast with 22:70 (see below), Jesus's answer σὺ λέγεις, 'You say so' (23:3), is understood by Pilate to be a denial, as his response shows (23:4) (Bond, *Pilate*, 152).
[15] Walaskay, *Rome*, 40–1.
[16] ἀνάγκην δὲ εἶχεν ἀπολύειν αὐτοῖς κατὰ ἑορτὴν ἕνα 'for he had to release one [prisoner] to them at passover' is found as v. 17 or v. 19 in various manuscripts (notably the uncials ℵ D W Θ Ψ), but is clearly a scribal addition based on Matt 27:15; Mark 15:6 (Metzger, *Commentary* (2nd ed.), 153; Johnson, *Luke*, 371).
[17] A. N. Sherwin-White, *Roman Society and Roman Law in the New Testament* (Grand Rapids, MI: Baker, 1963 repr. 1981), 27.
[18] By contrast with 23:3 (see above) ὑμεῖς λέγετε ὅτι ἐγώ εἰμι, 'You say that I am', is presented as an affirmative answer, albeit ironic, since condemnation immediately follows (22:71) (cf. Robert C. Tannehill, *Luke*, ANTC (Nashville, TN: Abingdon, 1996), 330).

Thus Pilate faces the test of trying an innocent Jesus, and fails, for he finds himself agreeing to his death and releasing a convicted criminal and violent political activist in order to pacify the Jewish 'rent a mob' outside his home early in the morning. Bond observes, 'The weak Pilate has let down first himself and Herod, second the Roman administration he represents'.[19] Pilate's actions form a fascinating contrast with Jesus's response to testing in 4:1–11, where he resists the temptation to deny his destined path.

Luke does not regard Pilate as solely responsible for the death of Jesus – far from it. Acts 4:27 makes clear that Pilate is simply one of an array of enemies gathered against Jesus, along with Herod, the gentiles (i.e. the Romans) and the Jews of Jerusalem (as ἐν τῇ πόλει ταύτῃ 'in this city' implies; cf. Acts 13:28).[20] But Pilate is culpable for his part in this opposition to God's way and thus adjudged by the divine court to have failed as a man and as a Roman administrator – if this is typical of the empire, the empire stands condemned. Thus when God acts to raise Jesus from the dead, part of the vindication of Jesus is a vindication against the Roman empire's verdict on him (note the link in Acts 13:28, 30). More than that, God's hand was in control of events so that God's purpose was carried out in spite of human opposition to Jesus (Acts 4:28).

II. Paul before Gallio in Corinth (Acts 18:12–17)

Scholarship divides over the proconsul Gallio. For some, he is the archetypal Roman ruler, dispensing justice fairly and acting properly.[21] For others, he is a weakling and a coward, biased and antisemitic to the extent that he is ready to turn a blind eye to Sosthenes the Jew being beaten up.[22] Our assessment of Luke's portrait of the Roman empire and its servants is affected by how we assess this debate. Several critical exegetical decisions are determinative for this.

First, there is the nature of the charge brought by 'the Jews' (v. 12) to Gallio against Paul. Luke portrays a united (ὁμοθυμαδόν, v. 12) attack, presumably of those unpersuaded by Paul, for some of the Jewish community have become believers (v. 8). There may be a certain opportunism in coming to Gallio early in his one-year

---

[19] Bond, *Pilate*, 159.
[20] Jack T. Sanders, *The Jews in Luke-Acts* (London: SCM, 1987), esp. ch. 3, wrongly understands Luke to regard the entire Jewish race to be responsible for the death of Jesus, but misses key phrases such as this, and fails to observe that the gentiles referred to here cannot be *all* gentiles (so rightly, Robert L. Brawley, *Luke-Acts and the Jews: Conflict, Apology, and Conciliation*, SBLMS 33 (Atlanta, GA: Scholars, 1987), 146–7). For cogent critique of Sanders's overall position, see Jon A. Weatherly, *Jewish Responsibility for the Death of Jesus in Luke-Acts*, JSNTSup 106 (Sheffield: Sheffield Academic, 1994), esp. chs 2–3.
[21] E.g. William M. Ramsay, *St Paul the Traveller and Roman Citizen* (London: Hodder & Stoughton, 1895), 258–9; Bruce W. Winter, "Rehabilitating Gallio and His Judgement in Acts 18:14-15," *TynBul* 57 (2006): 291–308.
[22] E.g. Richard J. Cassidy, *Society and Politics in the Acts of the Apostles* (Maryknoll, NY: Orbis, 1987), 91–3; Harry W. Tajra, *The Trial of St Paul: A Juridical Exegesis of the Second Half of the Acts of the Apostles*, WUNT II/35 (Tübingen: Mohr Siebeck, 1989), 56, 59, 61; Warren Carter, *The Roman Empire and the New Testament*, Abingdon Essential Guides (Nashville, TN: Abingdon, 2006), 40; Jerome Murphy-O'Connor, *St Paul's Corinth: Texts and Archaeology*, 3rd ed. (Collegeville, MN: Liturgical, 2002), 168–9.

proconsulship, seeking to influence him before he knew better. The charge they bring is centred on Paul acting 'against the law' (παρὰ τὸν νόμον, fronted for emphasis in their speech,[23] v. 13) – but which law?

One possibility is that they are appealing to an edict such as that of Claudius concerning Egypt, which permitted Jews to practise their faith without harassment.[24] Tajra takes the issue to be that they were seeking specifically to assert that Paul's messianic gathering should be seen as outside the bounds of Judaism, and therefore not entitled to the protection of such an edict.[25] However, we lack evidence for such an edict in relation to Roman Corinth.[26]

Another possibility is that they accused Paul, in similar manner to the Jews of Thessalonica (17:7), of bringing a rival to Caesar in encouraging people to worship god (σέβεσθαι τὸν θεόν, v. 13) contrary to the law – they were thus accusing Paul of rejecting the imperial cult.[27] This would be rather opportunistic and somewhat ironic for Jews, and there is no explicit indication that this was their charge.

A third possibility is that Gallio understood them rightly when he interpreted their charge as being concerning the νόμου τοῦ καθ' ὑμᾶς 'law which governs[28] you'.[29] If so, Luke is presenting the Corinthian Jews consistently with other Jewish accusers of Paul who attack him for faithlessness towards his ancestral faith (18:6; cf. 13:50–51; 14:2, 19; 17:5; 19:9). Such a charge would certainly not stand up for long in a Roman court, and would be consistent with Gallio's speedy dismissal.

A key clue may be the verb used by the Jews concerning Paul's activities: they assert that ἀναπείθει, which is usually translated 'he persuades'.[30] This is an NT *hapax legomenon* and, at one level, 'persuades' is an adequate translation: this verb is a compound of πείθω, used in 18:4 for Paul's activities in the synagogue 'persuading' both Jews and Greeks. But in other usage this compound verb carries a negative sense of *deceptive* persuasion and that is the sense the major NT and classical lexica propose here.[31] *The Message* renders the verb as 'seduce', which certainly gets its 'atmosphere'

---

[23] C. K. Barrett, *A Critical and Exegetical Commentary on the Acts of the Apostles*, 2 vols., ICC (Edinburgh: T&T Clark, 1994, 1998), 2:872.
[24] Josephus, *Ant.* 19.5.2-3 §§278–91, esp. 290; Sherwin-White, *Society*, 102–3.
[25] Tajra, *Trial*, 56; so also Joseph A. Fitzmyer, *The Acts of the Apostles: A New Translation and Commentary*, AB 31 (Garden City, NY: Doubleday, 1998), 629–30.
[26] Eckhard J. Schnabel, *Early Christian Mission*, 2 vols. (Downers Grove, IL: InterVarsity Press, 2004), 2:1193; cf. Tessa Rajak, "Was There a Roman Charter for the Jews?," *JRS* 74 (1984): 107–23, showing that the edicts and decrees we have concerning the Jews in the Roman empire are confined to local situations (Corinth does not come among her examples, which are taken from Josephus and Philo). It should be noted that we have few edicts of *any* kind relating to Roman Corinth (I owe this point to Dr David Gill).
[27] Schnabel, *Mission*, 2:1193–94.
[28] BDAG 512 κατά §5.a.α.
[29] Rudolf Pesch, *Die Apostelgeschichte*, 2 vols., EKKNT (Zürich: Benzinger, 1986), 2:150 argues that Paul's encouragement to worship a crucified Messiah was seen as against the Torah, since the Torah recorded a curse on one crucified.
[30] E.g. NRSV, RSV, NIV, TNIV, NASB, NLT, HCSB, ESV.
[31] BDAG 70 s.v.; LSJ s.v. §3; examples of this sense include Herodotus 3.148.2; LXX Jer 36:8 [MT 29:8]; 1 Macc 1:11; Bruce W. Winter, "Gallio's Ruling on the Legal Status of Early Christianity (Acts 18:14-15)," *TynBul* 50 (1999): 213–24, here 216, gives other examples from the papyri. cf. Cassidy, *Society*, 195 n. 30.

right. On this view, Paul is being accused of being a con-artist who is either deliberately misleading people or misleading people with evil intent, and those would be charges that a Roman court would consider.

A second issue is the meaning and tone of Gallio's ruling (vv. 14–15). For some, Gallio is very dismissive of the Jews' complaint and handles the situation in a high-handed way.[32] Thus Cassidy asserts that Gallio's address, 'O Jews' (v. 14) 'reflects disdain'.[33] However, the phrasing of Gallio's answer seems rather more careful than that, including a number of key legal terms.[34]

Gallio's reply consists of two conditional constructions. The first (v. 14b) is 'contrary to fact', assuming a protasis that is unlikely to be true,[35] and thus includes two categories of crime which Gallio understands Paul not to have committed: ἀδίκημα (roughly 'felony') and ῥᾳδιούργημα πονηρόν (a political misdemeanour[36]). The apodosis of this conditional construction includes the verb ἀνεσχόμην, a technical term which denotes that Gallio would proceed with the case,[37] and the expression κατὰ λόγον, which here refers to the legal basis of their charge.[38] The whole clause thus means, 'I would have begun a hearing to consider the legal basis of your complaint'.

The second conditional construction (v. 15a) has the protasis assumed true,[39] and here Gallio gives the basis for his ruling in the previous verse. The proconsul assesses that the complaint is merely περὶ λόγου καὶ ὀνομάτων καὶ νόμου τοῦ καθ' ὑμᾶς. περὶ λόγου may denote a particular legal immunity which the Jews had in relation to the imperial cult, which meant that they were not required to worship or pray to the emperor.[40] ὀνομάτων may refer to 'names' as opposed to deeds, for in Roman law people were held accountable for actions rather than 'any name they professed'.[41] νόμου τοῦ καθ' ὑμᾶς clarifies that it is under *Jewish* law that the issue exists, rather than being a matter of concern in *Roman* law. Gallio thus grants legal immunity to Paul and the believers against the complaint brought by the Jews and *de facto* treats the group meeting in Titius Justus's house as a subspecies of Judaism. He may thereby be permitting the believing community in Corinth an exemption from active participation in the imperial cult.[42]

And what of Gallio's address to the complainants as ὦ Ἰουδαῖοι 'O Jews' (v. 14)? Barrett observes that Luke's usage of ὦ with the vocative is classical rather than

---

[32] E.g. Cassidy, *Society*, 91–3.
[33] Cassidy, *Society*, 92.
[34] I therefore now wish to nuance my earlier comments on Gallio in Steve Walton, "The State They Were In: Luke's View of the Roman Empire," in *Rome in the Bible and the Early Church*, ed. Peter Oakes (Carlisle: Paternoster, 2002), 1–41, here 24.
[35] Barrett, *Acts*, 2:874.
[36] Winter, "Ruling," 218; LSJ 1447 πονηρός §III.3.
[37] BDAG 78 ἀνέχω §3.
[38] Winter, "Ruling," 219; cf. BDAG 601 λόγος §2.d; LSJ λόγος §III.1; in spite of Barrett, *Acts*, 2:873–74.
[39] Barrett, *Acts*, 2:874 calls it an 'open' condition.
[40] Winter, "Ruling," 219.
[41] Wendy Cotter, "The Collegia and Roman Law: State Restrictions on Voluntary Associations," in *Voluntary Associations in the Graeco-Roman World*, ed. John S. Kloppenborg and S. G. Wilson (London: Routledge, 1996), 74–89, here 82.
[42] Winter, "Ruling," 222–3.

Hellenistic, so that its inclusion is the 'default' form and does not indicate any special warmth.[43] Certainly the term Ἰουδαῖοι is neutral, neither warm nor distant – how else could Gallio address a group of Jewish people collectively? However, the polite address using the classical form underlines the sense that Gallio is giving a formal ruling.[44]

The third key consideration in assessing how Gallio is presented here is his actions subsequent to his ruling. He first ἀπήλασεν them from the tribunal (v. 16); NRSV renders 'dismissed', but this is rather mild for this verb – it is closer to 'drove away',[45] and is yet another NT *hapax legomenon* which may have a legal sense. It rather implies that Gallio called his lictors with their rods to eject the Jewish accusers forcibly.[46]

Following the expulsion, πάντες 'all'[47] turned on Sosthenes the ἀρχισυνάγωγος 'synagogue ruler', and Gallio 'did not concern himself with any of these things' (v. 17).[48] πάντες could refer to the Jewish community, disappointed at the failure in the tribunal under Sosthenes's leadership,[49] or to the people of the city taking the chance to express antisemitism[50] or support for Caesar's recent expulsion of the troublesome Jews from Rome (Acts 18:2),[51] or some combination of the two.[52] From poor Sosthenes's point of view, events probably *felt* little different! The natural referent of τούτων 'these things' of which Gallio took no notice appears to be the attack on Sosthenes,[53] rather than a continuing reference to the same τούτων that the Jewish delegation had brought up in the tribunal, and which Gallio declined to judge (v. 15).[54] This (in-)action by Gallio is widely reckoned to show at least his collusion with antisemitism.[55] Winter proposes that Gallio acted properly in ignoring events outside his tribunal,[56] but this seems overstated given the proper concern a proconsul would have for order within his province. Gallio's collusion with Sosthenes's beating may thus represent

---

[43] Barrett, *Acts*, 2:874; so also MHT 3:33. Cf. Daniel B. Wallace, *Greek Grammar beyond the Basics: An Exegetical Syntax of the New Testament* (Grand Rapids, MI: Zondervan, 1996), 69, arguing that in Acts a vocative with ὦ at the front of a sentence is emphatic and emotional, but that when it is in the middle of a sentence (as here), it is merely polite.

[44] Cf. Winter, "Rehabilitating," 301.

[45] BDAG 101 ἀπελαύνω; so also Ernst Haenchen, *The Acts of the Apostles*, trans. R. McL. Wilson (Oxford: Blackwell, 1971), 536 (citing Zahn).

[46] Even Winter, "Rehabilitating," 302 concedes this point, seeing Gallio's forceful action as illustrative of Gallio's unwillingness to be manipulated.

[47] This is the likeliest reading in light of support by 𝔓⁷⁴ ℵ A B; so Metzger, *Commentary* (2nd ed.), 411; Barrett, *Acts*, 2:875.

[48] Taking οὐδέν as accusative of respect, rather than as nominative subject of the verb ἔμελεν; see discussion in Barrett, *Acts*, 2:876; C. F. D. Moule, *An Idiom-Book of New Testament Greek*, 2nd ed. (Cambridge: Cambridge University Press, 1959), 28.

[49] Fitzmyer, *Acts*, 630–1. The minuscules 36 and 453 read πάντες οἱ Ἰουδαῖοι 'all the Jews'.

[50] Cassidy, *Society*, 92; cf. Haenchen, *Acts*, 536–7. This is the interpretation of Western and later Byzantine manuscripts, which read πάντες οἱ Ἕλληνες 'all the Greeks' – so D E H L P Ψ 33 1739 Byz, as well as numerous versions and Fathers; see Josep Rius-Camps and Jenny Read-Heimerdinger, *The Message of Acts in Codex Bezae: A Comparison with the Alexandrian Tradition*, 4 vols., JSNTSup/LNTS 257, 302, 365, 415 (London: T&T Clark, 2004–9), 3:368.

[51] Suggested by Winter, "Rehabilitating," 303.

[52] Barrett, *Acts*, 2:875.

[53] So Haenchen, *Acts*, 537.

[54] So Winter, "Rehabilitating," 303, tentatively.

[55] E.g. Robert C. Tannehill, *The Narrative Unity of Luke-Acts: A Literary Interpretation*, 2 vols. (Minneapolis, MN: Fortress, [1986] 1990), 2:228.

[56] Winter, "Rehabilitating," 305.

the antisemitism which was omnipresent in Roman society, even if a little below the surface much of the time[57] – and there may thus be an element of antisemitism behind his judgement in vv. 14–15, expressed in Roman legalese.

Given this conclusion, how should we see these events? Luke gives the key clue in vv. 9–10, where the Lord appears to Paul to encourage him to continue his ministry in Corinth, saying that οὐδεὶς ἐπιθήσεταί σοι τοῦ κακῶσαί σε ('No-one will lay hands on you to do you harm'). Paul is not promised that no-one will attack him, but that no harm will come to him. This incident shows the Lord's protection of Paul,[58] for Paul is almost completely peripheral to the tribunal scene in vv. 12–17 and yet is freed and vindicated. Indeed, Paul can be said to be a passive participant, for on the only two occasions he is named in this story, he is inactive: he is accused by the Jews (v. 12) and he is about to speak when Gallio gives his ruling (v. 14). Thus Luke's literary focus in presenting this incident appears to be his concern for God's action in taking the mission forward, and thus in protecting his servants, rather than the role of the Roman proconsul. Gallio is one chess piece who acts under the control of God and gives a legal ruling which benefits the renewed people of God, even if Gallio's actions and motives may be questionable. In presenting the story this way, from God's point of view, Luke is very much in tune with the biblical tradition.[59] Such a conclusion puts the Roman empire very much in its place, for it operates under the sovereign power of God and thus (implicitly) its officials should not get too big for their boots. The similarity of thought to Romans 13:1–7 is striking.

III. Paul before Felix in Caesarea (Acts 23–24)

In Jerusalem Paul is taken into custody (presumably in the Fortress Antonia on the boundary of the temple precincts[60]) by the tribune Claudius Lysias, initially to quell an apparent riot (21:31–33). When examined, Paul discloses to the centurion that he is a Roman citizen, thus making it illegal both to chain him and to flog him (22:24–29, esp. 29).[61] Lysias seeks to find out the basis of the accusation against Paul by seeking

---

[57] Haenchen, *Acts*, 541 observes that Gallio's brother, Seneca the Younger, was known for his antisemitic views. The main evidence for this is Augustine, *Civ.* 6.11, citing Seneca's lost work *De Superstitione*, stating that the Jews were 'a most criminal race' (*sceleratissima gens*; discussion: Hermann Lichtenberger."Jews and Christians in Rome in the Time of Nero: Josephus and Paul in Rome," *ANRW* 26.3:2142–76, here 2155).

[58] So also Haenchen, *Acts*, 540; Tannehill, *Unity*, 2:229; Luke T. Johnson, *The Acts of the Apostles*, SP 5 (Collegeville, MN: Liturgical, 1992), 334.

[59] Cf. (for example) Isa 45:1, where God calls the pagan king Cyrus 'my anointed'. See my survey of the whole book of Acts from this point of view in Steve Walton, "Acts, Book of," in *Dictionary for Theological Interpretation of the Bible*, ed. Kevin J. Vanhoozer, Craig G. Bartholomew, Daniel J. Treier and N. T. Wright (London: SPCK, 2005), 27–31.

[60] Brian M. Rapske, *The Book of Acts and Paul in Roman Custody*, BAFCS 3 (Carlisle: Paternoster, 1994), 137–8.

[61] Thus (e.g.) Cicero protests against the tribune Titus Labienus allowing a Roman citizen to be beaten before a proper trial, *Rab. Perd.* 4.12; see the full and helpful discussion in Rapske, *Paul*, 47–56.

advice from the Sanhedrin (22:30),[62] but the hearing falls into chaos when Paul self-identifies as a Pharisee, dividing the council along party lines (24:6-9). Lysias again steps in to subdue the violence and takes Paul to safety in the barracks (24:10). Luke includes a note of the Lord appearing to Paul and encouraging him to keep up his courage and keep testifying for the Lord (23:11), in broadly similar terms to the Lord's encouragement in Corinth (18:9-10).

On learning of a plot to assassinate Paul from Paul's nephew (23:12-22), the tribune decides to send Paul to the Roman administrative capital of Caesarea, for Paul's own safety (23:23-24). Lysias writes a letter, which is a rather economical with the truth in order to present himself in the best possible light,[63] to the governor Felix (23:25-30) to brief him, making clear that he sees the issue as an intra-Jewish debate which does not merit any serious penalty for Paul (23:29).[64]

At this point Felix steps into the story as ἡγεμών 'governor', technically procurator.[65] What we know of Felix from extra-biblical sources suggests that he could be a harsh governor who did not hesitate to use military means to keep the peace, and who was willing to cooperate with the *sicarii* terrorists to have the high priest killed.[66] That said, the positive *captatio benevolentiae* of Tertullus's speech is neither mere flattery nor simply disingenuous. Ananias, the high priest who led the delegation to Felix (24:1), and his predecessor Jonathan had pressed Claudius to appoint Felix as procurator.[67] It was an unusual appointment for a mere freedman rather than one of equestrian rank.[68] The Jewish delegation was thus compelled to support Felix's administration. Further, Felix had not long before brought peace following a rebellion led by an Egyptian,[69] and Tertullus's comments (24:2) may allude to this incident.

Luke presents Felix as acting properly, at least initially, in handling Paul's case. First, he establishes whether Paul falls under his jurisdiction by enquiring which province he comes from (23:34). Cilicia was probably at this time under the legate of Syria,

---

[62] It is not therefore a Sanhedrin *trial*, but simply a means of advising Lysias of the nature of the charges against Paul, with Rapske, *Paul*, 146-7; Barrett, *Acts*, 2:1091.

[63] It was not on learning that Paul was a Roman citizen that Lysias rescued him (24:27b), for example. More fully, see Rapske, *Paul*, 152-3; Ben Witherington, III, *The Acts of the Apostles: A Socio-Rhetorical Commentary* (Carlisle: Paternoster, 1998), 700-1.

[64] E. A. Judge in *NewDocs* 1:77-78, on the basis of the use of τύπος (23:25) plausibly suggests that Luke may be drawing on material from official sources in quoting Claudius Lysias's letter.

[65] Greek ἐπίτροπος, see Josephus, *J.W.* 15.11.4 §406 and discussion in Brian M. Rapske, "Roman Governors of Palestine," in *Dictionary of the Later New Testament and Its Developments*, ed. Ralph P. Martin and Peter H. Davids (Leicester: Inter-Varsity Press, 1997), 979-84, here 979; Tajra, *Trial*, 110-13.

[66] Respectively, Josephus, *Ant.* 20.8.7 §§173-78; *J.W.* 2.13.7 §§266-70 and *Ant.* 20.8.5 §162; *J.W.* 2.13.3. §§254-7. See the helpful brief treatments in Rapske, "Governors," 982-83; *ABD* 2:783 and, more fully, David W. J. Gill, "Acts and Roman Policy in Judaea," in *The Book of Acts in its Palestinian Setting*, ed. Richard Bauckham, BAFCS 4 (Carlisle: Paternoster, 1995), 15-26, here 21-6.

[67] Tacitus, *Ann.* 12.54. Bruce W. Winter, "The Importance of the *Captatio Benevolentiae* in the Speeches of Tertullus and Paul in Acts 24:1-21," *JTS* ns 42 (1991): 505-31, here 515-16; F. F. Bruce, *New Testament History*, revised ed. (London: Oliphants, 1971), 325.

[68] Claudius Lysias and Tertullus address Felix as 'most excellent' (κράτιστος, 23:26; 24:3), a title undoubtedly used for those of equestrian rank, but not exclusively for such people (Loveday Alexander, *The Preface to Luke's Gospel: Literary Convention and Social Context in Luke 1.1-4 and Acts 1.1*, SNTSMS 78 (Cambridge: Cambridge University Press, 1993), 133; *BegC* 2:505-507).

[69] Josephus, *J.W.* 2.13.5. §§261-63; Acts 21:38.

Felix's line manager, and so for Felix to fail to hear the case would be to risk appearing to waste the legate's time with a minor matter.[70] In any case, the transfer of an accused person to his own province was optional at this time.[71]

Second, Felix wishes to hear first-hand from Paul's accusers (23:35a; cf. 25:16).[72] When Tertullus and Paul present their arguments before Felix (24:1–21), Paul makes the point that at least some of the accusers are not present (24:19), thus implying that the charges were invalid.[73] Their absence is reflected in the reduced claims which Tertullus makes, asserting only that Paul 'attempted' to profane the temple (ἐπείρασεν, 24:6), whereas the missing Asian Jews had claimed that Paul 'had defiled' the temple (κεκοίνωκεν, 21:28).

Felix then acts within his powers in deciding to await testimony from the tribune Lysias (24:22), since he needs advice to help him decide between the two contradictory testimonies he has heard.[74] Luke does not tell us whether Felix was never able to consult Lysias or whether a consultation took place but was inconclusive – either way, Paul remained in custody at governor Felix's pleasure (as the British judicial system charmingly puts it). In the situation of waiting for Lysias's testimony, Felix can afford to relax Paul's conditions of detention, and does so (24:23).[75]

Strikingly, Paul's confinement does not prevent him testifying to the gospel, for Felix wishes to hear him on the subject on numerous occasions (24:24–26), thus partially fulfilling the Lord's word to Paul (23:11). As Skinner notes, this situation gives Paul access to some of the most powerful people in Judaea,[76] and thus Paul the prisoner is Paul the *missionary*-prisoner.[77]

As well as conducting procedures properly, Felix's response to Paul shows another, less savoury, side to his actions; in rapid succession, Luke highlights three issues.[78]

First, Felix becomes fearful at Paul's talk 'concerning righteousness and self-control and judgement to come' (24:25) and therefore sends Paul away. These qualities imply a call to repent, a key feature of evangelistic proclamation in Acts.[79] However, they may be particularly apposite for Felix as a governor who should act with righteousness and self-control, for Felix had deceptively drawn Drusilla away from her former husband into his arms[80] – ἐγκράτεια may thus focus on *sexual* self-control.[81] Thus 'judgement to come' would be an unwelcome thought to Felix if his conscience was at all sensitive to what Paul said. Interestingly, Paul is portrayed here as 'turning the tables' on Felix,

---

[70] Sherwin-White, *Society*, 55–7; Rapske, *Paul*, 155. Cilicia was probably not formally a province at this time, but this distinction does not affect the point noted.
[71] Sherwin-White, *Society*, 55.
[72] Sherwin-White, *Society*, 17; Tajra, *Trial*, 115.
[73] Johnson, *Acts*, 417; Fitzmyer, *Acts*, 737.
[74] Sherwin-White, *Society*, 53.
[75] On the possible form of relaxation, see Rapske, *Paul*, 167–72.
[76] Matthew L. Skinner, *Locating Paul: Places of Custody as Narrative Settings in Acts 21–28*, AcBib 13 (Atlanta, GA: SBL, 2003), 137–8.
[77] The expression is from Rapske, *Paul*, e.g. 429–36.
[78] Cf. Cassidy, *Society*, 105–6.
[79] E.g. 2:38; 3:19; 5:31; 11:18; 17:30; 20:21; 26:20.
[80] Josephus, *Ant.* 20.7.1 §§141–44; Gerhard Schneider, *Die Apostelgeschichte*, 2 vols., HTKNT (Freiburg: Herder, [1980] 1982), 2:351–2.
[81] BDAG 274 s.v.

his judge, by speaking to Felix of the values which (ironically) should be guiding his judgement.[82]

Second, Felix hoped for a bribe from Paul, and not just on one occasion, but repeatedly (24:26).[83] This was not uncommon among judges in the Roman empire,[84] although illegal under the *Lex Iulia de Repetundis*[85] and Luke takes a dim view of it,[86] for it results in Paul continuing to be held even though the tribune Lysias had written to Felix that Paul has not committed any crime worthy of death or imprisonment (23:29). As often in Luke-Acts, how possessions are handled is an index of a person's standing with God.[87]

Third, Felix is motivated by pleasing the Jewish leaders in keeping Paul confined on his departure from office (24:27). This is politically understandable in the sensitive climate of first-century Judaea, particularly because Roman legions based in Syria were occupied with peacekeeping duties on that front, and could not be relied upon to help in Judaea.[88] To free Paul would be to arouse the hostility of the Jewish leadership who had sought to persuade Felix to punish him as a troublemaker – and Tertullus had darkly hinted at this danger in stressing the peace which Judaea had enjoyed under his procuratorship (24:2). But to show such bias towards the politically powerful, even against a Roman citizen such as Paul, cannot be seen as good. It is striking, as Tannehill observes, that Felix never declares Paul innocent, by contrast with Lysias and (as we shall see) Festus and Agrippa.[89] Felix's appearance in Acts is thus the portrait of a man who is a tragic figure, for he is attracted to Paul and his gospel, and has the chance (many chances!) to respond positively both to the gospel and to Paul as the Lord's gospel-witness and fails to take it.[90] The resemblance to Pilate is clear.[91]

IV. Paul before Festus in Caesarea (Acts 25–26)

On Festus's arrival as procurator, he inherits Paul as a prisoner. Presumably the procurator's archives contained Lysias's letter and a record of the earlier hearing under

---

[82] Cf. Cassidy, *Society*, 106.
[83] Although πυκνότερον is formally a comparative form, the lack of anything to compare with forces a superlative sense to be present, meaning 'very often' (with MHT 3:30; Barrett, *Acts*, 2:1116; *pace* BDF §244(1), who assert it to be ambiguous).
[84] E.g. Albinus, as reported by Josephus, *J.W.* 2.14.1 §§272–73. Rapske, *Paul*, 65-7 lays out the evidence for such corruption in the judicial system.
[85] Introduced in 59 BC to prevent corruption of this kind in the provinces; see Tajra, *Trial*, 131.
[86] Beverly R. Gaventa, *Acts*, ANTC (Nashville, TN: Abingdon, 2003), 330 suggests that Felix is portrayed in the image of the unjust judge of the parable (Luke 18:1–8).
[87] For discussion of this theme in Luke, see Luke T. Johnson, *The Literary Function of Possessions in Luke-Acts*, SBLDS 39 (Missoula, MT: Scholars, 1977), 144–58.
[88] Gill, "Policy," 22.
[89] Tannehill, *Unity*, 2:304; so also Haenchen, *Acts*, 658–9.
[90] A point astutely observed by Tannehill, *Unity*, 2:303. Johnson, *Acts*, 423 sums up Felix's actions as 'an altogether shameless performance'. cf. Barrett, *Acts*, 2:1092–93.
[91] As Bond, *Pilate*, 142–3 notes.

Felix, and perhaps a record of Felix's decision to leave Paul in prison at the end of his governorship.[92]

The Jewish leaders take the opportunity of a new governor to seek a review of Paul's case, to be held in Jerusalem as a favour[93] to them (25:2–3) – in similar manner to our suggestion that the Corinthian Jews came to Gallio early in his proconsulship. Festus decides to hear the case in Caesarea, providentially as Luke notes, for the plan was to ambush and kill Paul *en route* to Jerusalem (25:3b); it seems likely that we should see Festus's decision as a partial fulfilment of the Lord's promise of protection (23:11).

Like Gallio, Festus sits on the raised dais from which he gave judgement (ἐπὶ τοῦ βήματος, 25:6; cf. 18:12) and hears the case of the Jewish leaders (25:7) and Paul's defence (25:8). Luke simply states the broad outline of the case and Paul's defence, presumably because we are to fill this gap with Tertullus's speech and Paul's defence before Felix (24:2–8, 10–21). Festus's bias is made clear by Luke at this point: θέλων τοῖς Ἰουδαίοις χάριν καταθέσθαι 'wanting to do a favour for the Jews' (25:9) is almost a verbatim echo of Felix's motivation in 24:27,[94] and a clear echo of the Jewish leaders' desire in 25:3.

Paul should not expect justice from such a judge, and will get injustice if handed over to the Jewish authorities, Luke implies, and Paul therefore appeals to the emperor (25:11c). Paul's thinking in reaching this conclusion is obscured by NRSV, which rather strangely translates v. 10, 'I *am appealing* to the emperor's tribunal', thus making it appear that Paul appeals to the emperor at the beginning of his speech. The verb is the periphrastic ἑστώς εἰμι, 'I am *standing*', referring to Paul's *present* location,[95] and the prepositional phrase ἐπὶ τοῦ βήματος Καίσαρος '*before* the tribunal of Caesar' echoes Festus's question, for he asks whether Paul wishes to be tried in Jerusalem ἐπ᾽ ἐμοῦ '*before* me'.[96] Thus, Paul is asserting that where he now is, before Festus, is the imperial tribunal – that is the correct place for him, as a Roman citizen, to be tried. He does not wish to be handed over to the Jewish authorities, for he has done no wrong to them (v. 10b) and they do not have jurisdiction over him (v. 11a). Paul's further observation, 'no-one is able *to hand* me *over* [χαρίσασθαι] to them' (v. 11b) ironically echoes the uses of the noun χάρις as 'favour' which we have just noticed – we might hear the echo by translating, 'no-one is able to hand me over to them *as a favour*'. Festus is not going to grant Paul justice, and so Paul appeals beyond him to the emperor.

Cassidy detects 'a quality akin to outrage' in Paul's words in vv. 10–11,[97] but such a tone of voice is hard to recognize without textual signals in support. Certainly, Paul

---

[92] Bruce W. Winter, "Official Proceedings and the Forensic Speeches in Acts 24–26," in *The Book of Acts in its Ancient Literary Setting*, ed. Bruce W. Winter and Andrew D. Clarke, BAFCS 1 (Carlisle: Paternoster, 1993), 305–36, here 307–9, provides evidence for careful preservation of court records and argues cogently that such a process went on with hearings of Paul before Felix and Festus.

[93] χάριν, echoing Felix's decision to grant the Jews χάριτα (24:27).

[94] The main difference is in the form of χάρις, shifting from one accusative form (χάριτα, 24:27) to another (χάριν, 25:9), with no difference in meaning (MHT 2:132; BDF §47(3)). A's reading χάριτα in 25:9 looks like a scribal harmonization of spelling in the two passages.

[95] BDAG 482 ἵστημι §C.2.b; the intransitive perfect of this verb has the force of a present.

[96] Gaventa, *Acts*, 334.

[97] Cassidy, *Society*, 108.

implicitly accuses Festus of dissembling by the phrase 'as you yourself (emphatic personal pronoun σύ) know very well' (v. 10),[98] but Luke does not say that Paul was angry or that he raised his voice. Johnson may be nearer the mark in seeing desperation on Paul's part,[99] but Gaventa may be the closest of all in identifying Paul's decision as the outcome of the Lord's word that he will stand before the emperor (23:11),[100] for these events, as with the earlier meetings with Felix, are under the overarching control of the Lord.

Festus seeks advice from his *consilium* and grants Paul's appeal to the emperor (25:12). Festus then takes the opportunity of Agrippa and Berenice's visit to seek further advice on what to do with Paul. He presents himself, as Lysias had earlier, as the model of propriety in his handling of the case: he stresses his concern for proper procedure in the accused meeting the accusers face to face and having the right to make a defence (25:16); he intimates that he acted expeditiously in hearing the case (ἀναβολὴν μηδεμίαν ποιησάμενος, 'making no delay', 25:17); he recognized that there was no case to answer under Roman law since the questions were intra-Jewish issues (25:18–19); and thus he offers the accused the chance to be tried before his own people (25:20).

Moreover, when Paul appears before Festus and Agrippa the next day, Festus underlines in this highly public, but Roman, setting (25:23) that he, the just and judicious governor, saved Paul from wild and unsubstantiated attacks: the whole Jewish community (τὸ πλῆθος τῶν Ἰουδαίων) were shouting (βοῶντες) for his death (25:24); Festus himself, however (note the emphatic ἐγὼ δέ, v. 25), came to recognize through the proper rational processes of enquiry (κατελαβόμην,[101] v. 25) that Paul had done nothing deserving death. However, his hands were tied by Paul's appeal to Caesar (25:25; cf. 26:32). Festus would therefore like advice from Agrippa in composing his advice to the emperor to accompany the other documents which would be sent to Rome (25:26–27).[102]

Throughout his encounter with Agrippa, Festus is presenting himself in the best possible light,[103] perhaps by contrast with Felix at a number of points. Festus does not mention his real motive, currying favour with the Jewish leaders (25:9), and somewhat distorts Paul's appeal in implying that Paul *wanted* to stay in Roman custody (25:21) – whereas Paul wanted to be free to proclaim the gospel, and denied that the charges against him had any substance (24:12–13; 25:8). The story ends with the third statement in the trials in Judaea that Paul has committed no crime under Roman law (26:31; cf. 23:29; 25:25), paralleling Pilate's three declarations of Jesus's innocence (Luke 23:4, 13, 22). Similarly, Agrippa's role as Jewish adviser parallels that of Herod in the trial of Jesus (Luke 23:7–12), coming to the same conclusion of innocence. Luke thus invites his readers to consider Paul's hearings in the light of Jesus's trial.

---

[98] Gaventa, *Acts*, 334.
[99] Johnson, *Acts*, 422.
[100] Gaventa, *Acts*, 335.
[101] BDAG 519 καταλαμβάνω §4.a.
[102] Probably at least Claudius Lysias's letter and the court record of the hearing before Felix; see Winter, "Official Proceedings," 309.
[103] As Cassidy, *Society*, 111–12 recognizes.

Festus does not come out of this situation well – but it should be noted that in at least some aspects of Paul's situation, Festus had been painted into a corner by the actions of his predecessor, Felix. Had Felix dealt summarily and correctly with Paul's case and acted on Lysias's recognition that there was no case to answer, Festus would never have met Paul. We are considering gradations of colour here, rather than clear red (for guilt)[104] or clear white (for innocence), but Felix seems considerably deeper pink than Festus.

In the midst of this situation, it is Paul who speaks for God – and thus for Luke – in identifying what is really going on. Two things are happening in this sequence of events: first, God is helping Paul to testify to the death and resurrection of the Messiah, Jesus (26:22–23a); and second, the exalted Messiah is himself proclaiming the truth to Jew and gentile alike (26:23b).[105] As always in Acts, God is the main actor in the story, and whatever human opposition there is, it cannot ultimately resist his purposes – and in speaking to Festus and his Roman court together with Agrippa and Berenice, Paul has a gentile-plus-Jew audience before him. As in Corinth, the purposes of God cannot be frustrated by the interference of the empire and its servants.

V. Conclusion

In sum, we have found significant continuities in the portrayal of the Roman empire and its provincial-level servants – prefects, procurators and proconsuls – in the four accounts we have considered. Their verdicts on Jesus and Paul are consistently of innocence, but Pilate finds himself giving sentence for the innocent Jesus to die to satisfy the Jewish leaders, and Felix holds Paul in prison for two years on a charge from the Jewish leaders which is without foundation. Festus is more interested in political expediency, under pressure from the Jewish leaders, than in rejecting what he recognizes to be an insubstantial case. Even Gallio, in many ways nearest to the epitome of Roman justice, may be acting from antisemitic motives – ironically, the reverse of pleasing the Jewish leaders – in finding in favour of Paul. Bond observes acutely that although the governors as representatives of Roman justice consistently find Jesus and his followers innocent, their character flaws can mean that justice is delayed or denied in practice.[106]

The Roman empire's servants are shown to be far from perfect – although not as corrupt as they might be – and yet the centre of Luke's attention does not lie there, but in the purposes of God that the gospel shall reach 'the end of the earth' (Acts 1:8). If we consider the major views of Luke's view of the Roman empire in scholarship in recent times,[107] there is something to be said for the claim that Luke is uninterested in politics.

---

[104] I use 'red' on the basis of Isa 1:18.
[105] This is one of a number of indications that Jesus is not absent from the story of Acts, as is frequently asserted. More fully, see the excellent discussion of Beverly R. Gaventa, "The Presence of the Absent Lord: The Characterization of Jesus in the Acts of the Apostles" (Paper given at SBL Annual Meeting, 2003), and her acute observation that here 'the proclaimed has become the proclaimer' (Gaventa, *Acts*, 348).
[106] Bond, *Pilate*, 142–3.
[107] See my discussion in Walton, "State," 2–12.

Franklin argues that Luke is focused on the triumph of God's purpose in bringing Paul to Rome,[108] and we have seen that there is substance to this. Jervell likewise argues that the empire is no real threat to the gospel's progress to the end of the earth.[109]

But this is not the whole story, for Luke, our omniscient narrator, speaks for God in presenting these servants of the empire in some of the negative ways we have seen. Thus Cassidy has a point in proposing that Luke is both warning his readers of the grave dangers of Christian testimony and encouraging them to show the same faithfulness under trial as Jesus and Paul.[110] And yet, too, there are times when the empire protects believers, of which Gallio's actions in Corinth are a prime example. We might add the freedom Paul had in Rome to speak 'unhindered' (28:20), using a legal term which implies Paul's innocence.[111]

The portrait of the empire which emerges from this study is thus a mixed one, falling (as I have suggested elsewhere[112]) at *both* ends of the spectrum between the views of the Roman state found in Romans 13 and Revelation 13. It is in the midst of this setting that Luke both tells the story of the spread of the Christian testimony and encourages his readers to become part of the story themselves. Perhaps most notably among his readers, Luke's addressee Theophilus is addressed as κράτιστε in similar manner to both Felix and Festus,[113] and thereby invited to consider how he resembles them, for good or ill, and how he might find himself (as we might say) on the side of the angels in the gospel story through repentance and faith in Jesus – and that would be a true turning of the tables!

---

[108] Eric Franklin, *Christ the Lord: A Study in the Purpose and Theology of Luke-Acts* (London: SPCK, 1975), 134–9.
[109] Jacob Jervell, *The Theology of the Acts of the Apostles*, NT Theology (Cambridge: Cambridge University Press, 1996), 105–6.
[110] Cassidy, *Society*, 160.
[111] ἀκωλύτως, see Barrett, *Acts*, 2:1253; Tajra, *Trial*, 192–3.
[112] Walton, "State," 35.
[113] Luke 1:3; Acts 23:26; 24:3; 26:25.

9

What Does 'Mission' in Acts Mean in Relation to the 'Powers That Be'?[1]

My wife and I have recently worked our way through all seven seasons of *The West Wing* on DVD and greatly enjoyed the experience. This is a fascinating series which portrays a devout Christian President of the United States and his staff engaging in the world of politics. One incident caught my attention recently in reflecting on this topic – for those interested, it is in season 4 episode 11, called 'Holy Night', set just before Christmas at the end of President Bartlet's first term of office. A new character, Will Bailey, has been introduced to the West Wing world, and he is now helping Toby Ziegler, the White House Director of Communications, with the President's second inaugural address, presently as a temporary appointment for three months. Bailey is cautious of power and has been working in a hotel and meeting Ziegler in the lobby of the White House to discuss drafts of the inaugural which they are preparing. This is frustrating for Ziegler, and early in the episode Ziegler moves Bailey to the office next to his. They have given the President a draft of a section of the inaugural and get three notes back from the President on this section, for review; what Bailey doesn't know is that one of these notes is deliberately mistaken and is there as a test of whether he will notice it is wrong and say so to the President. Bailey raises his concerns about this 'bad note' to Ziegler, but when Bailey has two opportunities – one alone with the President, and one with the President, Toby Ziegler and Leo McGarry (the President's Chief of Staff) – to mention his concerns to the President, he does not do so. This conversation follows during the second occasion, in the Oval Office:

> 'In his defence', Ziegler tells McGarry in front of Bailey, 'he caught the bad note. He came to me, he made it important … He wasn't distracted by the fact that his office was filled with bicycles'.
> 'Excuse me?' Bailey interrupts, 'You said that I caught the bad note?'
> 'Yeah, that was planted there to see how you'd do telling truth to power', Ziegler tells Bailey.

---

[1] A shorter version of this chapter was presented at the Luke-Acts Section of the Evangelical Theological Society in San Francisco in November 2011. I am grateful to the steering committee for their kind invitation to contribute this chapter to this session.

'Not very well so far', the President muses.

'I have no difficulty, Sir, telling truth to power'.

'Okay, except when I asked you to come into the Oval Office', the President says (referring to a previous opportunity), 'You said, "No. No, no. No, no, no, no."'

'And I was firm in my convictions'.

Leo McGarry interrupts. 'Can we get back to why you think'. And finally Bailey makes his point. 'Maybe', McGarry says. 'But I'm not convinced and that's 'cause you haven't convinced me. This isn't Tillman at the Stanford Club or the California 47th. This is big-boy school, Mr Bailey. You understand?'

'Yes, sir, I do'.

One of the hardest things to do in political life – and in life in general – is to tell the truth to power, especially when the person with power has the power to affect your own life and career. And yet what politicians need around them as advisers is not people who are 'yes' men and women, but people who will tell them the truth, however unpalatable. The thesis I want to suggest is that the essence of the way Luke portrays the earliest Christians' engagement with the 'powers' of their day is *speaking truth to power*.

Recent study of the New Testament has increasingly engaged with questions of politics, notably how the earliest Christians engaged (or not) with the Roman empire in its various manifestations, and (more broadly) the human 'powers' and authorities in the ancient world.[2] In this chapter, we shall consider the specific question of what we mean when we speak of 'mission' in relation to these human powers and authorities.

To ask this question is necessarily to ask what we mean by 'mission', both in general and in the book of Acts, and our first task will be to seek a working definition, so that we know what we are looking for. Our question also requires consideration of the range of 'powers that be' which are found in Acts, and our second task will be to consider the variety of people and institutions which come under this umbrella. We shall then be in a position to sample some encounters between the earliest Christians and these powers, before drawing some interim conclusions. Our conclusions will necessarily be provisional, as a fuller study would be required to provide a comprehensive answer to our question; hopefully, we shall have considered sufficiently typical examples to enable us to come to interim conclusions which will stand up to further scrutiny.

---

[2] E.g. Loveday Alexander, ed., *Images of Empire*, JSOTSup 122 (Sheffield: JSOT, 1991); Allen Brent, *A Political History of Early Christianity* (London: T&T Clark, 2009); Christopher Bryan, *Render to Caesar: Jesus, the Early Church, and the Roman Superpower* (Oxford/New York: Oxford University Press, 2005); Warren Carter, *The Roman Empire and the New Testament*, Abingdon Essential Guides (Nashville, TN: Abingdon, 2006); Richard J. Cassidy and Philip J. Scharper, eds, *Political Issues in Luke-Acts* (Maryknoll, NY: Orbis, 1983); David Rhoads, David Esterline and Jae Won Lee, eds, *Luke-Acts and Empire: Essays in Honor of Robert L. Brawley*, Princeton Theological Monographs 151 (Eugene, OR: Pickwick, 2011); Kazuhiko Yamazaki-Ransom, *The Roman Empire in Luke's Narrative*, LNTS 404 (London: T&T Clark, 2010); C. Kavin Rowe, *World Upside Down: Reading Acts in the Graeco-Roman Age* (Oxford/New York: Oxford University Press, 2009).

I. What Is 'Mission' in Acts?

In thinking about constructing a New Testament understanding of 'mission', the passages which come most quickly to mind are not in Luke's corpus: they are Matt 28:18-20 and John 20:21-23. Both include statements by the risen Jesus in which he sends his followers with a task: in Matthew, the task is to make disciples (the imperative μαθητεύσατε is the main verb of the command); in John, the task involves bringing and declaring forgiveness of sins.

Acts 1:8 is sometimes understood to be a similar statement, but it is worth noticing a significant difference from the Matthean and Johannine passages, namely that Acts 1:8 contains no explicit command. Rather, it is a statement by the risen Jesus of what will happen: there is no imperative verb; there is no statement that the disciples are being sent. The same applies to Luke 24:47-49: the verbs there are indicatives, not imperatives – Jesus does not command the disciples to go out, but tells them that they are witnesses of the crucial events of his suffering, death and resurrection. Let us explore Acts 1:8 further.

I.a. Acts 1:8

Several Isaianic echoes reverberate through Acts 1:7-8.[3] Luke reads Isa 32:15 LXX ἕως ἂν ἐπέλθῃ ἐφ᾽ ὑμᾶς πνεῦμα ἀφ᾽ ὑψηλοῦ 'until a spirit from on high comes upon you', which is located in a passage about Israel's new exodus restoration, in terms of the Spirit's coming to empower for witness. Isa 43:10-12 sits in a passage about the role of God's servant, Israel (43:1), and proclaims 'you are my witnesses'.[4] Isa 49:6 speaks of the role of God's servant not only as restoring Israel, but also as 'a light to the nations, that my salvation may reach to the end of the earth'.[5] Isa 49:6 LXX is echoed in Acts 1:8 and will be directly quoted in Acts 13:47, in the context of the mission turning towards gentiles. These Isaianic echoes signal that the disciples are to take part in God's restoration of Israel (which is the Isaianic servant's ministry) in order to bring light to the nations, in conjunction with Jesus the Messiah (cf. Acts 3:19-21). In this task they are to follow Jesus's example and lead.[6] Empowered by the Spirit, they will reach beyond and through the restored Israel to the world – a servant ministry in which Paul, too, will participate.[7]

Jesus's response here thus reshapes the disciples' assumptions in their question, 'Are you at this time restoring the kingdom to Israel?' (v. 6). There is an eschatological

---

[3] Max Turner, *Power from on High: The Spirit in Israel's Restoration and Witness in Luke-Acts*, JPTSup 9; (Sheffield: Sheffield Academic, 1996), 300-1; David W. Pao, *Acts and the Isaianic New Exodus*, BSL (Grand Rapids, MI: Baker Academic, 2002), 91-6; Peter Mallen, *The Reading and Transformation of Isaiah in Luke-Acts*, LNTS 367 (London: T&T Clark, 2007), 78-84; Thomas S. Moore, "'To the End of the Earth': The Geographic and Ethnic Universalism of Acts 1:8 in Light of Isaianic Influence on Luke," *JETS* 40 (1997): 389-99; D. E. Johnson, "Jesus against the Idols: The Use of Isaianic Servant Songs in the Missiology of Acts," *WTJ* 52 (1990): 343-53, here 346-9.
[4] MT: LXX has 'be [γένεσθε] my witnesses'; cf. also 44:8.
[5] LXX ἕως ἐσχάτου τῆς γῆς, echoed precisely in Acts 1:8.
[6] Luke 2:32; Mallen, *Reading*, 81-2.
[7] Mallen, *Reading*, 84-93.

hope of Israel's restoration, but the restoration's shape will not be Israel *ruling over* the nations, but *incorporation of* the nations into Israel's hope through Israel's Messiah – the restored and reshaped Israel will *serve* the nations as light-bringer, rather than rule them.[8] It is not, however, that the disciples' Spirit-empowered witness 'to the end of the earth' is the substance of the restoration of Israel, but rather that this witness is the means by which the way is prepared for what will become ἀποκαταστάσεως πάντων 'the restoration *of all things*', 3:21).[9] Verse 7 clarifies (in similar vein to 3:20–21) that the timing of this (final) restoration is in the Father's hands. The need for witness 'to the end of the earth' implies that the promised return of Jesus (v. 11) will not be immediate.[10]

By contrast (ἀλλά 'but', v. 8) with the lack of clarity over the timing of restoration, Jesus expresses confidence over what will happen next: the Spirit will come and bring power for witness throughout the world. Luke signals that the purpose of the Spirit's coming (a coming expressed in the subordinate genitive absolute clause ἐπελθόντος τοῦ ἁγίου πνεύματος 'the Holy Spirit having come') is that the disciples will receive power (main clause: λήμψεσθε δύναμιν) for witness. This is the heart of Luke's understanding of the Spirit's role, although it is not the *only* facet of the Spirit's work in Acts.[11]

The disciples' vocation as witnesses flows from the coming of the Spirit: ἔσεσθε is indicative 'you shall be' rather than imperative 'be!'[12] Jesus makes a promise that the disciples shall be witnesses as a result of divine enabling, rather than giving a direct exhortation to witness.[13] For Luke's readers this saying certainly signals that the heartbeat of the believing community is witness to the gospel, and also that with this great responsibility comes the promise of great power by divine enabling: to this extent Jesus's words contain (as Haenchen puts it well) 'at once gift and obligation'.[14]

Luke stresses the boldness of the believers' testimony at a number of points,[15] identifying their boldness as stemming from divine empowerment (Acts 2:4, 14; cf. 8:29; 10:19; 11:12; 13:2, 4; 16:6–7). Thus Peter confidently announces to the Jerusalemites that they were responsible for killing Jesus (2:29) – hardly the way to win friends and influence people. Peter and John speak boldly to the Sanhedrin (4:9–10,

---

[8] Cf. Richard Bauckham, "The Restoration of Israel in Luke-Acts," in *Restoration: Old Testament, Jewish and Christian Perspectives*, ed. James M. Scott, JSJSup 72 (Leiden: Brill, 2001) 435–87, here 477. Anthony Buzzard, "Acts 1:6 and the Eclipse of the Biblical Kingdom," *EvQ* 66 (1994): 197–215, esp. 203–14, rightly highlights that the disciples' question is a natural one, but does not recognize how much the scriptural hope of Israel's restoration is reshaped in Acts.

[9] Bauckham, "Restoration," 476–7; Turner, *Power*, 299–300.

[10] John T. Carroll, *Response to the End of History: Eschatology and Situation in Luke-Acts*, SBLDS 92 (Atlanta, GA: Scholars, 1988), 124 notes that the parallel questions in Luke 19:11 (implied) and 21:7 receive a similar answer which suggests a period of time before the End.

[11] Agreeing with what Menzies affirms (Robert P. Menzies, *Empowered for Witness: The Spirit in Luke-Acts*, JPTSup 6 (Sheffield: Sheffield Academic, 1994)), but rejecting what he denies (with Turner, *Power*, esp. 431–3).

[12] *Contra* Eckhard J. Schnabel, *Early Christian Mission*, 2 vols. (Downers Grove, IL: IVP, 2004), 1:371 n. 240, who treats the future as having 'imperatival meaning'.

[13] See the excellent summary, with references, in Turner, *Power*, 92–103. That the Spirit enables inspired speech is a commonplace in Jewish expectation of this period.

[14] Ernst Haenchen, *The Acts of the Apostles* (Oxford: Blackwell, 1971), 144.

[15] Using παρρησία and παρρησιάζομαι; see Allison A. Trites, *The New Testament Concept of Witness*, SNTSMS 31 (Cambridge: Cambridge University Press, 1977), 151–3.

13). Barnabas and Paul speak boldly in Antioch and Iconium (13:47; 14:3). Paul speaks boldly in the synagogue in Ephesus (19:8), before Agrippa (26:26), and while under house arrest in Rome (28:31).

μου μάρτυρες ('my witnesses') portrays the group both as witnesses who belong to Jesus (and are thus sent and authorized by him) and as witnesses whose testimony concerns Jesus – we need not torture the genitive μου to choose one or other alternative.[16] This phrase suggests that Lesslie Newbigin (in an otherwise helpful article) overstates when he writes, 'It is the Holy Spirit who is the Witness, and the Witness of the Apostles (words and "signs") is subordinate',[17] for *the disciples are the witnesses* – empowered, for sure, by the Spirit. 'Witness' is a judicial term, used metaphorically concerning testimony which these disciples will offer in order to persuade people to come to the right verdict concerning Jesus. The word group is widespread in Acts: the noun μάρτυς 'witness' is found at 1:8, 22; 2:32; 3:15; 5:32; 6:13; 7:58; 10:39, 41; 13:31; 22:15, 20; 26:16; the nouns μαρτυρία and μαρτύριον 'testimony' at 4:33; 7:44; 22:18; the verb μαρτυρέω 'I testify' at 6:3; 10:22, 43; 13:22; 14:3; 15:8; 16:2; 22:5, 12; 23:11; 26:5; and the verb μαρτύρομαι 'I testify' at 20:26; 26:22.[18] There are a number of courtroom or quasi-judicial scenes in Acts where such testimony takes place,[19] but 'witness' terminology is not restricted to these places.[20] This term's use signals Luke's wider purpose of providing apostolic testimony in writing Acts:[21] Luke does not use 'witness' language of the believing community at large, but uses it predominantly as a semi-technical term for ear- and eye-witness testimony to Jesus by people qualified to offer such testimony, principally the apostles (2:32; 3:15; 4:33; 5:32; 10:39, 41; 13:31), but also Paul (13:30; 22:15; 26:16) and Stephen (22:20).[22] Hence, the qualifications for the replacement for Judas include the experience which will allow them to give eyewitness testimony (1:21–22), and the preface to Luke's Gospel signals the importance of eyewitness testimony, clearly referring to the apostolic band (Luke 1:1-4). However, Jesus's commission in Luke 24:44-49 does not distinguish between the apostles and those with them.[23] Further, the group being addressed here in Acts, mentioned rather vaguely in v. 6 as οἱ ... συνελθόντες 'those who had come together', may include the larger group mentioned in vv. 14, 21.[24]

---

[16] Cf. the same *double entendre* in Isa 43:12.
[17] Lesslie Newbigin, "Witness in a Biblical Perspective," *MisSt* 3 (1986): 80–4, here 82, citing Acts 1:6–8; 5:32.
[18] See Trites, *Concept*, 128; Peter Bolt, "Mission and Witness," in *Witness to the Gospel: The Theology of Acts*, ed. I. Howard Marshall and David Peterson (Grand Rapids, MI; Cambridge: Eerdmans, 1998), 191–214, here 192–4 for helpful analysis of this word group.
[19] Acts 4:5–22; 5:27–41; 6:12–7:60; 16:16–40; 17:6–9; 18:12–17; 21:27–26:32; cf. Luke 12:9–12; 21:12–15; see Allison A. Trites, "The Importance of Legal Scenes and Language in the Book of Acts," *NovT* 16 (1974): 278–84; Johnson, "Jesus," 347–8.
[20] Trites, *Concept*, ch. 9.
[21] Cf. Trites, *Concept*, 140.
[22] Bolt, "Witness," esp. 196–210.
[23] αὐτῶν (second use), αὐτοῖς and αὐτούς 'them' in vv. 36, 44 include 'the eleven and their companions' and the two who walked to Emmaus, v. 33; see John Nolland, *Luke*, WBC 35A-C, 3 vols. (Dallas, TX: Word, 1989–93), 3:1220.
[24] Haenchen, *Acts*, 142–3; *contra* Nelson P. Estrada, *From Followers to Leaders: The Apostles in the Ritual of Status Transformation in Acts 1-2*, JSNTSup 255 (London: T&T Clark, 2004), 47, who

Trites helpfully identifies that their testimony in Acts concerns Jesus in at least three senses.[25] They witness to: (i) the facts of Jesus's ministry (1:21-22; 2:22-24; 10:36-42); (ii) Jesus's character of holiness and righteousness which gave rise to his deeds of power and healing (3:14; 10:38); (iii) the Christian faith, in the sense that their testimony calls for a verdict of repentance and trust in Jesus (2:38; 3:22-23; 10:43). Their witness to Jesus is also interpreted in Acts as witness to the kingdom of God (28:23) in continuity with the Gospel (cf. 1:3).[26] However they do not 'take on Jesus's mantle' in the way that Elisha did after Elijah – the apostles are Jesus's witnesses, not his successors.[27]

The testimony will spread in a series of growing circles which are widely understood to signal the structure of Acts.[28] First, they will testify in Jerusalem (chs 1-7); then persecution will drive them into Judaea and Samaria (ch. 8), before the call of the key witness who will go to the end of the earth, Saul (ch. 9), and the beginnings of including gentiles (10:1-11:18).[29] However, Acts does not follow such a structure tidily, since it returns on several occasions to Jerusalem (9:26-30; 11:2-18; 15:4-29; 19:21; 21:15-23:24). This statement, rather, reorders the disciples' perception of space,[30] for the land of Israel – and Jerusalem, and its temple in particular – is no longer central to God's ordering of the world: instead, the whole of the inhabited world becomes 'sacred space', for God meets people in the whole world, and Jesus sends his disciples into the whole world.

In sum, this verse clarifies the nature of the restoration of Israel which the disciples ask about (v. 6) by highlighting two features: the restoration will be empowered by the Holy Spirit who will shortly come upon the disciples; and the route to the final restoration of all things will be the Spirit-empowered witness of the disciples. For Luke's readers, there is an implicit call to participate in this task, but (to repeat) there is no call to 'go' or sending vocabulary here. Luke's Jesus simply identifies that the disciples will be witnesses to, for and of Jesus. Thus our central question, about the nature of the early believers' *mission* in the sphere of earthly power, can now be rephrased and clarified as a question about the nature of their *witness* in this sphere.

I.b. Luke's 'Mission' Vocabulary

All that said, Luke does speak of people as 'sent', and he includes commands to 'go' and to 'speak' at a number of places. Let us explore how those terms contribute to our study.

---

maintains that Acts 1 has an exclusive focus on the apostles. For fuller critique of Bolt's view, see Mallen, *Reading*, 191-3.

[25] Trites, *Concept*, 144.
[26] Augustín del Agua, "The Evangelization of the Kingdom of God," in *The Unity of Luke-Acts*, ed. J. Verheyden, BETL 142 (Leuven: Peeters, 1999), 639-61, here 655.
[27] *Contra* Estrada, *Followers*, 96.
[28] E.g. Conzelmann, *Acts*, 7; James D. G. Dunn, *Beginning from Jerusalem* (Grand Rapids, MI; Cambridge: Eerdmans, 2009), 145.
[29] It is noticeable that it is not those present who mainly accomplish the later parts of the mission, to gentiles (Giancarlo Biguzzi, "Witnessing Two by Two in the Acts of the Apostles," *Bib* 92 (2011): 1-20, here 3-6).
[30] Matthew Sleeman, *Geography and the Ascension Narrative in Acts*, SNTSMS 146 (Cambridge: Cambridge University Press, 2009), 70-2.

The theme of being 'sent' is fairly common in Luke-Acts.[31] Frequently, *God* is the sender, whether of angels (Luke 1:19, 26; Acts 12:11), Jesus himself (Luke 4:18 [quoting Isa 61:1–2], 43; 9:48; 10:16; Acts 3:26[32]), John the baptizer (Luke 7:27, echoing Mal 3:1), or biblical prophets and Moses (Luke 4:26; 13:34; Acts 7:34, 35[33]). In Luke's Gospel, *Jesus* sends disciples, in the missions of the twelve (9:2), those going ahead of him as he travelled to Jerusalem (9:52), and the seventy (10:1–3). *Jesus, God or the Spirit* sends in Acts: the exalted Jesus sends Ananias to Saul (9:17); Cornelius's messengers are sent by God at the angel's instigation (10:8, 17, 20, 22, 29, 32, 33; 11:13); Barnabas and Saul are sent out by the Spirit (13:4); Paul is sent by Jesus to Jews and gentiles (22:21; 26:17, both in accounts of his Damascus road experience); and the gospel message itself can be described as 'sent' by God (10:36; 13:26). In addition, Jesus sends the Spirit on the disciples to empower them for the task of witness (Luke 24:48–49), and Jesus himself will be sent at his return (Acts 3:20).

In addition, Luke's Gospel contains commands to 'go', notably in the mission of the seventy (Luke 10:3). In Acts, Philip is told to 'go' to a place where he meets the Ethiopian eunuch (Acts 8:26,[34] 29), and Peter is told to 'go down' to Cornelius's messengers (10:20) – both are rather specific commands, as opposed to general calls to 'go'. Paul is told to keep speaking for Jesus (18:9), and Paul's re-tellings of the Damascus road story include clear statements that Paul has an assigned task (22:10, 21; 26:16). Paul's task of testimony[35] must be carried out in both Jerusalem and Rome, the Lord assures him (23:11).

Luke's use of 'sending' and 'go' language provides evidence that the mission of testimony is both initiated and empowered by God, Jesus and the Spirit; it is not a human initiative – rather, as I have argued elsewhere, the believers are frequently playing catch-up with the divine driver who expands the mission beyond the circles and circumstances in which the believers are comfortable.[36]

I.c. Summary

Let us draw breath and review the point we have reached. The 'mission' in Acts is a divine mission, which will ultimately result in the restoration of all things. It is a mission which will ultimately go to 'the end of the earth' (Acts 1:8), a phrase which echoes Isaiah 49:6 and Jesus's statement that the disciples will go to 'all nations' (πάντα τὰ ἔθνη, Luke 24:47), and signals the universality of the mission.[37] Such a claim is

---

[31] The key terms used are πέμπω and compounds, ἀποστέλλω, ἐξαποστέλλω, ἀπολύω.
[32] And, implicitly, in the parable of the wicked tenants, where Jesus is the son (Luke 20:9–19).
[33] Cf. again the parable of the wicked tenants, where the servants are surely the prophets (Luke 20:9–19).
[34] Luke echoes the imperatives ἀνάστηθι καὶ πορεύου 'get up and go' (8:26) precisely in Philip's ready obedience: καὶ ἀναστὰς ἐπορεύθη 'he got up and went' (v. 27).
[35] Using διαμαρτύρομαι, a 'witness' verb, which incidentally shows that it is not only the eyewitnesses who can testify to Jesus.
[36] See Steve Walton, "The Acts – of God? What is the 'Acts of the Apostles' All About?," *EvQ* 80 (2008): 291–306 [in this volume, 15–30]; Steve Walton, "Acts, Book of," in *Dictionary for Theological Interpretation of the Bible*, ed. Kevin J. Vanhoozer, Craig G. Bartholomew, Daniel J. Treier and N. T. Wright (London: SPCK; Grand Rapids, MI: Baker Academic, 2005), 27–31.
[37] See helpful summary of discussion of this phrase in Schnabel, *Mission*, 1:372.

implicitly critical of the claims of the Roman empire to govern the world, exemplified in Augustus's claim that he had subjected 'the whole world' (*orbem terrarum*) to the Romans (Preface, *Res. gest. divi Aug.*), or Ovid's statement, 'The land of other nations has a fixed boundary: the circuit of Rome is the circuit of the world' (*Fasti* 2.684 [Goold, LCL]).[38] What form did the testimony take, then, when it encountered the 'powers that be', whether Roman or other 'powers' subordinate to Rome, such as the Jewish authorities or local officials in cities around the empire? To this question we turn.

II. The 'Powers That Be' in Acts

To speak of the 'powers that be' is to throw together into a bucket category a variety of different 'powers', and so it is worthwhile first to distinguish these different authorities and their different realms and ranges of authority.[39]

II.a. The Roman Empire

At the top of the pile in the first century AD was Rome, focused in the emperor.[40] He, in conjunction with the Imperial Senate, led the Roman empire, which dominated its territory. In the first century the empire was divided into provinces, some under direct imperial authority and some under senatorial control. In charge of each province was a governor, normally of senatorial rank, supported by a (usually very small) staff under his immediate control. Only in frontier or troublesome provinces, such as Judaea, were significant numbers of Roman troops present, in order to preserve Roman control and political stability. A key member of the governor's staff was the procurator, whose duties could include the collection of taxes, as well as looking after the emperor's interests.[41]

---

[38] Cf. Acts 10:36; Steve Walton, "The State They Were In: Luke's View of the Roman Empire," in *Rome in the Bible and the Early Church*, ed. Peter Oakes (Carlisle: Paternoster; Grand Rapids, MI: Baker Academic, 2002), 1–41, here 26–8; James S. Romm, *The Edges of the Earth in Ancient Thought: Geography, Exploration, and Fiction* (Princeton, NJ: Princeton University Press, 1992), 121–7.

[39] Cf. the helpful overview of trials and authorities in the ancient world in Matthew L. Skinner, *The Trial Narratives: Conflict, Power, and Identity in the New Testament* (Louisville, KY: Westminster John Knox, 2010), 13–32.

[40] For fuller accounts of Roman administration, see the following: Joyce Reynolds, "Cities," in *The Administration of the Roman Empire 241 BC-AD 193*, ed. David C. Braund, Exeter Studies in History 18 (Exeter: University of Exeter, 1988) 15–51; Fergus Millar, *The Roman Empire and its Neighbours*, 2nd ed. (London: Duckworth, 1981); David W. J. Gill, "The Roman Empire as a Context for the New Testament," in *Handbook to Exegesis of the New Testament*, ed. Stanley E. Porter, NTTS 25 (Leiden: Brill, 1997) 389–406; David W. J. Gill Conrad H. Gempf (eds), *The Book of Acts in its Graeco-Roman Setting*, BAFCS 2 (Carlisle: Paternoster; Grand Rapids, MI: Eerdmans, 1994); Andrew Lintott, *Imperium Romanum: Politics and Administration* (London/New York: Routledge, 1993), esp. chs. 3–4, 8; A. H. M. Jones, *The Greek City from Alexander to Justinian* (Oxford: Clarendon, 1940), esp. chs IV, VIII, XI; Anthony D. Macro, "The Cities of Asia Minor under the Roman Imperium," *ANRW* 7.2:658–97. Helpful collections of sources in English translation can be found in: W. K. Lacey and B. W. J. G. Wilson, *Res Publica: Roman Politics and Society according to Cicero* (London: Oxford University Press, 1970); Jo-Ann Shelton, *As the Romans Did: A Sourcebook in Roman Social History*, 2nd ed. (Oxford: Oxford University Press, 1998), esp. sections X, XII.

[41] Judaea and Egypt were exceptions to this structure in NT times, not having their own governor, but rather a procurator or prefect of equestrian rank: Emil Schürer, Geza Vermes and Fergus Millar,

Within a province there would be a number of communities with 'city' (πόλις) status, and the nature of this status could vary considerably from one community to another.[42] Among its inhabitants, some were citizens of the city, and a smaller group (often much smaller) were Roman citizens. Philippi, Corinth and Pisidian Antioch were Roman colonies, all of whose citizens were Roman citizens – many were former soldiers granted citizenship on their retirement from the army.[43] Athens, by contrast, retained the feel of a Greek city with the Areopagus as its ruling council.[44] In this case, the Romans had taken an established Greek city and permitted its own civic structures to continue, but now overseen by the governor of the province of Achaia and his staff. As long as the city ran smoothly and peacefully, and Roman taxes were paid promptly, the governor would not be likely to interfere.

Typically a πόλις in the eastern empire would consist of an urban centre which controlled a surrounding territory, usually containing villages under the centre's jurisdiction – thus, to think of a modern 'city' does not give quite the right picture. When the emperor granted the status of πόλις to an existing place, he would allow the people to appoint (or, in the case of an established city, to continue to appoint) a council (βουλή) which could pass local laws, and to elect their own magistrates annually,[45] who dispensed justice in many matters and had their own subordinate officials.[46] Cities usually had a citizen assembly (ἐκκλησία), but under the Romans it was increasingly subject to the council, which tended to consist of members of the wealthy social élite.[47] Magistrates were frequently appointed from the council members, and on appointment were required to contribute financially to the city's affairs,[48] further limiting those who could afford to be candidates for office.

The powers of these local magistrates, councils and assemblies were circumscribed by those of the governor. Hence the Ephesian town clerk warns the citizens that the city is in danger of being charged with rioting (Acts 19:40), which could lead to the governor disbanding the citizen-assembly, punishing city officials or taking away privileges already granted to the city.[49]

The History of the Jewish People in the Age of Jesus Christ (175 BC-AD 135), revised ed., 4 vols. (Edinburgh: T&T Clark, 1973–86), 1:358.

[42] See Reynolds, "Cities," 23 for a helpful taxonomy.

[43] David W. J. Gill, "Macedonia," in *The Book of Acts in its Graeco-Roman Setting*, ed. David W. J. Gill and Conrad H. Gempf, BAFCS 2 (Carlisle: Paternoster; Grand Rapids, MI: Eerdmans, 1994), 397–417, here 411–13.

[44] Gill, "Achaia," 433–53, here 441–3, 447.

[45] Luke gets the designation and jurisdiction of these officials right in place after place; see Colin J. Hemer, *The Book of Acts in the Setting of Hellenistic History*, WUNT 49 (Tübingen: J. C. B. Mohr [Paul Siebeck], 1989), 115 (on 16:22), 119 (on 17:34), 121 (on 19:31), 122 (on 19:35), 123 (on 19:38), 153 with n 152 (on 28:7).

[46] Cicero, *Att.* VI.1.15 (written c. 50 BC) says that he allowed Greeks to try cases between provincials under their own laws. Methods of election varied considerably across the empire: Reynolds, "Cities," 26–7.

[47] Millar, *Empire*, 87.

[48] Reynolds, "Cities," 36.

[49] Paul R. Trebilco, "Asia" in *The Book of Acts in its Graeco-Roman Setting*, ed. David W. J. Gill and Conrad H. Gempf, BAFCS 2 (Carlisle: Paternoster; Grand Rapids, MI: Eerdmans, 1994), 291–362, here 344–5 (where examples are given).

More specifically, cases which could result in death or exile were reserved for the governor's judgement, as well as cases involving Roman citizens,[50] and some cases involving commercial questions or public order.[51] The governor would travel annually to various cities within his province to try such cases, and others which the local magistrates could not resolve.[52] In Achaia, Luke records Gallio hearing the Jews' case against Paul in Corinth, the governor's seat (Acts 18:12–17).[53] In Judaea, this comports well with John's assertion that the Jews were not allowed to 'put anyone to death' (John 18:31).[54]

It is within this setting that the Acts accounts of encounter between the Christians and the 'powers that be' should be seen. This limits the number of *direct* contacts between the Christians and the Roman empire.[55] Specifically, Paul encounters the proconsuls Sergius Paulus in Cyprus (13:4–12) and Gallio in Corinth (18:12–17), the tribune Claudius Lysias in Jerusalem (22:26–30; 23:16–30), the governors Felix (23:33–24:26) and Festus (24:27–25:12).

In terms of more local officials, we also encounter the magistrates in Philippi (16:16–40), the politarchs in Thessalonica (17:1–15), the Areopagus in Athens (17:16–34),[56] the Asiarchs and the town clerk in Ephesus (19:23–41),[57] the client king Agrippa in Caesarea (25:13–26:32), and the first man of the island in Malta (28:7).

II.b. Judaea

A particular question is the role of the Sanhedrin in Judaea, presented in the NT as 'the Jewish supreme court of justice'.[58] The believers have several encounters with this body in Acts (4:5–22; 5:17–41; 6:12–7:60; 22:30–23:10; 24:20), and its powers seem to have been considerable, although in the first century it was not allowed to administer the death penalty (John 18:31; cf. Josephus, *J.W.* 2.17.1 §405; *y. Sanh.* 18a, 24b; *b. Sanh.*

---

[50] Macro, "Cities," 671. Hence the Philippian magistrates are taken aback when they realize they have beaten Roman citizens, thus acting in a case over which they have no jurisdiction (Acts 16:37–39).
[51] Bruce W. Winter, *Seek the Welfare of the City: Christians as Benefactors and Citizens* (Carlisle: Paternoster; Grand Rapids, MI: Eerdmans, 1994), 107–8.
[52] See G. P. Burton, "Proconsuls, Assizes and the Administration of Justice under the Empire," *JRS* 65 (1975): 92–106, for a careful description of the system of travelling assizes.
[53] Most governors had at least one legal advisor among their personal staff (cf. Acts 25:12), whereas Gallio, a noted jurist, gives his own judgement without consulting advisors.
[54] Supported by Josephus, *J.W.* 2.8.1 §117. See discussion (and further references) in George R. Beasley-Murray, *John*, WBC 36 (Dallas, TX: Word, 1987), 308–10; D. A. Carson, *The Gospel according to John* (Leicester: Inter-Varsity Press; Grand Rapids, MI: Eerdmans, 1991), 590–2.
[55] See the study of the three most direct Pauline encounters with imperial representatives, Steve Walton, "Trying Paul or Trying Rome? Judges and Accused in the Roman Trials of Paul in Acts," in *Luke-Acts and Empire: Essays in Honor of Robert L. Brawley*, ed. David Rhoads, David Esterline and Jae Won Lee, Princeton Theological Monographs 151 (Eugene, OR: Pickwick, 2011), 122–41 [in this volume, 107–21].
[56] See Bruce W. Winter, "On Introducing Gods to Athens: An Alternative Reading of Acts 17:18-20," *TynBul* 47 (1996): 71–90, esp. 75–80, for the role of the Areopagus.
[57] As well as the off-stage proconsuls, v. 38.
[58] Schürer, Vermes and Millar, *History*, 2:206; Graham H. Twelftree, "Sanhedrin" in *DNTB*, 1061–5, here 1063. See Schürer, Vermes and Millar, *History*, 2:199–226 and Twelftree, "Sanhedrin" for the debate over the nature of the Sanhedrin(s) and its (their) authority.

41a).⁵⁹ The high priest presided over its meetings and, under the Romans, this body seems to have had considerable powers over Judaea, but not other provinces within Palestine (and this may explain why they did not act against Jesus until he came to Judaea⁶⁰). However, Luke presents the high priest as having sufficient authority (perhaps moral rather than judicial) to write letters authorizing Saul to arrest believers in Damascus (Acts 9:1-2). Thus the appearances of believers before the Sanhedrin were significant occasions on which the Jewish judiciary sought to quash the Jesus movement in its infancy, as they had sought to suppress Jesus himself.

II.c. Political or Religious?

A key point to recognize is that in all of these levels of power within the Roman empire, the two categories which we today distinguish, religion and politics, were inextricably intertwined.

Roman officials regularly functioned as priests, offering sacrifice to the gods in order to seek their favour. What westerners today would consider 'political' decisions were taken in the light of auguries, haruspicy, necromancy and omens. Leaders were expected – nay required – not only to participate in cultic activities, including imperial cultic activities, but also to preside over them.⁶¹

In a different way, the same was true of the Jewish Sanhedrin. All of its members were significant people within Judaism and their decision-making was governed by the legal framework provided by Scripture and 'religious' oral tradition.

This means that to try to distinguish and separate 'political' and 'religious' authorities and spheres in the ancient world is to make a category error. The ancient world had them joined inextricably together, and we should not seek to put them asunder. Peter Oakes provides a helpful example in considering a (reconstructed) family who were bakers in Philippi.⁶² Half their bread is sold to three well-off families from the social élite as a regular order; the rest is sold from their shop. Simias, the father of the family, is a member of a burial club which provides for its members to have a good burial,

---

⁵⁹ The murder of Stephen in what appears to be a Sanhedrin meeting looks more like a lynching than a judicial execution (Acts 7:54-60). The inscriptions in Latin and Greek in the Jerusalem temple at the edge of the Court of the Women that any gentile who crossed that line was liable to be killed looks, similarly, like a warning against mob action (CIJ 1400 n 85; cf. Josephus, J.W. 5.5.2 §§193-94).

⁶⁰ Twelftree, "Sanhedrin," 1064.

⁶¹ E.g. Duncan Fishwick, *The Imperial Cult in the Latin West, vol. 3, part 3: Provincial Cult*, RGRW 147 (Leiden: Brill, 2004), 360 notes three elements in imperial religion: 'dedications to the gods on behalf of the emperor's *salus*, sacrifice to the gods performed by the emperor himself, rites to the emperor modelled on the cult of the gods.' Bruce W. Winter, *Divine Honours for the Caesars: The First Christians' Challenge* (Grand Rapids, MI: Eerdmans, 2015), ch. 3) exemplifies these three elements in one inscription from Sardis, *IGR* IV 1756 lines 6-21; I am grateful to Dr Winter for sharing this material and references with me. Mary Beard, John A. North and Simon R. F. Price, *Religions of Rome*, 2 vols. (Cambridge: Cambridge University Press, 1998) document priesthoods and offices as augur held by emperors and senators, including the emperor's role as *pontifex maximus*, intermediary between the people and the gods (1:186-96), and the roles of priestly figures who were magistrates in haruspicy (interpreting prodigies) and augury (establishing the gods' will through various techniques) (1:19-24).

⁶² Peter Oakes, *Philippians: From People to Letter*, SNTSMS 110 (Cambridge: Cambridge University Press, 2000), 89-93.

paid for by a regular subscription. At club meetings, Simias meets other bakers and these contacts are very helpful if they get a big order and he suddenly needs extra oven space. The burial club meets for meals on the anniversaries of the death of former members, and eats together at the former member's tomb and prays to the gods for their dead friend. What would it mean for such a family to become Jesus-believers? Simias would either withdraw from the burial club or miss meetings on anniversaries of death, since he would no longer be willing to participate in prayer to the gods. This would damage his friendship with others in the club, and that alone might lead to some of his regular customers withdrawing their trade and buying their bread elsewhere. It would also mean that fellow-bakers refused to help him when he needed extra oven space for a big order, so he would lose trade. Problems would arise at the shop, too. Simias and Ianthe, his wife, would remove the shrine of the god popular among bakers from the counter of their baker's shop, and this would rapidly be noticed by their customers and people would mutter that they were dishonouring the gods. The effect would be that people would assume the baker's family were now being disloyal to the city of Philippi – for they were disloyal to a town god – and thus people would stop buying bread in their shop, probably including at least one of the three élite families who are their biggest customers. In addition, their regular supplier of flour would stop supplying them so that they had to buy from another supplier at about 10% extra cost. Oakes's example is more extended, but this gives you the picture that for this family to become Jesus-believers would be costly, both economically and socially, precisely because the 'religious' and 'political' spheres were so intertwined in a city like Philippi.

III. The Believers Encountering the 'Powers That Be'

We turn, then, to sample encounters between the believers and the authorities. After noting Lukan promises of help by the Spirit or Jesus when the disciples encounter the powers, we shall briefly consider key features of engagement with Jewish authorities (Peter and John before the Sanhedrin), city authorities (Paul before the Areopagus and in Philippi), and imperial representatives (Paul before Felix), before drawing together some key features which emerge from these stories.

III.a. The Promises of Jesus in Luke's Gospel[63]

Luke's Jesus twice promises his disciples help when they are in front of the powers, in Luke 12:12 and 21:15.

Luke 12:12 appears in teaching about the importance of public confession of Jesus (12:8–10) and particularly in the context of trials before the authorities (12:11a). This teaching is addressed in the first instance to his disciples (12:1a) with the crowd

---

[63] See fuller discussion of these promises in Steve Walton, "Whose Spirit? The Promise and the Promiser in Luke 12:12," in *The Spirit and Christ in the New Testament in Christian Theology*, ed. I. Howard Marshall, Volker Rabens and Cornelis Bennema, FS Max Turner (Grand Rapids, MI: Eerdmans, 2012), 35–51.

overhearing (12:1b). In that setting, Jesus assures his disciples that the Spirit will teach them what to say (12:12) and thus that they need not worry in advance about how to defend themselves (12:11b).

There are parallels to Luke 12:12 in the other synoptic Gospels (Matt 10:19–20; Mark 13:11) and Luke himself has an interesting parallel (21:12–15; cf. Matt 24:9–13). There are clear similarities and differences among these four passages: (i) all are placed in a context of trial, although there is considerable variation in the specified authorities; (ii) structurally, Luke 12, Matthew 10 and Mark 13 begin with a generalizing ὅταν ('whenever') clause, whereas Luke 21 does not, for this seems to refer to a *specific* time of trials; (iii) Jesus calls his disciples not to worry (μὴ μεριμνήσητε/προμεριμνᾶτε) in advance in Luke 12, Mark 13 and Matthew 10, whereas Luke 21 simply specifies that the disciples must not prepare (μὴ προμελετᾶν) in advance; (iv) Luke 12, Matthew 10 and Mark 13 mention the Spirit as the one who will give the disciples words to say (although Matthew alone specifies that it is the Father's Spirit), whereas Luke 21 says that Jesus himself will give them words to speak; (v) Luke alone (in 12:11 and 21:14) uses the language of 'defence' (ἀπολογέομαι), a word found only in these passages in Luke and only here in the Gospels, although it is also used in Acts in forensic contexts.[64]

The Lukan promises are specific to the situation of judicial trial before authorities (Luke 12:11; 21:12), and thus stand alone among the promises of the Spirit to the disciples in the synoptic Gospels in being situation-specific. Other Spirit-promises (granted that there are not many) are more general, concerning the role of the Spirit in equipping the disciples as witnesses to Jesus (notably Luke 24:49). Jesus's assurance of the Spirit's help in judicial trials prepares for the trials of believers in Acts, where Luke draws attention to the Spirit filling Peter and John when they respond to the charges against them in the Sanhedrin (Acts 4:8), and also Stephen on trial (Acts 7:51, 55; cf. 6:9–10).[65]

The parallel promises in Luke 12:12 and 21:14–15 are suggestive, too, for the relationship of Jesus and the Spirit. Both relate the promise of aid during trials to the instruction not to prepare a defence in advance, both use the rare ἀπολογέομαι ('I defend'), and both explain the basis of this statement with a γάρ ('for') clause. However, the one providing the aid in 12:12 is the Spirit, whereas in 21:15 it is Jesus himself (emphatic ἐγώ, 'I myself'). This theme develops and expands in Acts, for while often it is the Spirit who empowers and leads the disciples in witness (Acts 4:8–12; 6:10; 8:29; 10:19; 13:2–4), sometimes it is Jesus (Acts 7:55–56; 9:4–5, 10–16; 18:9–10; 22:7–10,

---

[64] Acts 19:33; 24:10; 25:8; 26:1–2, 24; the only other NT uses are Rom 2:15; 2 Cor 12:19.
[65] Both Joseph B. Fitzmyer, *Luke*, AB 28A–B, 2 vols. (Garden City, NY: Doubleday, [1981] 1985), 2:966 and Darrell L. Bock, *Luke*, IVPNTC (Downers Grove, IL: InterVarsity Press; Leicester: Inter-Varsity Press, 1994), 2:1144 draw attention to the immediacy of the promise (ἐν αὐτῇ τῇ ὥρᾳ 'in that very hour', v. 12) and compare Philo's retelling of the angel's instruction to Balaam: 'Pursue your journey. Your hurrying will avail you nought. I shall prompt the needful words without your mind's consent, and direct your organs of speech as justice and convenience require. I shall guide the reins of speech, and, though you understand it not, employ your tongue for each prophetic utterance' (*Moses* 1:274 [Colson, LCL]). Philo goes on to tell how 'the prophetic spirit entered' Balaam (προφητικοῦ πνεύματος ἐπιφοιτήσαντος, 1:277) with the result that he prophesied (θεσπίζει, 1:278). However, this is not strictly parallel, since it is about prophetic inspiration, rather than inspiration when on trial.

17–21; 23:11; 26:14–18).⁶⁶ It is thus hard to agree with Green, if his implication is that it is *exclusively* by the Spirit that Jesus will be present to his disciples, when he writes:

> Jesus thus portends his continual presence with the disciples even as they face the tribunal, following his death; only with the onset of Acts we understand fully that he will be present to the community of his followers by means of the Holy Spirit poured out among them.⁶⁷

Buckwalter points to an interesting parallel: in the OT, action by YHWH from heaven is described in similar terms to action by the Spirit, and YHWH is not limited to appearing on earth *as or by* the Spirit; in Luke-Acts, action by *the exalted Jesus* from heaven is described in similar terms to action by the Spirit, and again, Jesus is not limited to appearing on earth *as or by* the Spirit.⁶⁸ It is thus plausible that the parallel actions of Jesus and the Spirit in empowering and enabling speech when the disciples are on trial (in Luke 12 and 21) entail a relationship of Jesus in relation to the Spirit which is similar to that of YHWH and the Spirit.⁶⁹ Not only that, but the ability of the exalted Jesus to be present with disciples in different times and places when they are on trial shows Jesus (and the Spirit) to have the same multi-locational ability as YHWH.⁷⁰

III.b. Peter and John before the Jewish Authorities (Acts 4:5–22)

Peter and John appear before the Sanhedrin in Acts 4:5–22 as a result of the healing of the man at the Beautiful Gate (3:1–10). The question put to them is, 'By what power or by what name did you do this?' Luke then records the Spirit's enabling to do this before they respond (v. 8). The Sanhedrin's question both invites and enables them to focus on witness directly about Jesus in their response. They address the Sanhedrin respectfully, as 'Rulers of the people and elders',⁷¹ and then assert that it is through Jesus that the man has been healed. Not only that, but they boldly identify the Sanhedrin's part in Jesus's death, 'whom *you* (emphatic ὑμεῖς) crucified'. Jack T. Sanders mistakenly understands this as placing responsibility for Jesus's death on the Jewish people as a whole,⁷² whereas vv. 5–6 make it clear that it is the Jewish leaders in Jerusalem who are in view here.⁷³ The greatness of their error is highlighted by the contrasting divine verdict: God raised Jesus from the dead. Peter calls on Ps 117:21 LXX (MT 118:22) as

---

⁶⁶ See discussion, Douglas Buckwalter, *The Character and Purpose of Luke's Christology*, SNTSMS 89 (Cambridge: Cambridge University Press, 1996), 197–204.
⁶⁷ Joel B. Green, *The Gospel of Luke*, NICNT (Grand Rapids, MI/Cambridge: Eerdmans, 1997), 737.
⁶⁸ Buckwalter, *Character*, ch. 8.
⁶⁹ Buckwalter, *Character*, 203–4.
⁷⁰ Robert H. Stein, *Luke*, NAC 24 (Nashville, TN: Broadman, 1992), 518–19. He goes on to suggest that we should therefore 'describe Jesus as possessing an *essence* different from others' (519, his italics).
⁷¹ This phrase functions as a *captatio benvolentiae*, and is respectful without being fawning (Marion L. Soards, *The Speeches in Acts: Their Content, Context, and Concerns* (Louisville, KY: Westminster John Knox, 1994), 45)
⁷² Jack T. Sanders, *The Jews in Luke-Acts* (London: SCM, 1987), 238–9.
⁷³ With Jon A. Weatherly, *Jewish Responsibility for the Death of Jesus in Luke-Acts*, JSNTSup 106 (Sheffield: Sheffield Academic, 1994), 69; Skinner, *Trial*, 111.

witness to the crucial place which Jesus now has, as 'head of the corner', after being rejected by '*you* builders' – the insertion of ὑμῶν into the biblical citation hammers the contrast of verdicts home.

The evident boldness of Peter and John causes comment (v. 13), and clearly comes from their sense of compulsion to speak (v. 20). Verse 29 will further clarify that such boldness is a divine gift flowing from being filled with the Spirit (v. 31). This boldness stops the Sanhedrin in its tracks, and they go into private session to decide what to do. Their discussion is striking for its lack of mention or consideration of God and God's purposes, by contrast with the bold speech of Peter and John. They cannot even bring themselves to mention the name of Jesus: they use 'that name' (v. 18) instead.

By contrast with the Sanhedrin's failure to speak about God, Peter and John identify the issue as being what God wants (v. 19). Thus the apostles turn the tables on the Sanhedrin by speaking truth to power: they have Peter and John on trial, but the apostolic κρίνατε ('you judge!') puts the Sanhedrin on trial concerning their assessment of Jesus. The issue is not just their assessment of Jesus, but also their impotence in the face of what God is now doing: they lack any legal ground to punish the apostles and their verdict is at variance with the people's (v. 21). The apostles are those who speak for God, rather than the Sanhedrin. Haenchen rightly notes that Luke wishes to bring

> home to the reader the justice and obligation of preaching Christ, and showing from the example of the apostles ... how the Christian, certain of divine assistance, should fearlessly bear witness for his Lord, unquelled by police, arrest or official interdict.[74]

III.c. Philippi: Engagement with Local Magistrates (Acts 16:16–40)

By contrast with the plain speaking of Peter and John in Jerusalem, Paul and Silas are silent in what passes for a trial in Philippi. Here, they are attacked because of the economic consequences of Paul's deliverance of the slave girl who has a 'python spirit' (Acts 16:16–19). The owners of the slave girl have lost their source of income because she can no longer do divination for fees, and their (carefully chosen) claim against Paul and Silas is that they are advocating Jewish customs which Roman law prohibits (vv. 20–21). In the midst of what seems to be a disorderly crowd situation (v. 22a), Luke does not record any speech by Paul and Silas – after addressing the spirit to deliver the girl (v. 18), their next words in the story are to sing hymns to God (v. 25), not to address any human audience. After they receive a flogging, Paul and Silas are put in the innermost part of the prison (v. 24), presumably for security. However, God acts in an earthquake which opens the doors, and we next hear Paul and Silas speak in response to the jailer's question, 'What must I do to be saved?', in response to which they lead him to faith in Jesus and baptize him and his household.

Verse 40 suggests that Paul and Silas return to prison after eating at the jailer's home; it is there, on the next morning, that the magistrates (οἱ στρατηγοί) seek to

---

[74] Haenchen, *Acts*, 223–4.

have them leave quietly. They send the lictors (ῥαβδοῦχος, v. 35) as messengers, and the jailer relays the message to them (v. 36). It is at this point that Paul engages the magistrates, and sends a message back to them to the effect that they have acted unlawfully in beating Roman citizens without proper trial and imprisoning them, and that he is not now willing to leave quietly (v. 38). What is going on here? Why does Paul now seem to stand on his dignity, rather than earlier in this story? It may be partly that the earlier 'trial' moved so speedily that it was not possible to object, but it is more significant that it is only following the earthquake that the magistrates decide to free Paul and Silas, and their desire to send them away quietly is designed to avoid the embarrassment of admitting that divine action by Paul and Silas's god had persuaded them that they should release the two men – at this point, they do not know that Paul and Silas are Roman citizens. Thus Paul wants to insist that the earthquake demonstrated that God has vindicated him and Silas against the city authorities, and plays the card of Roman citizenship to force the authorities to come and apologize. Here is speaking truth to power which is double-edged. There is a delicious irony in this about-turn, for the charge against Paul and Silas was anti-Roman behaviour (vv. 20–21) and the authorities have to apologize for *their* anti-Roman behaviour (vv. 38–39).

Paul and Silas thus insist on the claims of God and the name of Jesus not being marginalized by the city authorities; these believers are prepared to require the authorities to act justly, and this should be seen as really a part of Paul and Silas's testimony to Jesus as Paul's deliverance of the slave girl 'in the name of Jesus the Messiah' (v. 18).

III.d. Athens: Paul before the Areopagus (Acts 17:16–34)

The Areopagus's powers in Athens as the 'standing committee' of the citizen assembly (the *Demos*) were considerable and included jurisdiction over the introduction of new gods into the city and therefore over the construction of new temples. In an important article, Bruce Winter argues that this power is a key context for Paul's speech to the council.[75] Paul, Winter argues, would have been perceived as seeking to introduce new gods into the city: 'He seems to be a proclaimer of foreign deities' (Acts 17:18), and it may be that he was seen as proclaiming Jesus and Anastasis as two gods. The Athenians took Paul to the Areopagus, and the council there stated that they had the legal right (δυνάμεθα = 'we have the power') to decide (γνῶναι = 'to form a judgement') (v. 19). They go on in v. 20 to say that they wish to make a judgement on what is being claimed by Paul. This is a polite enquiry, not a prosecution.[76] The council is concerned whether Paul's new gods could be acceptable to join the Athenian pantheon. Were the Areopagus to accept Paul's gods – or recommend to the *Demos* that they do so – Paul would be expected to purchase

---

[75] Winter, "Gods," citing R. Garland, *Introducing New Gods: The Politics of Athenia Religion* (London: Duckworth, 1992).
[76] Winter, "Gods," 83.

land, built a sacrificial altar, defray the costs at least of an annual dinner in the god's honour, and probably also of cultic officials.

Paul's Athens speech takes on a new light in responding to their question understood this way, for he declares that he is not introducing new gods, but one they already worship, albeit as 'unknown' (v. 23). There was no requirement to acquire land for this god, for Israel's God was the creator of all land (v. 24a) – indeed, this god did not live in hand-made temples (v. 24b), and so it was pointless to consider building a new temple for him. Paul thus undercuts the assumptions of the council, and denies that there is any need for further evidence for them to honour this god among their pantheon, for this god provides for all and does not need human attendants (v. 25). The quest for more gods to add to the statues in Athens was a mistake (v. 29).

Paul turns the tables on his interlocutors, for he asserts that the resurrection of Jesus – ironically – shows that the council, rather than making judgements *about* gods, faces judgement *from* the one true God through Jesus (vv. 30–31).

Luke thus presents Paul as undermining his hearers' world view and offering them a replacement worldview drawn from Jewish monotheism re-understood in the light of Jesus's resurrection. Thus witness to Jesus in Athens in front of the Areopagus, a political body, involves speaking truth to power in the form of argument about world view, including engagement with and critique of the council's assumptions. The speech is apologetic, but not as we often think of apologetics in today's world and situations, for it does not involve argument about Jesus and his identity – those things are assumed and asserted, rather than argued.

III.e. Paul before the Governor Felix in Caesarea[77]

Felix enters the story of Acts as governor (technically, procurator) of Palestine who meets Paul after his arrest in Jerusalem. The tribune Claudius Lysias sends a letter to brief Felix on Paul's case (Acts 23:26–30) – a letter which is rather economical with the truth, although it does make clear that the tribune regards the issue as an intra-Jewish matter which does not merit any serious penalty being applied to Paul (v. 29).

What we know of Felix from extra-biblical sources suggests that he could be a harsh governor who did not hesitate to use military means to keep the peace, and who was willing to cooperate with the *sicarii* terrorists to have the high priest killed.[78] However, Tertullus's positive introduction that seeks Felix's goodwill and attention (*captatio benevolentiae*, 24:2b–3[79]) is neither mere flattery nor simply disingenuous. Ananias, the high priest who led the delegation to Felix (24:1), and Ananias's predecessor

---

[77] See fuller discussion in Walton, "Trying," 132–6 [in this volume 114–17].

[78] Respectively, Josephus, *Ant.* 20.8.7 §§173–78; *J.W.* 2.13.7 §§266–70 and *Ant.* 20.8.5 §162; *J.W.* 2.13.3. §§254–57. See the helpful brief treatments in Brian M. Rapske, "Roman Governors of Palestine" in *DLNT*, 979–84, here 982–83; *ABD* 2:783 and, more fully, David W. J. Gill, "Acts and Roman Policy in Judaea" in *The Book of Acts in its Palestinian Setting*, ed. Richard Bauckham, BAFCS 4 (Carlisle: Paternoster; Grand Rapids, MI: Eerdmans, 1995) 15–26, here 21–6.

[79] Bruce W. Winter, "The Importance of the *Captatio Benevolentiae* in the Speeches of Tertullus and Paul in Acts 24:1–21," *JTS* ns 42 (1991): 505–31.

Jonathan had pressed Claudius to appoint Felix as procurator.[80] It was an unusual appointment for a mere freedman rather than someone of equestrian rank.[81] The Jewish delegation was thus compelled to support Felix's administration. Further, not long before this, Felix had brought peace following a rebellion led by an Egyptian.[82] Tertullus's comments (24:2) may allude to this incident.

Luke presents Felix as acting properly, at least initially, in handling Paul's case. First, he establishes whether Paul falls under his jurisdiction by enquiring which province he comes from (23:34). Cilicia was probably at this time under the legate of Syria, Felix's line manager. So for Felix to fail to hear the case and pass it on to the legate of Syria would be to risk appearing to waste the legate's time with a minor matter[83] – even though the transfer of an accused person to his own province was optional at this time.[84]

Second, Felix wishes to hear first-hand from Paul's accusers (23:35a; cf. 25:16), as was normal in Roman law.[85] Paul's defence speech (24:10–21) initially focuses on the charges made against him and denies that they are valid (vv. 12–13). Paul then turns to testify to his faith as a valid form of Judaism, worshipping the God of the Jewish ancestors and holding to the Jewish Scriptures (v. 14), and a faith which entails resurrection hope (v. 15). Paul makes the point that at least some of the accusers are not present (24:19), thus implying that the charges were invalid.[86] Their absence is reflected in the reduced claims that Tertullus makes, asserting only that Paul 'attempted' to profane the temple (ἐπείρασεν, 24:6), whereas the missing Asian Jews had claimed that Paul 'had defiled' the temple (κεκοίνωκεν, 21:28).

Felix then acts within his powers in deciding to await testimony from the tribune Lysias (24:22), since he needs advice to help him decide between the two contradictory testimonies he has heard.[87] Luke does not tell us whether Felix was able to consult Lysias or whether a consultation took place but was inconclusive. Whatever the case, Paul remained in custody at governor Felix's pleasure (as the British judicial system charmingly puts it). In the situation of waiting for Lysias's testimony, Felix can afford to relax Paul's conditions of detention, and so he does (24:23).[88]

---

[80] Tacitus, *Ann.* 12.54. Winter, "Importance," 515–16; F. F. Bruce, *New Testament History* (London: Oliphants, 1977), 325.

[81] Claudius Lysias and Tertullus address Felix as 'most excellent' (κράτιστος, 23:26; 24:3), a title undoubtedly used for those of equestrian rank, but not exclusively for such people (Loveday Alexander, *The Preface to Luke's Gospel: Literary Convention and Social Context in Luke 1.1-4 and Acts 1.1*, SNTSMS 78 (Cambridge: Cambridge University Press, 1993), 133; BegC 2:505–507).

[82] Josephus, *J.W.* 2.13.5. §§261–63; Acts 21:38.

[83] A. N. Sherwin-White, *Roman Society and Roman Law in the New Testament* (Grand Rapids, MI: Baker, 1963 repr. 1981), 55–7; Brian M. Rapske, *The Book of Acts and Paul in Roman Custody*, BAFCS 3 (Carlisle: Paternoster; Grand Rapids, MI: Eerdmans, 1994), 155. Cilicia was probably not formally a province at this time, but this distinction does not affect the point noted.

[84] Sherwin-White, *Society*, 55.

[85] Sherwin-White, *Society*, 17; Harry W. Tajra, *The Trial of St Paul: A Juridical Exegesis of the Second Half of the Acts of the Apostles*, WUNT II/35 (Tübingen: Mohr Siebeck, 1989), 115.

[86] Luke T. Johnson, *The Acts of the Apostles*, SP 5 (Collegeville, MN: Liturgical, 1992), 417; Joseph A. Fitzmyer, *The Acts of the Apostles: A New Translation and Commentary*, AB 31 (Garden City, NY: Doubleday, 1998), 737.

[87] Sherwin-White, *Society*, 53.

[88] On the possible nature of the relaxation of conditions, see Rapske, *Book*, 167–72.

Strikingly, Paul's confinement does not prevent him from testifying to the gospel, for Felix wishes to hear him on the subject on numerous occasions (24:24–26), thus partially fulfilling the Lord's word to Paul (23:11). As Skinner notes, this situation gives Paul access to some of the most powerful people in Judaea.[89] Thus Paul the prisoner is Paul the *missionary*-prisoner.[90]

Paul persists in being Jesus's witness with Felix, speaking about 'faith in Jesus the Messiah' (24:24), but the deal-breaker for Felix seems to be the moral demands of Paul's testimony. Felix becomes fearful at Paul's talk 'concerning righteousness and self-control and judgement to come' (24:25) and therefore sends Paul away. These qualities imply a call to repent, a key feature of evangelistic proclamation in Acts.[91] However, they may be particularly apposite for Felix as a governor who should act with righteousness and self-control, but had deceptively drawn Drusilla away from her former husband into his arms.[92] Self-control (ἐγκράτεια) may thus focus here on *sexual* self-control.[93] In this light, 'judgement to come' would be an unwelcome thought to Felix if his conscience was at all sensitive to what Paul said. Paul is portrayed here as 'turning the tables' on Felix, his judge, by speaking to Felix of the values which (ironically) should be guiding his judgement.[94] Testimony to Jesus involves speaking uncomfortable truth to power at times.

Not only that, but testimony to Jesus involves rejecting underhand ways out, for Felix hoped for a bribe from Paul, and not just on one occasion, but repeatedly (24:26).[95] This was not uncommon among judges in the Roman empire,[96] although illegal under the *Lex Iulia de Repetundis*.[97] Luke takes a dim view of it,[98] for it results in Paul continuing to be held even though the tribune Lysias had written to Felix that Paul had not committed any crime worthy of death or imprisonment (23:29). As is often the case in Luke-Acts, how possessions are handled is an index of a person's standing with God,[99] and on that index Paul's stock is high and Felix's is low.

---

[89] Matthew L. Skinner, *Locating Paul: Places of Custody as Narrative Settings in Acts 21-28*, AcBib 13 (Atlanta, GA: SBL, 2003), 137–8.
[90] The expression is from Rapske, *Book*, e.g. 429–36.
[91] E.g. 2:38; 3:19; 5:31; 11:18; 17:30; 20:21; 26:20.
[92] Josephus, *Ant.* 20.7.1 §§141–44; Gerhard Schneider, *Die Apostelgeschichte*, HTKNT, 2 vols. (Freiburg: Herder, 1980, 1982), 2:351–52.
[93] BDAG 274 s.v.
[94] Cf. Richard J. Cassidy, *Society and Politics in the Acts of the Apostles* (Maryknoll, NY: Orbis, 1987), 106.
[95] Although πυκνότερον is formally a comparative form, the lack of anything to compare suggests a superlative sense, meaning 'very often'; with MHT, 3:30; C. K. Barrett, *A Critical and Exegetical Commentary on the Acts of the Apostles*, ICC, 2 vols. (Edinburgh: T. & T. Clark, 1994, 1998), 2:1116; *pace* BDF §244[1], who assert it to be ambiguous.
[96] E.g. Albinus, as reported by Josephus, *J.W.* 2.14.1 §§272–73. Rapske, *Book*, 65-7 lays out the evidence for such corruption in the judicial system.
[97] Introduced in 59 BC to prevent corruption of this kind in the provinces; see Tajra, *Trial*, 131.
[98] Beverly R. Gaventa, *Acts*, ANTC (Nashville, TN: Abingdon, 2003), 330 suggests that Felix is portrayed in the image of the unjust judge of the parable (Luke 18:1–8).
[99] For discussion of this theme in Luke, see Luke T. Johnson, *The Literary Function of Possessions in Luke-Acts*, SBLDS 39 (Missoula, MT: Scholars, 1977), 144–58.

IV. Summarizing What We Have Seen

We have seen the earliest believers engaging in a variety of contexts with the powers-that-be. Of necessity, we have sampled rather than attempted to be exhaustive, but some themes come through consistently and clearly concerning the shape which speaking truth to power – witness to and for Jesus – takes in these encounters.

First, testimony about Jesus himself is normally present, usually including some key moments from the gospel story being told or mentioned, notably Jesus's death, resurrection, understood as vindication by God, and his coming again to judge.

Secondly, believers speaking truth to power can involve direct attribution of responsibility for Jesus's death, as Peter and John do in Jerusalem.[100] The believers' testimony to the powers involves telling the powers when they have committed sin, and in this case sin of enormous magnitude. We have suggested that a similar theme is present in the scenes in Athens and with Felix.

Thirdly, testimony to Jesus can involve calling the powers to act justly when they fail to do so, as Paul does with the magistrates in Philippi and with Felix in Caesarea. This is not only because to get them to act justly will (as we might say) open more doors for the gospel, but also (I suggest) because justice itself is part of the gospel the believers proclaim, for it is a key feature of the Christian God's character and a key Christian hope for the world to come; by contrast, injustice, in the sense of distinguishing between citizens and non-citizens, between élite and non-élite, was just the way the world was.

---

[100] Note the shift from 'you' bearing this responsibility when speaking in Jerusalem (Acts 4:10–11) to speaking of 'them' – the Jerusalemites and their rulers – as hearing that responsibility when speaking in Antioch (Acts 13:27–29).

Part III

Theological Themes in Acts

10

Jesus, Present and/or Absent? The Presence and Presentation of Jesus as a Character in the Book of Acts

I. An Absentee Christology?

Hans Conzelmann's view that the ascension means that Jesus has departed to heaven and is, in consequence, now absent from the sphere of earth,[1] has been highly influential on subsequent scholarship, especially as mediated (and qualified) by C. F. D. Moule's influential essay, 'The Christology of Acts'.[2] Conzelmann asserts that Luke considers that, after the ascension, Jesus is now exalted as the living Lord in a distant heaven, and at some point in the future will return and judge the world. Jesus's primary role in Acts is thus as a character of the *past*, whose teaching and deeds offer a source of teaching and inspiration for believers. Hence, readers of Acts meet reports of Jesus's past actions and the promise of his future return, but they do not meet Jesus himself as an active and present character within the story of Acts.

Two key passages are cited in support of this view. The first is the ascension scene in Acts 1:9–11, where Jesus is removed from human sight (v. 9), and the viewers are told that he is now in heaven and will return from heaven (v. 11). Similarly, 3:20–21 presents Jesus as remaining in heaven[3] until the restoration of all things (v. 20), which occurs at the return of Jesus.[4]

Moule further argues (against Conzelmann) that the Christology of Acts is more developed than that of Luke's Gospel.[5] In the Gospel Jesus is almost never referred to as ὁ κύριος 'the Lord' by humans,[6] except in the narrator's voice, other than when people

---

[1] Hans Conzelmann, *The Theology of St Luke*, trans. Geoffrey Buswell (London: Faber & Faber, 1960), 170–206.
[2] C. F. D. Moule, "The Christology of Acts," in *Studies in Luke-Acts*, ed. Leander E. Keck and J. Louis Martyn (London: SPCK, 1968), 159–85.
[3] ὃν δεῖ οὐρανὸν μὲν δέξασθαι 'whom heaven must receive' (v. 20).
[4] This is the majority interpretation of 'the restoration of all things' in scholarship, e.g. Luke T. Johnson, *The Acts of the Apostles*, SP 5 (Collegeville, MN: Liturgical, 1992), 74; Kevin L. Anderson, *'But God Raised Him from the Dead': The Theology of Jesus' Resurrection in Luke-Acts*, PBM (Milton Keynes: Paternoster, 2006), 228.
[5] Moule, "Christology," 160–1.
[6] This descriptor is used by angels in Luke 2:11.

address Jesus using the vocative κύριε, which is simply a respectful form of address and might be translated, 'Sir.' Moule notes two exceptions, when Elizabeth speaks of Mary as 'the mother of my Lord (τοῦ κυρίου μου)' (1:43), and when Zechariah speaks of John as one who will go 'before the Lord (ἐνώπιον κυρίου)' (1:76) – although Moule argues that the referent of 'the Lord' as Jesus in 1:76 is only clear with Christian hindsight.[7] By contrast, after the resurrection, both in the Gospel and throughout Acts, Jesus is referred to as ὁ κύριος by people (notably Luke 24:34; Acts 10:36).[8]

If Jesus is absent, Conzelmann and others understand the Spirit to mediate or to substitute for the presence of the absent Jesus.[9] Conzelmann characterizes the Spirit in Acts as 'no longer the eschatological gift, but the substitute in the meantime for the possession of ultimate salvation'.[10]

This view has not gone unchallenged.[11] Its significance for this essay is that there is evidently a tension within Acts between the physical absence of Jesus from earth following his ascension, including statements about him as a figure of the past in the evangelistic speeches, and Luke's presentation of the exalted Jesus as now *active from heaven* within the narrative.[12] In order to address this tension, we shall study both the means by which Luke characterizes Jesus in Acts, and the content of Luke's characterization of Jesus. For both clarity and brevity, we shall organize our discussion around the various means of characterization which Luke uses. We shall then synthesize our discussion in dialogue with the recent category of 'divine identity' Christology, before returning to the question of how we should understand Luke's portrait of Jesus's presence and absence in Acts.

II. Means of Characterizing Jesus in Acts

Robert Alter helpfully identifies a 'scale of means' for characterization in biblical narrative, which he understands to be 'reliable third-person [narration]'.[13] He identifies

---

[7] Moule, "Christology," 160, 172; discussion of these exceptions forms part of the challenge to Moule in Eric Franklin, *Christ the Lord: A Study in the Purpose and Theology of Luke-Acts* (London: SPCK, 1975), 49–55. For an alternative, narrative reading of 1:76, arguing that this verse should be read as part of a thread running from 1:43 to 3:4–6, and thus 'Lord' in 1:76 refers to Jesus *in Luke's narrative context*, see C. Kavin Rowe, *Early Narrative Christology: The Lord in the Gospel of Luke*, paperback ed. (Grand Rapids, MI: Baker, 2009), 69–77.

[8] Moule goes on to identify similar shifts in usage for Jesus as prophet, the son of man, saviour, and son ("Christology," 162–5).

[9] E.g. C. K. Barrett, *Luke the Historian in Recent Study* (London: Epworth, 1961), 67; F. F. Bruce, "The Holy Spirit in the Acts of the Apostles," *Int* 27 (1973): 166–83, esp. 178–9; Bo Reicke, "The Risen Lord and His Church: The Theology of Acts," *Int* 13 (1959): 157–69, esp. 162, 166; Arland J. Hultgren, *Christ and His Benefits. Christology and Redemption in the New Testament* (Philadelphia, PA: Fortress, 1987), 81, 85.

[10] Conzelmann, *Theology*, 97.

[11] E.g. Robert F. O'Toole, "Activity of the Risen Jesus in Luke-Acts," *Bib* 62 (1981): 471–98; Mikeal C. Parsons, *The Departure of Jesus in Luke-Acts: The Ascension Narratives in Context*, JSNTSup 21 (Sheffield: JSOT, 1987), 160–2.

[12] For the latter, see Matthew Sleeman, *Geography and the Ascension Narrative in Acts*, SNTSMS 146 (Cambridge: Cambridge University Press, 2009), throughout, e.g. 72–80.

[13] Robert Alter, *The Art of Biblical Narrative* (London: Allen & Unwin, 1981), 116–17, quotations are from 116; cf. the slightly longer exposition, with helpful examples, in J. L. Resseguie, *Narrative*

a series of means of revealing character which he sees as providing increasing degrees of explicitness and confidence: (i) the actions of a character and description of the character's appearance ('showing'); (ii) what other characters say about a character; (iii) the character's own speech to others; (iv) the character's 'interior monologue' (a category which is absent in Acts); (v) the narrator's statements about the character's views, intentions and attitudes ('telling'). These are also the means which an author uses to guide readers in evaluating characters, for the author's choice of terms, presentation, speech, manner, and so forth will lead readers to sympathize, empathize or be antipathetic towards a character.[14]

Let us consider how Jesus is characterized in Acts using these means.

II.a. Jesus's Actions and Appearance ('Showing')

There is relatively little 'showing' of Jesus, i.e. description of his appearance and actions, which is hardly surprising since he is not physically present for the vast majority of the story in Acts – this Conzelmann recognizes accurately. The only physical description may be that he shines (9:3). This reticence is shared with most ancient narrative. There are mentions of Jesus's deeds in the past (e.g. 2:22; 1:1–11; 10:38), most notably of his death and resurrection (e.g. 2:23–24; 3:13–15; 4:10; 10:39b–41; 13:27–31; 17:18, 31), and of what Jesus does now: he causes Saul to be blind (9:9), and he heals Aeneas (9:34). Further, through Jesus's name forgiveness is available (2:38) and the man with a congenital disability is healed (3:6).

The last two references are the tip of an iceberg of mentions of the power of Jesus's name (or 'the name') in the present of the Acts story,[15] including: baptism 'in the name of Jesus the Messiah' (2:38; 8:16; 10:48; 19:5; 22:16); forgiveness through the name of Jesus (2:38; 10:43); healing through the name (3:6, 16; 4:7, 10); signs and wonders performed through the name (4:30–31; 8:12 with 8:3–8); salvation given through the name (2:21; 4:12). We shall learn more about 'the name of Jesus' when we look at other characters' speech about Jesus below.

In sum, the contribution of description of Jesus's actions and appearance to our understanding of Luke's characterization of Jesus is small, just as, according to Alter's model, it is less explicit and significant. Other means of characterization will be more useful in developing a well-grounded understanding.

Criticism of the New Testament. An Introduction (Grand Rapids, MI: Baker Academic, 2005), 130–2. For a treatment of characterization by a literary critic which has been influential in Biblical Studies, and which makes similar points, see Wayne C. Booth, *The Rhetoric of Fiction* (Chicago: University of Chicago Press, 1961), 3–20. Cf. also Malbon's five means of characterization of Jesus in Mark: what the narrator and other characters say about Jesus; what Jesus says in response to what others say to and of him; what Jesus says about himself and God; what Jesus does; and what other characters do which is related to what Jesus says and does; in Elizabeth S. Malbon, *Mark's Jesus. Characterization as Narrative Christology* (Waco, TX: Baylor University Press, 2009). Her approach, while useful for studying a Gospel, is less helpful for Acts, because of Jesus's physical absence for most of the narrative.

[14] Mark Allan Powell, *What Is Narrative Criticism?* (London: SPCK, 1993), 53–4; Daniel Marguerat and Yves Bourquin, *How to Read Bible Stories* (London: SCM, 1999), 66–9.

[15] See John A. Ziesler, "The Name of Jesus in the Acts of the Apostles," *JSNT* 4 (1979): 28–41.

II.b What Other Characters Say about Jesus

This is one of the two largest groups of references concerning Jesus in Acts (the other is the author's comments on Jesus). Notable here is the variety of appellations predicated of Jesus by a number of characters,[16] as well as the focus on divine testimony to Jesus (notably by his resurrection and exaltation), and the powerful effect of Jesus's name.

II.b.i. Calling Jesus Names[17]

Lord Jesus is called 'Lord' κύριος in a number of places in a way which goes beyond the polite address of the vocative κύριε ('Sir') by characters in Luke's Gospel. It is, of course, likely that some uses of κύριος in Acts refer to God rather than Jesus;[18] nevertheless, some characters use this appellation of Jesus in striking ways.

One cluster of uses features address to Jesus in prayer, notably Stephen's dying prayer to κύριε Ἰησοῦ 'Lord Jesus' (7:59). Similarly, 'the Lord' speaking in a vision to Ananias undoubtedly suggests a divine 'Lord', and thus the combination 'the Lord Jesus' portrays Jesus speaking from heaven, and thus acting in the place of YHWH (9:10, 13, 17; see further below).[19] This kind of combination of names is echoed in regular uses of the collocation ὁ κύριος Ἰησοῦς [Χριστός] 'the Lord Jesus [Messiah]' by believing speakers (1:21; 4:33; 11:17, 20; 15:11, 26; 16:21; 20:21 with 24, 35; 21:13; 28:31) who are reliable characters.

Stephen's prayer follows hot on the heels of Jesus's appearance to Stephen at God's right side (7:55-56), sharing God's rule. Stephen identifies Jesus as 'the son of man', echoing the exalted 'son of man' of Dan 7:13-14 who is given universal rule and authority.[20] The Sanhedrin's response in both stopping their ears[21] and stoning Stephen to death indicates that they understand Stephen's statements about Jesus as

---

[16] I use 'appellations' in preference to 'titles' because older approaches considered Christology almost exclusively through 'titles', which tended to assume that the most significant factor in interpreting Jesus was the 'titles' applied to Jesus, and that these 'titles' had a pre-existing meaning which Jesus was recognized as fitting. By contrast, it seems more likely that early Christian encounter with Jesus in the flesh and through the life of the believing communities shaped how these 'titles' were understood. On the importance of early Christian 'religious experience' for understanding early Christian interpretation of Jesus, see, *inter alia*, Larry W. Hurtado, *Lord Jesus Christ. Devotion to Jesus in Earliest Christianity* (Grand Rapids, MI; Cambridge: Eerdmans, 2003); Luke T. Johnson, *Religious Experience in Early Christianity* (Minneapolis, MN: Fortress, 1998).

[17] See the helpful summaries in Larry W. Hurtado, "Christology in Acts. Jesus in Early Christian Belief and Practice," in *Issues in Luke-Acts. Selected Essays*, ed. Sean A. Adams and Michael W. Pahl, Gorgias Handbooks 26 (Piscataway, NJ: Gorgias, 2012), 217-37, here 221-6.

[18] See discussion in J. D. G. Dunn, "ΚΥΡΙΟΣ in Acts," in his *The Christ and the Spirit. Collected Essays of James D. G. Dunn.* vol. 1 *Christology* (Edinburgh: T&T Clark; Grand Rapids, MI: Eerdmans, 1998), 241-53.

[19] Josep Rius-Camps and Jenny Read-Heimerdinger, *The Message of Acts in Codex Bezae. A Comparison with the Alexandrian Tradition*, JSNTSup/LNTS 257, 302, 365, 415, 4 vols. (London: T&T Clark, 2004-9), 2:186-7.

[20] F. F. Bruce, *The Acts of the Apostles*, 3rd ed. (Leicester: Apollos, 1990), 211; C. F. D. Moule, *The Origin of Christology* (Cambridge: Cambridge University Press, 1977), 11-22.

[21] Eckhard J. Schnabel, *Acts*, ZECNT 5 (Grand Rapids: Zondervan, 2012), 390; Alan F. Segal, *Two Powers in Heaven: Early Rabbinic Reports about Christianity and Gnosticism*, SJLA 25 (Leiden: Brill, 1977), 94-5.

blasphemous, for stoning is a punishment for blasphemy, including the worship of false gods.[22] Luke's authorial observation that Stephen is πλήρης πνεύματος ἁγίου 'filled with the Holy Spirit' when he sees Jesus exalted (7:55) indicates that Stephen speaks as a reliable character – what Stephen says is to be trusted, and the Sanhedrin have understood it correctly.

Ananias encounters 'the Lord' in a vision (9:10), and this character is consistently referred to as 'the Lord' (9:11, 13, 15). Ananias himself then clarifies that 'the Lord' is Jesus when he speaks with Saul, and that identification is a crucial point of continuity with Saul's vision: 'the Lord (ὁ κύριος), Jesus (Ἰησοῦς)[23] *who appeared to you on your way here*, has sent me' (9:17, my italics; cf. 9:5).

Stephen and Ananias both speak of Jesus as Lord and as a figure of the present. Jesus is certainly located in heaven, but he engages with the world of people from there, by appearance and speech – he is truly 'Lord of all' (πάντων κύριος, 10:36).

Messiah Jesus is also 'Messiah', notably in 2:36, where Peter signals that God's action in raising Jesus from the dead and exalting Jesus to his right side (2:33) causes him to be known as 'both Lord and Messiah'.[24] The controversy over the healing of the man with a congenital disability at the temple gate is peppered with references in believers' speeches to Jesus as Messiah, without reference to him as 'Lord'. The healing itself takes place through 'the name of Jesus the Messiah', and Peter and John's speeches identify Jesus as Messiah (3:6, 18, 20; 4:10). In response to the ban on speaking in the name of Jesus, the believers pray and identify Jesus as the 'Messiah' of Ps 2:2 (4:26). Proclamation is thus of Jesus as Messiah (5:42; 8:5; 9:22; 10:36; 11:17), and his messianic name brings deliverance from demonization (16:18).

'Messiah' in first-century Judaism is a word with variegated reference.[25] Χριστός is cognate with the verb χρίω (cf. 4:27; 10:38) and thus has the sense 'anointed one', which connotes kingship.[26] Use of 'Messiah' points to the *present* kingly rule of Jesus, demonstrated in his sovereign actions of salvation and healing. His rule as Messiah (and, indeed, Lord) necessarily challenges others who claim *absolute* rule, including Caesar.[27] I am not suggesting by this that Luke understands earliest Christianity to be

---

[22] E.g. Lev 24:13–16; Deut 17:2–7.

[23] Ἰησοῦς is absent from 𝔐 sa^ms, but its overwhelming support in primitive witnesses (𝔓45, 74 ℵ A B C D E most minuscules vg) makes its presence extremely probable; with C. K. Barrett, *A Critical and Exegetical Commentary on the Acts of the Apostles*, ICC, 2 vols. (Edinburgh: T&T Clark, 1994, 1998), 1:457; Bruce M. Metzger, *A Textual Commentary on the Greek New Testament*, 2nd ed. (Stuttgart: Deutsche Bibelgesellschaft/United Bible Societies, 1994), 320.

[24] I take ἐποίησεν here to signal not that Jesus has acquired a status he did not previously possess, but that through the resurrection and ascension of Jesus, and his pouring out the Spirit (2:33), Jesus is now known to be Messiah and Lord. See the valuable discussions in C. K. Rowe, "Acts 2:36 and the Continuity of Lukan Christology," NTS 53 (2007): 37–56; I. Howard Marshall, *Luke: Historian and Theologian* (Exeter: Paternoster, 1970), 166–7.

[25] See, e.g., N. T. Wright, *The New Testament and the People of God*, Christian Origins and the Question of God 1 (London: SPCK, 1992), 307–20 and literature there cited.

[26] Moule, *Origin*, 31–2.

[27] For fuller discussion, see Steve Walton, "The State They Were In: Luke's View of the Roman Empire," in *Rome in the Bible and the Early Church*, ed. Peter Oakes (Carlisle: Paternoster; Grand Rapids, MI: Baker Academic, 2002), 1–41; Steve Walton, "Trying Paul or Trying Rome? Judges and Accused in the Roman Trials of Paul in Acts," in *Luke-Acts and Empire. Essays in Honor of Robert L. Brawley*, ed. David Rhoads, David Esterline and Jae Won Lee, Princeton Theological Monographs 151

(or that it should be) aggressively anti-imperial in its words and actions; importantly, there is little evidence – especially in Acts – that Roman rulers understood the lives and actions of believers that way.[28] I *am* suggesting that the kingly connotations of Χριστός for Jesus necessarily implied that, where there was a clash of loyalties between Jesus and Caesar (such as over offering sacrifices to Caesar), Luke calls believers to put Caesar second. It may well be the recognition of this greater status of Jesus which stands behind the claim of Paul's opponents that he announces Jesus as 'another king' (βασιλέα ἕτερον, 17:7).[29]

Servant Jesus is further identified as God's παῖς 'servant' (3:13, 26; 4:27, 30), exclusively by believers – a designation which echoes Isa 52:13. In 3:13 Peter goes on to speak of Jesus's rejection, suffering, death and exaltation, picking up further themes from Isa 52:13–53:12,[30] and thus invites Luke's readers to listen carefully to this echo – the quotation from this Isaianic passage in 8:32–33 underlines its importance. This name also echoes descriptions of both Israel and David as God's 'servant';[31] these echoes may suggest that the term both connotes and shapes Jesus's role as Israel's king, a king who 'sums up' the nation in his own person.[32] Mention of Jesus as God's servant is, interestingly, focused on his past deeds, rather than his present actions.

Saviour Jesus is called σωτήρ 'saviour' only twice in Acts (5:31; 13:23), both in speeches by believers to not-yet-believing audiences. Nevertheless, Jesus's activity of saving people is prominent – the verb σῴζω 'I save/heal' is what Jesus does for people (2:21; 4:9, 12; 11:14; 14:9; 15:1, 11; 16:30–31; 27:20, 31), particularly in the programmatic summary, 'we believe that we will be saved (σωθῆναι) through the grace of the Lord Jesus, just as they will' (15:11). Similarly, in speeches, 'salvation' (σωτηρία, σωτήριον) is what Jesus – and no-one else – brings (4:12; cf. 13:26, 47; 16:17; 28:28). There are uses of this word group which focus on healing as the present activity of Jesus (e.g. 4:9; 14:9), although the majority of uses on believers' lips concern Jesus's role in saving people from judgement, specifically by making forgiveness for sins available (2:38 with 2:21; 5:31; 10:43 with 11:14; 13:38 with 13:26, 47; 26:18).[33] Jesus is characterized as one who saves, and that in the present as well as the future.

Other names Several other designations are used, although none is as common as those discussed above.

Holy and righteous one Jesus is ὁ ἅγιος καί δίκαιος 'the holy and righteous one' (3:14). Holiness and righteousness are characteristics of YHWH in Scripture: YHWH is

---

(Eugene, OR: Pickwick, 2011), 122–41 [in this volume 107–21]; Steve Walton, "What Does 'Mission' in Acts Mean in Relation to the 'Powers That Be'?," *JETS* 55 (2012): 537–56 [in this volume 123–42].

[28] See the very valuable discussions in C. Kavin Rowe, *World Upside Down. Reading Acts in the Graeco-Roman Age* (Oxford/New York: Oxford University Press, 2009), esp. 91–176.

[29] With Joseph A. Fitzmyer, *The Acts of the Apostles. A New Translation and Commentary*, AB 31 (Garden City, NY: Doubleday, 1998), 596.

[30] For details, see Darrell L. Bock, *Proclamation from Prophecy and Pattern: Lucan Old Testament Christology*, JSNTSup 12 (Sheffield: JSOT, 1987), 188–9.

[31] *Israel*: Luke 1:54; cf. Isa 42:1; 44:1–2, 21; 45:4; *David*: Luke 1:69; Acts 4:25; cf. Isa 37:35.

[32] Cf. 1 Sam 5:1–5, where the tribes gather to anoint David and say to him, 'We are your bone and flesh,' language which suggests representation.

[33] See Marshall, *Historian*, 138–41, 169–75.

'the holy one of Israel',[34] and is righteous.[35] Jesus has been called 'the holy one of God' by demons (Luke 4:34), and is described as 'the righteous one' by Jewish believers (Acts 7:52; 22:14). These uses focus on Jesus's past, rather than his present, notably in the context of his death.

Author of life Jesus is ὁ ἀρχηγὸς τῆς ζωῆς 'the author/leader of life' (3:15) or simply ἀρχηγός 'leader' (5:31). This term is widely used in LXX (and elsewhere) for 'leader',[36] and that is most probably its sense here: Jesus as leader leads the way to life.[37] The deeply ironic claim in 3:14 is that Jesus was the author of life at the point where the Jerusalemites had him killed. 3:14 is a statement about the past, whereas in 5:31 Jesus is *now* the 'leader and saviour' who presently gives repentance and forgiveness to Israel. Characters' use of this designation, then, spans both past and present activities of Jesus.

Prophet like Moses In the same speech as the previous two designations, Jesus is also seen as the 'prophet like Moses' (3:22–23). Peter quotes Deut 18:15, where Moses promises that YHWH will send a prophet like him, whom Peter here identifies as Jesus, as does Stephen (7:37). Other Jews expected such a prophet, so identifying Jesus as that prophet was significant.[38] The point of this identification is that the people should listen to Jesus: Peter quotes Lev 23:29 to underline the point (3:23). This description of Jesus roots his identity in Scripture, as many other designations do, and highlights Jesus as one who conveys the very words of God. The focus is thus on the past of Jesus: 'God will raise up' may well focus on Jesus's resurrection, for Peter has already spoken of Jesus's earthly ministry (3:13b–15) – and if 'God will raise up' is a further reference to Jesus's pre-resurrection ministry, there would be no possibility of repentance for those who rejected him then.[39]

A man Jesus is also referred to as 'a man', both by believers, using the specifically masculine term ἀνήρ (2:22; 17:31), and by unbelievers, using the generic human term ἄνθρωπος (5:28) – it is unlikely that there is any significance to the difference in term between believers and unbelievers, although the unbelievers, of course, believe that Jesus is *only* human. Peter also identifies Jesus's humble beginnings in Nazareth: he is ὁ Ναζωραῖος (also 3:6; 4:10; 6:14; 22:8; 26:9; cf. Luke 18:37), confirming his human origins. There is no 'Ebionite' suggestion here that Jesus began as human and later became God's son, for Luke has made it clear that Jesus was God's son from his

---

[34] E.g. Pss 71:22 (LXX 70:22); 78:41 (LXX 77:41); 89:18 (LXX 88:19); Isa 1:4; 5:19; 12:6; Jer 50:29 (LXX 27:29].

[35] E.g. Deut 32:4; 1 Sam 2:2; 2 Chron 12:6; Ezra 9:15; Neh 9:33; Pss 7:11 (LXX 12); 11:7 (LXX 10:7); 116:5 (LXX 114:5); 129:4 (LXX 128:4); Isa 45:21; Tob 3:2; 2 Macc 1:24; 3 Macc 2:3.

[36] E.g. Exod 6:14; Num 10:4; 13:2, 3 (MT 3,4); 14:4; 24:17; Deut 32:21; 1 Chr 5:24; Neh 2:9; 7:70, 71; Isa 3:6, 7; 30:4; Jdt 14:2; 1 Macc 9:61. For extra-biblical uses, see Barrett, *Acts*, 1:197. For other senses found in Greek literature, see David L. Jones, "The Title 'Author of Life (Leader)' in the Acts of the Apostles," in *SBL 1994 Seminar Papers*, SBLSP 33 (Atlanta, GA: SBL, 1994), 627–36, here 627 nn. 3–6.

[37] τῆς ζωῆς is genitive of direction. BDF §166; cf. Mic 1:13 LXX ἀρχηγὸς ἁμαρτίας αὐτή ἐστιν 'she is the one who leads to sin'.

[38] E.g. 1QS 9.11; 4QTest 175 5–7; see also Julie E. Robb, "The Prophet Like Moses. Its Jewish Context and Use in the Early Christian Tradition" (PhD diss., King's College London, 2003), ch. 2; J. Jeremias, Μωυσῆς, *TDNT* 8:857–64, 867–73.

[39] Robb, "Prophet," 100; Gerhard Krodel, *Acts*, ProcC (Philadelphia, PA: Fortress, 1981), 29; Anderson, *But God*, 231–2.

origins (Luke 1:35).[40] Peter believes that Jesus is more than human, but not less than human – and Paul's claim in Athens that God will judge the world through 'a man' (17:31) suggests that he understands the present, exalted Jesus as *still* human, although, again, more than human as the agent of God's judgement (cf. 10:42). Jesus's humanity is thus a past, present and future feature of his characterization.

Gracious It is 'the grace (χάρις) of the Lord Jesus' which saves believers (15:11), and the choice of χάρις in this subjective genitive construction (it is Jesus acting graciously which is in view) presents Jesus in similar colours to God himself (cf. 11:23; 13:43; 14:26; 20:24, 32) as a generous giver. It is striking that 15:11 is the only place in Acts where grace is predicated of Jesus, amidst a sea of references to God's grace. Jesus's grace is a present reality, for it saves people now.

II.b.ii. Divine Testimony to Jesus

As well as human speech about Jesus, we should also consider divine testimony to Jesus in Acts. This is never explicit divine speech (contrast Luke 3:22 – perhaps audible to Jesus alone; 9:35); it is usually found in the form of human speeches which speak of God's actions and testimony to Jesus.

Deeds of power Jesus's own actions were divine testimony, says Peter on the day of Pentecost (2:22), for they were δυνάμεσιν καὶ τέρασιν καὶ σημείοις 'deeds of power and wonders and signs'. These terms echo the prophecy of Joel quoted by Peter (2:19, citing Joel 2:30 [LXX 3:3]), except that in Joel they are YHWH's deeds. It may be that we should connect the deeds of power with God's anointing of Jesus (4:27), a further piece of divine testimony. As we noted above, anointing marked kings and signalled authority.[41]

The resurrection It is consistently the resurrection of Jesus to which the apostolic band are to bear witness (1:22; 2:24, 31, 32; 4:2, 33; 17:3, 18, 31, 32; 25:19; 26:23; cf. 23:6; 24:15, 21).[42] This action is regularly presented as God's action of vindicating Jesus against human injustice in putting him to death (2:23–24, 32; 3:13–15; 4:10; 5:30; 10:29–30; etc.), and thus is the centre of the apostolic testimony (4:33).[43] The verbs used, either ἀνίστημι or ἐγείρω,[44] have God as active: it is never that 'Jesus rose', but rather that 'God raised Jesus'.[45] Implicit in the resurrection, then, is Jesus's innocence, a theme stressed in Luke's crucifixion account: Jesus is explicitly declared innocent no less than six times (Luke 23:4, 14, 15, 22, 41, 47). The innocent Jesus dies in the place of a guilty man, Barabbas: 23:25 sharply juxtaposes Barabbas's guilt and his replacement by Jesus. The resurrection has two implications: first, that Jesus is now

---

[40] Against Ernst Haenchen, *The Acts of the Apostles*, trans. R. McL. Wilson (Oxford: Blackwell, 1971), 187; with Hans Conzelmann, *Acts of the Apostles*, Hermeneia, trans. James Limburg, A. Thomas Kraabel and Donald H. Juel (Philadelphia, PA: Fortress, 1987), 20, 21.

[41] See the discussion of 'Messiah' above, 149–50.

[42] More fully, see Anderson, *But God*, 34–5.

[43] See the fine exposition of the latter theme in Daniel Marguerat, "The Resurrection and Its Witnesses in the Book of Acts," in *Reading Acts Today: Essays in Honour of Loveday C. A. Alexander*, ed. Steve Walton, Thomas E. Phillips, Lloyd K. Pietersen and F. Scott Spencer, LNTS 427 (London: T&T Clark, 2011), 171–85.

[44] ἀνίστημι: 2:24, 32; 13:33, 34; ἐγείρω: 3:15; 4:10; 5:30; 13:30, 37.

[45] With Anderson, *But God*, 127.

alive and available to his people (e.g. Acts 2:38); and secondly, that his innocent death has dealt with sin – forgiveness and transformation are now available through Jesus (e.g. Acts 2:38; 3:26; 4:12; 5:31; 10:43; 13:38; 26:18). Thus Jesus's past act of humiliation now issues in his present ability to 'save' (4:12).

Scripture A further piece of divine testimony to Jesus is the voice of Scripture.[46] When speaking about Jesus at Pentecost, Peter turns to Scripture to interpret recent events, citing Joel and two Psalms (16; 110) (2:16–20, 25–28, 31, 34–35). When answering the Sanhedrin, Peter directs his hearers to Ps 118:22 as identifying Jesus as the stone which the builder rejected, but which is now the cornerstone (4:11). When praying, the believing community see the recent events of Jesus's trial, death and resurrection through the lens of Ps 2 (4:25–28): Scripture provides divine interpretation of what has happened in Jesus's lifetime and is *now* happening during the time of his reign from God's right side. When Philip meets the Ethiopian eunuch, he finds him reading Isa 53, and responds to the eunuch's question, 'About whom ... does the prophet speak?' (8:34) by 'starting with that scripture' and telling him 'the good news about Jesus' (8:35). In the synagogue at Pisidian Antioch, Paul cites Ps 2:7 (13:33), Isa 55:3 (13:34), and Ps 16:10 (13:35), and uses the language of fulfilment/completion to describe the relationship between Scripture and Jesus (πληρόω, 13:27; ἐκπληρόω 13:33; τελέω 13:29).[47] Further examples could be multiplied,[48] but the point is clear: God's voice in Scripture testifies to and interprets both the past and present of Jesus and his people.

II.b.iii. The Power of Jesus's Name

We noted the 'name (of Jesus)' above as a means by which Jesus acts.[49] It is frequently found on believers' lips. Thus believing characters are (ironically) proud of the dishonour they suffer for 'the name' (5:41; 21:13; 26:9); risk their lives 'for the name' (15:26); speak 'in the name' (4:17–18; 5:28, 40; 8:12; 9:14, 15); call 'on the name' (9:21; 22:16); and are characterized as a people 'for his name' (15:14). A good outcome of evangelism in a city is that 'the name' is held in honour (19:17).

In particular, Jesus's name is called upon in prayer. The believers whom Saul goes to persecute are characterized by Ananias and the Damascene people at large as 'those who call on (ἐπικαλουμένους) your name' (9:14, 21). Stephen calls upon 'Lord Jesus' as he is being stoned (7:59).

Baptism is into 'the name', programmatically so in 2:38.[50] There is variation in the preposition: it can be ἐπί (2:38), εἰς (8:16) or ἐν (10:48), but there seems no discernible

---

[46] More fully, see Bock, *Proclamation*; Mark L. Strauss, *The Davidic Messiah in Luke-Acts: The Promise and Its Fulfillment in Lukan Christology*, JSNTSup 110 (Sheffield: Sheffield Academic, 1995).

[47] See David Peterson, "The Motif of Fulfilment and the Purpose of Luke-Acts," in *The Book of Acts in Its Ancient Literary Setting*, ed. Bruce W. Winter and Andrew D. Clarke, BAFCS 1 (Carlisle: Paternoster; Grand Rapids: Eerdmans, 1993), 83–104; John T. Squires, *The Plan of God in Luke-Acts*, SNTSMS 76 (Cambridge: Cambridge University Press, 1993).

[48] See the full treatment in I. Howard Marshall, "Acts," in *Commentary on the New Testament Use of the Old Testament*, ed. G. K. Beale and D. A. Carson (Grand Rapids, MI: Baker Academic; Nottingham: Apollos, 2007), 513–606.

[49] See above, 147.

[50] See Max Turner, *Power from on High. The Spirit in Israel's Restoration and Witness in Luke-Acts*, JPTSup 9 (Sheffield: Sheffield Academic, 1996), 358–60.

difference in meaning. Older studies, notably W. Heitmüller, understood baptism 'into the name' as signifying becoming the possession of the one into whose name one was baptized;[51] however the variation in preposition tells against such a specific idea being involved. It seems more likely that the name of Jesus was invoked in connection with the rite of baptism, by either or both of the baptizer and the candidate.[52] Baptism is a ritual act of entering into the group of Jesus-believers marked by invoking his name, both as a component of the rite and as giving the rite its power. Thus in 22:16, 'Now what are you waiting for? Get up, be baptized and (epexegetical καί) wash away your sins by calling upon his name.' Similarly, when Paul baptizes the Ephesian twelve *in Jesus's name* and lays hands on them, the Holy Spirit falls – the rite is effective – whereas in their previous state as disciples of John the baptizer, they did not even know of the Spirit (19:2–7).

Healing, too, takes place through Jesus's name, and particular play is made of this in the healing of the man with the congenital disability at the Temple. There, Peter commands him to stand and walk 'in the name of Jesus the Messiah' (3:6), and the man does so. The Sanhedrin's question to Peter and John is 'by what name' the healing took place (4:7), and Peter is clear that it is 'by the name of Jesus the Messiah of Nazareth' (4:10). Jesus himself can intervene in the present story to heal too, as Aeneas discovers (9:34) – this is a remarkable piece of evidence that Luke understands Jesus to be presently active in the apostolic community.

Deliverance from evil spirits takes place through the name of Jesus, such as the slave girl in Philippi (16:18). This usage parallels the invocation of a powerful name in spells and on amulets of the period.[53] People were prepared to use any name that was effective, as we learn comically in Ephesus, for the sons of Sceva discover that the name of Jesus is not a magical word to overpower spirits (19:13). Rather, a relationship with the Jesus whose name is invoked is critical.[54]

II.b.iv. Summary

As we have seen, the claims come from a variety of characters; they are 'focalized' through different characters.[55] This means that, in assessing Luke's portrait of Jesus in Acts, we must take into account how reliable Luke considers the characters who speak to be – for example, Petrine and Pauline testimony is clearly of high value, for these are people full of the Spirit, whereas the testimony of opponents (e.g. in 17:7) needs handling with more care, as I sought to do above. Bearing this in mind, a very wide range of characterizing features are provided through the means of other (reliable)

---

[51] Wilhelm Heitmüller, 'Im Namen Jesu.' Eine sprach.- u. religionsgeschichtliche Untersuchung zum Neuen Testament, speziell zur altchristlichen Taufe, FRLANT I/2 (Göttingen: Vandenhoeck & Ruprecht, 1903).
[52] Lars Hartman, 'Into the Name of the Lord Jesus': Baptism in the Early Church, SNTW (Edinburgh: T&T Clark, 1997).
[53] For examples, see Hans Dieter Betz, ed., The Greek Magical Papyri in Translation. Including the Demotic Spells, vol. 1. Text, 2nd ed. (Chicago: University of Chicago Press, 1992).
[54] See my "Evil in Ephesus: Acts 19.8-40" in Evil in Second Temple Judaism and Early Christianity, ed. Chris Keith and Loren Stuckenbruck, WUNT II/417 (Tübingen: Mohr Siebeck, 2016), 224–34.
[55] For a helpful brief introduction to focalization, see Marguerat and Bourquin, How to Read, 72–4.

characters' speech about Jesus, and they add up to a substantial testimony to him as human and much more than human. This testimony is not only concerning 'titles', as older scholarship thought, but also deeds and actions 'in the name of Jesus'.

Having studied other characters' speech about Jesus, we have a greater sense of Luke's own view of Jesus as a character. Some of the themes which were merely suggested by what Luke writes of Jesus's own actions are developed and delineated by Luke's reliable characters – and even sometimes unknowingly reinforced by less reliable characters.

II.c. Jesus's Own Speech

Understandably, this is rare in Acts, for Jesus is off stage most of the time. He is not inactive, but he is not centre stage. However, when he does speak after his ascension, and he does this to Saul of Tarsus, his words are fascinating (9:5; 22:8b; 26:16b). Jesus asks Saul why he is persecuting Jesus, a question which implicitly identifies Jesus with his followers whom Saul is persecuting – and thus a question which entails Jesus's being present in several different places, with his persecuted people, a portrait which Max Turner dubs 'soteriological omnipresence'.[56] Jesus is thus characterizing himself as one who shares God's ability to be present in multiple places simultaneously – a remarkable claim.

II.d. Authorial Comments

This is the second largest group of factors, although very much smaller in number than those by characters.

Luke as author uses a number of appellations we considered earlier on characters' lips, notably: Lord (5:14; 8:12, 16; 9:1, 17, 28, 42; 10:48; 11:20) and Messiah (8:5; 9:22; 10:48). With Stephen as focalizer for the observation, Luke reports Jesus at God's right side (7:55), in the position of power in the universe, reinforcing the point addressed by Peter in the Pentecost sermon (2:33).

Jesus is identified by Luke as the subject of proclamation or teaching by believers: Philip tells the good news (εὐηγγελίσατο) concerning Jesus to the eunuch (8:35); Saul proclaims (ἐκήρυσσεν) Jesus in the Damascene synagogues (9:20) and demonstrates (συμβιβάζων) that Jesus is the Messiah (9:22); the Cypriot and Cyrenian believers tell the good news concerning Jesus (εὐαγγελιζόμενοι); and the Cypriot proconsul Sergius Paulus is astonished by 'the teaching about the Lord' (τῇ διδαχῇ τοῦ

---

[56] Max Turner, "The Spirit of Christ and 'Divine' Christology," in *Jesus of Nazareth. Lord and Christ. Essays on the Historical Jesus and New Testament Christology* ed. Joel B. Green and Max Turner (Carlisle: Paternoster; Grand Rapids: Eerdmans, 1994), 413–36, here 421. Some might think of Paul's statement that he could be present 'in spirit' with the Corinthian congregations when they met (1 Cor 5:4) as a potential parallel. However, Paul qualifies his role there, for his spirit is present 'with the power of our Lord Jesus' (σὺν τῇ δυνάμει τοῦ κυρίου ἡμῶν Ἰησοῦ), and Paul's judgement is pronounced 'in the name of the Lord Jesus' (ἐν τῷ ὀνόματι τοῦ κυρίου Ἰησοῦ). Indeed, Paul does not speak of the believing communities as belonging to him, as Jesus does in Acts; rather they are 'the church(es) of God' (1 Cor 10:32; 11:16, 22; 15:9; Gal 1:3; 1 Thess 1:1; 2:14; 2 Thess 1:1, 4).

κυρίου, 13:12). This theme can be expressed as proclaiming the good news concerning the name of Jesus the Messiah (εὐαγγελιζομένῳ περὶ ... τοῦ ὀνόματος Ἰησοῦ Χριστοῦ, 8:12). Of course, baptism, as we noted earlier, is into Jesus's name, and we hear this point in Luke's narrator's voice (8:16; 10:48) too. To focus attention on a person in this way, rather than on following a person's teaching, was distinctive in the ancient world, and shows that Luke's understanding of Jesus is one who is accessible now to his people, rather than merely a figure of the past – through the proclamation he can be encountered: in Joppa, Jesus is the *object of faith* (9:42), whereas among Jewish people, YHWH alone would deserve such allegiance and trust.

Thus, at this 'highest' level of Alter's types of characterization, Luke as author points his readers to Jesus as the focus and centre of his world view, and as one whom he invites his readers to begin to trust or to continue to trust.

III. The Content of Luke's Characterization of Jesus in Acts

To assess the overall impact of Luke's characterization of Jesus in Acts, we shall place it alongside the recent category of 'divine identity Christology' developed by Richard Bauckham. In his book *God Crucified*, Bauckham seeks to go beyond sterile debates about functional versus ontological approaches to Christology, and instead asks what makes God God in second temple Judaism. His answer is twofold: God is the sole creator and sole ruler of all things.[57] For example, Nebuchadnezzar recognizes God's sovereignty over all when he comes to his senses after a period of madness:

> I blessed the Most High,
> and praised and honoured the one who lives forever.
> For his sovereignty is an everlasting sovereignty,
> and his kingdom endures from generation to generation.
> All the inhabitants of the earth are accounted as nothing,
> and he does what he wills with the host of heaven
> and the inhabitants of the earth.
> There is no one who can stay his hand
> or say to him, 'What are you doing?'
> (Dan 4:34–35)

Isa 40:28 similarly marks out YHWH as the creator of the universe:

> Have you not known? Have you not heard?
> The LORD is the everlasting God,

---

[57] Richard Bauckham, *God Crucified: Monotheism and Christology in the New Testament*, Didsbury Lectures 1996 (Carlisle: Paternoster, 1998), 1–22.

the Creator of the ends of the earth.
He does not faint or grow weary;
his understanding is unsearchable

In consequence, YHWH alone is worth of worship: monolatry (worship of one God alone) follows from monotheism (belief that there is one God alone). Hence, Israel mocked idolatry, such as in the barbed critique of Isa 44:9–20. This critique is predicated on YHWH's exclusive status: 'I am the first and I am the last; besides me there is no god' (Isa 44:6). Against the Hellenistic belief in many gods, Israel was marked by its belief in the one true God. Bauckham shows that his approach is fruitful in reading Paul,[58] and Hays has further shown than this approach illuminates the Gospel-writers' reading of key Old Testament passages.[59] This opens the possibility that such an approach might help us understand Luke's characterization of Jesus in Acts. In other words, we can look at the passages we have studied in Acts to seek to understand what the book is communicating in its presentation of Jesus as a character. So let us interrogate our data from Acts to see if these features can be found concerning Jesus.

Jesus is presented as reigning, for he is exalted to heaven (1:9). The cloud which hides Jesus from the disciples' eyes echoes the cloud of Dan 7:13–14, which is also a cloud travelling to heaven: on Daniel's cloud the 'son of man' is taken to the Ancient of Days and given universal sovereignty. Jesus, further, is now located in heaven (1:11) at God's right side (2:33), and is now Lord of the Spirit, dispensing the Spirit to his own. To give the Spirit is an ability YHWH alone possesses in second temple Jewish understanding.[60] Thus Luke never speaks of believers giving the Spirit to others. Rather, believers pray for *God* to give the Spirit (Acts 8:15); thus Peter objects to Simon's request to buy the ability to lay hands on people in order that they might receive the Spirit, since the gift of the Spirit is 'God's gift' (Acts 8:20). The implication is that for Luke to record that Jesus, having received the Spirit from the Father, now pours out the Spirit, is to place Jesus in the same category as YHWH, and thus to invite worship of Jesus.

This point can be developed further, for Jesus is given the divine *name* as 'Lord of all' (10:36). Franklin writes, 'Luke's understanding, however, does not allow for any deification',[61] and there can be no doubt Franklin is right within a first-century Jewish framework of thought. It is worth reflecting on two passages in the Third Gospel which help us see more of Luke's theologizing. In 3:3–6, Luke quotes Isa 40:3–4 and applies it to John the baptizer: John is the one who prepares the way for the Lord to come, and in the context of Isaiah, that must mean YHWH. However, in the Third Gospel, the one who comes after John is Jesus, and he comes to baptize with the Holy Spirit and fire (3:16–17). This places Jesus in the YHWH position in the Isaiah quotation: *Jesus* is the Lord whose way John prepares. Luke makes a similar

---

[58] Bauckham, *God*, 25–42.
[59] Richard B. Hays, *Reading Backwards: Figural Christology and the Fourfold Gospel Witness* (Waco, TX: Baylor University Press, 2014).
[60] See Turner, *Power*, 277–9; Turner, "Divine," esp. 420; Turner, "The Spirit of Christ and Christology," in *Christ the Lord: Studies in Christology Presented to Donald Guthrie*, ed. Harold H. Rowdon (Leicester: Inter-Varsity Press, 1982), 168–90.
[61] Franklin, *Christ*, 54.

hermeneutical move in 7:27. There Luke's Jesus quotes Mal 3:1, concerning the messenger whom God sends to prepare for God's own coming. Jesus applies this to John the baptizer: he is the messenger. But John's role is to prepare the way for *Jesus* to come, which again places Jesus in the YHWH position in the Malachi quotation.[62] As Hays observes, these texts (and others) 'ascribe to Jesus roles and actions that are reserved in Israel's Scripture for God alone.'[63] By them Luke is pointing to Jesus as sharing the divine identity.

Prayer to Jesus, which we have already observed as a remarkable feature, underlines the identity of Jesus further. Stephen prays to the Lord Jesus as he dies (Acts 7:59).[64] Peter, in his Pentecost speech, quotes Joel 2:32 (LXX 3:5) in 2:21, concerning calling on the name of the Lord. The response required in 2:38 is 'be baptised in the name of *Jesus*'. The likelihood is that baptism 'in the name of Jesus' is shorthand for baptism in which the baptizand calls upon Jesus's name for salvation, as the parallel description of Saul's baptism suggests: 'Get up, be baptized, and have your sins washed away, calling on his name' (22:16). This is all the more remarkable when we consider uses of the phrase 'call on the name' in relation to YHWH in Scripture:

> Then we will never turn back from you; give us life, and *we will call on your name*. (Ps 80:18)
>
> And you will say in that day: Give thanks to the LORD, *call on his name*; make known his deeds among the nations; proclaim that his name is exalted. (Isa 12:4)
>
> At that time I will change the speech of the peoples to a pure speech, that *all of them may call on the name of the* LORD and serve him with one accord. (Zeph 3:9)
>
> And I will put this third into the fire, refine them as one refines silver, and test them as gold is tested. *They will call on my name*, and I will answer them. I will say, 'They are my people'; and they will say, 'The LORD is our God.' (Zech 13:9)

To 'call on' Jesus is an unprecedented innovation, for while Jewish people recognized beings who were divine agents, such as angels, personified Wisdom, and the like, none of them were addressed in prayer in this way.[65]

Bauckham helps us to take the thought one stage further, for having concluded that the earliest believers innovated by placing Jesus alongside YHWH as an object for prayer and worship, he suggests that to do this redefines the God of Israel as one who suffers: 'In this act of self-giving, God is most truly himself and defines himself for the world.'[66] Can we find evidence of such reflection in Acts? Yes, we can, for Acts emphasizes the suffering of Christ as the necessary prelude to his glorification. Thus

---

[62] Cf. Hays, *Backwards*, 62–4; Professor Hays kindly acknowledges a conversation about Luke's divine identity Christology which we had (xx).

[63] Hays, *Backwards*, 62–3.

[64] The verb is ἐπικαλέω, which is used for calling upon a deity (BDAG 373 s.v §1); so also (e.g.) Richard I. Pervo, *Acts*, Hermeneia (Minneapolis, MN: Fortress, 2009), 198–9; Haenchen, *Acts*, 293 (comparing the prayer to 'an ancient Jewish evening-prayer [Ps 31.5]').

[65] Hurtado, *Lord*, 199; Craig S. Keener, *Acts: An Exegetical Commentary*, 4 vols (Grand Rapids: Baker Academic, 2012–15), 2:1459.

[66] Bauckham, *God*, 69.

in 2:23–24, he suffered because of the Jerusalemites and their leaders' actions, and God then reversed this human verdict; in 3:13–15 they killed the author of life (itself a wonderfully self-contradictory thing to do!) and rejected him, but God raised Jesus from the dead and glorified him (cf. Phil 2:5–11[67]); in 8:32–35 Philip finds the eunuch reading Isa 53:7–8 and interprets the servant who suffers as Jesus.

IV. Conclusion: Presence and/or Absence?

In the light of our discoveries, we can return to the Conzelmann thesis, that Jesus is absent from the scene in Acts. There are several features we have noticed which suggest that Jesus is now personally active in the world, and not simply by means of the Spirit. Certainly he is active *from heaven*, for he is now located at God's right side.[68]

To start at the beginning, Acts 1:1 sets the book up as being about what Jesus *continues* to do and teach, and 1:2 further shows that Jesus instructs the apostles. 1:8 identifies the apostles as his witnesses, and suggests thereby that their teaching and preaching is Jesus's work. The major event of the early part of Acts is Pentecost, and Peter interprets this as Jesus's being active in pouring out the Spirit (2:33).

As we have noted, Jesus is present in the narrative by appearing to Stephen standing at God's right side (7:56), and by appearing to Saul of Tarsus (9:1–9). The repeated charge that Saul has been persecuting *Jesus* (not merely his followers) implies Jesus's identification and presence with his followers (9:4; 22:7; 26:14 – this is a constant feature in each telling of the Damascus road experience). Jesus himself directs Saul to Damascus (9:6) and sends Ananias to him (9:11, 15–16) – indeed, he has to send Ananias twice because Ananias argues with him! Paul later says that he has received his ministry from the Lord Jesus (20:24), and surely thereby refers to the Damascus road experience. Aeneas is healed by Jesus the Messiah himself, not merely in Jesus's name (9:34).

Saul continues to experience personal visitations by Jesus: Jesus appears to Saul on his first post-Damascus road visit to Jerusalem in the Temple to tell him to flee the city and go to the gentiles (22:17–18, 21). 'The Lord' who visits to assure Paul in Corinth may well be Jesus (18:9–10).[69] Paul declares, strikingly, that it is *Jesus himself* who is announcing light to Israel and the gentiles (26:23) – thus Paul's proclamation is not merely Paul speaking, but Jesus himself at work (cf. 1:2, 8). 26:23 echoes the parallel missions to gentiles and Israel of Luke 2:32 and thus Isa 49:6.

---

[67] See Gorman's valuable discussion of Phil 2:5–11 which suggests that God's very nature is to give of himself in service. Michael J. Gorman, *Inhabiting the Cruciform God. Kenosis, Justification, and Theosis in Paul's Narrative Soteriology* (Grand Rapids, MI: Eerdmans, 2009), 9–39.

[68] In what follows, I am drawing on an excellent conference paper, Beverly R. Gaventa, "The Presence of the Absent Lord: The Characterization of Jesus in the Acts of the Apostles" (Paper given at SBL Annual Meeting, 2003). Professor Gaventa has summarized some of this thinking in her article "Acts of the Apostles," *NIDB* 1:33–47.

[69] Identifying the 'Lord' here as Jesus is suggested by the immediately preceding use, which speaks of believing 'in the Lord' (18:6), a verb normally used in Acts with Jesus as object (when it has an object) (11:17; 16:31; 19:4).

Taken together, these features of Luke's characterization of Jesus in Acts suggest that Jesus is now present in heaven, at God's right side, but in such a way that he can continue to be active on earth in the *missio Dei*, guiding his people and drawing others into the body of Jesus-believers.[70] Jesus thus shares the characteristics of the God of Israel,[71] and is therefore rightly treated as deserving of the same veneration and honour as the one true God.

---

[70] For a recent, very rich, discussion of Acts using spatial theory to engage with Jesus's location in heaven and activity on earth, see Sleeman, *Geography*.

[71] Cf. this interesting treatment of the characterization of God in Acts: Ling Cheng, *The Characterisation of God in Acts: The Indirect Portrayal of an Invisible Character*, PBM (Milton Keynes: Paternoster, 2011).

11

Identity and Christology: The Ascended Jesus in the Book of Acts

I. Introduction

Luke alone in the New Testament gives Jesus's exalted status narrative expression (Luke 24:51; Acts 1:9–11), and thereby signals its significance for him. Nevertheless, Luke is far from alone in recognizing this status of Jesus to which the ascension points, as numerous scholars recognize.[1] Thus, Hebrews emphasizes Jesus's position of rule and authority in heaven (e.g. 1:3), Revelation highlights Jesus's reign as a key encouragement to beleaguered believers (e.g. 3:21; 5:6–14; 7:17), and Paul assumes Jesus's present rule in writing of Jesus's expected return (e.g. Rom 8:34; Phil 2:9; 1 Thess 1:10; 4:16; cf. Eph 1:20; 4:7–13; Col 3:1; 1 Tim 3:16). The synoptic Gospels similarly speak of Jesus as 'ἐρχόμενον with the clouds' (e.g. Matt 24:30; 26:64; Mark 14:62; Luke 21:27), denoting either his 'going' to God to be given power and authority (Dan 7:13) or his 'coming' from heaven to earth bearing divine power and authority[2] – for our purpose, either option signals that Jesus is to be revered alongside God. John's Gospel speaks of Jesus's 'glorification' (e.g. 7:39; 8:54; 12:16; 14:13; 17:5), which denotes the son's journey back to his Father in heaven through death, resurrection and exaltation (3:13; 13:1–3; 16:5, 28).

Two questions focus our reflection on the contribution of Acts to this widespread New Testament theme. First, we shall consider the portrait of Jesus as ascending and ascended by studying the Acts account of the ascension (Acts 1:9–11), references to Jesus's status in speeches in Acts 2–7 (located in Jerusalem), and the ascended Jesus's engagement with the story of Acts, particularly in relation to Saul/Paul.

Forming this portrait opens up our second question, which is the extent to which Jesus is portrayed as having 'divine identity', a category developed by Richard Bauckham and now used by a number of scholars working on New Testament Christology. This

---

[1] See, e.g., the helpful collection of references in Douglas Farrow, *Ascension and Ecclesia: On the Significance of the Doctrine of the Ascension for Ecclesiology and Christian Cosmology* (Edinburgh: T&T Clark, 1999), 275–77.
[2] For the former view, see N. T. Wright, *Jesus and the Victory of God* (London: SPCK, 1996), 360–5; for the latter, see (on Mark 13:26): Joel Marcus, *Mark*, AB 27, 27A, 2 vols. (New Haven, CT: Yale University Press, 1999, 2009), 2:908–9.

will allow us to engage with the discussion about how Luke's Christology is best characterized.

II. Acts' Portrayal of Jesus as Ascending and Ascended

Acts' portrait of the ascension event begins in 1:2 with the statement ἄχρι ἧς ἡμέρας… ἀνελήμφθη 'until the day when … he was taken up'. The verb is a 'divine' passive, denoting God as actant. NRSV and NIV 2011 both add 'into heaven', although the equivalent words are not present in the Greek text. However, Dupont rightly argues against van Stempvoort that the verb denotes the ascension of Jesus, rather than his passing from this world in death, and so those two English versions are making explicit a claim made implicitly by the verb choice.[3] In support of this interpretation, we note that the same verb in the passive voice is used in LXX for Elijah and Enoch passing from this world into heaven (4 Kgdms 2:9, 10, 11; 1 Macc 2:58; Sir 48:9; 49:14), and by Peter when speaking of Jesus going to heaven (Acts 1:22, in similar wording to 1:2).[4]

II.a. Luke's Description of the Ascension Acts 1:9–11

The primary portrait of the event is in 1:9–11, and several points are crucial to note: the rich visual vocabulary, and the phrase εἰς τὸν οὐρανόν 'into heaven'; the verb voices; the cloud; the interpretive words of the two men in white; the implications suggested concerning Jesus's status; and the portrait of Jesus's presence.

II.a.i. Visual Vocabulary and 'into Heaven'

The rich visual vocabulary is frequently noted as a feature of this passage; there are five verbs of seeing in these two sentences: βλεπόντων 'as they were watching', ἀπὸ τῶν ὀφθαλμῶν αὐτῶν 'from their eyes (sc. sight)', ἀτενίζοντες 'as they were staring', ἰδού 'see!', and ἐμβλέποντες 'looking intently'.[5] This collocation of verbs of seeing is remarkable, and these terms are different from the terms generally used for visionary experiences.[6] Thus Barrett observes that βλεπόντων 'places the Ascension in the same

---

[3] A. van Stempvoort, "The Interpretation of the Ascension in Luke and Acts," NTS 5 (1958-9): 30–42; Jacques Dupont, "ἈΝΕΛΗΜΦΘΗ (Act. I. 2)," NTS 8 (1962): 154–7.
[4] Dupont, "ἈΝΕΛΗΜΦΘΗ," 156.
[5] Some mss have βλέποντες 'looking', but that does not affect the argument here; see Bruce M. Metzger, A Textual Commentary on the Greek New Testament, 2nd ed. (Stuttgart: Deutsche Bibelgesellschaft, 1994), 245.
[6] John B. F. Miller, Convinced That God Had Called Us: Dreams, Visions, and the Perception of God's Will in Luke-Acts, BibInt 85 (Leiden: Brill, 2007), 8 notes that four word most significant in Lukan dream-visions, ἐνύπνιον, ὀπτασία, ὄραμα and ὅρασις; he does not list any of the terms found here. Contra Rick Strelan, "Strange Stares: ἀτενίζειν in Acts," NovT 41 (1999): 235–55, there is no evidence that ἀτενίζω denotes entering an altered state of consciousness through a self-induced trance.

category of events as any other happening in the story of Jesus'[7] – indeed, this point is stronger, given the collocation of five such verbs.

Not only this, but Luke's account stresses the destination to which the ascending Jesus travels as εἰς τὸν οὐρανόν 'into heaven' (vv. 10b, 11), while playing on the dual reference of the phrase by having the two men ask why the bystanders are looking 'into heaven' (v. 10a), which could mean 'into the skies' or 'into the realm of God'.

However, to notice these linguistic features is to raise the question: what actually happened? If we had been there with a video camera, what would we have recorded? David Strauss observes:

> The first impression from this narrative is clearly this: that it is intended as a description of a miraculous event, an actual exaltation of Jesus into heaven, as the dwelling-place of God, and an attestation of this by angels; as orthodox theologians, both ancient and modern, correctly maintain.[8]

Strauss is clear, of course, that no such event could have taken place. James Dunn (who quotes Strauss[9]) insists that Luke cannot be describing events within space-time, but that Luke, because of his worldview, is compelled to express his belief in Jesus's location at the Father's right side and his consequent reign using 'concrete' imagery.[10] Dunn claims that the *only* worldview open to Luke is a 'three-decker' universe. He quotes from Bultmann's famous observation about what 'modern man' (*sic*) can believe:

> *Man's knowledge and mastery of the world* have advanced to such an extent through science and technology that it is no longer possible for anyone seriously to hold the New Testament view of the world – in fact, there is no one who does. What meaning, for instance, can we attach to such phrases in the creed as 'descended into hell' or 'ascended into heaven'? We no longer believe in the three-storied universe which the creeds take for granted. The only honest way of reciting the creeds is to strip the mythological framework from the truth they enshrine – that is, assuming that they contain any truth at all, which is just the question that theology has to ask. No one who is old enough to think for himself supposes that God lives in a

---

[7] C. K. Barrett, *A Critical and Exegetical Commentary on the Acts of the Apostles*, ICC, 2 vols. (Edinburgh: T&T Clark, 1994, 1998), 1:81.

[8] David F. Strauss, *The Life of Jesus Critically Examined* (London: SCM, 1973), 750.

[9] James D. G. Dunn, "The Ascension of Jesus: A Test Case for Hermeneutics," in *Auferstehung – Resurrection: The Fourth Durham-Tübingen Research Symposium: Resurrection, Transfiguration, and Exaltation in Old Testament, Ancient Judaism, and Early Christianity (Tübingen, September 1999)*, ed. Friedrich Avemarie and Hermann Lichtenberger, WUNT 135 (Tübingen: Mohr Siebeck, 2001), 301–22, here 308–9.

[10] Dunn, "Ascension"; see also his earlier dialogue with David Gooding, provoked by James D. G. Dunn, "Demythologizing – The Problem of Myth in the New Testament," in *New Testament Interpretation*, ed. I. Howard Marshall (Exeter: Paternoster, 1977), 285–307; David W. Gooding, "Demythologizing Old and New, and Luke's Description of the Ascension: A Layman's Appraisal," *IBS* 2 (1980): 95–119; James D. G. Dunn, "Demythologizing the Ascension – A Reply to Professor Gooding," *IBS* 3 (1981): 15–27; David W. Gooding, "Demythologizing the Ascension – A Reply," *IBS* 3 (1981): 46–54. Dunn's most recent statement is James D. G. Dunn, *Beginning from Jerusalem* (Cambridge/Grand Rapids, MI: Eerdmans, 2009), 145–51.

local heaven. There is no longer any heaven in the traditional sense of the word. The same applies to hell in the sense of a mythical underworld beneath our feet. And if this is so, the story of Christ's descent into hell and of his Ascension into heaven is done with.[11]

Dunn observes:

> This is not simply the way Luke conceived the ascension; it was the *only* way he could conceive of it … The departure of Jesus to heaven as narrative could not be conceptualized except as an ascension. And if we want to speak of the event behind the narrative, we have also to say that the event could not be experienced except as the witness of an ascension.[12]

This presents us, says Dunn, with 'the problem of a conceptualization of reality which we today do not, cannot share, but do not know how to reconceptualize'.[13] He goes on to argue that to ask what happened in any detail is to miss the point: what was important for the 'earliest tradents of the ascension tradition' was the *theme* of Jesus's exaltation to God's right side.[14] Dunn is considerably less clear – as he concedes – about the 'event-character' of the ascension.[15] Thus he concludes that the ascension is 'a story which clothes a still vivid metaphor'.[16]

I report Dunn's views at length because I judge that they are both widely held and deeply mistaken. The prime mistake is the one from which others flow, and that is the claim that Luke had only one way of seeing the world open to him, a 'three-decker' universe in which heaven was 'up'. We note two primary objections.

First, this is manifestly not so, for we know of a number of writers from the sixth century BC onwards who held different views of cosmology, and the widespread nature of these views, temporally and geographically, means it is highly likely that Luke and others of his day knew of them. Prominent Greeks thinkers, notably Pythagoras and his followers, rejected the 'flat earth' view which was previously universal in our ancient sources, and conceived the earth as spherical.[17] In the second millennium BC, Babylonian and Chinese astronomers knew the planets Mercury, Venus, Mars, Jupiter and Saturn.[18] Astronomers thus faced the challenge of conceptualizing a universe with such bodies, and by the first century AD worked with models which included

---

[11] Rudolf Bultmann, "New Testament and Mythology," in *Kerygma and Myth: A Theological Debate*, ed. Hans-Werner Bartsch, trans. Reginald H. Fuller, 2 vols. (London: SPCK, 1953, 1962), 1:1–44 (4, his italics). This is a fuller quotation than Dunn's.
[12] Dunn, "Ascension," 312.
[13] Dunn, "Ascension," 313 (his italics).
[14] Dunn, "Ascension," 317.
[15] Dunn, "Ascension," 317.
[16] Dunn, "Ascension," 322.
[17] See the masterly survey of Edward Adams, "Graeco-Roman and Ancient Jewish Cosmology," in *Cosmology and New Testament Theology*, ed. Jonathan T. Pennington and Sean M. McDonough, LNTS 355 (London: T&T Clark, 2008), 5–27. For what follows I am also in debt to my student, Dr David Larsen.
[18] A. Sachs, "Babylonian Observational Astronomy," *Philos. Trans. Royal Soc. A* 276 (1974): 43–50.

a spherical universe beyond which nothing physical existed, but beyond which an 'unmoved mover' – god – who brought the whole universe into being might exist, and who must be eternal (Aristotle, *Met.* 12.7.2 = 1073a). Such models did not necessitate picturing a realm outside the universe as 'up'. In Jewish thought, reality is described by the merism 'heaven and earth',[19] although 'heaven' can denote either the skies or the divine realm. There is no agreement among Jewish writers of our period about the structure of reality, e.g. apocalyptic writers described 'tours' of heaven from which visitors returned (e.g. 1 En. 17–36; 2 En. 3–66), although without precision about heaven's location; and Philo adapted Greek understanding in discussing creation (e.g. *Creation*, which synthesizes Gen 1–3 and Plato's *Timaeus*), but again without clarity about the relation of the heavenly to physical reality. There were quite a number in Luke's time who distinguished (in our terms) outer space from the divine realm.

Secondly, the use of 'up' in this context is necessary metaphorical and (as we would say) earth-centred, for many ancients (but not all[20]) held a geocentric view of the universe. Luke necessarily describes things in the language of his day; but for him to speak of Jesus rising into the air and then being taken into heaven no more implies that heaven is physically 'up' than a person today speaking of 'sunrise' should be taken to believe that the sun rotates around the earth – both are metaphorical, observer-centred language. To suggest that the ancients did not recognize that they used metaphorical language in speaking of the location of the divine realm in relation to the earthly is a rather flat-footed way of handling metaphor when we know the ancients discussed it with some sophistication.[21]

In addition, the line of thought that we know better than Luke because of our scientific discoveries, and thus his presentation of the ascension must be rejected, entails a modernist confidence in 'objective' knowledge which is untenable in a postmodern world where we recognize the necessarily perspectival nature of knowledge claims, including those of scientific knowledge.

Thus, unless we adopt an antisupernaturalist rejection of phenomena beyond our experience, Luke's description of the event, that Jesus was elevated from the ground and passed into a cloud which obscured him from the sight of the onlookers, interpreted (probably through the lens of Dan 7:13) as transferring him into the divine realm, is both coherent and consistent. Luke records post-resurrection accounts which portray Jesus as both disappearing and appearing (Luke 24:31, 36), so the ascension account is adding little to these descriptions. To take the description this way is not to deny that some features are *also* understood symbolically, but it is to reject the view that they are merely 'apocalyptic stage props', a way of speaking of Jesus's exalted status without

---

[19] See discussion in Jonathan T. Pennington, "Dualism in Old Testament Cosmology: *Weltbild* and *Weltanschauung*," *SJOT* 18 (2004): 260–77, arguing cogently that OT cosmology is predominantly bipartite (heaven and earth) rather than tripartite (including an underworld).

[20] Aristarchus of Samos (fourth/third centuries BC) held a heliocentric model: Thomas Heath, *Aristarchus of Samos: The Ancient Copernicus* (Oxford: Clarendon, 1913).

[21] E.g. Aristotle, *Poet.* 21–22; *Rhet.* 3.2.6–4.4, 3.10.7–11.15. See brief discussion in Michael S. Silk, "Metaphor and Simile," *OCD* (4th online ed.; 2012) https://oxfordre.com/classics/view/10.1093/acrefore/9780199381135.001.0001/acrefore-9780199381135-e-4151?rskey=uvb7hI&result=1 (accessed December 2021).

describing a space-time event.[22] Jesus's ascension is portrayed as no less a space-time event than any of his other resurrection appearances.

Why is this significant? As we shall see, Luke both implies theological claims about Jesus and his present status on the basis of the ascension story, and presents that story as an event within the space-time universe. To deny the space-time-ness of the event is thus to deny the implications which Luke suggests flow from it – as so often in Scripture, history and theology are not easily separable categories, and nor are historical and theological claims easy to split from one another. This certainly seems to be so with Luke's portrayal of the ascension.

II.a.ii Verb Voice, Subject and Object

Luke's choice of verb voice, subject and object to describe Jesus's movement in this section stands out. There are a number of 'divine passive' uses, uses of passive voice verbs where Jesus is the subject but with no stated actant, which imply that God performs the action:[23] ἐπήρθη 'he was lifted up' (v. 9),[24] πορευομένου 'as [he] was going' (v. 10), ἀναλημφθείς '[who] was taken' and πορευόμενον '[who] was going' (v. 11). Further, Jesus is the object of the verb ὑπέλαβεν 'took him up' (v. 9), and the verb's subject is νεφέλη 'a cloud', which is to be understood as acting under the guidance of its Creator (see further below).

These features signify that Luke presents the God of Israel as acting to elevate Jesus, in both physical lifting and being raised in standing and esteem. This implication is explicit in Peter's Pentecost speech (2:33–36).

II.a.iii The Cloud

A singular cloud ὑπέλαβεν Jesus from (ἀπό) their sight. The verb here is sometimes translated 'hid' (NIV 2011, 1984), whereas its more usual sense is 'take up' or 'receive up'.[25] Haenchen observes that the verb 'covers the moment of both concealment and separation, either of which may be expressed by ἀπό'.[26] None of this implies that the cloud is a means of transport to heaven.[27]

---

[22] E.g. Dunn, "Ascension," 318: 'The point is that such apocalyptic language would be widely recognized even then as having symbolic rather than literal force.' To say this is, of course, to concede that ancients could distinguish metaphor from literal description.

[23] Cf. passive verbs used when Luke speaks of Jesus's resurrection, also implying that God raised Jesus; see Steve Walton, "Jesus, Present and/or Absent? The Presence and Presentation of Jesus as a Character in the Book of Acts," in *Characters and Characterization in Luke-Acts*, ed. Frank Dicken and Julia A. Snyder, LNTS 548 (London: Bloomsbury T&T Clark, 2016), 123–40, here 132 [in this volume, 145–60, here 152].

[24] With (e.g.) Joseph A. Fitzmyer, *The Acts of the Apostles: A New Translation and Commentary*, AB 31 (Garden City, NY: Doubleday, 1998), 210.

[25] BDAG s.v. So NRSV.

[26] Ernst Haenchen, *The Acts of the Apostles* (Oxford: Blackwell, 1971), 149 n. 4; see BDAG 105 ἀπό §§1.b, d.

[27] *Contra* Fitzmyer, *Acts*, 210; with Eckhard Schnabel, *Acts*, ZECNT (Grand Rapids, MI: Zondervan, Expanded digital ed., 2012) on 1:9.

What echoes might we hear when Luke mentions this cloud? Two passages in the Third Gospel resonate with this use, each with further biblical echoes. First, when Jesus speaks of the cloud (singular) in which the son of man comes or goes with power and glory (Luke 21:27), the cloud portrays Jesus as (most probably[28]) going to God as the son of man of Dan 7:13–14, to be given universal authority and rule.

Secondly, at the transfiguration a (singular) cloud overshadows Jesus and his three disciples, and a voice from the cloud declares, 'This is my beloved son. Listen to him!' (Luke 9:34–35). Here biblical echoes are multiple. There is Ps 2:7, as at the baptism of Jesus (Luke 3:22), although there the voice addresses Jesus directly, '*You are* my beloved son.'[29] The description of the cloud in Luke 9:34 as overshadowing (ἐπεσκίαζεν) them points to the cloud which overshadowed the tent of meeting and prevented Moses entering (Exod 40:35), and reverberates with the echo of the travelling cloud of God's presence with the wandering Israelites led by Moses (Exod 13:21–22). These echoes invite readers to see the transfiguration cloud as marking God's presence and (thus) to hear the voice as God's.

Together, the Lukan and biblical echoes of this cloud mark the ascension scene as Jesus's exaltation by God to a divinely-occupied place of universal rule and authority, confirmed by a divine voice, which here comes through angels (v. 11).

II.a.iv. The Words of the Two in White

The two figures in white (v. 10), most probably angels, speak to interpret the disciples' experience (v. 11). Luke's ἰδού 'look!' (untranslated in many versions) signals that readers should pay particular attention to the following words, which give God's perspective on the ascension. This interpretation contrasts with other second temple Jewish heavenly journeys, which frequently involve a human travelling into the divine realm and then returning with a message for their earth-bound hearers and readers.[30] Here, rather, the angels bring the message, which promises the return of Jesus from heaven at a future date in a similar manner to his ascension. *Contra* the assumptions of Conzelmann, this passage neither says nor implies anything about a 'delay' of Jesus's future coming;[31] in fact, it says nothing about the timing of the event, in line with Jesus's statement that the disciples will not know (v. 7).

II.a.v. Jesus's Presence as a Theme in the Ascension Scene

Throughout the ascension scene and its immediate antecedent, the presence of Jesus is a significant theme. In response to the question about Israel's restoration, Jesus

---

[28] For references see n. 2.
[29] See Max Turner, *Power from on High: The Spirit in Israel's Restoration and Witness in Luke-Acts*, JPTSup 9 (Sheffield: Sheffield Academic, 1996), 197–201.
[30] E.g. 1 En. 17–36; Philo, *Spec. Leg.* 3.1–6; Rev 1:10–11, 19; for brief discussion, see James D. Tabor, "Heaven, Ascent to," *ABD* 3:91–94; James M. Scott, "Heavenly Ascent in Jewish and Pagan Tradition," *DNTB*, 447–51.
[31] Hans Conzelmann, *The Theology of St Luke*, trans. Geoffrey Buswell (London: Faber & Faber, 1960), 95–136.

speaks of himself as represented by his witnesses, those with whom he speaks (v. 8, taking genitive μου as 'on my behalf'). The Spirit's coming follows Jesus's ascension into heaven, suggesting that Luke also indicates here that Jesus is present through the Spirit, who empowers his witnesses.

The threefold 'into heaven' (vv. 10, 11 [twice]) signals Jesus's presence in heaven, and Peter's Pentecost speech clarifies that Jesus is now in the position of power at God's right side (2:33), ruling over the universe. It is hard to accept Strelan's antithesis concerning εἰς τὸν οὐρανόν: 'This is not a spatial or locative description; it means that Jesus now participates in the rule of God.'[32] We do not have to choose between location as denotation of the phrase 'into heaven' and rule as connotation – both are natural understandings of this phrase.

The presence of Jesus in heaven will not be permanent, for he will return to earth, promise the duo in white (v. 11). That will be the time of 'universal restoration' (3:21), when history is wrapped up and all things are restored to match the Creator's intentions.

The combination of Jesus's temporary presence in heaven with the Spirit's coming during that period, and then Jesus's return signalling and effecting the restoration of all things, portrays Jesus as having immense power and authority, of a kind which YHWH alone was understood to have in second temple Jewish thought.

II.a.vi. Jesus's Exaltation to the Place of Power

Two other implications flow from the exaltation of Jesus, as we look back to Luke's account at the end of his Gospel, and forward into the following chapters of Acts.

Looking back, it is striking that Luke describes the disciples as *worshipping* (προσκυνήσαντες) Jesus after he is taken up to heaven (Luke 24:52). The only other use of προσκυνέω in the Third Gospel is where the devil invites Jesus to worship him, and Jesus rejects that invitation with a quotation from Deut 6:13 which specifies that it is the Lord your God *alone* who should be worshipped (4:7–8).[33] Luke gives no indication that the disciples are misguided in 24:52 – rather the reverse – and thus that parallel indicates that it is appropriate to treat Jesus as YHWH alone should be treated.

Looking forward into the Acts narrative, Jesus's ascension opens traffic flow between heaven and earth. The Spirit will come (Acts 2), angels will appear in the narrative (e.g. 5:19; 8:26; 10:3; 12:7), signs and wonders will be performed, enabled by divine power (e.g. 2:43; 5:12; 6:8), people will be healed and delivered from evil spirits in the name of Jesus (e.g. healing: the sequence 3:6–7, 16; 4:10; cf. 9:34; deliverance: 16:16–18). The entry of Jesus into heaven opens the door for heaven to come to earth.

---

[32] Rick Strelan, *Strange Acts: Studies in the Cultural World of the Acts of the Apostles*, BZNW 126 (Berlin: de Gruyter, 2004), 39.
[33] With Richard B. Hays, *Reading Backwards: Figural Christology and the Fourfold Gospel Witness* (Waco, TX: Baylor University Press, 2014), 69.

II.b. Interpretation of Jesus's Exaltation through Speech in Acts 2–7

We turn from the account of the ascension to four passages in Acts 2–7 which both state and interpret Jesus's present exalted status: Peter's Pentecost speech (esp. 2:33–36), Peter's speech in the temple courts after the healing of the man at the Beautiful Gate (esp. 3:20–21), Peter and the apostles' speech to the Sanhedrin (esp. 5:31), and Stephen's dying words (7:56–60).

II.b.i. Acts 2:33–36

The key to understanding the Pentecost speech's claims about Jesus's status is v. 33. Jesus is now 'exalted (ὑψωθείς, a further 'divine passive') at the right hand of God' and in this position 'has received from the Father the promise which is the Holy Spirit'. Thus the one who has 'poured out[34] what you see and hear' is Jesus – he continues to be the verb subject throughout the sentence. 'What you see and hear' refers to the phenomena of vv. 1–4: the rushing wind, the tongues of fire, and the speaking in other languages, which are markers of the Spirit's coming (v. 4b).

The key to interpreting this verse is to ask, in second temple Jewish understanding, who pours out the Spirit.[35] The answer is YHWH and YHWH alone: no one else has this ability, for God's Spirit '*was a way of speaking of the active* (usually self-revealing) *personal presence of the transcendent God himself*'.[36] Luke prepares for this sentence by the presence of 'God declares' (λέγει ὁ θεός) in Acts 2:17. This phrase, absent from Luke's source text (Joel 2:28–32), presents God himself as speaking of the promise of the Spirit (Acts 2:17–21) – *God* will pour out the Spirit in the last days, not any human being or angel or other creature. So when Peter speaks in v. 33 to say that *Jesus himself* is the one who has poured out the Spirit at Pentecost – not even that Jesus *mediates* the Spirit from YHWH – this implies that Jesus, exalted to God's right hand, is Lord of the Spirit and the Spirit is his 'executive power'.[37] The Spirit is now related to Jesus as the Spirit has been related to God: 'God the Father grants Jesus *the same authority as himself* to pour out the Spirit'.[38] Indeed, Luke has Jesus say that he himself will send the Father's promise, i.e. the Spirit (Luke 24:49, emphatic ἐγώ). Heaven is now 'open' for much greater traffic to earth as a result of Jesus's ascension – hence a sound comes from there (v. 2), and hence the Spirit comes from the exalted Jesus.

Peter wastes no time in spelling these implications out by contrasting Jesus with David, who did not ascend to heaven (v. 34), and identifying Jesus as the 'Lord' of Ps 110:1.[39] Thus Jesus is the one who now sits at God's right side awaiting his enemies

---

[34] Echoing Joel 3:1–2 LXX (MT 2:28–29).
[35] For what follows, see my essay, "Whose Spirit? The Promise and the Promiser in Luke 12:12," in *The Spirit and Christ in the New Testament and Christian Theology*, ed. I. Howard Marshall, Volker Rabens and Cornelis Bennema (Grand Rapids, MI: Eerdmans, 2012), 35–51, here 47–8.
[36] Turner, *Power*, 277 (his italics).
[37] Turner, *Power*, 278; cf. Douglas Buckwalter, *The Character and Purpose of Luke's Christology*, SNTSMS 89 (Cambridge: Cambridge University Press, 1996), 194–6.
[38] Buckwalter, *Character*, 195 (his italics); cf. *TDNT* 6:405: Jesus is 'not a pneumatic, but the Lord of the Spirit'.
[39] Cf. Jesus's use of Ps 110:1 in a similar argument about David and the Messiah (Luke 20:42–3).

being made his footstool: he is both Lord and Messiah (v. 36). As Barrett observes, '[h]e who shares the throne of God shares his deity; and he who is God is what he is from and to eternity – otherwise he is not God'.[40] In the setting of v. 33, Jesus is now in the same category as Israel's God as 'Lord', and that is why he is the one whose name people must call on to be saved (vv. 21, 38), for he is 'Lord of all', as Peter later says (10:36).

II.b.ii. Acts 3:20-21

A key claim of Peter's speech in the temple courts (3:11-26), following the healing of the man at the Beautiful Gate (3:1-10), is about the present position and role of Jesus. He is now in heaven (v. 21), a (divinely) necessary (δεῖ) state of affairs.[41] From there he will be sent (by God) at the restoration of all things, the time when cosmic renewal and regeneration will take place. The echo of ἀποστέλλω (v. 20) from 1:11 makes this connection sure – it is Jesus's return which will coincide with (and probably trigger) cosmic restoration.[42] Jesus not only restores Israel,[43] but the entire universe. In the absence of demiurges and the like in Judaism, this can only mean that Jesus is placed in a role which YHWH was expected to accomplish.[44]

II.b.iii. Acts 5:31

Peter and the apostles respond to the Sanhedrin's reproach for continuing to speak in Jesus's name after being forbidden to do so (4:17-18; 5:28) with a theo- and Christocentric answer. Not only is God the one who must be obeyed rather than mere humans (v. 29; cf. 4:19), but this same God has reversed the Sanhedrin's verdict by raising Jesus from the dead (v. 30) and has exalted Jesus to his right side as ἀρχηγός and σωτήρ (v. 31). This passage echoes the themes of 2:33-35, which suggests that the ascension and its implications are also in view here. Σωτήρ is predicated of Jesus in Luke 2:11 (and not since in Luke-Acts) and the following reference here to repentance and forgiveness indicates what Jesus saves from. It is not widely noticed that σωτήρ is a common biblical designation of God, as well as (far less) human deliverers sent by God.[45] The following purpose clause indicates that God gives repentance and

---

[40] Barrett, *Acts*, 1:152.
[41] See the fine discussion in Charles H. Cosgrove, "The Divine ΔΕΙ in Luke-Acts: Investigations into the Lukan Understanding of God's Providence," *NovT* 26 (1984): 168-90.
[42] Again we notice, *contra* Conzelmann, that there is no indication of the time – short or long – in which this return will take place, with Hans F. Bayer, "Christ-Centred Eschatology in Acts 3:17-26," in *Jesus of Nazareth, Lord and Christ: Essays on the Historical Jesus and New Testament Christology*, ed. Joel B. Green and Max Turner (Grand Rapids, MI: Eerdmans; Carlisle: Paternoster, 1994), 236-50 (250).
[43] See Richard Bauckham, *The Jewish World around the New Testament: Collected Essays I*, WUNT 233 (Tübingen: Mohr Siebeck, 2008), 325-70, esp. 361-6; Bayer, "Eschatology."
[44] See the valuable discussions of OT and later Jewish 'restoration of Israel' themes in James M. Scott, ed., *Restoration: Old Testament, Jewish, and Christian Perspectives*, JSJSup 72 (Leiden: Brill, 2001).
[45] God: e.g. LXX Deut 32:15; 1 Sam 10:19; Pss 23:5; 24:5; 26:1 (MT 27:1); 61:3 (MT 62:2); 94:1 (MT 95:1); Isa 12:2; 17:10; 45:15, 21; 62:11; Bar 4:22; Jdt 9:11; 1 Macc 4:30; 3 Macc 6:29, 32; 7:16. Human deliverers: Judg 3:9, 15; Neh 9:27. By New Testament times it may well have become a messianic

forgiveness to the people as a consequence of Jesus's exaltation, or perhaps that Jesus himself is the one who does the giving: it is not completely clear who is the actant of the infinitive δοῦναι (v. 31).

II.b.iv. Acts 7:55-60

Towards the end of Stephen's speech, he sees the exalted Jesus at God's right side (v. 55) and identifies him as the son of man, most probably alluding to Dan 7:13, which is also in a martyr context.[46] In response to this sight, Stephen prays to Jesus: 'Lord Jesus, receive my spirit' (v. 59). Luke's specific expression is that Stephen 'calls on' (ἐπικαλούμενον), and this is 'cultic practice' language, as Hurtado notes.[47] Acts 9:14, 21 characterize the believers as those who 'call on the name (of Jesus)' (cf. 22:16). However, in (OT) Scripture, it is God alone who is the proper recipient of prayer,[48] so to include Jesus with God as one who is given 'public, corporate, cultic reverence'[49] is a remarkable innovation in a Jewish context which 'drew a sharp line between any such figure and the one God in the area of cultic practice, reserving cultic worship for the one God'.[50]

II.b.v. Summary

The passages we have considered provide a body of evidence that early believers understood Jesus to be exalted to the place of honour at God's right side in heaven, and that from there he exercised authority and rule to the extent that he took the God of Israel's distinctive role in both giving (the Spirit, phenomena, repentance, and forgiveness) and receiving (prayer).

II.c. Narrative Portrayal of Jesus as Acting and Appearing from Heaven

Let us then turn to consider how Jesus is portrayed as acting and appearing from heaven in the narrative portions of Acts.[51] Because space is limited, we focus on Jesus's appearance to Saul of Tarsus, a highly significant event, for Luke tells it three times (Acts 9, 22, 26), and some examples – chosen from a number – where healing and deliverance come through Jesus or his name.

---

designation (1 En. 48.7; 51.5a; see J. C. O'Neill, *The Theology of Acts in its Historical Setting*, 2nd ed. [London: SPCK, 1970], 144).

[46] C. F. D. Moule, *The Origin of Christology* (Cambridge: Cambridge University Press, 1977), 17. This is the only New Testament use of 'the son of man' outside the Gospels.

[47] Larry W. Hurtado, *Lord Jesus Christ: Devotion to Jesus in Earliest Christianity* (Grand Rapids, MI/Cambridge: Eerdmans, 2003), 198.

[48] Cf. 'call on the name', referring to the name of YHWH, in Ps 80:19; Isa 12:4; Zeph 3:9; Zech 13:9.

[49] Hurtado, *Lord*, 199.

[50] Hurtado, *Lord*, 47-8.

[51] See the more detailed study in Matthew Sleeman, *Geography and the Ascension Narrative in Acts*, SNTSMS 146 (Cambridge: Cambridge University Press, 2009).

II.c.i. Saul of Tarsus Acts 9, 22, 26

Luke tells the story of Jesus's appearances to Saul of Tarsus on the road to Damascus three times. While there are differences among the stories, the core presentation of Jesus who appears is consistent among the three.[52] Here we observe factors signalling key features of the identity of Jesus.

First, the one who appears from heaven is Jesus himself, and he is characterized as 'Lord'. In response to Saul's question, he announces himself as 'Jesus, whom you are persecuting' (9:5; 22:8; 26:15). Ananias speaks of 'the Lord Jesus' as the one who appeared to Saul (9:17), and this interprets the uses of 'Lord' in vv. 10, 11, 13, 15. Further, he is the Lord 'who rescues' (ἐξαιρούμενος, 22:17), something predicated only of YHWH in LXX.[53]

Secondly, as we noticed above, the one who appears is identified with his suffering followers: *he* is being persecuted: This implies that Jesus now has multi-locational ability – he is not merely said to be identified with his people, but he himself is being persecuted in the persecution of his people.

Thirdly, the Jesus who appears stage-manages events by visiting Ananias and directing him to visit Saul (9:10–16). This much resembles the 'divine appointments' of Philip and the Ethiopian eunuch (8:26–40) and Peter and Cornelius (10:1–11:18) which surround this story in the Acts narrative. In both of those stories, it is clear that divine action brings the two protagonists together (8:26, 29; 10:3–7, 19–20, 30–33; 11:11–12, 17–18) and the same is true here – except that it is explicitly 'the Lord Jesus ... [who] has sent me' (9:17).

Finally, Jesus strikes Saul blind and directs him to await instruction (9:6, 8–9; 22:10–11). Illness, including the removal of sensory powers – and even death, is frequently a divine action, or the action of a divine delegate in Scripture.[54] Direction from God to await instruction is similar,[55] as is commissioning to a divine task (26:16–18).[56]

II.c.ii. Healing and Deliverance

Jesus himself acts in healing and deliverance in Acts. Healing can happen by Jesus explicitly being stated to be the actant, such as in the healing of Aeneas: 'Aeneas, Jesus the Messiah heals you' (9:34). It can also happen through the powerful effect of the name of Jesus, which stands for him in action, such as in the healing of the man at the Beautiful Gate: 'in the name of Jesus the Messiah the Nazarene, walk!' (3:6; cf. 3:16; 4:7, 17, 30).[57]

---

[52] For a detailed study, see Timothy W. R. Churchill, *Divine Initiative and the Christology of the Damascus Road Encounter* (Eugene, OR: Pickwick, 2010), esp. 191–249.

[53] Churchill, *Initiative*, 170–1 with the vast array of references in footnotes – 131 uses in LXX. See also John J. Scullion "God in the OT," *ABD* 2:1014–48, here 1044 §3 "God Who Rescues."

[54] E.g. divine: 1 Cor 10:1–5; divine delegate: Luke 1:20; Acts 13:6–12; see valuable discussion of this theme in John Christopher Thomas, *The Devil, Disease and Deliverance: Origins of Illness in New Testament Thought*, JPTSup 13 (Sheffield: Sheffield Academic, 1998), with summary 297–301.

[55] E.g. Exod 24:12; Num 9:8; Pss 38:15; 106:13.

[56] Churchill, *Initiative*, 245–6.

[57] More fully, see my essay, "Jesus," 133–4 [in this volume 153–4].

Deliverance from evil spirits similarly happens through the name of Jesus, illustrated positively by Paul's deliverance of the slave girl in Philippi (16:18), and comically in the failure of the Jewish exorcists in Ephesus, who are overcome by a demonized man because, although they use the name of Jesus, they are not in the kind of relationship with him which the believers are (19:13–17).[58] The conclusion of the episode states that 'the name of Jesus' is honoured (19:17).

II.c.iii. Acts 26:23

Finally, in this necessarily selective discussion, the exalted Jesus is active in the world *himself*, for as Messiah he proclaims light to both Jews and gentiles (26:23). This is a remarkable statement, as Beverly Gaventa notes: 'In Luke's understanding, it is entirely possible for Jesus to be at the right hand of God and simultaneously at work in Christian witness and work.'[59]

II.d. Summary

This is a remarkable collection of data from Acts: we have seen that Luke locates Jesus after his ascension at the place of power at the Father's right side, that the apostolic message both proclaims and explains that status, and that Jesus exercises authority from there by continuing to act within the earthly sphere. To what extent can we take the further step of seeing Luke as in some sense identifying Jesus with the God of Israel?

III. Acts and 'Divine Identity' Christology

'Divine identity Christology' has recently entered scholarly conversation about the early church's understanding of Jesus. Richard Bauckham introduces this category to answer the question what, according to second temple Judaism, makes God God. The failure to answer this question directly left older debate on Christology in ultimately sterile debates between ontology and function, or between 'high' and 'low' Christologies. I shall suggest that this category is a helpful lens through which to consider the data of Acts.

III.a. What Is 'Divine Identity' Christology'?

Bauckham first (to my knowledge) writes of how to recognize Israel's God as God in *God Crucified*, a superb short discussion of New Testament Christology.[60] His short answer is that God is known to be God because he is the sole creator and the sole

---

[58] See discussion in my essay, "Evil in Ephesus: Acts 19:8-40," in *Evil in Second Temple Judaism and Early Christianity*, ed. Chris Keith and Loren T. Stuckenbruck, WUNT II/417 (Tübingen: Mohr Siebeck, 2016), 224–34, here 229–33.
[59] Beverly R. Gaventa, "Acts of the Apostles," in *NIDB* 1:33–47, here 43.
[60] Richard Bauckham, *God Crucified: Monotheism and Christology in the New Testament* (Carlisle: Paternoster, 1998), now incorporated into Richard Bauckham, *Jesus and the God of*

ruler of all things.⁶¹ Key OT examples include Nebuchadnezzar's recognition of God's rule: 'his sovereignty is an everlasting sovereignty' (Dan 4:34) and the vision of YHWH as creator in Isa 40–55, such as 'The Lord is the everlasting God, the creator of the ends of the earth' (Isa 40:28).

YHWH's sovereign status leads to monolatry – worship of this God alone. second temple Judaism mocked idolatry and the multiple gods of other nations (e.g. Isa 44:9–20) because of the exclusive status of YHWH: 'I am the first and I am the last; besides me there is no god' (Isa 44:6).

Bauckham himself applies this line of thinking to Paul and John, very fruitfully,⁶² and Richard Hays has recently used 'divine identity Christology' as a tool to interrogate how the four Gospels read Scripture.⁶³ Our question in relation to our ascension data in Acts is this: to what extent does Acts portray Jesus as sharing the divine identity of YHWH?

III.b. Does Jesus in Acts Share YHWH's Divine Identity?

Acts portrays Jesus as now exalted to the position of power at God's right side (1:9, 11; 2:33), and this means he is able to give the Spirit (2:33; 8:20), an ability which belongs to YHWH alone in second temple Jewish understanding. Jesus is given the divine name in consequence, 'Lord' (2:36), even 'Lord of all' (10:36), heralding his universal power and rule (and implicitly challenging any other 'lords' who claimed universal sovereignty).

The exalted Jesus is appropriately addressed in prayer, notably by Stephen (7:59), but also by implication in the phrase 'call on the Lord's name', where the 'Lord' is Jesus (2:21, 38; cf. 22:16).⁶⁴ This links into the question of monolatry, for second temple Judaism regarded YHWH alone as a proper object of prayer. Hurtado has further documented the early believers' devotional practices in relation to Jesus in Acts, and argues cogently that they bespeak a regard for Jesus as in the same category as YHWH.⁶⁵

Jesus is not only exalted, but he is present with his followers: he is persecuted when they are persecuted (9:4; 22:7; 26:14). Acts is a record of what Jesus *continues* to do and teach (1:1). Thus Jesus acts from heaven on earth, in giving commands and instructions in divine fashion (9:6, 11, 15–16; 20:24) and in healing and deliverance (esp. 9:34, along with references to the 'name' of Jesus in such acts).

While there is thus no doubt that Jesus in Acts shares YHWH's sovereign position and rule, as well as YHWH's ability to be present in different places at the same time, the part of divine identity Christology which is missing in Acts is Jesus as creator. There are clear mentions of God as creator (e.g. 17:24), but no explicit statements that Jesus/

Israel: God Crucified and Other Studies on the New Testament's Christology of Divine Identity (Grand Rapids, MI/Cambridge: Eerdmans, 2008). References are to the 1998 edition.
[61] Bauckham, *God*, 1–22; see my fuller summary in Walton, "Jesus," 136–7 [in this volume 156–9], where I discuss a wider range of data from Acts.
[62] Bauckham, *God*, 25–69.
[63] Hays, *Backwards*; more fully Richard B. Hays, *Echoes of Scripture in the Gospels* (Waco, TX: Baylor University Press, 2016).
[64] See Walton, "Jesus," 133–4 [in this volume 153–4].
[65] Hurtado, *Lord*, 177–216.

the son engaged in creating the universe, by contrast with such statements in John, Colossians and Hebrews.[66] Nevertheless, the 'ascension evidence' in Acts for Jesus as sharing in the sovereign rule of YHWH is widespread and cogent – and this case can be expanded into other features of the narrative.[67]

One further point is worth noting. Bauckham observes that through the New Testament portrait of Jesus as sharing the divine identity a new feature of the God of Israel is made known, namely that God is a God who suffers in Christ.[68] Not only that, through Christ's suffering it becomes clearer that God identifies with the pain of his creation and enters into it, standing alongside people who are lowly, weak, poor or suffering. This novel feature of the understanding of Israel's God is present in Acts too, for the exalted Jesus is one who suffered in his earthly life, and especially in his passion at the hands of sinful people (2:23–24; 3:13–15). This Jesus is to be identified as YHWH's servant who suffers on behalf of the people of God to redeem them (8:32–35), and now suffers with his people (9:4).

---

[66] John 1:3; Col 1:15–17; Heb 1:2.
[67] See Walton, "Jesus."
[68] Bauckham, *God*, 69–77.

12

'The Heavens Opened': Cosmological and Theological Transformation in Luke and Acts

In Luke's story, both heaven and earth are transformed through Jesus and by the Spirit. This process of transformation affects even how God is to be seen and understood, for there is now a human being in heaven at God's right hand – and he pours out the Spirit upon God's people to equip them to reclaim creation for its Creator.

Luke's Gospel and Acts are unique in two important respects for this study. First, Luke[1] alone of the Evangelists provides a 'volume two' telling the story of the establishment of the earliest Christian communities. This allows us to see how the remarkable intervention of Israel's God in human history through Jesus is played out among those who follow Jesus. By writing Acts, Luke portrays the universal claims of Jesus with particular clarity.

Second, Luke alone among the NT writers narrates the ascension of Jesus, and he does so twice (Luke 24; Acts 1). By contrast with angels, who come from heaven and return there, Jesus is a human being who enters heaven. Jesus both shares the rule of God over the universe and continues to intervene in the story of his followers, both in his own person and by the Spirit. In piercing the barrier between earth and heaven, Jesus restructures how reality is understood, both now and in the days to come.

To explore Luke's engagement with cosmology, we shall first review his perspective on the key cosmological terms and ideas which he uses. We shall then focus on the shift of perspective which the ascension of Jesus brings. This will lead into discussion of those who invade this realm of earth from heaven, notably angels, the Spirit and Jesus himself after his ascension, repulsing the occupying forces of Satan, demons, and unclean and evil spirits. Finally, we shall consider some key passages in Acts where there seems to be explicit dialogue with rival accounts of cosmology, particularly those which centre on the Jerusalem temple, on paganism, or on the role of Caesar.

---

[1] For the purpose of this study we make no assumption about the identity of the author of Luke and Acts, other than his gender.

I. Naming Space(s): Key Terms

Luke uses οὐρανός ('heaven' or 'sky') 61 times in his two books. The Lukan favourite ὕψιστος ('highest') can denote the heavenly realm as well. Luke also has a number of uses of ᾅδης 'Hades' (4 of 10 NT uses are in Luke-Acts). By contrast, Luke does not use the κτίζω ('create') word group at all, and uses κόσμος ('world') only four times. Luke does use γῆ, variously translated as 'earth', 'soil', 'land', 58 times, notably for our purpose in combinations with οὐρανός. This impression is borne out by more detailed examination. Thus *prima facie* Luke shows a strong interest in the heavenly realm and its interaction with the earthly.

Luke's preference for 'heaven and earth' language over κόσμος is rather unexpected given that Luke is writing into a Graeco-Roman setting, where κόσμος is more common than 'heaven and earth' as a label for the universe. Plausibly, this is an example of Luke imitating the LXX, where usage is similar.[2]

I.a. Heaven/the Heavens,[3] the Highest, and Hades

The large majority of Lukan uses of οὐρανός occur in prepositional phrases.

The Lukan assumption of an above/below metaphor for the division of heaven and earth is seen in the expression 'under heaven' (ὑπὸ τὸν οὐρανόν), in each use suggesting universality (Luke 17:24; Acts 2:5; 4:12).

Likewise, movement 'into heaven' (εἰς τὸν οὐρανόν) is upwards in relation to earth, especially in Jesus's ascension (Luke 24:51; Acts 1:9–11). Peter contrasts Jesus with David, who did not ascend (ἀνέβη) there (Acts 2:34). Jesus is now in an exalted position of power in the realm of God (cf. Acts 3:21; 7:56).[4] The angels depart into heaven (Luke 2:15), and the sheet in Peter's vision is taken up into heaven (Acts 10:16; 11:10). The above/below metaphor is expressed in relation to prayer in the tax collector who will not lift his eyes εἰς τὸν οὐρανόν (Luke 18:13) and Jesus looking up (ἀναβλέψας) into heaven when he gives thanks (Luke 9:16). In these cases 'heaven' stands for the realm of God, as it does in the prodigal son's affirmation that he has sinned 'against heaven' (Luke 15:18, 21), and in Stephen seeing 'into heaven' (Acts 7:55).

The expression 'from heaven' (ἐκ τοῦ οὐρανοῦ, ἐξ οὐρανοῦ or ἀπὸ τοῦ οὐρανοῦ) indicates intervention from that realm into the earthly. Often this is positive intervention from the divine realm in the form of sound (Luke 3:22; Acts 2:2; 11:9) or sight (Acts 9:3; 11:5; 22:6) or great signs (Luke 21:11). However, judgement in the

---

[2] As a rough and ready measure, the 71 LXX uses of κόσμος are completely outweighed by 621 uses of οὐρανός and 3043 uses of γῆ. I am grateful to Dr Jonathan Pennington for suggesting the link with the LXX to me.

[3] I have excluded uses of οὐρανός for 'sky' or 'air' (such as τὰ πετεινὰ τοῦ οὐρανοῦ 'the birds of the air', found five times in Luke-Acts), but have focused on those of greater cosmological and theological significance.

[4] It is hard to accept Strelan's antithesis concerning the threefold use of εἰς τὸν οὐρανόν in 1:10–11: 'This is not a spatial or locative description; it means that Jesus now participates in the rule of God' (Rick Strelan, *Strange Acts: Studies in the Cultural World of the Acts of the Apostles*, BZNW 126 [Berlin: de Gruyter, 2004], 39) – why can location not be the denotation and rule the connotation of the expression?

form of fire can come from heaven (Luke 9:54; 17:29), and Satan fell from heaven (Luke 10:18). As previously, 'heaven' is the divine realm, where the Father is (Luke 11:13; cf. 20:4).

By contrast with these present-oriented expressions, ἐν τῷ οὐρανῷ 'in heaven' is often used in future settings. Those who follow Jesus will receive a reward or treasure in heaven (Luke 6:23; 12:23; 18:22), and their names are written in heaven (Luke 10:20). There is rejoicing in heaven when sinners repent (Luke 15:7; cf. 15:10). Rejoicing happens ἐν ὑψίστοις 'in the highest' (Luke 2:15; 19:38). Heaven is also a place of peace and glory (Luke 19:38).

Heaven, however, is not to be attained easily: Capernaum will not be exalted to heaven (ἕως οὐρανοῦ), but brought down to Hades (Luke 10:15). Hades is a realm of pain and suffering (Luke 16:23; although a parable, this draws on popular assumptions about the nature of the after-life[5]). Ps 15:10 LXX (MT 16:10) is quoted in Acts 2:27, 31, and read as a prophecy of the Messiah not being abandoned to Hades. In mentioning Hades, Luke may now be using a 'three decker' model of the universe, with earth in the middle, heaven 'above' and Hades 'below'.[6]

Most striking for our study are uses of οὐρανός as closed or open. Jesus speaks of the famine in Elijah's time in which 'the heaven was closed [ἐκλείσθη ὁ οὐρανός] for three years and six months' (Luke 4:25). The closure of heaven is clearly a reference to the lack of rain from the sky, but probably also implies that God had ceased to care for the people of Israel because of Ahab's sin and their idolatry.[7] Conversely, to speak of heaven as open indicates that intercourse between God and earthly beings is taking place – indeed 'I saw heaven opened' is a standard apocalyptic formula for God revealing himself.[8] Jesus has a vision of heaven opened at his baptism (Luke 3:21); Stephen sees the heavens opened as he is being stoned and recognizes the exalted Jesus in heaven (Acts 7:56); and Peter sees heaven opened when he has the vision of the sheet (Acts 10:11). This language is highly suggestive, for it indicates that God is communicating with his creation, both with Jesus while he is on earth and, after his ascension, with Jesus's followers.

I.b. Earth,[9] the World

A number of times the pair 'heaven and earth' expresses the totality of existence. God made them and is their Lord (Acts 4:24; 14:15; 17:24). Heaven is God's throne and earth his footstool (Acts 7:49, quoting Isa 66:1). In an intriguing pair of sayings, Jesus asserts that it is easier for heaven and earth to pass away than for the smallest

---

[5] John Nolland, *Luke*, WBC 35A–C, 3 vols. (Dallas, TX: Word, 1989–93), 2:557.
[6] Cf. Leslie Houlden, "Beyond Belief: Preaching the Ascension," *Theology* 94 (1991): 173–80, here 177.
[7] I. Howard Marshall, *The Gospel of Luke*, NIGTC (Exeter: Paternoster, 1978), 188.
[8] E.g. Ezek 1:1 LXX; John 1:51; Rev 19:11; see the surveys of Jewish apocalyptic in Markus Bockmuehl, *Revelation and Mystery in Ancient Judaism and Pauline Christianity*, WUNT II/36 (Tübingen: Mohr Siebeck, 1990) and Christopher Rowland, *The Open Heaven: A Study of Apocalyptic in Judaism and Early Christianity* (London: SPCK, 1982).
[9] I exclude here uses of γῆ for 'soil', 'land' (i.e. a country) or 'land' (by contrast with sea or lake); these account for about 25 uses from a total of 58 in Luke-Acts.

character to be dropped from the law (Luke 16:17), and yet says that heaven and earth *will* pass away, but his words will not (Luke 21:33). Heaven and earth clearly possess a certain durability, but not greater durability than Jesus's teaching! Luke thus hints at the coming renewal of the universe.

Elsewhere heaven and earth stand in contrast: the sheet Peter sees is let down from heaven to earth (Acts 10:11) and, suggestively, Saul falls to the earth after the light from heaven shines around him (Acts 9:3–4). Here the superiority of the realm of God is asserted over the human, earthly realm.

Where γῆ occurs without οὐρανός it is used to speak of life here and now by implicit contrast with life in heaven (e.g. Acts 8:33 [quoting Isa 53:8 LXX]; 22:22). Thus Jesus's birth brings peace upon earth (Luke 2:14) and he has authority on earth (Luke 5:24). The future of which he warns will include distress and suffering on earth (Luke 21:23, 25, 35), and his own ministry will bring fire rather than peace (Luke 12:51, 49). In Acts the expression ἕως ἐσχάτου τῆς γῆς 'to the end of the earth', derived from Isa 49:6, is a keynote for the breadth of the believers' mission (Acts 1:8), a mission which they gradually come to see includes gentiles (Acts 13:47) – thus, all the earth's families will be blessed (Acts 3:25, echoing Gen 12:3).

I.c. The Universe as God's Creation

Luke does not use the κτίζω 'create' word group at all, but the idea of the universe as God's creation is clear, particularly where believers are encountering pagans. In Athens, Paul presents God as the one 'who made [ὁ ποιήσας] heaven and earth' and who (in consequence) is 'Lord of heaven and earth' (Acts 17:24). This God is no deistic watchmaker, for he continues to give[10] πᾶσι ζωὴν καὶ πνοὴν καὶ τὰ πάντα '*to all* people life and breath and all things' (v. 25), and (quoting a pagan poet) 'in him we live and move and exist' (v. 28).[11] Luke also presents Jesus as referring to God's kindly providence towards the birds and the flowers of the field and thus, *a fortiori*, for people made in his image (Luke 12:24–28).

This theme can also be seen in Stephen's speech (Acts 7:50, quoting Isa 66:2), where God's 'hand' is synecdoche for God himself – his power in particular; in the prayer of the believers (Acts 4:24); and in Paul's words in Lystra (Acts 14:24).[12] In the latter two cases, the sequence 'the heaven and the earth and the sea and everything in them' follows that in the creation story of Gen 1:1–2:3, further underlining the claim that the God of the believers is the Creator. God's creation of the universe is also hinted at in the idea of 'the foundation of the world' (Luke 11:50), which presupposes a beginning,

---

[10] The present participle διδούς (v. 25) suggests an ongoing giving; with C. K. Barrett, *A Critical and Exegetical Commentary on the Acts of the Apostles*, ICC, 2 vols. (Edinburgh: T&T Clark, 1994, 1998), 2:841.

[11] See further below on Luke's engagement with alternative cosmologies.

[12] Both 4:24 and 14:15 echo LXX Exod 20:11; Neh 9:6; Ps 145:6 (MT 146:6); Isa 37:16, while not being an exact quotation of any of them.

although hints of creation in Luke's Gospel are rare – it is only in the wider mission in Acts that this theme becomes explicit.[13]

II. Changing Space(s): The Ascension[14]

Luke alone narrates Jesus's ascension, and does so twice (Luke 24:50–53; Acts 1:6–11); other NT authors assume its existence or spell out its significance.[15] Luke's double telling shows the importance of the ascension, which provides the basis for much that follows in Acts, as well as being the appropriate climax to the Gospel's story.[16] It marks Jesus's stepping from the realm of earth into heaven, from whence he continues to act; it marks a watershed in his life and in the way the universe is seen and experienced. Because the ascension is so significant for the cosmology of Luke-Acts, we shall focus on it first, and then consider how Luke's Gospel prepares for this remarkable event.

The ascension of Jesus marks the close of the forty-day period of resurrection appearances (Acts 1:3), and vividly shows the risen Jesus entering heaven – εἰς τὸν οὐρανόν 'into heaven' comes three times in Acts 1:10–11. Luke 24:50–53 appears to relate the same event, but with no time frame provided: v. 50 is linked to v. 49 only by the vague δέ.[17] This account contains the same note of Jesus entering heaven (v. 51). It is beyond the scope of this essay to debate the precise relationship of resurrection and ascension; the view taken here is that the resurrection and ascension, although they should be seen together, are distinct moments in the process of Jesus's exaltation to God's right hand.[18] The ascension may then be seen as the culmination of the process

---

[13] It is also worth observing that, while God's fatherhood is linked in the OT and second temple Jewish writings with creation, this link is not made in Luke-Acts. For references and discussion, see Diane G. Chen, *God as Father in Luke-Acts*, StBibL 92 (Frankfurt am Main: Peter Lang, 2006), 84–5, 136–7.

[14] A number of significant issues concerning the ascension, including its historicity, are beyond the scope of this limited study. Significant studies include: Strelan, *Strange*, 33–49; A. W. Zwiep, *The Ascension of the Messiah in Lukan Christology*, NovTSup 87 (Leiden: Brill, 1997); Mikeal C. Parsons, *The Departure of Jesus in Luke-Acts: The Ascension Narratives in Context*, JSNTSup 21 (Sheffield: JSOT, 1987), with useful review of previous work on 14–18; Gerhard Lohfink, *Die Himmelfahrt Jesu: Untersuchungen zu den Himmelfahrts- und Erhöhungstexten bei Lukas*, SANT 26 (München: Kösel, 1971) (convenient summary in English: François Bovon, *Luke the Theologian: Fifty-five Years of Research (1950–2005)*, 2nd revised ed. [Waco: Baylor University Press, 2006], 190–8); see also the bibliography in the dogmatics-oriented study of Farrow (see n. 15 below).

[15] See Douglas Farrow, *Ascension and Ecclesia: On the Significance of the Doctrine of the Ascension for Ecclesiology and Christian Cosmology* (Edinburgh: T&T Clark, 1999), 15–40, 275–80; Thomas F. Torrance, *Space, Time, and Resurrection* (Edinburgh: Handsel, 1976), 106–22.

[16] Cf. Eric Franklin, *Christ the Lord* (London: SPCK, 1975), 35.

[17] Although δέ can be used as a marker of change of temporal setting; with Stephen H. Levinsohn, *Textual Connections in Acts*, SBLMS 31 (Atlanta, GA: Scholars, 1987), 87. There is thus no basis to claims that Luke's Gospel presents the departure as happening on the day of Jesus's resurrection in contradiction of Acts, e.g., Ernst Haenchen, *The Acts of the Apostles* (Oxford: Blackwell, 1971), 141.

[18] See the helpful summaries in Kevin L. Anderson, *'But God Raised Him from the Dead': The Theology of Jesus' Resurrection in Luke-Acts*, PBM (Milton Keynes: Paternoster, 2006), 6–10, 41–7; Robert F. O'Toole, "Luke's Understanding of Jesus' Resurrection-Ascension-Exaltation," *BTB* 9 (1979): 106–14. I share the view of Anderson and P. A. Van Stempvoort, "The Interpretation of the Ascension in Luke and Acts," *NTS* 5 (1958-9): 30–42, *contra* Lohfink, *Himmelfahrt*, 80–98, 270; Joseph A. Fitzmyer, "The Ascension of Christ and Pentecost," in his *To Advance the Gospel: New Testament Studies*, 2nd ed. (Grand Rapids, MI: Eerdmans, 1998), 265–94, esp. 265–77; Zwiep, *Ascension*.

of Jesus's exaltation and the point at which Jesus is visually exalted to heaven, thereby providing the disciples with a visual demonstration of the truth of Jesus's exalted status. Hence, Acts 1:9–10 uses a rich visual vocabulary which stresses the reality of the event, for the terms used are not visionary or dream language: βλεπόντων, τῶν ὀφθαλμῶν αὐτῶν, ἀτενίζοντες,[19] ἐμβλέποντες, ἐθεάσασθε.

II.a. What the Ascension Implies

Given the stress Luke places on the ascension and heavenly session of Jesus, what intersection does it have with cosmological issues? At least six points come to mind.

First, the ascension and exaltation of Jesus to God's right hand imply that *Jesus now reigns alongside God from heaven*; it is now appropriate to call him κύριος ('Lord') as well as Χριστός ('Messiah'), for God himself has done so in exalting Jesus to his right hand (Acts 2:36). His ascension is 'into heaven' (Luke 24:51;[20] Acts 1:10, 11). The account of the ascension is brought to a close for the disciples by a cloud (Acts 1:9), a cloud which echoes the singular cloud of Luke 21:27 upon which the son of man comes (contrast Mark 13:26; Matt 24:29). It therefore appears that Luke intends an echo of Luke 21:27 in Acts 1:9, and thereby makes a connection to Dan 7:13 concerning the son of man who comes to the Most High on the clouds. The prominent use of a cloud in the transfiguration (three times in Luke 9:34–35) further reinforces the likelihood that the ascension cloud connotes God's presence and glory.[21]

Alongside these links, Luke explicitly states that, after Jesus ascended, 'they worshipped him' (Luke 24:52). Since for Jews worship is to be given to God alone, Jesus is here being placed alongside YHWH as an object of worship.[22] His entry into heaven is thus different from those of Elijah or Enoch, for his entry follows his resurrection.[23] Thus the way 'God' is understood changes:

> [T]he way that Luke narrates the ascension of an eschatologically transformed, fleshly human being inevitably alters the life of ... God and forever breaks the bounds of any cosmology, ancient or modern, that portrays the gap that needs

---

[19] Strelan, *Strange*, 38–9 unconvincingly seeks to argue that ἀτενίζοντες implies entering into a trance-like state, which is unlikely – the verb here (as elsewhere) denotes intent looking or staring at something or someone (BDAG 148 s.v.). Even if Strelan were correct about ἀτενίζοντες, Luke has used numerous other visual words which carry no such implication; cf. Barrett, *Acts*, 1:81 on βλεπόντων, whose use 'places the Ascension in the same category of events as any other happening in the story of Jesus'.

[20] ℵ* D some Old Latin manuscripts and the Sinaitic Syriac lack καὶ ἀνεφέρετο εἰς τὸν οὐρανόν, 'and he was carried up into heaven', but these words are read by 𝔓75 and the rest of the manuscript tradition, and seem to be presupposed by Acts 1:2; with Bruce M. Metzger, *A Textual Commentary on the Greek New Testament*, 2nd ed. (Stuttgart: Deutsche Bibelgesellschaft/United Bible Societies, 1994), 162–3.

[21] Cf. the thoughtful argument of Strelan (*Strange*, 36) for early Christian appropriation of Pss 8, 46 to connect Jesus's exaltation with reigning, as well as his helpful tracing of references to clouds connoting God's presence (37–8).

[22] Larry W. Hurtado, *Lord Jesus Christ: Devotion to Jesus in Earliest Christianity* (Grand Rapids, MI; Cambridge: Eerdmans, 2003), 345.

[23] This is the diametrical opposite of the puzzling view of Franklin, *Christ*, 35, that it was the ascension rather than the resurrection which marked Jesus out as 'other than one of the prophets'.

overcoming between God and humanity as primarily ontological rather than harmatological.[24]

Second, the two white-robed interpreters tell the disciples that *Jesus's ascension presages his return from heaven to earth* (Acts 1:11).[25] This return to earth will be the time of cosmic renewal and restoration promised in Scripture (Acts 3:20–21) as well as of judgement (Acts 17:31). The cloud also became emblematic of the return of Jesus, as he was to come from the presence of God which the cloud symbolizes (cf. 1 Thess 4:17; Rev 1:7; 14:14–16). It is possible that this parousia symbolism may have further encouraged Luke to report the cloud as enveloping Jesus.

Third, *heaven's gift, the Holy Spirit, flows from Jesus's exaltation to God's right hand* (Acts 2:33). Heaven is open (Acts 2:2 speaks of a sound coming 'from heaven') and the Spirit is poured upon God's people as a result of Jesus's exaltation, which itself marks him as Lord of the Spirit (Acts 2:36).[26] The futuristic present ἀποστέλλω (Luke 24:49) and the emphatic ἐγώ show that Jesus himself will send the Holy Spirit as 'power from on high' (cf. Acts 1:5). The Spirit here and in Acts 2:33–36 is the executive power of the exalted Jesus, by which he exercises his sovereignty over the world.[27] This same Spirit will be the means of empowering the believers for the task of calling creation back to God as they witness to Jesus (Acts 1:8),[28] in preparation for the day of Jesus's return.

Fourth, *the heavenly Jesus will welcome and receive believers.* This seems to be the significance of the appearance of Jesus to Stephen (Acts 7:55–56).[29] Jesus is named as 'the son of man' (v. 56), uniquely outside the Gospels. He has fulfilled Dan 7:13 and therefore has received the universal jurisdiction given to the son of man. Stephen's murderers recognize this (to them) blasphemous claim by refusing to hear it further and by stoning Stephen (vv. 57–58). Daniel 7 was, of course, addressed to a martyr context of the people of God suffering against the pagans, portrayed as wild beasts (vv. 2–8), immediately before the Ancient of Days enters the scene to find in favour of his people.[30] It is thus particularly appropriate that Daniel 7 is alluded to here.[31]

Fifth, *Stephen provides an example of a wider category of Jesus's appearances and actions from heaven.* These flow from Jesus's role at God's right hand as God's 'chief

---

[24] Andy Johnson, "Resurrection, Ascension and the Developing Portrait of the God of Israel in Acts," *SJT* 57 (2004): 146–62, here 147; see also Douglas Buckwalter, *The Character and Purpose of Luke's Christology*, SNTSMS 89 (Cambridge: Cambridge University Press, 1996), esp. 180–92.
[25] Torrance, *Resurrection*, 150–8.
[26] Max Turner, *Power from on High: The Spirit in Israel's Restoration and Witness in Luke-Acts*, JPTSup 9 (Sheffield: Sheffield Academic, 1996), 278; Max Turner, "'Trinitarian' Pneumatology in the New Testament? – Towards an Explanation of the Worship of Jesus," *AsTJ* 57 (2003): 167–86, here 178; Buckwalter, *Character*, 194–6.
[27] See, much more fully, Turner, *Power*, 290–315.
[28] I here take 'the end of the earth' as a reference to 'everywhere', in tune with the echo of Isa 49:6, with, *inter alia*, Luke T. Johnson, *The Acts of the Apostles*, SP 5 (Collegeville, MN: Liturgical, 1992), 26–7. Note also that the crowd at Pentecost come 'from every nation *under heaven*' (Acts 2:5) – while all of these are Jews, the choice of term hints at the universality of the concerns of God.
[29] For interpretive options, see Barrett, *Acts*, 1:384–85.
[30] N. T. Wright, *The New Testament and the People of God* (London: SPCK, 1992), 291–7.
[31] C. F. D. Moule, *The Origin of Christology* (Cambridge: Cambridge University Press, 1977), 17.

executive agent' – Luke has no 'absentee Christology'.³² Hence Jesus appears from heaven to Saul of Tarsus on the road to Damascus and exercises his power by striking him blind (Acts 9:8). Jesus is not absent from earth, for he is identified with the believers whom Saul is persecuting – to persecute them is to persecute Jesus himself (Acts 9:5). The Jesus who reigns with the Father is also the Jesus who suffers with his people, thereby sharing God's own ability to be present in many locations at once – and this illustrates our human difficulty with using the language of 'presence' and 'absence' in relation to the exalted Jesus.³³

Not only does Jesus meet Saul directly, but he goes on to prepare for Saul's integration into the believing community by speaking to Ananias (Acts 9:10–16).³⁴ The exalted Jesus stage-manages events to his own ends, and thus exercises his sovereignty over the universe. Similarly, it is Jesus who pours out the Spirit (Acts 2:33). It is Jesus who heals Aeneas (Acts 9:34) and, when other healings take place in the name of Jesus, the name stands for his person too (e.g. Acts 3:6, 16; 4:7, 17, 30)³⁵ and shows his present, earthly exercise of power: 'What believers do in Jesus's name is in effect being done by Jesus himself.'³⁶ That power is also seen in deliverance from evil spirits (Acts 16:18 and, comically, 19:13, 17).³⁷ Indeed, so powerful is Jesus's name that it is the unique and sole instrument of salvation (Acts 4:12), so that new believers are baptized into Jesus's name (Acts 2:38; cf. 10:43; 22:16)³⁸ and proclamation of the message is proclamation of the name of Jesus (Acts 9:15, 27, 28). Prayer, too, is calling upon the name of Jesus (Acts 9:14, 21).

Sixth, the ascension of Jesus, his piercing the barrier between earth and heaven, means that *heaven is open to earth*. To be sure, heaven has been invading earth in and through the ministry of the earthly Jesus, but the flurry of angelic activity in the early chapters of Acts is unprecedented, directing, saving and emboldening believers and bringing God's judgement to Herod (Acts 1:10–11; 5:19; 8:26; 10:3; 12:7–11, 23; cf. 27:23–24). The repeated coming and action of the Holy Spirit is a further important instance of heaven invading earth (e.g. Acts 2:1–4; 4:8, 31; 6:10; 7:55; 8:17; 9:17; 10:44; 11:28; 13:2, 9, 52), as are the healings and exorcisms which take place. The exorcisms, in particular, drive back the occupying forces of evil and free people from bondage to belong to God's people (e.g. Acts 5:16; 8:7; 16:16–18; 19:12). 'Signs and wonders'

---

[32] See Turner, *Power*, 295–6 for the point and the specific phrases, *contra* (famously) Hans Conzelmann, *The Theology of St Luke*, trans. Geoffrey Buswell (London: Faber & Faber, 1960), throughout, esp. 204.

[33] I owe this point to an unpublished paper presented by Prof. Beverly Gaventa to the Book of Acts Section at the SBL Annual Meeting of November 2003; I gratefully acknowledge her kindness in providing me with a copy.

[34] It is natural to take ὁ κύριος (v. 10) as Jesus, since he has recently been called 'Lord' by Saul (v. 5) and there has been no intervening mention of God as 'Lord'. It is a little surprising that Dunn's otherwise comprehensive discussion does not engage with this passage (James D. G. Dunn, "KURIOS in Acts," in his *The Christ and the Spirit: Collected Essays of James D. G. Dunn: vol. 1 Christology* [Edinburgh: T&T Clark; Grand Rapids, MI: Eerdmans, 1998], 241–53).

[35] John A. Ziesler, "The Name of Jesus in the Acts of the Apostles," *JSNT* 4 (1974): 28–41, here 35–7.

[36] Buckwalter, *Character*, 184; see 182–4 for a helpful discussion.

[37] John Goldingay, "Are They Comic Acts?," *EvQ* 69 (1997): 99–107, here 102–4.

[38] This may be a reference to entering into the ownership of Jesus. See discussion in Ziesler, "Name," 29–32; Lars Hartman, *'Into the Name of the Lord Jesus': Baptism in the Early Church*, SNTW (Edinburgh: T&T Clark, 1997), 37–50, 127–45.

occur at the beachheads of the invasion (e.g. Acts 2:22, 43; 4:30; 5:12; 6:8; 14:3; 15:12). Those who outwardly join God's renewed people, but who lie to the heavenly Spirit, are judged (Acts 5:1–11). Further, God's word is an active agent within the mission of God (Acts 6:7; 12:24; 13:48–49; 20:32),[39] and acts as a further agent of God's heavenly invasion of earth (cf. Isa 55:10–11). By contrast with previous times, both in the OT and in the ministry of Jesus, heaven is now 'open for business' on a permanent basis.

III. Space Invaders: Heaven Coming to Earth

We have discovered thus far that the exaltation of Jesus, visually represented and culminated in the ascension, initiates a new chapter in the life of heaven and earth. There is now a human being reigning alongside God, and earth is open to heaven in a fresh way. How far does Luke's Gospel prepare for this?

The time of Jesus's birth bristles with divine activity. God sends angels to announce both the birth of John, the forerunner of Jesus, and Jesus himself (Luke 1:11–20, 26–38; 2:8–14). The Holy Spirit inspires speech to announce what God is now doing (Luke 1:41–45, 67–79; 2:25–32). Most notably of all, the Spirit causes Mary to become pregnant (Luke 1:35),[40] a fresh creative act which reflects God's desire to intervene anew in his universe in and through Jesus.

At Jesus's baptism the apocalyptic expression ἀνεῳχθῆναι τὸν οὐρανόν 'the heaven was opened' (Luke 3:21) presages a significant disclosure from God.[41] Here, 'after a period of apparent inactivity God himself comes down to act in power.'[42] Jesus's vision of the Spirit's descent is interpreted by the heavenly voice, echoing Ps 2:7 and Isa 42:1: Jesus is empowered by the Spirit for his messianic task as 'great David's greater son'.[43] Luke repeatedly underlines Jesus's empowerment by the Spirit, for Jesus returns from Jordan 'filled with the Holy Spirit' and is then 'led by the Spirit' (Luke 4:1). Jesus emerges from the temptations 'in the power of the Spirit' (Luke 4:14), and announces in Nazareth that he is the one anointed with the Lord's Spirit for his mission (Luke 4:18–19, quoting Isa 61:1–2; 58:6).[44] This mission is God's work through Jesus, so that his exorcisms are to be understood as demonstrating the power of God (Luke 11:20) – his ministry is progressively bringing down Satan's empire (Luke 10:18).[45] Jesus's healing

---

[39] See the valuable discussion in David W. Pao, *Acts and the Isaianic New Exodus*, BibStL (Grand Rapids, MI: Baker, 2002), 160–7.
[40] With Turner, *Power*, 155–60, *contra* Robert P. Menzies, *Empowered for Witness: The Spirit in Luke-Acts*, JPTSup 6 (Sheffield: Sheffield Academic, 1994), 111–16.
[41] Cf. Acts 10:11; John 1:51; Rev 4:1; 19:11 and Isa 64:1; Ezek 1:1; T. Levi 2.6; 2 Bar 22.1.
[42] Marshall, *Gospel*, 152.
[43] See discussion in Turner, *Power*, 197–201, *contra* James D. G. Dunn, *Baptism in the Holy Spirit* (London: SCM; Philadelphia: Westminster, 1970), 23–37; Menzies, *Empowered*, 132–9.
[44] Discussion: Turner, *Power*, 213–64.
[45] The image of Satan falling ὡς ἀστραπὴν ἐκ τοῦ οὐρανοῦ 'as lightning from heaven' likely continues an echo of Isa 14 found in Luke 10:15. 10:15 applies the Isaianic imagery of being exalted to heaven and being thrown down to Hades (Isa 14:11, 13–15) to Capernaum which rejects Jesus. So Luke T. Johnson, *The Gospel of Luke*, SP 3 (Collegeville, MN: Liturgical, 1992), 169; full discussion in Susan R. Garrett, *The Demise of the Devil: Magic and the Demonic in Luke's Writings* (Minneapolis, MN: Fortress, 1989), 46–57.

ministry similarly restores people to full participation in the people of God, notably a man with leprosy (Luke 5:12-14); the woman who was haemorrhaging for twelve years (Luke 8:43-48), who would be unclean because of her bleeding; and the woman who had been bent over for eighteen years because of a spirit (Luke 13:10-17), whom Jesus regards as a 'daughter of Abraham' (v. 16) and thus a member of God's people.

Not only is Jesus himself empowered by God through the Spirit, but we already know from John that the coming one is also the one who baptizes with the Holy Spirit (Luke 3:16) – Jesus is thus pivotal to God's purpose to open heaven to earth afresh by enabling the Spirit to come. Luke makes it clear that he sees the fulfilment of this promise at Pentecost by Jesus's statement that 'John baptized with water, but you will be baptized with the Holy Spirit not many days from now' (Acts 1:5). Thus the beginnings of Jesus's ministry point forward to the time when the believers will be equipped to serve God by calling all in creation back to him.

When we focus on Jesus's death and resurrection, non-earthly beings and phenomena are again present.[46] The darkness at the cross (Luke 23:44-45a) suggests that creation is turning its back on the suffering Messiah, Jesus.[47] Even God is turning away from Jesus as he suffers, for darkness symbolizes both God's absence and the presence and dominance of evil, just as light symbolizes God's presence.[48]

In the midst of the darkness the temple curtain is torn in two (Luke 23:45b). Readers frequently see this incident through the eyes of Heb 10:20, which pictures Jesus opening a new way to God through the curtain, and thus interpret the tearing of the curtain as symbolizing access to God.[49] However, it seems likely that the tearing may rather focus on the emptiness of the Holy of Holies, to demonstrate that this is not where God is to be found (cf. Ezek 10; 2 Bar 6:7; 8:2), and thus this event portends the ultimate destruction of the temple.[50] This likelihood is increased by two features of Acts. First, Stephen's speech (Acts 7) is critical of the elevation of the temple as *the* place where God is known, although not of its foundation or existence. Stephen's speech claims that the temple's time is over, for God is active and available apart from the temple – he is not limited to this particular holy space (Acts 7:48).[51] Second, God makes himself known to people in Acts away from the holy space of the temple, such as in the desert to a eunuch (8:26-40), in an unclean gentile household in Joppa (10:1-48), and in many places outside the land of Palestine during Paul's travels.[52] The temple,

---

[46] It is textually unlikely that the angel in Gethsemane (Luke 22:43-44) is original (Metzger, *Textual Commentary* 2nd ed., 151), so it is omitted from discussion here.

[47] Cf. Josephus, *Ant*. 14.12.3 §309, a comment from a letter of Mark Antony to Hyrcanus concerning his opponents in battle: 'the sun turned away his light from us, as unwilling to view the horrid crime they were guilty of in the case of Caesar.'

[48] Cf. Luke 22:53 and note the contrast with Luke 1:79, where Jesus's birth is as the dawn rising; so Raymond E. Brown, *The Death of the Messiah*, ABRL, 2 vols. (London: Geoffrey Chapman; Garden City, NY: Doubleday, 1994), 2:1042; cf. Joseph A. Fitzmyer, *Luke*, AB 28, 2 vols. (Garden City, NY: Doubleday, 1981, 1985), 2:1518-19; Joel B. Green, *The Gospel of Luke*, NICNT (Grand Rapids, MI/Cambridge: Eerdmans, 1997), 825.

[49] See the useful enumeration of possibilities in Nolland, *Luke*, 3:1157.

[50] Marshall, *Gospel*, 875; Brown, *Death*, 2:1101-06.

[51] Steve Walton, "A Tale of Two Perspectives? The Temple in Acts," in *Heaven on Earth: The Temple in Biblical Theology*, ed. T. Desmond Alexander and Simon J. Gathercole (Carlisle: Paternoster, 2004), 135-49, here 138-43 [in this volume, 75-87, here 77-82].

[52] Walton, "Tale," 146-8 [in this volume 85-6].

whose destruction Jesus has prophesied (Luke 21:6), becomes functionally redundant, for access to God is through Jesus and by the Spirit.[53]

At the tomb of Jesus, the women meet two men in dazzling clothes, who are angels and announce Jesus's resurrection (Luke 24:4–5, 23). These angels form an *inclusio* with the angels who announce Jesus's birth in Luke 1–2, and provide heaven's commentary on the empty tomb.

Luke's Gospel prepares for the fuller picture seen in Acts by portraying phenomena which show that heaven is entering the earthly realm to reclaim the world for its Creator. The angels who surround the beginning and end of Jesus's ministry will be active in the church's ministry. The same Spirit who empowered Jesus for his messianic task will empower his followers for their missionary task. The cosmological change of Jesus's presence in heaven at God's right hand produces a theological change in how God is to be seen, understood and known – it is now through Jesus and by the Spirit that he is to be known, and that by the gentiles as well as the Jews (Acts 1:8).

IV. Space(d) Out? Challenging Other Cosmologies

Finally, we briefly consider some places where there appears to be dialogue between a Christian cosmology and other cosmologies.

We have already noticed Stephen's speech (Acts 7), for here Stephen implicitly critiques a cosmology which gives a unique and special place to the Jerusalem temple as *the* earthly place of access to God. Instead, Stephen asserts, God has made himself known in pagan lands (e.g. vv. 2, 9, 29–34, 44). He presents the temple's status as ambiguous, in tune with the ambiguity in the dedication of the temple (1 Kgs 8:15–53, esp. 27).[54] When the Sanhedrin respond in rage to the suggestion that they oppose the Holy Spirit (vv. 51–54), Stephen's vision of Jesus, the son of man, vindicated and exalted to God's right hand (vv. 55–56), announces that it is through Jesus that access to God is now found – hence Stephen's prayer is for Jesus to receive him (v. 59). The latter point combines the claims that it is Jesus who receives people into heaven – normally God's prerogative – and that it is appropriate to pray to Jesus, rather than God alone.[55]

Second, this cosmology critiques the claimed place of Caesar in the Roman empire. Rather than Caesar being the one with universal jurisdiction and worthy of worship, Jesus should receive the highest honours.[56] This theme underlies a number of events

---

[53] Cf. Green, *Luke*, 825–6, who seeks to combine the best of both positions.
[54] Walton, "Tale," 141–2 [in this volume 80–1].
[55] ἐπικαλούμενον is used for 'calling upon' God in prayer, BDAG 373 s.v. §1.
[56] E.g. Julius Caesar is described as 'the god made manifest' (*SIG*³ §760) and Claudius as 'god who is saviour and benefactor' (*IGRR* IV §584); more fully, see the listing of evidence in Steve Walton, "The State They Were In: Luke's View of the Roman Empire," in *Rome in the Bible and the Early Church*, ed. Peter Oakes (Carlisle: Paternoster; Grand Rapids, MI: Baker Academic, 2002), 1–41, here 26–8; Jacob Jervell, *Die Apostelgeschichte*, KEK, 17th ed. (Göttingen: Vandenhoeck & Ruprecht, 1998), 434 with n. 175.

and speeches in Acts, not least 17:7, where Jesus is recognized as being 'another king' in place of Caesar.[57]

Third, this cosmology engages highly critically with pagan cosmologies which see a multiplicity of gods controlling various elements of the universe. Paul engages in Lystra with uneducated pagans (Acts 14:11–18) and in Athens with highly educated pagans (Acts 17:16–31) who hold such views. It is interesting that, in Lystra, Paul does not speak explicitly of Jesus in response to the crowds' desire to offer sacrifice to him and Barnabas, although our expectation as Luke's readers is that when Paul speaks (14:9), it is about Jesus. Paul critiques paganism by focusing on the oneness of the true God as Creator and implicitly that he alone should be worshipped (14:15–17).

In Athens,[58] by contrast, Paul explicitly speaks about Jesus and his resurrection (and thus, presumably, his exaltation), and this provokes the invitation to the Areopagus (17:18).[59] Paul engages with Stoics and Epicureans (17:18)[60] and both held cosmologies different to the Christian one.[61]

The Stoics collapsed god and the universe into one in pantheistic fashion; however, it seems likely that at least some Stoic thinkers also deified natural forces: Jupiter was the sky-god, Neptune controlled the sea, and so on. Stoics were materialistic, and believed there to be no real realm outside the visible universe. They were highly deterministic, and used augury and haruspicy to seek what the gods were going to do, but did not regard the gods as personally 'knowable' by humans. Against Stoicism, Paul insists that the Creator is distinct from his creation (v. 24), and that God is knowable (v. 27). More, rather than the gods having control of particular elements or lands, the true God allocated where all peoples lived (v. 26). It is a mistake to identify elements within creation for worship, for this is idolatry (vv. 24–25, 28).[62] Paul asserts firmly that the way that God is known is through Jesus, whom God has raised from the dead and who will be the one who will judge all on the Day (v. 31). One can see why Stoics would be doubtful of the resurrection (v. 32a), and also why it is the climax and centrepiece of Paul's speech, for it is Jesus's exaltation by God which gives Jesus the status and right to judge.

---

[57] For a well-argued and plausible proposal that the 'decrees of Caesar' (17:7) which Jason was accused of breaking were those banning voluntary associations, see Justin K. Hardin, "Decrees and Drachmas at Thessalonica: An Illegal Assembly in Jason's House (Acts 17.1–10a)," *NTS* 52 (2006): 29–49.

[58] For very useful discussions, see Eckhard Schnabel, *Early Christian Mission*, 2 vols. (Downers Grove, IL: InterVarsity Press, 2004), 2:1169–80; Bruce W. Winter, "On Introducing Gods to Athens: An Alternative Reading of Acts 17:18-20," *TynBul* 47 (1996): 71–90.

[59] If Winter's reconstruction is correct, the invitation was to offer grounds for building a temple to Jesus in Athens (Winter, "Gods," esp. 71–80, 87–9). If so, Paul's speech is particularly acute, for he rejects the premise that gods require temples, and asserts that, rather than humans building a temple for God, the one true God has created the world where he should be worshipped.

[60] See Bruce W. Winter, "Introducing the Athenians to God: Paul's Failed Apologetic in Acts 17?," *Them* 31 (2005): 38–59, esp. 48–57.

[61] For a helpful overview of the various positions held in the ancient world, see Cicero, *Nat. d.*, written around the middle of the first century BC, and identifying the Stoics, the Epicureans and the sceptical Academicians.

[62] If Paul asserted this in Ephesus, it is easy to see why the silversmiths, who made souvenir models of the temple of Artemis, would be upset (Acts 19:23–29)! It is possible that 'pure' Stoicism reject idols; if so, Paul is critiquing a popularized version of Stoicism (although see Winter, "Athenians," 54 for a contrary view).

The Epicureans shared the Stoics' materialism and rejected ideas of life after death. They portrayed the gods in human form since they believed human form to be the most beautiful. However, the gods were uninterested in human affairs, so there was no point in offering sacrifice, for the gods would not involve themselves in earthly life. Worship was offered, but only to change the worshipper. Against this backcloth, Paul argues not only that God is the Creator, but that he desires to know his creatures and be known by them (vv. 24, 27). While Paul makes common ground with the Epicureans in presenting God as not needing humans (v. 25), he is critical in claiming that God nevertheless is interested in his creation and wants people to respond to him through Jesus (vv. 30–31).

Paul's response, after building common ground with his interlocutors, is to focus on Jesus and his exaltation, via resurrection, to the place of judgement over the cosmos (v. 31). As elsewhere in Acts, the evangelism of the earliest believers centres on how God is now knowable through Jesus. The risen Jesus has ascended to heaven to reside at God's right hand, thus transforming both cosmological and theological perspectives: he is now the pathway for his people to join him. Heaven is indeed open – to everyone who comes to God through Jesus.

13

Turning Anthropology Right Side Up: Seeing Human Life and Existence Lukewise

Luke[1] rarely gets a mention when anthropology is discussed – the Third Gospel gets lumped in with the other synoptic Gospels, and Acts is placed in the pending tray never to emerge.[2] Yet, when we read Luke and Acts with care, a strong and clear perspective on the nature of human beings, their relationships with God and one another, including across gender and ethnic boundaries, and what it means to be human, emerges.[3] This essay seeks to map that perspective.

We shall proceed by considering first how we may draw out an idea (anthropology) from a story, for the documents we are considering are narrative, rather than directly didactic. This will lead us to note the important device of reversal, which Luke is recognized to use as a storytelling technique, but which can be seen more widely in contrasts between Luke's view of humanity and those found in society and culture. The examination of the Lukan text will then focus on four themes which are particularly relevant to anthropology: the transformation of sinful humanity, explored through the evangelistic speeches of Acts; Jesus as humanity *par excellence*, explored through Jesus-Peter-Paul parallels; human physicality re-understood, explored through comparing Luke's writings and the physiognomic tradition; and the refiguring of community of men and women among believers (and wider hints at community life) in Luke and Acts.

---

[1] As is customary, I use 'Luke' as the name of the author of the Third Gospel and Acts, without any necessary implication as to the author's identity.
[2] See the valuable survey in Christoph W. Stenschke, *Luke's Portrait of Gentiles Prior to Their Coming to Faith*, WUNT II/108 (Tübingen: Mohr Siebeck, 1999), 9–50, esp. 9–11.
[3] I here assume both the common authorship of the Third Gospel and Acts and that there is common intentionality and message to them. See, e.g., I. Howard Marshall, "Acts and the 'Former Treatise,'" in *The Book of Acts in its Ancient Literary Setting*, ed. Bruce W. Winter and Andrew D. Clarke, BAFCS 1 (Carlisle: Paternoster; Grand Rapids, MI: Eerdmans, 1993), 163–82; Joel B. Green, "Luke-Acts, or Luke and Acts? A Reaffirmation of Narrative Unity," in *Reading Acts Today: Essays in Honour of Loveday C. A. Alexander*, ed. Steve Walton, Thomas E. Phillips, Lloyd K. Pietersen and F. Scott Spencer, LNTS 427 (London: T&T Clark, 2011), 101–19.

I. How Does Narrative Teach?

In seeking to study the anthropology of two narrative texts, Luke and Acts, we are asking how an author communicates ideas through story and stories. Our question is particularly acute given that the speeches – where it is commonly assumed that we hear Luke's ideology[4] – are not focused on the understanding of humanity so much as the understanding of God and how God is made known and available to people in and through Jesus. What features of Luke's 'double work' will enable us to recognize what Luke understands by the nature and roles of human beings and humanity collectively?

First, the example and model of Jesus are significant. Luke does not explicitly state that Jesus models what humanity is meant to be in the way that Paul does (e.g. Rom 5:12–21; Phil 2:1–11). Nevertheless, Luke is clear that Jesus is human, rather than the kind of visiting deity known from Graeco-Roman myths:[5] in Acts, he is twice called 'a man' (ἀνήρ) in strategic speeches, by Peter at Pentecost (2:22) and by Paul in Athens (17:31).[6] Luke's Jesus is a man filled with the Spirit and exercising his ministry 'in the Spirit' (e.g. Luke 3:21–22; 4:1, 14, 18), and the oft-noted parallels between Jesus, Peter and Paul in Luke-Acts[7] are suggestive that Luke is modelling his portrait of restored humanity (Peter, Paul) on Jesus as a human being *par excellence*.

Secondly, statements about how people need to respond to the message of Jesus and the apostolic band signal how Luke understands God's purposes for humanity, for they indicate ways in which humanity is out of kilter, and how God, through Jesus and the Spirit, is bringing people back in tune with God's purposes for humanity and the world.

Thirdly, healings and deliverance stories signal that illness and demonization are no part of God's purpose for humanity, for God acts to change them. This is so in Jesus's ministry, where his actions are intrinsic to his message of the kingdom of God – God's rule brings restoration of people to God's creational purposes and hopes.[8] It is also so in the healing and deliverance stories in Acts, where the physical/spiritual restoration performed also restores people to community in general, and to an active engagement

---

[4] See, e.g., the seminal essay "The Speeches in Acts and Ancient Historiography," in Martin Dibelius, *Studies in the Acts of the Apostles* (London: SCM, 1956), 138–85. For critical response, see Marion L. Soards, *The Speeches in Acts: Their Content, Context, and Concerns* (Louisville, KY: Westminster John Knox, 1994), 6–11.

[5] E.g. Ovid tells the story of Zeus and Hermes visiting an elderly couple, Baucis and Philemon (*Metam.* 8.621–96; cf. Acts 14:11), and (notoriously) Zeus engaged in sexual intercourse in human guise (e.g. Apollodorus, *Library* 3.10).

[6] Jesus is also referred to as ἄνθρωπος, a generic 'human being', by the Sanhedrin (Acts 5:28).

[7] See Susan M. Praeder, "Jesus-Paul, Peter-Paul, and Jesus-Peter Parallelisms in Luke-Acts: A History of Reader Response," *SBL 1984 Seminar Papers*, SBLSP 23 (Chico, CA: Scholars, 1984), 23–39; Steve Walton, *Leadership and Lifestyle: The Portrait of Paul in the Miletus Speech and 1 Thessalonians*, SNTSMS 108 (Cambridge: Cambridge University Press, 2000), 34–40; Andrew C. Clark, *Parallel Lives: The Relation of Paul to the Apostles in the Lucan Perspective*, PBTM (Carlisle: Paternoster, 2001), 63–73.

[8] Cf. Turner's valuable discussion, arguing that the close connection of the kingdom of God with healing and deliverance suggests the latter are an instance of the former's presence, in Max Turner, *Power from on High: The Spirit in Israel's Restoration and Witness in Luke-Acts*, JPTSup 9 (Sheffield: Sheffield Academic, 1996), 319–33.

in the people of God in particular. For example, in the healing of the man with a congenital disability at the Beautiful Gate, Luke stresses that he now enters the temple 'walking and leaping and praising God' (Acts 3:8 *bis*, 9) – his physical restoration means he no longer sits dependent as a beggar, unable to join in the temple worship, but can now participate fully in the life of the people of God.

Fourthly, external sources provide a helpful comparison. Specifically, Graeco-Roman sources offer an understanding of the nature and being of humanity collectively and as individual persons, and we may compare (and frequently contrast) such pictures with that emerging from Luke.[9] In particular, Mikeal Parsons argues cogently that the ancient physiognomic tradition offers a valuable dialogue partner, for that tradition assumes that physical appearance speaks of character and a person's nature, and necessarily makes assumptions about what it means to be truly and fully human.[10] Further, the Old Testament provides a rich and important source for Luke's reflection and writing about the events of Jesus and the apostolic church. It is well known that Luke (in common with most other NT writers) cites Isaiah and the Psalms most frequently. Luke also cites and echoes Genesis, a key source of understanding of humanity's origins, destiny and purposes in the OT,[11] and these echoes can help us in reflecting on Luke's anthropology.

Sensitized to these possibilities, we next note a major Lukan literary technique which will be important for our study.

II. Luke's Reversal Theme

It is widely recognized that Luke uses reversal as a literary device to contrast how something/someone appears or is reckoned to be with how it/they actually is or should be.[12] For example, the parable of the rich man and Lazarus involves an overturning of expectations, in that the rich man – normally understood to be blessed by God because of his wealth – goes to Hades in the after-life, and poor Lazarus is taken to that blessed place (Luke 16:19–31). Similarly, the parable of the Pharisee and the tax collector overturns expectations, for the deeply devout Pharisee is not 'justified', whereas the hated tax collector is (Luke 18:9–14) – indeed, Jesus makes the reversal explicit: 'all who exalt themselves will be humbled, and all who humble themselves will be exalted' (v. 14).

Luke uses this reversal theme to communicate positively and negatively, as do other ancient writers who use this theme.[13] By contrast with other ancient writers, however,

---

[9] A fine recent example is Brittany E. Wilson, *Unmanly Men: Refigurations of Masculinity in Luke-Acts* (New York: Oxford University Press, 2015); we shall consider her arguments in discussing masculinity and the relationship of the sexes below.

[10] Mikeal C. Parsons, *Body and Character in Luke and Acts: The Subversion of Physiognomy in Early Christianity* (Grand Rapids, MI: Baker Academic, 2006).

[11] See Peter Mallen, "Genesis in Luke-Acts," in *Genesis in the New Testament*, ed. Maarten J. J. Menken and Steve Moyise, LNTS 466 (London: Bloomsbury T&T Clark, 2012), 60–82.

[12] See valuable surveys in John O. York, *The Last Shall Be First: The Rhetoric of Reversal in Luke*, JSNTSup 46 (Sheffield: JSOT, 1991), 10–38; Frederick W. Danker, *Luke*, ProcC, 2nd ed. (Philadelphia, PA: Fortress, 1987), 47–57.

[13] For Graeco-Roman examples, see York, *Last*, 173–81.

Luke is clear that God stands behind the reversals which he portrays.[14] Positively, Luke signals that God – rather than mere chance or fate – stands with people who are lowly, poor, outcast or marginal. These qualities are attractive to Jesus and to his people, especially where they are combined with humility and recognition of need. Negatively, Luke signals that God stands against people who are rich, self-satisfied, proud of their own achievements or oppressive of poor people, especially where these qualities are combined with, or expressive of, arrogance towards God in religious dress. York suggests that Luke regularly presents 'bi-polar' reversal, that is, that an opposition is reversed: high status becomes low status and vice versa; '*good* becomes *bad* and *bad* becomes *good*'.[15]

In what follows, we shall see ways in which Luke's anthropological understanding forms a reversal of a number of features of the way people are understood in Luke's time and cultural setting(s). We shall consider the way that humans are sinful and need transformation by God-in-Jesus through the Spirit. We shall see a portrait of true humanity in the life and service of Jesus, and in God's vindication of Jesus in the resurrection, and God's exaltation of Jesus in the ascension. We shall reflect on the contrast between Luke's presentation of human physicality in relation to human nature and the physiognomic tradition. We shall look at the nature of human community as transformed in Christ, including the relations of gentiles and Jews, and women and men. Not for nothing did the people of Thessalonica describe Paul and Silas as people 'who have turned the world upside-down' (Acts 17:6) – and the change to right-side-up (as Luke would see it) includes a different view of humankind in these dimensions.

III. Sinful Humanity Transformed

It is well-recognized that salvation is a – if not *the* – major theme in Luke-Acts: Jesus comes 'to seek and to save the lost' (Luke 19:10).[16] This recognition necessarily entails two questions: *from* what do people need to be saved, and *to* what do they need to be saved?[17] However, the question is never answered by Luke in Acts in the direct way that he answers the question *how* people are saved in Paul's answer to the Philippian jailer (Acts 16:30–31), and this lack forces us to look for less direct statements and hints, including in the Third Gospel.[18]

---

[14] York, *Last*, 181–2.
[15] York, *Last*, 42 (his italics); discussion of several clear examples on 44–92.
[16] E.g. I. Howard Marshall, *Luke: Historian and Theologian* (Exeter: Paternoster, 1970), esp. chs IV–VIII; I. Howard Marshall and David Peterson (eds), *Witness to the Gospel: The Theology of Acts* (Grand Rapids, MI/Cambridge: Eerdmans, 1998), esp. the essays of John Nolland (63–81), Joel B. Green (83–106), H. Douglas Buckwalter (107–23), Christoph Stenschke (125–44) and Ben Witherington III (145–66).
[17] Cf. 'If we can find the answer to this question [sc. to whom the message of Jesus Christ comes], we can also conclude what kind of salvation it must be which will save such a man, and also how he can lay hold of it', W. G. Kümmel, *Man in the New Testament*, trans. John J. Vincent, revised ed. (London: Epworth, 1963), 16–17.
[18] Christoph W. Stenschke, "The Need for Salvation," in *Witness to the Gospel: The Theology of Acts*, ed. I. Howard Marshall and David Peterson (Grand Rapids, MI/Cambridge: Eerdmans, 1998), 125–44, here 128.

The question of how to respond is put clearly twice in Acts: one in a gentile setting, on the lips of the Philippian jailer, as we noted above, 'Sirs, what must I do (τί με δεῖ ποιεῖν) to be saved?' (16:30); the other in a Jewish setting, on the lips of the Pentecost crowd, 'What shall we do (τί ποιήσωμεν), brothers and sisters?' (2:37). Exploring the context, both literary and cultural, of these questions will help us to understand why humanity – both Jewish and gentile – needs saving, and what the gospel message offers under the name 'salvation'.

III.a. The Pentecost Question

The Pentecost question is provoked by a change to the crowd's inner state: they had been divided in their response to the pentecostal events, with some 'astonished and perplexed' (v. 13) and some sceptical (v. 14). Peter's speech has focused their attention on Jesus, and their response is to be 'cut to the heart' (κατενύγησαν τὴν καρδίαν, v. 14). They experience sharp pain, doubtless remorse for their part in Jesus's death (note ἀνείλατε 'you put to death', v. 23) and want to know how to respond. Peter calls them to a response which includes at least five elements. The first four – repentance, baptism, forgiveness, and the gift of the Spirit – are widely recognized. Less widely recognized is that v. 39, connected to v. 38 by γάρ 'for', offers further explanation of the response required. Let us consider these elements of response, which are both personal and corporate, and the light they shine on Luke's anthropology.

Repentance includes both change of mind and change of life-direction in consequence.[19] Repentance is a characteristic response to the gospel message elsewhere, in both Jewish and gentile settings.[20] Here it includes the specific element of repudiating the killing of Jesus, for the speech holds those present responsible (v. 23).[21] In both Jewish and gentile settings, repentance involves two assumptions about people: that they are going in the wrong direction, and that they are thinking the wrong way – their lifestyle and mindset need to change. Luke is thus no naïve optimist about human nature, although he does expect that people can recognize that they are out of sync with God's intentions for them – people in general are not 'so far gone' that this is impossible. It is, of course, also necessary for God to draw people to himself by opening people's minds[22] to the gospel message. The need for repentance shows that there is material for God to work with in human beings.

Baptism is the second element. The passive imperative βαπτισθήτω 'be baptized' calls people to submit to baptism, illustrating that what they receive from God (forgiveness and the Spirit) is gift. The verb is plural, which places baptism in the corporate sphere,

---

[19] Guy D. Nave, *The Role and Function of Repentance in Luke-Acts*, SBLAcBib 4 (Leiden: Brill, 2002), 199.
[20] Jewish: 3:19; 5:31; cf. Luke 3:3, 8; 5:32; 10:13; 13:3, 5; 15:7, 10; 16:30; 17:3, 4; gentile: 11:18; 17:30; cf. 20:21; 26:20; Luke 24:47.
[21] Contrast speeches outside Jerusalem to Jewish audiences, which speak of 'they' who killed Jesus, e.g. 13:27–29. See discussion in Jon A. Weatherly, *Jewish Responsibility for the Death of Jesus in Luke-Acts*, JSNTSup 106 (Sheffield: Sheffield Academic, 1994), 50–98.
[22] 'Minds' is today's term: in common with OT writers, Luke uses 'heart' for the realm of understanding and will, e.g. 2:37; 8:22; 16:14.

but combined with a singular personal pronoun, ἕκαστος 'each one', which underlines the personal nature of the response. Household baptisms elsewhere in Acts, where each individual is baptized – rather than the head of the household being baptized on behalf of all (e.g. 16:15, 33) – further demonstrate both the individual and corporate nature of the response. Baptism is ἐπὶ τῷ ὀνόματι Ἰησοῦ Χριστοῦ 'in the name of Jesus Messiah', most probably with the sense 'having in mind' or 'with regard to' the name of Jesus Messiah.[23] Such usage connects with the expression 'call upon' (ἐπικαλέω) used in v. 21 and, strikingly, implies that *Jesus* – rather than YHWH – is the name upon which believers are to call. Similarly, 22:16 suggests that a baptizand calls upon the name of Jesus for forgiveness. To call on the name of Jesus, to be baptized in the name of Jesus, is to invoke the power of the one who is at God's right side, the one with whom authority thus rests. This picture shows the radical nature of conversion in Acts, for people are unable to save themselves: they need and require outside power to change, symbolized and enacted in water baptism.

Those who respond in repentance and baptism receive forgiveness and the gift of the Holy Spirit. The emphasis continues to be on the Godward side of human change, as well as the need for change.

Forgiveness of sins entails two movements: the one forgiving first acknowledges that they have been done wrong by the other party, and then commits themself not to continue to hold the wrong against the other party.[24] Thus Luke's usage on the lips of Peter here indicates that the audience are in the wrong in relation to God, and yet may have that situation reversed. The combination of repentance and baptism leads to (εἰς) 'forgiveness of sins' (ἄφεσις τῶν ἁμαρτιῶν, a distinctively Lukan phrase). Luke has prepared carefully for this use: John the baptizer's ministry is prophesied by his father Zechariah to bring salvation to the people ἐν ἀφέσει ἁμαρτιῶν αὐτῶν 'by the forgiveness of their sins' (Luke 1:77), and such forgiveness is the focus of his baptism of repentance (3:3); Jesus has announced forgiveness to the man with paralysis (5:20) and to the woman who pours ointment on his feet in the house of Simon the Pharisee (7:47–48), in each case scandalizing his hearers (5:21; 7:49); the disciples' prayer is to include asking for forgiveness of sins (11:4); and the risen Jesus tells his disciples that 'repentance and forgiveness of sins' will be heralded to all nations (24:47).[25] Forgiveness of sins continues to be prominent in Acts: people, both Jewish and gentile, are urged to receive the forgiveness God-in-Jesus offers, frequently with repentance as the road which leads to forgiveness (Acts 3:19; 5:31; 10:43; 13:38–39; 22:16; 16:17–28). Luke's anthropology here is universal: the breadth of use of 'forgiveness of sins' in Luke-Acts indicates that the wrong-standing with God which requires forgiveness is a universal human characteristic, and not confined to those in Jerusalem who have particular culpability for Jesus's death, and that the offer of forgiveness is made to all kinds of people without distinction.

---

[23] Lars Hartman, *'Into the Name of the Lord Jesus': Baptism in the Early Church*, SNTW (Edinburgh: T&T Clark, 1997), 42–3. See discussion in my forthcoming commentary on Acts in the Word Biblical Commentary on 2:38.

[24] See the excellent discussion in Miroslav Volf, *Free of Charge: Giving and Forgiving in a Culture Stripped of Grace* (Grand Rapids, MI: Zondervan, 2006), esp. 129–31, 165–77.

[25] See discussion in Tim Carter, *The Forgiveness of Sins* (Cambridge: James Clarke, 2016), esp. ch. 8.

The gift of the Holy Spirit, in combination with λήμψεσθε 'you will receive', signals that the change required comes from outside a person: the Spirit is *received* from another, not taken for oneself. Peter's appropriation of Joel's promise of a universal gift of the Spirit (Joel 2:28–32 [LXX 3:1–5], quoted in vv. 17–21) to explain the pentecostal outpouring prepares for this promise – anyone who repents and is baptized can expect to receive the Spirit.[26] Pentecost is a Jewish setting, but the expectation of the Spirit's coming to gentiles who similarly repent and are baptized is clear as the story of Acts develops: 8:16 (in Samaria) should be heard as Luke speaking with raised eyebrows – it is a surprise that the Spirit has not yet fallen on the Samaritans who have believed;[27] and the Ephesian twelve receive the Spirit after baptism in the name of Jesus (19:1–10). The Spirit in Acts, as Turner rightly argues, is given not only to empower God's people for mission, but is also a vital necessity for the life of believers and believing communities, both in bringing people into the experience of salvation and in equipping them to continue to live that way.[28] Anthropologically, then, the picture of humanity as dependent on God for the ability to live in tune with God is further reinforced.

Renewed community Peter's explanation of the nature of the response required continues into the next sentence (v. 39), where it becomes even clearer that it is not a purely individual matter: others near and far are implicated and involved. A Jewish audience – indeed, any ancient audience – would hear 'the promise is to you and your children' as entailing family solidarity with the head of household's response. 'All who are far away (πᾶσιν τοῖς εἰς μακράν)' echoes Isa 57:19 LXX 'peace upon peace to those far away (τοῖς μακρὰν … οὖσιν) and to those near', and 'whoever the Lord our God calls to himself (ὅσους ἂν προσκαλέσηται κύριος ὁ θεὸς ἡμῶν)' echoes Joel 3:5 LXX 'whom the Lord has called (οὓς κύριος προσκέκληται)', a phrase not quoted in vv. 17–21. The eschatological pilgrimage which Joel and others portray includes far-flung diaspora Jews and some gentiles coming to Jerusalem.[29]

People in the ancient world – and the large majority today, especially in the two-thirds world – think of themselves as members of a community first, and as individuals only far later (if at all).[30] So the question of human identity is about the community to which a person belongs. To speak, as Peter does, of a community which will include household-members and 'all who are far away', identifies that a new kind of community is in process of being formed, for it is not constituted by ethnicity, by blood-relationships; rather, it is constituted by a relationship to God-in-Jesus. It took some time for the

---

[26] Thus Turner, *Power*, 358–9 considers 2:38 to be programmatic, signalling the elements which Luke understands to be constitutive of Christian conversion.
[27] See Max Turner, "Interpreting the Samaritans of Acts 8: The Waterloo of Pentecostal Soteriology and Pneumatology?," *Pneuma* 23 (2001): 265–86, esp. 267–8, 278.
[28] Turner, *Power*, 405–27; with James D. G. Dunn, *Baptism in the Holy Spirit* (London: SCM, 1970), 90–102; *contra* Robert P. Menzies, *Empowered for Witness: The Spirit in Luke-Acts*, JPTSup 6 (Sheffield: Sheffield Academic, 1994), 172–225.
[29] E.g. Zech 8:20–23; Isa 2:1–3; 56:6–8; cf. Isa 49:6; Sib. Or. 3:616–17, 772–73; Pss. Sol. 17:34–35; see E. P. Sanders, *Jesus and Judaism* (London: SCM, 1984), 212–18; Michael F. Bird, *Jesus and the Origins of the Gentile Mission*, LNTS 331 (London: T&T Clark, 2006), 26–9, both with further ancient references.
[30] For discussion, see Bruce J. Malina, *The New Testament World: Insights from Cultural Anthropology*, 3rd ed. (Louisville, KY: Westminster John Knox, 2001), 58–79.

implications of this change to sink in: even after the 'Jerusalem council' (Acts 15:6–29), the question of Jew-gentile relationships within the believing communities rumbled on, to the extent that Paul was later asked to show his Jewish credentials and loyalty by participating in a temple vow (Acts 21:20–24). To form a community across the great Jew-gentile divide was remarkable and difficult. The quantity of Luke's use of Jewish Scripture in Acts, not least in understanding the inclusion of gentiles in the people of God,[31] shows that Luke does not think the Jews as a people are being rejected in favour of the gentiles: rather, gentiles are being included in the renewed people of God – once the 'tent of David' is rebuilt, that is, once Israel's restoration is well in process, then inclusion of gentiles is fitting (Amos 9:11–12, quoted in Acts 15:16–18).[32] Ethnicity, then, is not to be regarded as a prime anthropological reality concerning membership of the people of God, and nor are markers of ethnicity, such as circumcision.

III.b. The Philippian Jailer's Question

The jailer's question, 'What must I do to be saved?' (Acts 16:30) is sometimes suggested to be about how the jailer can escape punishment for the prisoners' escape.[33] However, at the point in the story where the jailer speaks, he has already been assured that the prisoners are there by Paul (v. 28) and has confirmed this by bringing in lights (v. 29a).[34] As happens elsewhere with gentiles, his first reaction is to fall before the believers (v. 29b; cf. 10:25), most probably expressing fear, for he had treated these men harshly (vv. 23b–24) and now saw that an earthquake had seemingly vindicated them. He would most naturally assume that the earthquake was a deed of Paul and Silas's god,[35] and thus feared retribution from their god.[36] His desire to know how to be saved was based on this fear, and need not be understood to include a personal sense of sin. It was only Paul and Silas's answer which opened his understanding to 'salvation' more broadly, as they pointed him to the Lord Jesus as the source of salvation (v. 31).

What is it from which gentiles need saving? Christoph Stenschke summarizes well, identifying seven key features of gentiles prior to faith in Christ:[37] (i) *ignorance*: they do not recognize God and how God has made himself known in nature (Acts 17:16,

---

[31] See Joseph B. Tyson, "The Gentile Mission and the Authority of Scripture in Acts," *NTS* 33 (1987): 619–31; James A. Meek, *The Gentile Mission in Old Testament Citations in Acts: Text, Hermeneutic, and Purpose*, LNTS 385 (London: T&T Clark, 2008).

[32] See discussion in Turner, *Power*, 312–15; Richard Bauckham, "James and the Jerusalem Church," in *The Book of Acts in its Palestinian Setting*, ed Richard Bauckham, BAFCS 4 (Carlisle: Paternoster; Grand Rapids, MI: Eerdmans, 1995), 415–80 (452–62); Richard Bauckham, "James and the Gentiles (Acts 15:13-21)," in *History, Literature, and Society in the Book of Acts*, ed. Ben Witherington III (Cambridge: Cambridge University Press, 1996), 154–84; Meek, *Gentile Mission*, 77–94; contra Jack T. Sanders, *The Jews in Luke-Acts* (London: SCM, 1987), who considers Luke to be anti-Jewish and to regard the whole Jewish nation as responsible for Jesus's death.

[33] E.g. C. K. Barrett, *A Critical and Exegetical Commentary on the Acts of the Apostles*, ICC, 2 vols. (Edinburgh: T&T Clark, 1994, 1998), 2:796-77; although Barrett does go on to note that Luke could hardly have been unaware of the overtones of 'saved' for Christian readers.

[34] With Stenschke, *Portrait*, 200.

[35] Or, indeed, that they were gods, a possible interpretation of his addressing them as κύριοι (30); cf. 14:11-13. See discussion in Stenschke, *Portrait*, 202 with n. 469.

[36] Stenschke, *Portrait*, 201.

[37] Stenschke, *Portrait*, 378–82.

22–25); (ii) *rejection* of God's purpose and revelation in history: they discard ways in which God has made himself known to the Jewish people, and despise God's historic people and their city, Jerusalem (Luke 21:24; Acts 16:20–21), and in particular were complicit in the death of Jesus (Acts 4:25–27); (iii) *idolatry* marks gentile ignorance and rejection of revelation; gentiles worship the wrong things in place of the one true God – they are deeply 'religious', but in erroneous ways (Acts 8:9–11; 15:20, 28; 19:23–37), and thus are unable to differentiate adequately between divine and human beings (Acts 8:9–11; 12:20–23; 19:35; 28:4–6); (iv) *materialism* is the centre of their concerns, and drives their decision-making and preoccupations – they even seek to manipulate spiritual forces to this end (Luke 12:29–30; Acts 16:16–24; 19:24–28); (v) *moral failure* marks their lives, although such sins are the outworking of their sinful state of living in independence of the true God – thus the death of Jesus is an expression of their rejection of God (Acts 4:25–27). They can and do act above the level of this state in showing kindness (e.g. Acts 27:3; 28:2); (vi) *under Satan's power*: gentiles are under the rule of the Evil One (e.g. Acts 26:18; cf. Luke 4:5–6), although they are not thereby removed from culpability for their other failures noted previously;[38] (vii) *under God's judgement*: gentiles face future judgement by God, and divine actions of judgement in history prefigure and actualize this judgement before the Last Day (e.g. Acts 7:7).

When gentiles are invited to faith, it is their spiritual failure which comes to the fore: for example, Simon Magus has been wicked (Acts 8:22–23), and the Athenians are called to repentance from past ignorant idolatry (Acts 17:29–30). The remedy for this spiritual failure is radical forgiveness, not merely tidying up their lives (cf. Luke 1:77)[39] or moral correction[40] (although teaching and change follows once they have become believers[41]). Interestingly, gentiles who respond to the message of salvation are most frequently godfearers,[42] rather than 'devout pagans' (e.g. Cornelius: Acts 10:1–2; Antiochenes: 13:42–49; Lydia: 16:13–15; Thessalonians: 17:4; Beroeans: 17:12; Titius Justus and other Corinthians: 18:6–7). Such people have some understanding and knowledge of God through their association with the synagogues and Jewish groups; yet they – like Jewish people – are called to repent and receive salvation, rather than needing only correction (e.g. Acts 13:38–39; cf. 17:30–31).

---

[38] Stenschke, *Portrait*, 382 observes that (e.g.) Satan is not held responsible for the Ephesian riot, and comments that 'Luke does not clarify the bearing of Satan's dominance on human responsibility' (see also 242).

[39] Stenschke, *Portrait*, 384–5; *contra* Hans Conzelmann, *The Theology of St Luke*, trans. Geoffrey Buswell (London: Faber & Faber, 1960), 228–9, who claims that sin is predominantly an ethical concept in Luke-Acts (and thus implies that character improvement is all that is required).

[40] Stenschke, *Portrait*, 100, 240, 318; *contra* Jens-Wilhelm Taeger, *Der Mensch und sein Heil: Studien zum Bild des Menschen und zur Sicht der Bekehrung bei Lukas*, SNT 14 (Gütersloh: Mohn, 1982), esp. 105–224, and note 'Der Mensch ist kein salvandus, sondern ein corrigendus' ('Humanity is not something to be saved, but something to be corrected', 227; my translation). See Stenschke's good summary in English of Taeger's overall argument: Stenschke, *Portrait*, 36–45.

[41] Stenschke, *Portrait*, 386 cites Acts 8:24; 11:28–29; 20:7–12; 19:18–19 as examples.

[42] On this disputed category, see (e.g.) Craig S. Keener, *Acts: An Exegetical Commentary*, 4 vols (Grand Rapids, MI: Baker Academic, 2012–15), 2:1750–5; Conrad H. Gempf, "The God-Fearers," in Colin J. Hemer, *The Book of Acts in the Setting of Hellenistic History*, ed. Conrad H. Gempf, WUNT 49 (Tübingen: Mohr Siebeck, 1989), 444–8.

What, then should we make of passages which have been understood to indicate gentile kinship to God, most notably the Athens speech (Acts 17:16–31), upon which some have almost entirely based their understanding of Lukan anthropology?[43] Vielhauer declared that Luke's portrait of Paul's proclamation to gentile pagans in Athens was at odds with the portrait found in Rom 1:18–32, for in Romans the statement of human kinship to God resulted in God's wrath, whereas in Acts 17 the result was simply the need for education and enlightenment.[44]

Paul's speech responds to a question (17:19–20) which is likely to be about why the Areopagites should allow Paul to build a temple to Jesus in Athens.[45] The council had authority to determine whether new deities were to have temples, and thus required evidence that the temple would be viable, i.e. that there were sufficient worshippers of the deity to provide the money to buy land and build the temple with an altar for sacrifice, and perhaps a statue of the god, as well as to endow an annual feast.[46] Thus their question has the sense, '[W]e possess the legal right to judge what this new teaching is that is being spoken by you.'[47] Paul's response undermines and rejects the presuppositions of their question: he is not bringing a new god to Athens, but one they already worship, but as unknown (vv. 22–23); no plot of land to build a temple is required, for this god does not live in hand-built places (v. 24), but is himself the creator of all things (v. 25); and no statue or image of this god is required, since humans are themselves this god's offspring (vv. 28–29). Instead, Paul's speech makes clear that, rather than them judging this god, Jesus judges them and seeks their repentance (vv. 30–31).

Given Paul's declaration of his hearers' ignorance (ἄγνοια, v. 30; cf. ἀγνοοῦντες, v. 24), how should we understand his opening statement that they are ὡς δεισιδαιμονεστέρους (v. 22)? This phrase can mean 'deeply religious' or 'deeply superstitious', and thus can signal a positive or negative approbation of Paul's hearers.[48] In favour of the latter, it comes in a context where Luke has expressed Paul's distress at the city's idolatry (v. 16), Luke uses other terms to express a positive view of non-believers' religious sensibilities, notably the participle of σέβομαι, sometimes with τὸν θεόν as object,[49] and the rest of the speech offers an acerbic critique of the Athenians' idolatry, notably v. 29.[50] It could be that the term was understood by Paul (and Luke) negatively, but might be heard in the opening part of the speech as positive, for the audience had not yet heard the rest of the speech,[51] but the context makes clear that Luke's Paul regards

---

[43] E.g. Phillip Vielhauer, "On the Paulinism of Acts," in *Studies in Luke-Acts*, ed. Leander E. Keck and J. L. Martyn (London: SPCK, 1968), 33–50 (34–7); Kümmel, *Man*, 89; Dibelius, *Studies*, 47–57.

[44] Vielhauer, "Paulinism," 36–7.

[45] Bruce W. Winter, "On Introducing Gods to Athens: An Alternative Reading of Acts 17:18-20," *TynBul* 47 (1996): 71–90.

[46] Robert Garland, *Introducing New Gods: The Politics of Athenian Religion* (London: Duckworth, 1991), 21.

[47] Winter, "Gods," 82.

[48] For the view that it is 'cautiously appreciative', see Ernst Haenchen, *The Acts of the Apostles* (Oxford: Blackwell, 1971), 520 n. 7.

[49] Acts 13:43, 50; 16:14; 17:4, 17; 18:7 – contrast 18:13; 19:27.

[50] Stenschke, *Portrait*, 211, 213–18; Conrad H. Gempf, "Athens, Paul at," in *DPL* 51–4, here 52.

[51] So Rudolf Pesch, *Die Apostelgeschichte*, EKKNT, 2 vols. (Zürich: Benzinger, 1986), 2:136, who calls it 'zweideutig' (ambiguous); cf. Stenschke, *Portrait*, 211; C. Kavin Rowe, *World Upside Down: Reading Acts in the Graeco-Roman Age* (Oxford/New York: Oxford University Press, 2009), 33–4.

the term negatively – and thus signals that Luke regards humans as not 'naturally' near to knowing the true God. This distance from God in practical gentile experience is underlined by the use of the tentative εἰ ἄρα γε 'if then, perhaps' with the optative verb εὕροιεν 'might find' (v. 27): although people have an instinct to seek the true God and that God is actually not far from them (vv. 27b–28), they are unlikely in their groping around (ψηλαφήσειαν, v. 27, also optative) to find him.[52] Taeger notes this failure: 'the Athenians actually do not come by themselves to accurate knowledge and remain trapped in ignorance'.[53]

The Areopagus speech, in sum, seeks to 'change the frame'[54] of the Athenians' thinking and living by showing them their ignorance about the one true God, and calling for a change in their thinking and living, and for submission to the judge of all, Jesus. In more traditional language, gentiles are sinners who live in idolatry and ignorance and need to repent. Their sins may differ from those of their Jewish contemporaries, but those sins are nonetheless offensive to God, so that gentiles require repentance and baptism in order to receive forgiveness and the empowering Spirit.

III.c. Summary

Jews and gentiles alike are called to repentance and faith, expressed in baptism, in the light of their sinfulness. This sinfulness goes beyond particular deeds and words to life-orientation – and that is why only God, in Christ and by the Spirit, can achieve effective and lasting change in people's lives. People are saved into a new community, which includes both gentile and Jew, and in which relationships are being restored to the Creator's pattern. We move on now to consider that pattern as modelled and exemplified in Jesus, and then its implications for re-understanding human physicality and refiguring human community.

IV. Jesus as Humanity Par Excellence

The parallels between Luke's portraits of Jesus, Peter and Paul have frequently been noted and explored.[55] A key implication in relation to this essay is that Jesus is presented as a *model human being* whom others will imitate – as we noted above, he is designated 'a man' (ἀνήρ, Acts 2:22; 17:31). For sure, others do not imitate Jesus without the enabling of the Spirit – hence the transformation of the apostles after

---

[52] Rowe, *World*, 199 n. 155 rightly criticizes RSV and others for translating in a way which suggests that they have found God. On the verbs, see Gempf, "Athens," 52; Barrett, *Acts*, 2:844–46.
[53] Taeger, *Mensch*, 101 (my translation).
[54] I owe the image to Rowe, *World*, 39. Rowe's whole discussion of the speech is judicious and helpful (27–41).
[55] See Praeder, "Jesus-Paul"; Clark, *Lives*, 35–8, 39–49, 63–73; Graham H. Twelftree, *People of the Spirit: Exploring Luke's View of the Church* (Grand Rapids, MI: Baker Academic; London: SPCK, 2009), 30–51; Robert F. O'Toole, SJ, "Parallels between Jesus and His Disciples in Luke-Acts: A Further Study," *BZ* 27 (1983): 195–212 (with literature there cited); Robert F. O'Toole, SJ, *The Unity of Luke's Theology*, GNS 9 (Wilmington, DE: Michael Glazier, 1984), 62–95; and my discussion in Walton, *Leadership*, 34–40 and literature there cited.

Pentecost – but Luke portrays Peter and Paul's actions and attitudes coming more into line with those of Jesus. This section considers some major parallels in order to substantiate this claim.[56]

First, *Jesus, Peter and Paul are agents of deliverance, signs and wonders, and healings*.[57] One of Jesus's first actions is to deliver a man from an unclean demon (Luke 4:31–37), and Peter's summary of Jesus's ministry is that he 'went about doing good and healing all who were oppressed by the devil' (Acts 10:38). Within the time of Jesus's ministry, the Twelve receive power and authority over all demons (Luke 9:1), and the seventy(-two)[58] rejoice that the demons submit to them in Jesus's name (Luke 10:17); both groups would include Peter. Such deliverance ministry is a feature of Peter and Paul's lives in Acts (5:16; 16:16–18; 19:11–12). More specifically: Jesus heals a person who is paralysed (παραλελυμένος, Luke 5:18, 24), and so does Peter (παραλελυμένος, Acts 9:33; cf. Philip, 8:7) – although Peter is clear that it is the exalted Jesus Christ who is healing Aeneas (9:34); Jesus, Peter and Paul are the agents of a person being raised from the dead (Luke 7:1–11; Acts 9:36–43; 20:7–12); Jesus, Peter and John, and Paul are agents of healing people with impairments of the lower limbs (χωλός, Luke 7:22; Acts 3:2; 14:8; again cf. Philip, 8:7). Jesus, Peter (as one of the apostles) and Paul are all said in Acts to perform 'signs and wonders' (σημεῖα καὶ τέρατα, 2:22, 43; 5:12; 14:3; 15:12; cf. Stephen, 6:8). The fact that Peter and Paul (and other believers) do such things demonstrates that it is not necessarily Jesus's divine status which enables him to act thus[59] – they are performed through empowerment by the Spirit, which is common to Jesus and his followers in Luke-Acts.

Secondly, developing the previous point, *Jesus, Peter and Paul are all empowered by the Spirit*, who enables these signs and wonders to happen. There is a cluster of key 'Spirit' references surrounding the beginning of Jesus's public ministry in Luke: Jesus sees the Spirit come down on him at his baptism (3:21–22); he is filled with the Spirit and then led by the Spirit in the wilderness (4:1); he returns from the wilderness in the power of the Spirit and thus begins to teach (4:14–15); and in the Nazareth synagogue he reads from Isaiah 61:1, identifying himself as the one upon whom the Lord's Spirit rests (4:18) – the Spirit will be the power of his ministry.[60] Moreover, Jesus's parting words in both the Gospel and Acts instruct his followers to wait in Jerusalem for the Spirit's power to rest on them as the Spirit had rested on Jesus (Luke 24:49; Acts 1:4–5). It is thus no great surprise to readers of Luke's double work when the Spirit is poured

---

[56] In addition to Peter and Paul, other characters in Acts – notably Stephen – exemplify key qualities shown by Jesus (Twelftree, *People*, 34–6). The wider believing community – and not prominent leaders alone – is presented as imitating Jesus.

[57] Note the valuable study of Leo O'Reilly, *Word and Sign in the Acts of the Apostles: A Study in Lucan Theology*, AnGr 243 (Rome: Editrice Pontificia Università Gregoriana, 1987) on this theme.

[58] The manuscripts are divided between 'seventy' and 'seventy-two', an issue which is not significant for our purposes. For discussion, see (e.g.) Bruce M. Metzger, *A Textual Commentary on the Greek New Testament*, 2nd ed. (Stuttgart: Deutsche Bibelgesellschaft/United Bible Societies, 1994), 126; I. Howard Marshall, *The Gospel of Luke: A Commentary on the Greek Text*, NIGTC (Exeter: Paternoster; Grand Rapids, MI: Eerdmans, 1978), 414–15.

[59] On Jesus's divine identity in Luke, see Richard B. Hays, *Reading Backwards: Figural Christology and the Fourfold Gospel Witness* (Waco, TX: Baylor University Press, 2014), 55–74.

[60] For discussion, see Turner, *Power*, 188–212; Dunn, *Baptism*, 23–37; Menzies, *Empowered*, 132–56.

out on and fills the believers at Pentecost (Acts 2:1–4, 16–18, 33) and is promised to others who believe (2:38). The most natural reading of the description of the life of the earliest community in Jerusalem as contiguous with the Pentecost account is that in that description we see the outflow of their Spirit-empowered life into the believing community (2:42–47).[61] Indeed, the statement that 'many signs and wonders' (2:43) were done among the believers echoes Peter's statement that Jesus performed such deeds (2:22), thus showing that the Spirit is at work through the apostles in similar manner as through Jesus. Luke reports other occasions when Peter (sometimes as part of the apostolic band) is filled with or directed by the Spirit for particular tasks (4:8, 31; 10:19; 11:12).[62] Paul, too, is filled with the Spirit and thus empowered for his ministry (13:9; 20:22, 23; 21:4, 11). The programmatic and normative role of 2:38 suggests that the usual expectation is that believers will receive the Spirit at the point of water baptism[63] – indeed (as we saw above) Luke writes with raised eyebrows when this does not happen (8:16;[64] 19:2).

Thirdly, in particular, Jesus, Peter and Paul's *teaching and speaking is empowered by the Spirit*. In the case of Jesus, it is immediately following his return from the wilderness, filled with Spirit, that he begins to teach (4:14–15).[65] The apostles – notably Peter (who gives the first two major speeches in Acts, 2:14–36, 38–40; 3:12–26) – begin their teaching ministry following the Spirit's descent at Pentecost (Acts 2:42), and this ministry is critical to the church's life and growth (6:2, 4, 7). When they speak to a hostile audience, the Spirit empowers them, as Jesus had promised (4:8, 31 with Luke 12:11–12; cf. 5:32; 6:5, 8–10; 7:55).[66] S/Paul, likewise, begins to proclaim Jesus with great effectiveness after he is filled with the Holy Spirit (9:17, 19b–22). Paul's travels from Antioch are initiated by the Spirit (13:2, 4), and his speech is imbued by the Spirit (13:9).

Fourthly, *suffering* marks Jesus, Peter and Paul and is understood as a normal feature of faithful discipleship.[67] In the case of Jesus, suffering is focused in his death on the cross and the lead-up to that event (he is mocked and beaten, Luke 22:63–65). His death, of course, has redemptive significance seen in (e.g.) the exchange of the innocent Jesus for the guilty Barabbas (Luke 23:13–25), along with the stress on

---

[61] With Turner, *Power*, 412–14; Luke T. Johnson, *The Literary Function of Possessions in Luke-Acts*, SBLDS 39 (Missoula, MT: Scholars, 1977), 183–4; Matthias Wenk, *Community-forming Power: The Socio-ethical Role of the Spirit in Luke-Acts*, JPTSup 19 (Sheffield: Sheffield Academic, 2000), 261–3; *contra* Menzies, *Empowered*, 258; Gonzalo Haya-Prats, SJ, *Empowered Believers: The Holy Spirit in the Book of Acts*, trans. Scott A. Ellington (Eugene, OR: Cascade, 2011), 168–77.
[62] Cf. similar instances with Stephen (6:10; 7:55), Philip (8:29, 39), and Barnabas (11:24).
[63] For a clear statement of this view with supporting references, see Turner, *Power*, 358–60.
[64] Turner, "Samaritans," 267–8, 278.
[65] The imperfect ἐδίδασκεν (4:15) is inceptive, portraying the teaching as beginning and continuing.
[66] See my discussion of Luke 12:11–12 in the context of Luke-Acts: Steve Walton, "Whose Spirit? The Promise and the Promiser in Luke 12:12," in *The Spirit and Christ in the New Testament and Christian Theology*, ed. I. Howard Marshall, Volker Rabens and Cornelis Bennema (Grand Rapids, MI: Eerdmans, 2012), 35–51.
[67] Parts of what follows draw on my student Brian J. Tabb's PhD thesis, "Suffering and Worldview: A Comparative Study of Acts, Fourth Maccabees, and Seneca" (PhD diss.: London School of Theology/Middlesex University, 2013), published in revised form as *Suffering in Ancient Worldview: Luke, Seneca and 4 Maccabees in Dialogue*, LNTS 569 (London: Bloomsbury T&T Clark, 2017).

Jesus's innocent suffering in the passion narrative (e.g. Luke 23:14, 15, 22, 41, 47): in this respect Jesus's suffering is different from that of his followers. Nevertheless, Jesus teaches that his faithful followers should expect to suffer (e.g. Luke 12:11-12; 21:12-19), and Acts presents the fulfilment of Jesus's words: Peter and John are twice brought before the Jewish council to answer for their proclamation of Jesus as Messiah – once alone, and once with the other apostles (4:1-22; 5:17-41); and Peter is imprisoned by Herod and narrowly escapes execution because of an angelic intervention (12:3-11).[68] Paul – ironically, having been an imitator of persecution of believers (8:3; 9:1-2; 26:9-11) – regularly suffers, through being thrown out of cities (13:50-51), imprisonment (16:23; chs 21-28),[69] attempted and actual physical punishment and attack (14:5-6, 19; 16:22-23; 17:5; 20:3; 22:22-23, 24-29; 23:10, 12-15, 35), storm and shipwreck (27:13-44), being brought before the authorities (16:19-21; 18:12; 24:1-2), and riot (19:23-34; 21:27-36). The exalted Lord programmatically tells Ananias that suffering will mark Paul's path (9:15),[70] and Paul reflects on and theologizes about suffering with the Ephesian elders (20:19, 23-24, 29-30).[71] There are clear echoes of Jesus's promise of aid from the Spirit in such situations (Luke 12:11-12; cf. Acts 4:8; 5:32; 6:10; 7:55).[72]

Thus in a number of ways Luke presents Jesus as a model of what it means to be truly and fully human, as a model for imitation amidst the vicissitudes of human existence. For Luke, being fully human – which means living in relationship with God and his people – necessitates reliance upon the Spirit's enabling and transforming power; the Spirit is the active power of God to unite a disparate set of people.[73]

V. Human Physicality Re-understood

Mikeal Parsons highlights the significance of bodily form and life in ancient physiognomic traditions, whether Graeco-Roman, Jewish or early Christian.[74] He shows that ancient authors considered the physical form of the body as displaying character.[75] In particular, physical disabilities marked a person as morally inferior, as well as less than fully human. Parsons argues cogently that Luke – along with other Christian writers – critiques these physiognomic assumptions.

---

[68] For fuller discussion of persecution in Palestine, see Ernst Bammel, "Jewish Activity against Christians in Palestine according to Acts," in *The Book of Acts in Its Palestinian Setting*, ed. Richard Bauckham, BAFCS 4 (Carlisle: Paternoster; Grand Rapids, MI: Eerdmans, 1995), 357-64. On persecution in Luke-Acts, see Scott Cunningham, *'Through Many Tribulations': The Theology of Persecution in Luke-Acts*, JSNTSup 142 (Sheffield: Sheffield Academic, 1997); Wenk, *Power*.
[69] See the insightful studies Brian M. Rapske, *The Book of Acts and Paul in Roman Custody*, BAFCS 3 (Carlisle: Paternoster; Grand Rapids, MI: Eerdmans, 1994); Matthew L. Skinner, *Locating Paul: Places of Custody as Narrative Settings in Acts 21-28*, AcBib 13 (Atlanta, GA: SBL, 2003).
[70] See the fine discussion of 9:15-16 in Tabb, "Suffering," 164-9.
[71] On suffering in this speech, see Walton, *Leadership*, 87-9.
[72] See discussion in Walton, "Spirit."
[73] Alan J. Thompson, *The Acts of the Risen Lord Jesus: Luke's Account of God's Unfolding Plan*, NSBT 27 (Nottingham: Apollos; Downers Grove, IL: InterVarsity Press, 2011), 131-41.
[74] Parsons, *Body*.
[75] Parsons, *Body*, 28-34, 39-61.

For example, the man at the Beautiful Gate (Acts 3:1–10) is presented as having weak feet and ankles (v. 7). Of ankles, pseudo-Aristotle writes, 'Those who have strong and well-jointed ankles are brave in character; witness the male sex. Those that have fleshly and ill-jointed ankles are weak in character; witness the female sex' (810a25–29); and of feet, Pomelo writes, 'If you see contracted, strong feet, and their tendons are straight and strong, and their joints are evenly proportioned, these are the signs of powerful and mighty men. If the feet are very fleshly and soft, they indicate weakness, softness, and laxity' (5:15–19).[76] This man is being presented, thus, as morally weak and effeminate.[77] The story could be read, then, as following the ancient physiognomic expectations, for his physical healing results in him becoming a 'whole' person, able to participate in the praise of God's people (vv. 8, 9). However, the man does not adopt the steady, slow gait expected of a man of composure, but enthusiastically leaps (ἐξαλλόμενος 'jumping', ἀλλόμενος 'leaping', v. 8). Luke does not present the healed man as conforming to physiognomic expectations; rather, Luke presents the man's response to God as breaking those expectations.[78]

Membership of the people of God in Luke's understanding is not confined to those who fit with social norms of 'wholeness': 'God shows no partiality' (Acts 10:34). As well as the man at the Beautiful Gate, Parsons also highlights the woman bent double (Luke 13:11–17), Zacchaeus, who is small of stature (Luke 19:1–10), and the Ethiopian eunuch (Acts 8:25–40), and in each case shows that the ancient physiognomic traditions would regard them as sub-human and morally inferior because of their physical appearance or impairment.[79] Such attitudes would lead to social marginalization and exclusion. In some cases, they are healed and social inclusion – indeed, inclusion in the people of God – results: e.g. the man at the Beautiful Gate enters the temple, from which he would formerly have been excluded by his disability, participating in praising God (Acts 3:8–9), and associates with the believing community in their regular meeting place, Solomon's Portico (3:11; cf. 5:12). However, the Ethiopian eunuch continues to be a eunuch, and finds himself needing to ask whether anything prevents him being baptized (Acts 8:36) – a natural question in the light of his probable exclusion from anything close to full participation in temple worship, which was the purpose of his visit to Jerusalem (8:27). His 'rejoicing' (8:39) is the natural response to his inclusion in the people of God through baptism.

Gentiles are, of course, a particular and prominent example of such inclusion, and the Ethiopian eunuch provides a key example.[80] Barriers of physical deformity and ethnicity, which shut people out from full participation in the people of God (Deut 23:1), are overcome in belonging to the people of Jesus (cf. Isa 56:3–8, promising a

---

[76] Translations from Parsons, *Body*, 112, 113.
[77] On ancient attitudes to disability more widely, see Parsons, *Body*, 114–16.
[78] Parsons, *Body*, 119–21.
[79] See, respectively, Parsons, *Body*, 83–95, 97–108, 123–41.
[80] Interestingly, in the main, Ethiopians were not regarded with contempt in antiquity because of their dark skin colour; for example, Homer wrote of 'blameless Ethiopians' (*Il.* 1.423–24). See Parsons, *Body*, 132; Frank M. Snowden, Jr, *Blacks in Antiquity: Ethiopians in the Greco-Roman Experience* (Cambridge, MA: Harvard University Press, 1970), esp. 169–95; idem, *Before Color Prejudice: The Ancient View of Blacks* (Cambridge, MA: Harvard University Press, 1983), esp. 46–59.

day when foreigners and eunuchs will be joined to the people of God). The symbolic world of first-century Judaism is being reordered to include such outsiders. Through baptism, repentance and faith, the unclean and despised is made clean and accepted.

VI. Human Community Refigured

Two areas of human community in Luke-Acts require reflection here. Standard ancient social understandings of what it means to be a man or a woman are reshaped through the gospel, and thus the nature of being human-in-relationships looks different to the mainstream pictures.

It is a striking discovery – although disputed[81] – in recent studies that Luke's portrait of men does not comport with Graeco-Roman norms of masculinity.[82] In particular, a 'manly man' (Wilson's phrase) should not act in ways which women were expected to behave. Wilson characterizes 'manly man' expectations as including: the exercise of sexual and paternal power as 'head of the household'; the exercise of political and military power; the exercise of self-control in areas such as emotions, diet and exercise; and bodily autonomy, notably safety from the body being invaded or penetrated from outside.[83] These expectations are shattered by Luke's characterization of believing men as living in dependence on God's power, rather than exercising their own power – thus, Zechariah is silenced (Luke 1:20), Jesus is crucified (Luke 23), Paul is blinded by the exalted Jesus (Acts 9:8-9), and the Ethiopian eunuch has been emasculated prior to entering the story and is characterized consistently and solely as 'the eunuch' (Acts 8:27, 34, 36, 38, 39).[84] All four men are examples of loss of power, loss of self-control, and breach of bodily boundaries, and yet these are four of Luke's 'heroes', men whose example (once they bow to the power of God-in-Jesus) Luke commends and promotes.

However, it is interesting that Luke does not follow the example of his contemporaries and discuss these men using the standard vocabulary of manliness (ἀνδρεία),[85] or describe them as 'feminized' (ἐθηλύνετο) or that they have a 'female disease' (νόσον θήλειαν).[86] Luke is also relatively restrained in his descriptions of suffering: he does

---

[81] Some argue that Luke perpetuates elite images of masculinity in order to present the Christian gospel attractively to such men, e.g. the essays by Mary Rose D'Angelo, and Todd Penner and Caroline VanderStichele in Amy-Jill Levine and Marianne Blickenstaff, eds, *A Feminist Companion to the Acts of the Apostles*, FCNT 9 (Edinburgh: T&T Clark International, 2004), respectively 44–69, 193–209.

[82] Brittany E. Wilson, "Contextualizing Masculinity in the Book of Acts: Peter and Paul as Test Cases," in *Reading Acts in the Discourses of Masculinity and Politics*, ed. Eric D. Barreto, Matthew L. Skinner and Steve Walton, LNTS 559 (London: Bloomsbury T&T Clark, 2017); Wilson, *Men*; Bonnie J. Flessen, *An Exemplary Man: Cornelius and Characterization in Acts 10* (Eugene, OR: Pickwick, 2011); Sean D. Burke, *Queering the Ethiopian Eunuch: Strategies of Ambiguity in Acts*, Emerging Scholars (Minneapolis, MN: Fortress, 2013).

[83] Wilson, "Masculinity"; more fully, Wilson, *Men*, 39–75.

[84] See full discussion in Wilson, *Men*, chs 3–6.

[85] As shown by, e.g., the mother of the Jewish brothers martyred in 4 Maccabees is said to act like a man (ἀνδρειώσας, 15:23), to show manly endurance (ὑπομονὴν ἀνδρειοτέρα, 15:30), and to be found as a man (ἀνδρός, 16:14). I owe these references to Wilson, *Men*, 47 n. 29.

[86] Wilson, *Men*, 46 with n. 23 cites examples from Josephus, *J. W.* 1:59; and Philo, *Abr.* 135–6; *Contempl.* 59–61; *Spec.* 1.60.325.

not give detail on men's bodily suffering – and in this he contrasts with later Christian martyrological texts too.[87]

To be a believing man looks different from the way Graeco-Roman and Jewish societies of the day would think of masculinity, and that is so because to believe is to submit to God-in-Jesus known through the Spirit. It is to be filled with – and thus penetrated by – the Spirit, rather than one's standing reflecting personal authority and self-control (e.g. Acts 2:4; 4:8, 31; 6:3, 5; 7:55; 9:17; 11:24; 13:9, 52). Control is given to Another, and that Other can and does give male followers the promise of suffering and pain (e.g. Acts 9:15–16), so that Paul can describe himself as 'having been *bound* by the Spirit' (δεδεμένος...τῷ πνεύματι, 20:22), a strong image of being under the control of Another.

Luke's reshaping of masculinity in the light of his focus on God, and what God is doing in and through Jesus and by the Spirit, also reshapes his portrait of femininity. Luke's portrait of women characters has been controversial in recent times:[88] some (probably a majority) present him as generally positive towards women, while not anachronistically seeing him as a 'feminist';[89] others regard Luke's portrait of women as simply reflecting the norms of his time and place which place women as subordinate to men in both home and wider society.[90] A third group see a 'double message' in Luke's material including women, affirming both their presence and participation in the believing communities and traditions of masculine leadership.[91] Veronica Koperski has examined a number of such studies, focusing on the male-female pairs which are a prominent feature of Luke-Acts, and showing that they regularly portray the female partner positively.[92]

It is indeed striking that Luke's women are generally portrayed as better models of discipleship than the men. Mary and Zechariah spring quickly to mind as one such pair, for Mary's response is a believing one (Luke 1:38) and Zechariah's the opposite (Luke 1:20). More broadly in the infancy narratives, women hear about the coming of Jesus and model a positive response of praise and trust – Mary, Elisabeth and Anna (Luke 1:26–38, 39–45; 2:36–38; contrast Matthew's infancy narrative, told through the eyes of Joseph, Matt 1:20–21). Similarly Jesus is ready to receive help from wealthy women who provide for him in response to his provision for them (Luke 8:1–3). Mary, strikingly, is found in the posture of a disciple, sitting at Jesus's feet learning from him (Luke 10:38), and is affirmed by Jesus in this orientation (Luke 10:42). Luke alone

---

[87] Wilson, "Masculinity."
[88] For a valuable survey of key scholarship, see Beverly R. Gaventa, "What Ever Happened to Those Prophesying Daughters?," in *A Feminist Companion to the Acts of the Apostles*, ed. Amy-Jill Levine and Marianne Blickenstaff, FCNT 9 (Edinburgh: T&T Clark International, 2004), 49–60, here 50–3.
[89] E.g. Leonard Swidler, *Biblical Affirmations of Woman* (Philadelphia, PA: Westminster, 1979), ch. VIII.
[90] E.g. Shelly Matthews, *The Acts of the Apostles: Taming the Tongues of Fire*, PGNT 5 (Sheffield: Sheffield Phoenix, 2013), 47–9; Mary Rose D'Angelo, "Women in Luke-Acts: A Redactional View," *JBL* 109 (1990): 441–61.
[91] Notably Turid Karlsen Seim, *The Double Message: Patterns of Gender in Luke-Acts*, SNTW (Edinburgh: T&T Clark, 1994).
[92] Veronica Koperski, "Is 'Luke' a Feminist or not? Female-Male Parallels in Luke-Acts," in *Luke and His Readers: Festschrift A. Denaux*, ed. Reimund Bieringer, Gilbert Van Belle and Joseph Verheyden, BETL 182 (Leuven: Peeters, 2005), 25–48.

records parables which take their point from knowledge of the world which women experienced, such as the lost coin (Luke 15:8–10) and the persistent widow (Luke 18:1–8).

When we turn to Acts, we meet a number of passages where Luke signals that 'both men and women' were involved in the believing community's activities, frequently linked by the double conjunction τε καί 'both … and' (5:14; 8:3, 12; 9:2; 17:12, 34; 22:4). Such involvement included suffering and persecution, so these were no 'fair weather' followers (8:3; 9:2; 22:4). A similar point is in view in the emphasis on both men and women prophesying in the Joel quotation cited by Peter at Pentecost (2:17–18, quoting Joel 2:28–29 [LXX 3:1–2]). So where are these 'prophesying daughters' asks Beverly Gaventa?[93] As she notes, they do not disappear, but they are perhaps less prominent than we might expect after the prominent threefold statement about women and men in the Joel prophecy. Philip's daughters clearly fit the bill (Acts 21:8–9), although we never hear their voices. Other women take significant roles, such as Lydia hosting the church in Philippi (Acts 16:13–15), which suggests she takes leadership in some way. We do hear Lydia speak, albeit briefly (v. 15), but the brevity may simply be because Paul is the main vehicle of Luke's story at this point and others, both women and men, speak or act only insofar as they touch Paul's life and ministry.

Luke's picture of the believing communities includes both women and men, and hints that some – such as Lydia – take a leading role. It would be a huge anachronism to regard Luke as a 'feminist' if we construe that in twenty-first-century western terms. Nevertheless, this evidence suggests that Luke cannot simply be pigeonholed as a man of his day whose double-work simply reflects the values of his cultural setting(s). The invasion of the kingdom of God in and through Jesus, in the Third Gospel, and the spread of the gospel empowered by the Spirit, in Acts, are carried out in ways that include women and men together as both recipients and as proponents.

The Lukan portrait of believing communities stretches wider than the community of men and women, to include the sharing of possessions, both from individuals (e.g. Luke 8:1–3; Acts 2:44–45; 4:32–35) and from community to community (Acts 11:27–30).[94] This community fulfils the ideals both of Israel ('there was not a needy person among them', Acts 4:34 echoes Deut 15:4) and the Greek world,[95] and thus offers a model of community life which contributes to our picture of Luke's anthropology – humans are designed to live in relationships with one another which are mutually sustaining and supportive.

---

[93] Gaventa, "What Ever."
[94] On the sharing of possessions, see my student Fiona J. R. Gregson's PhD thesis, "Everything in Common? The Theology and Practice of the Sharing of Possessions in Community in the New Testament with Particular Reference to Jesus and his Disciples, the Earliest Christians, and Paul" (PhD diss.: London School of Theology/Middlesex University, 2012), published as *Everything in Common? The Theology and Practice of the Sharing of Possessions in Community in the New Testament* (Eugene, OR: Pickwick, 2017).
[95] Steve Walton, "Primitive Communism in Acts? Does Acts Present the Community of Goods (2:44–45; 4:32–35) as Mistaken?," *EvQ* 80 (2008): 99–111, here 104–5 [in this volume 63–73].

VII. Conclusion

Luke has led us on a fascinating journey as we have walked with him and sought to understand his understanding of what it means to be human. This journey has ranged from the darkness of human life apart from God's transforming power to the shining light of the new community of believers – not without its dark spots, it must be said – which includes people who are female and male, gentile and Jew, rich and poor, and able-bodied and disabled. Luke presents ideals of godly humanity alongside portraits of godless humanity, and is thus thoroughly realistic. He gives us food for thought and an invitation to action, that in our day believing communities might reflect the best of his vision of humanness.

Bibliography

Aarflot, Christine H. *God (in) Acts: The Characterization of God in the Acts of the Apostles.* Eugene, OR: Pickwick, 2020.

Adams, Edward. "Graeco-Roman and Ancient Jewish Cosmology." Pages 5–27 in *Cosmology and New Testament Theology.* Edited by Jonathan T. Pennington and Sean M. McDonough. LNTS 355. London: T&T Clark, 2008.

Adams, Edward. *The Earliest Christian Meeting Places: Almost Exclusively Houses?* LNTS 450. London: T&T Clark, 2013.

Alexander, Loveday. "Fact, Fiction and the Genre of Acts." *NTS* 44 (1998): 380–99.

Alexander, Loveday, ed. *Images of Empire.* JSOTSup 122. Sheffield: JSOT, 1991.

Alexander, Loveday. *The Preface to Luke's Gospel: Literary Convention and Social Context in Luke 1.1-4 and Acts 1.1.* SNTSMS 78. Cambridge: Cambridge University Press, 1993.

Allen, Brent. *A Political History of Early Christianity.* London: T&T Clark, 2009.

Allen, Leslie C. *Psalms 101-150.* WBC 21. Waco, TX: Word, 1983.

Alter, Robert. *The Art of Biblical Narrative.* London: Allen & Unwin, 1981.

Anderson, Kevin L. *'But God Raised Him from the Dead': The Theology of Jesus' Resurrection in Luke-Acts.* PBM. Milton Keynes: Paternoster, 2006.

Ball, David M. *'I Am' in John's Gospel: Literary Function, Background and Theological Implications.* JSNTSup 124. Sheffield: Sheffield Academic, 1996.

Bammel, Ernst. "Jewish Activity against Christians in Palestine according to Acts." Pages 357–64 in *The Book of Acts in Its Palestinian Setting.* Edited by Richard Bauckham. BAFCS 4. Carlisle: Paternoster; Grand Rapids, MI: Eerdmans, 1995.

Barrett, C. K. "Apollos and the Twelve Disciples of Ephesus." Pages 29–39 in vol. 1 of *The New Testament Age.* Edited by William C. Weinrich. 2 vols. Macon, GA: Mercer University Press, 1984.

Barrett, C. K. "Attitudes to the Temple in the Acts of the Apostles." Pages 345–67 in *Templum Amicitiae.* Edited by William Horbury. JSNTSup 48. Sheffield: JSOT, 1991.

Barrett, C. K. *A Critical and Exegetical Commentary on the Acts of the Apostles.* 2 vols. ICC. Edinburgh: T&T Clark, 1994, 1998.

Barrett, C. K. *Luke the Historian in Recent Study.* London: Epworth, 1961.

Bauckham, Richard. *God Crucified: Monotheism and Christology in the New Testament.* Didsbury Lectures 1996. Carlisle: Paternoster, 1998.

Bauckham, Richard. "James and the Gentiles (Acts 15.13–21)." Pages 154–84 in *History, Literature, and Society in the Book of Acts.* Edited by Ben Witherington, III. Cambridge: Cambridge University Press, 1996.

Bauckham, Richard. "James and the Jerusalem Church." Pages 415–80 in *The Book of Acts in its Palestinian Setting.* Edited by Richard Bauckham. BAFCS 4. Carlisle: Paternoster; Grand Rapids, MI: Eerdmans, 1995.

Bauckham, Richard. *Jesus and the God of Israel: God Crucified and Other Studies on the New Testament's Christology of Divine Identity.* Grand Rapids, MI/ Cambridge: Eerdmans, 2008.

Bauckham, Richard. "The Early Jerusalem Church, Qumran, and the Essenes." Pages 63–89 in *The Dead Sea Scrolls as Background to Postbiblical Judaism and Early Christianity: Papers from an International Conference at St Andrews in 2001*. Edited by James R. Davila. STDJ 46. Leiden: Brill, 2003.

Bauckham, Richard. *The Jewish World around the New Testament: Collected Essays I*. WUNT 233. Tübingen: Mohr Siebeck, 2008.

Bauckham, Richard. "The Restoration of Israel in Luke-Acts." Pages 435–87 in *Restoration: Old Testament, Jewish and Christian Perspectives*. Edited by James M. Scott. JSJSup 72. Leiden: Brill, 2001.

Bayer, Hans F. "Christ-Centred Eschatology in Acts 3:17–26." Pages 236–50 in *Jesus of Nazareth, Lord and Christ: Essays on the Historical Jesus and New Testament Christology*. Edited by Joel B. Green and Max Turner. Carlisle: Paternoster; Grand Rapids, MI: Eerdmans, 1994.

Beard, Mary, John A. North, and Simon R. F. Price. *Religions of Rome*. 2 vols. Cambridge: Cambridge University Press, 1998.

Beasley-Murray, George R. *John*. WBC 36. Dallas, TX: Word, 1987.

Bennema, Cornelis. "Character Reconstruction in the New Testament (1): The Theory." *ExpTim* 127 (2016): 365–74.

Bennema, Cornelis. "Character Reconstruction in the New Testament (2): The Practice." *ExpTim* 127 (2016): 417–29.

Bennema, Cornelis. *A Theory of Character in New Testament Narrative*. Minneapolis, MN: Fortress, 2014.

Betz, Hans Dieter, ed. *The Greek Magical Papyri in Translation: Including the Demotic Spells, vol. 1: Text*. 2nd ed. Chicago: University of Chicago Press, 1992.

Biggar, Nigel. "Showing the Gospel in Social Praxis." *Anvil* 8 (1991): 7–18.

Biguzzi, Giancarlo. "Witnessing Two by Two in the Acts of the Apostles." *Bib* 92 (2011): 1–20.

Bird, Michael F. *Jesus and the Origins of the Gentile Mission*. LNTS 331. London: T&T Clark, 2006.

Bock, Darrell L. *Luke*. IVPNTC. Downers Grove, IL: InterVarsity Press, 1994.

Bock, Darrell L. *Proclamation from Prophecy and Pattern: Lucan Old Testament Christology*. JSNTSup 12. Sheffield: JSOT, 1987.

Bockmuehl, Markus. *Revelation and Mystery in Ancient Judaism and Pauline Christianity*. WUNT II/36. Tübingen: Mohr, 1990.

Boismard, M.-É., OP. *Le texte occidental des Actes des Apôtres*. 2nd ed. EBib ns 40. Paris: Gabalda, 2000.

Bolt, Peter. "Mission and Witness." Pages 191–214 in *Witness to the Gospel: The Theology of Acts*. Edited by I. Howard Marshall and David Peterson. Grand Rapids, MI: Eerdmans, 1998.

Bond, Helen K. *Pontius Pilate in History and Interpretation*. SNTSMS 100. Cambridge: Cambridge University Press, 1998.

Booth, Wayne C. *The Rhetoric of Fiction*. Chicago: University of Chicago Press, 1961.

Bovon, François. *Luke the Theologian: Fifty-five Years of Research (1950–2005)*. 2nd revised ed. Waco. TX: Baylor University Press, 2006.

Branigan, Edward. *Narrative Comprehension and Film*. Sightlines. London: Routledge, 1992.

Brawley, Robert L. *Centering on God: Method and Message in Luke-Acts*. Louisville, KY: Westminster John Knox, 1990.

Brawley, Robert L. *Luke-Acts and the Jews: Conflict, Apology, and Conciliation*. SBLMS 33. Atlanta, GA: Scholars, 1987.

Brent, Allen. "John as *Theologos*: The Imperial Mysteries and the Apocalypse." *JSNT* 22 (2000): 87–102.
Brooke, George J. "Isaiah 40:3 and the Wilderness Community." Pages 117–32 in *New Qumran Texts and Studies: Proceedings of the First Meeting of the International Organization for Qumran Studies, Paris, 1992*. Edited by George J. Brooke and Florentino García Martínez. STDJ 15. Leiden: Brill, 1994.
Brown, Raymond E. *The Death of the Messiah*. 2 vols. ABRL. London: Geoffrey Chapman, 1994.
Bruce, F. F. *New Testament History*. revised ed. London: Oliphants, 1971.
Bruce, F. F. *The Acts of the Apostles*. 3rd ed. Leicester: Apollos, 1990.
Bruce, F. F. *The Book of Acts*. revised ed. NICNT. Grand Rapids, MI: Eerdmans, 1988.
Bruce, F. F. "The Holy Spirit in the Acts of the Apostles." *Int* 27 (1973): 166–83.
Bryan, Christopher. *Render to Caesar: Jesus, the Early Church, and the Roman Superpower*. Oxford: Oxford University Press, 2005.
Buckwalter, Douglas. *The Character and Purpose of Luke's Christology*. SNTSMS 89. Cambridge: Cambridge University Press, 1996.
Bultmann, Rudolf. "Is Exegesis without Presuppositions Possible?" Pages 289–96, 314–15 in *Existence and Faith: Shorter Writings of Rudolf Bultmann*. Edited by Schubert M. Ogden. London: Hodder & Stoughton, 1961.
Bultmann, Rudolf. "New Testament and Mythology." Pages 1–44 in vol. 1 of *Kerygma and Myth: A Theological Debate*. Edited by Hans-Werner Bartsch. Translated by Reginald H. Fuller. 2 vols. London: SPCK, [1953] 1962.
Burke, Sean D. *Queering the Ethiopian Eunuch: Strategies of Ambiguity in Acts*. Emerging Scholars. Minneapolis, MN: Fortress, 2013.
Burridge, Richard A. *What Are the Gospels? A Comparison with Graeco-Roman Biography*. SNTSMS 70. Cambridge: Cambridge University Press, 1992.
Burton, G. P. "Proconsuls, Assizes and the Administration of Justice under the Empire." *JRS* 65 (1975): 92–106.
Busch, Eberhard, ed. *Barth in Conversation: Volume 2, 1963*. Louisville, KY: Westminster John Knox, 2018.
Buzzard, Anthony. "Acts 1:6 and the Eclipse of the Biblical Kingdom." *EvQ* 66 (1994): 197–215.
Cadbury, Henry J. "Names for Christians in Acts." Pages 375–92 in vol. 5 of *The Beginnings of Christianity, Part I: The Acts of the Apostles*. Edited by F. J. Foakes Jackson and K. Lake. 5 vols. London: Macmillan, 1933.
Calvin, John. *Commentaries on the Minor Prophets, vol. 3: Jonah, Micah, Nahum*. Edinburgh: Calvin Translation Society, 1847.
Capper, Brian J. "Community of Goods in the Early Jerusalem Church." *ANRW* 26.2:1730–74. Part 2, *Principat*, 26.2. Edited by Hildegard Temporini and Wolfgang Haase. Berlin: de Gruyter, 1995.
Capper, Brian J. "'In der Hand des Ananias': Erwagungen zu 1QS 6:20 und der urchristlichen Gütergemeinschaft." *RevQ* 12 (1986): 223–36.
Capper, Brian J. "The Interpretation of Acts 5.4." *JSNT* 19 (1983): 117–31.
Capper, Brian J. "The Palestinian Cultural Context of Earliest Christian Community of Goods." Pages 323–56 in *The Book of Acts in its Palestinian Setting*. Edited by Richard Bauckham. BAFCS 4. Carlisle: Paternoster; Grand Rapids, MI: Eerdmans, 1995.
Capper, Brian J. "'With the Oldest Monks …' Light from Essene History on the Career of the Beloved Disciple?" *JTS* ns 49 (1998): 1–55.
Carroll, John T. *Response to the End of History: Eschatology and Situation in Luke-Acts*. SBLDS 92. Atlanta, GA: Scholars, 1988.

Carson, D. A. *The Gospel according to John*. Grand Rapids, MI: Eerdmans; Leicester: InterVarsity Press, 1991.
Carter, Tim. *The Forgiveness of Sins*. Cambridge: James Clarke, 2016.
Carter, Warren. *The Roman Empire and the New Testament*. Abingdon Essential Guides. Nashville, TN: Abingdon, 2006.
Casey, Maurice. *Son of Man: The Interpretation and Influence of Daniel 7*. London: SPCK, 1979.
Cassidy, Richard J. *Society and Politics in the Acts of the Apostles*. Maryknoll, NY: Orbis, 1987.
Cassidy, Richard J., and Philip J. Scharper, eds. *Political Issues in Luke-Acts*. Maryknoll, NY: Orbis, 1983.
Chance, J. Bradley. *Jerusalem, the Temple and the New Age in Luke-Acts*. Macon, GA: Mercer University Press, 1978.
Chen, Diane G. *God as Father in Luke-Acts*. StBibL 92. Frankfurt am Main/New York: Peter Lang, 2006.
Cheng, Ling. *The Characterisation of God in Acts: The Indirect Portrayal of an Invisible Character*. PBM. Milton Keynes: Paternoster, 2011.
Churchill, Timothy W. R. *Divine Initiative and the Christology of the Damascus Road Encounter*. Eugene, OR: Pickwick, 2010.
Clark, Andrew C. *Parallel Lives: The Relation of Paul to the Apostles in the Lucan Perspective*. PBTM. Carlisle: Paternoster, 2001.
Cole, R. A. *The New Temple*. Tyndale Monographs. London: Tyndale, 1950.
Collins, John J. *Daniel*. Hermeneia. Minneapolis, MN: Fortress, 1993.
Collins, John J. "Saints of the Most High." Pages 720–2 in *Dictionary of Deities and Demons in the Bible*. Edited by K. van der Toorn, Bob Becking and Pieter Willem van der Horst. 2nd ed. Leiden: Brill; Grand Rapids, MI/Cambridge: Eerdmans, 1999.
Conzelmann, Hans. *Acts of the Apostles*. Translated by James Limburg, A. Thomas Kraabel and Donald H. Juel. Hermeneia. Philadelphia, PA: Fortress, 1987.
Conzelmann, Hans. *The Theology of St Luke*. Translated by Geoffrey Buswell. London: Faber & Faber, 1960.
Cosgrove, Charles H. "The Divine ΔΕΙ in Luke-Acts: Investigations into the Lukan Understanding of God's Providence." *NovT* 26 (1984): 168–90.
Cotter, Wendy. "The Collegia and Roman Law: State Restrictions on Voluntary Associations." Pages 74–89 in *Voluntary Associations in the Graeco-Roman World*. Edited by John S. Kloppenborg and S. G. Wilson. London: Routledge, 1996.
Cunningham, Scott. *'Through Many Tribulations': The Theology of Persecution in LukeActs*. JSNTSup 142. Sheffield: Sheffield Academic, 1997.
D'Angelo, Mary Rose. "Women in Luke-Acts: A Redactional View." *JBL* 109 (1990): 441–61.
Dahl, Nils Alstrup. "'A People for His Name.'" *NTS* 4 (1958): 319–27.
Dahl, Nils Alstrup. "The Neglected Factor in New Testament Theology." Pages 153–63 in *Jesus the Christ: The Historical Origins of Christological Doctrine*. Edited by Nils Alstrup Dahl and Donald H. Juel. Minneapolis, MN: Fortress, 1991.
Danker, Frederick W. *Luke*. 2nd ed. ProcC. Philadelphia, PA: Fortress, 1987.
Del Agua, Augustín. "The Evangelization of the Kingdom of God." Pages 639–61 in *The Unity of Luke-Acts*. Edited by J. Verheyden. BETL 142. Leuven: Peeters, 1999.
Dibelius, Martin. *Studies in the Acts of the Apostles*. London: SCM, 1956.
Dicken, Frank and Julia A. Snyder, eds. *Characters and Characterization in Luke-Acts*. LNTS 548. London: Bloomsbury T&T Clark, 2016.

Dodd, C. H. *According to the Scriptures: The Sub-structure of New Testament Theology*. London: Nisbet, 1952.
Downs, David J. "Paul's Collection and the Book of Acts Revisited." *NTS* 52 (2006): 50–70.
Dunn, James D. G. *Baptism in the Holy Spirit*. London: SCM; Philadelphia: Westminster, 1970.
Dunn, James D. G. *Beginning from Jerusalem*. Grand Rapids, MI/Cambridge: Eerdmans, 2009.
Dunn, James D. G. "Demythologizing the Ascension – A Reply to Professor Gooding." *IBS* 3 (1981): 15–27.
Dunn, James D. G. "Demythologizing – The Problem of Myth in the New Testament." Pages 285–307 in *New Testament Interpretation*. Edited by I. Howard Marshall. Exeter: Paternoster, 1977.
Dunn, James D. G. *The Acts of the Apostles*. EC. London: Epworth, 1996.
Dunn, James D. G. "The Ascension of Jesus: A Test Case for Hermeneutics." Pages 301–22 in *Auferstehung – Resurrection: The Fourth Durham-Tübingen Research Symposium: Resurrection, Transfiguration, and Exaltation in Old Testament, Ancient Judaism, and Early Christianity (Tübingen, September 1999)*. Edited by Friedrich Avemarie and Hermann Lichtenberger. WUNT 135. Tübingen: Mohr Siebeck, 2001.
Dunn, James D. G. "ΚΥΡΙΟΣ in Acts." Pages 241–53 in his *The Christ and the Spirit: Collected Essays of James D. G. Dunn: vol. 1 Christology*. Edinburgh: T&T Clark; Grand Rapids, MI: Eerdmans, 1998.
Dupont, Jacques. "Note sur le 'Peuple de Dieu' dans les Actes des Apôtres." Pages 209–22 in *Unité et diversité dans l'Église*. Edited by Pontifical Biblical Commission. Teologia e filosofia 15. Vatican City: Libreria Editrice Vaticana, 1989.
Dupont, Jacques. "ἈΝΕΛΗΜΦΘΗ (Act. I. 2)." *NTS* 8 (1962): 154–7.
Dyas, Dee. "Where Is God in Luke-Acts?" (unpublished paper).
Eco, Umberto. *The Role of the Reader: Explorations in the Semiotics of Text*. Advances in Semiotics. London: Hutchinson, 1981.
Estrada, Nelson P. *From Followers to Leaders: The Apostles in the Ritual of Status Transformation in Acts 1–2*. JSNTSup 255. London: T&T Clark, 2004.
Farrow, Douglas. *Ascension and Ecclesia: On the Significance of the Doctrine of the Ascension for Ecclesiology and Christian Cosmology*. Edinburgh: T&T Clark, 1999.
Fee, Gordon D., and Douglas K. Stuart. *How to Read the Bible for All Its Worth*. 4th ed. Grand Rapids, MI: Zondervan, 2014.
Fishwick, Duncan. *The Imperial Cult in the Latin West, Vol. 3, Part 3: Provincial Cult*. RGRW 147. Leiden: Brill, 2004.
Fitzmyer, Joseph A. *Essays on the Semitic Background of the New Testament*. London: Geoffrey Chapman, 1971.
Fitzmyer, Joseph A. *Luke*. 2 vols. AB 28A-B. Garden City, NY: Doubleday, [1981] 1985.
Fitzmyer, Joseph A. *The Acts of the Apostles: A New Translation and Commentary*. AB 31. Garden City, NY: Doubleday, 1998.
Fitzmyer, Joseph A. "The Ascension of Christ and Pentecost." Pages 265–94 in his *To Advance the Gospel: New Testament Studies*. 2nd ed. Grand Rapids, MI: Eerdmans; Livonia. MI: Dove, 1998.
Fitzmyer, Joseph A. "The Designations of Christians in Acts and Their Significance." Pages 223–36 in *Unité et diversité dans l'Église*. Edited by Pontifical Biblical Commission. Teologia e filosofia 15. Vatican City: Libreria Editrice Vaticana, 1989.
Fitzmyer, Joseph A. *To Advance the Gospel: New Testament Studies*. 2nd ed. Biblical Resource series. Grand Rapids, MI: Eerdmans; Livonia, MI: Dove, 1998.

Flessen, Bonnie J. *An Exemplary Man: Cornelius and Characterization in Acts 10*. Eugene, OR: Pickwick, 2011.

Fletcher-Louis, Crispin H. T. *Luke-Acts: Angels, Christology and Soteriology*. WUNT II/94. Tübingen: Mohr Siebeck, 1997.

Foakes Jackson, F. J., and K. Lake, eds. *The Beginnings of Christianity, Part I: The Acts of the Apostles*. 5 vols. London: Macmillan, 1920–33.

Fowl, Stephen E. *Theological Interpretation of Scripture*. Cascade Companions. Eugene, OR: Cascade, 2009.

France, R. T. "Inerrancy and New Testament Exegesis." *Them* 1 (1975): 12–18.

Franklin, Eric. *Christ the Lord: A Study in the Purpose and Theology of Luke-Acts*. London: SPCK, 1975.

Fuller, Michael E. *The Restoration of Israel: Israel's Re-gathering and the Fate of the Nations in Early Jewish Literature and Luke-Acts*. BZNW 138. Berlin: de Gruyter, 2006.

Garland, Robert. *Introducing New Gods: The Politics of Athenian Religion*. London: Duckworth, 1992.

Garrett, Susan R. *The Demise of the Devil: Magic and the Demonic in Luke's Writings*. Minneapolis, MN: Fortress, 1989.

Gärtner, Bertil. *The Areopagus Speech and Natural Revelation*. Uppsala: Gleerup, 1955.

Gärtner, Bertil. *The Temple and the Community in Qumran and the New Testament: A Comparative Study in the Temple Symbolism of the Qumran Texts and the New Testament*. SNTSMS 1. Cambridge: Cambridge University Press, 1965.

Gaventa, Beverly R. *Acts*. ANTC. Nashville, TN: Abingdon, 2003.

Gaventa, Beverly R. "Acts of the Apostles." Pages 33–47 in vol. 1 of *New Interpreter's Dictionary of the Bible*. Edited by Katharine Doob Sakenfeld. 5 vols. Nashville, TN: Abingdon, 2006.

Gaventa, Beverly R. "The Presence of the Absent Lord: The Characterization of Jesus in the Acts of the Apostles." Paper presented at SBL Annual Meeting, 2003.

Gaventa, Beverly R. "What Ever Happened to Those Prophesying Daughters?" Pages 49–60 in *A Feminist Companion to the Acts of the Apostles*. Edited by Amy-Jill Levine and Marianne Blickenstaff. FCNT 9. Edinburgh: T&T Clark International, 2004.

Gempf, Conrad H. "Athens, Paul at." Pages 51–4 in *Dictionary of Paul and His Letters*. Edited by Gerald F. Hawthorne, Ralph P. Martin and Daniel G. Reid. Downers Grove, IL: InterVarsity Press; Leicester: Inter-Varsity Press, 1993.

Gempf, Conrad H. "Public Speaking and Published Accounts." Pages 259–303 in *The Book of Acts in Its Ancient Literary Setting*. Edited by Bruce W. Winter and Andrew D. Clarke. BAFCS 1. Carlisle: Paternoster; Grand Rapids, MI: Eerdmans, 1993.

Giles, Kevin N. "Luke's Use of the Term ἐκκλησία with Special Reference to Acts 20:28 and 9:31." *NTS* 31 (1985): 135–42.

Giles, Kevin N. *What on Earth Is the Church? A Biblical and Theological Enquiry*. London: SPCK, 1995.

Gill, David W. J. "Achaia." Pages 433–53 in *The Book of Acts in its Graeco-Roman Setting*. Edited by David W. J. Gill and Conrad H. Gempf. BAFCS 2. Carlisle: Paternoster; Grand Rapids, MI: Eerdmans, 1994.

Gill, David W. J. "Acts and Roman Policy in Judaea." Pages 15–26 in *The Book of Acts in its Palestinian Setting*. Edited by Richard Bauckham. BAFCS 4. Carlisle: Paternoster; Grand Rapids, MI: Eerdmans, 1995.

Gill, David W. J. "Macedonia." Pages 397–417 in *The Book of Acts in its Graeco-Roman Setting*. Edited by David W. J. Gill and Conrad H. Gempf. BAFCS 2. Carlisle: Paternoster; Grand Rapids, MI: Eerdmans, 1994.

Gill, David W. J. "The Roman Empire as a Context for the New Testament." Pages 389–406 in *Handbook to Exegesis of the New Testament*. Edited by Stanley E. Porter. NTTS 25. Leiden: Brill, 1997.

Gill, David W. J., and Conrad H. Gempf, eds. *The Book of Acts in Its Graeco-Roman Setting*. BAFCS 2. Carlisle: Paternoster; Grand Rapids, MI: Eerdmans, 1994.

Goldingay, John. "Are They Comic Acts?" *EvQ* 69 (1997): 99–107.

Goldingay, John. *Daniel*. WBC 30. Dallas, TX: Word, 1989.

Gooding, David W. "Demythologizing Old and New, and Luke's Description of the Ascension: A Layman's Appraisal." *IBS* 2 (1980): 95–119.

Gooding, David W. "Demythologizing the Ascension – A Reply." *IBS* 3 (1981): 46–54.

Gorman, Michael J. *Elements of Biblical Exegesis: A Basic Guide for Students and Ministers*. 3rd ed. Grand Rapids, MI: Baker Academic, 2020.

Gorman, Michael J. *Inhabiting the Cruciform God: Kenosis, Justification, and Theosis in Paul's Narrative Soteriology*. Grand Rapids, MI: Eerdmans, 2009.

Green, Joel B. "Acts of the Apostles." Pages 7–24 in *Dictionary of the Later New Testament and its Developments*. Edited by Ralph P. Martin and Peter H. Davids. Downers Grove, IL: InterVarsity Press; Leicester: Inter-Varsity Press, 1997.

Green, Joel B. "Luke-Acts, or Luke and Acts? A Reaffirmation of Narrative Unity." Pages 101–19 in *Reading Acts Today: Essays in Honour of Loveday C. A. Alexander*. Edited by Steve Walton, Thomas E. Phillips, Lloyd K. Pietersen and F. Scott Spencer. LNTS 427. London: T&T Clark, 2011.

Green, Joel B. *Practicing Theological Interpretation: Engaging Biblical Texts for Faith and Formation*. Grand Rapids, MI: Baker Academic, 2011.

Green, Joel B. *The Death of Jesus: Tradition and Interpretation in the Passion Narrative*. WUNT II/33. Tübingen: J. C. B. Mohr (Paul Siebeck), 1988.

Green, Joel B. *The Gospel of Luke*. NICNT. Grand Rapids, MI/Cambridge: Eerdmans, 1997.

Gregson, Fiona J. Robertson. *Everything in Common? The Theology and Practice of the Sharing of Possessions in Community in the New Testament*. Eugene, OR: Pickwick, 2017.

Gregson, Fiona J. Robertson. "Everything in Common? The Theology and Practice of the Sharing of Possessions in Community in the New Testament with Particular Reference to Jesus and his Disciples, the Earliest Christians, and Paul." PhD diss., London School of Theology/Middlesex University, 2012.

Grudem, Wayne A. *The Gift of Prophecy in the New Testament and Today*. Eastbourne: Kingsway, 1988.

Haenchen, Ernst. *The Acts of the Apostles*. Translated by R. McL. Wilson. Oxford: Blackwell, 1971.

Hardin, Justin K. "Decrees and Drachmas at Thessalonica: An Illegal Assembly in Jason's House (Acts 17.1–10a)." *NTS* 52 (2006): 29–49.

Harris, Murray J. *Jesus as God: The New Testament Use of Theos in Reference to Jesus*. Grand Rapids, MI: Baker, 1992.

Harrison, Everett F. *Acts: The Expanding Church*. Chicago: Moody, 1975.

Hart, H. StJ. "The Coin of 'Render unto Caesar …' (A Note on Some Aspects of Mark 12:13–17; Matt. 22:15–22; Luke 20:20–26)." Pages 241–8 in *Jesus and the Politics of His Day*. Edited by Ernst Bammel and C. F. D. Moule. Cambridge: Cambridge University Press, 1984.

Hartman, Lars. *'Into the Name of the Lord Jesus': Baptism in the Early Church*. SNTW. Edinburgh: T&T Clark, 1997.

Harvey, A. E. *Jesus on Trial: A Study in the Fourth Gospel*. London: SPCK, 1976.

Haya-Prats, Gonzalo, SJ. *L'Esprit, force de l'Église: sa nature et son activité d'après les Actes des apôtres*. LD 81. Paris: Éditions du Cerf, 1975.
Hays, Richard B. *Echoes of Scripture in the Gospels*. Waco, TX: Baylor University Press, 2016.
Hays, Richard B. *Reading Backwards: Figural Christology and the Fourfold Gospel Witness*. Waco, TX: Baylor University Press, 2014.
Head, Peter M. "Acts and the Problem of Its Texts." Pages 415–44 in *The Book of Acts in Its Ancient Literary Setting*. Edited by Bruce W. Winter and Andrew D. Clarke. BAFCS 1. Carlisle: Paternoster; Grand Rapids, MI: Eerdmans, 1993.
Head, Peter M. "The Temple in Luke's Gospel." Pages 101–19 in *Heaven on Earth: The Temple in Biblical Theology*. Edited by T. Desmond Alexander and Simon J. Gathercole. Carlisle: Paternoster, 2004.
Heath, Thomas L. *Aristarchus of Samos, the Ancient Copernicus*. Oxford: Clarendon, 1913.
Heitmüller, Wilhelm. *"Im Namen Jesu." Eine sprach.- u. religionsgeschichtliche Untersuchung zum Neuen Testament, speziell zur altchristlichen Taufe*. FRLANT I/2. Göttingen: Vandenhoeck & Ruprecht, 1903.
Hemer, Colin J. *The Book of Acts in the Setting of Hellenistic History*. Edited by Conrad H. Gempf. WUNT 49. Tübingen: J. C. B. Mohr (Paul Siebeck), 1989.
Hengel, Martin. *The Zealots: Investigations into the Jewish Freedom Movement in the Period from Herod I until 70 AD*. 2nd ed. Edinburgh: T&T Clark, 1989.
Hill, Craig C. *Hellenists and Hebrews: Reappraising Division within the Earliest Church*. Minneapolis, MN: Fortress, 1992.
Holtzmann, H. J. "Die Gütergemeinschaft der Apostelgeschichte." Pages 27–60 in *Strassburger Abhandlungen zur Philosophie. Eduard Zeller zu seinem siebenzigsten Geburtstag*. Edited. Tübingen: Akad. Verlagsbuchhandlung, 1884.
Horbury, William. "New Wine in Old Wine-Skins: IX. The Temple." *ExpTim* 86 (1974): 36–42.
Horbury, William. "Septuagintal and New Testament Conceptions of the Church." Pages 1–17 in *A Vision for the Church: Studies in Early Christian Ecclesiology in Honour of J. P. M. Sweet*. Edited by Markus Bockmuehl and Michael B. Thompson. Edinburgh: T&T Clark, 1997.
Horsley, Richard A. "Introduction to Building an Alternative Society." Pages 206–14 in *Paul and Empire: Religion and Power in Roman Imperial Society*. Edited by Richard A. Horsley. Harrisburg: Trinity Press International, 1997.
Houlden, Leslie. "Beyond Belief: Preaching the Ascension." *Theology* 94 (1991): 173–80.
Hultgren, Arland J. *Christ and His Benefits: Christology and Redemption in the New Testament*. Philadelphia, PA: Fortress, 1987.
Humphreys, W. Lee. *The Character of God in the Book of Genesis: A Narrative Appraisal*. Louisville, KY: Westminster John Knox, 2001.
Hurtado, Larry W. "Christology in Acts: Jesus in Early Christian Belief and Practice." Pages 217–37 in *Issues in Luke-Acts: Selected Essays*. Edited by Sean A. Adams and Michael W. Pahl. Gorgias Handbooks 26. Piscataway, NJ: Gorgias, 2012.
Hurtado, Larry W. *Honoring the Son: Jesus in Earliest Christian Devotional Practice*. Snapshots. Bellingham, WA: Lexham, 2018.
Hurtado, Larry W. *Lord Jesus Christ: Devotion to Jesus in Earliest Christianity*. Grand Rapids, MI/Cambridge: Eerdmans, 2003.
Jeremias, Joachim. *Jerusalem in the Time of Jesus*. London: SCM, 1969.
Jeremias, Joachim. *The Eucharistic Words of Jesus*. London: SCM, 1966.
Jervell, Jacob. *Die Apostelgeschichte*. 17th ed. KEK. Göttingen: Vandenhoeck & Ruprecht, 1998.

Jervell, Jacob. *The Theology of the Acts of the Apostles*. NT Theology. Cambridge: Cambridge University Press, 1996.
Jewett, Robert. *Romans*. Hermeneia. Minneapolis, MN: Fortress, 2007.
Jipp, Joshua W. "The Beginnings of a Theology of Luke-Acts: Divine Activity and Human Response." *JTI* 8 (2014): 23–44.
Johnson, Andy. "Resurrection. Ascension and the Developing Portrait of the God of Israel in Acts." *SJT* 57 (2004): 146–62.
Johnson, D. E. "Jesus against the Idols: The Use of Isaianic Servant Songs in the Missiology of Acts." *WTJ* 52 (1990): 343–53.
Johnson, Luke T. *Religious Experience in Early Christianity*. Minneapolis, MN: Fortress, 1998.
Johnson, Luke T. *The Acts of the Apostles*. SP 5. Collegeville, MN: Liturgical, 1992.
Johnson, Luke T. *The Gospel of Luke*. SP 3. Collegeville, MN: Liturgical, 1992.
Johnson, Luke T. *The Literary Function of Possessions in Luke-Acts*. SBLDS 39. Missoula, MT: Scholars, 1977.
Jones, A. H. M. *The Greek City from Alexander to Justinian*. Oxford: Clarendon, 1940.
Jones, Donald L. "The Title 'Author of Life (Leader)' in the Acts of the Apostles." Pages 627–36 in *Society of Biblical Literature 1994 Seminar Papers*. SBLSPS Atlanta, GA: SBL, 1994.
Käsemann, Ernst. "The Disciples of John the Baptist in Ephesus." Pages 136–48 in *Essays on New Testament Themes*. Edited by Ernst Käsemann. SBT 41. London: SCM, 1964.
Keener, Craig S. *Acts: An Exegetical Commentary*. 4 vols. Grand Rapids, MI: Baker Academic, 2012–15.
Kilgallen, John J. *The Stephen Speech: A Literary and Redactional Study of Acts 7,2-53*. AnBib 67. Rome: Biblical Institute Press, 1976.
Klijn, A. F. J. "Stephen's Speech – Acts VII. 2–53." *NTS* 4 (1957): 25–31.
Koperski, Veronica. "Is 'Luke' a Feminist or Not? Female-Male Parallels in Luke-Acts." Pages 25–48 in *Luke and His Readers: Festschrift A. Denaux*. Edited by Reimund Bieringer, Gilbert Van Belle and Joseph Verheyden. BETL 182. Leuven: Peeters, 2005.
Krodel, Gerhard. *Acts*. ACNT. Minneapolis, MN: Augsburg, 1986.
Krodel, Gerhard. *Acts*. ProcC. Philadelphia, PA: Fortress, 1981.
Kümmel, W. G. *Man in the New Testament*. Translated by John J. Vincent. Revised ed. London: Epworth, 1963.
Lacey, W. K., and B. W. J. G. Wilson. *Res Publica: Roman Politics and Society according to Cicero*. London: Oxford University Press, 1970.
Lawrence, Louise J. *Reading with Anthropology: Exhibiting Aspects of New Testament Religion*. Bletchley: Paternoster, 2005.
Lennartsson, Göran. *Refreshing and Restoration: Two Eschatological Motifs in Acts 3:19-21*. Lund: Lund University, Centre for Theology and Religious Studies, 2007.
Levine, Amy-Jill and Marianne Blickenstaff, eds. *A Feminist Companion to the Acts of the Apostles*. FCNT 9. Edinburgh: T&T Clark International, 2004.
Levinsohn, Stephen H. *Textual Connections in Acts*. SBLMS 31. Atlanta, GA: Scholars, 1987.
Lichtenberger, Hermann. "Jews and Christians in Rome in the Time of Nero: Josephus and Paul in Rome." *ANRW* 26.3:2142–76. Part 2, *Principat*, 26.3. Edited by Hildegard Temporini and Wolfgang Haase. Berlin: de Gruyter, 1996.
Lincoln, Andrew T. *Truth on Trial: The Lawsuit Motif in the Fourth Gospel*. Peabody, MA: Hendrickson, 2000.
Lindemann, Andreas. "The Beginnings of Christian Life in Jerusalem according to the Summaries in the Acts of the Apostles (Acts 2:42-47; 4:32-37; 5:12-16)." Pages 202–18

in *Common Life in the Early Church: Essays Honoring Graydon F. Snyder*. Edited by Julian V. Hills. Harrisburg, PA: Trinity Press International, 1998.

Lintott, Andrew. *Imperium Romanum: Politics and Administration*. London/New York: Routledge, 1993.

Lohfink, Gerhard. *Die Himmelfahrt Jesu: Untersuchungen zu den Himmelfahrts- und Erhöhungstexten bei Lukas*. SANT 26. München: Kösel, 1971.

Longenecker, Richard N. *Acts*. Expositor's Bible Commentary. Grand Rapids, MI: Zondervan, 1995.

Longenecker, Richard N. *Galatians*. WBC 41. Dallas, TX: Word, 1990.

Longenecker, Richard N. "The Acts of the Apostles." Pages 207–573 in Volume 9 of *The Expositor's Bible Commentary*. Edited by Frank E. Gaebelein. 12 vols. Grand Rapids, MI: Zondervan, 1981.

Longenecker, Richard N. *The Christology of Early Jewish Christianity*. SBT 2/17. London: SCM, 1970.

Lucas, Ernest. *Daniel*. AOTC 20. Leicester: Apollos, 2002.

Lüdemann, Gerd. *Early Christianity according to the Traditions in Acts: A Commentary*. London: SCM, 1989.

Macro, Anthony D. "The Cities of Asia Minor under the Roman Imperium." *ANRW* 7.2:658–97. Part 2, *Principat*, 7.2. Edited by Hildegard Temporini and Wolfgang Haase. Berlin: de Gruyter, 1980.

Maddox, Robert. *The Purpose of Luke-Acts*. SNTW. Edinburgh: T&T Clark, 1982.

Malbon, Elizabeth Struthers. *Mark's Jesus: Characterization as Narrative Christology*. Waco, TX: Baylor University Press, 2009.

Malherbe, Abraham J. *The Cynic Epistles: A Study Edition*. SBLSBS 12. Missoula, MT: Scholars, 1977.

Malina, Bruce J. *The New Testament World: Insights from Cultural Anthropology*. 3rd ed. Louisville, KY: Westminster John Knox, 2001.

Mallen, Peter. "Genesis in Luke-Acts." Pages 60–82 in *Genesis in the New Testament*. Edited by Maarten J. J. Menken and Steve Moyise. LNTS 466. London: Bloomsbury T&T Clark, 2012.

Mallen, Peter. *The Reading and Transformation of Isaiah in Luke-Acts*. LNTS 367. London: T&T Clark, 2008.

Marcus, Joel. *Mark*. 2 vols. AB 27, 27A. New Haven, CT: Yale University Press, [1999] 2009.

Marguerat, Daniel. "The Resurrection and Its Witnesses in the Book of Acts." Pages 171–85 in *Reading Acts Today: Essays in Honour of Loveday C. A. Alexander*. Edited by Steve Walton, Thomas E. Phillips, Lloyd K. Pietersen and F. Scott Spencer. LNTS 427. London: T&T Clark, 2011.

Marguerat, Daniel, and Yvan Bourquin. *How to Read Bible Stories*. London: SCM, 1999.

Marshall, I. Howard. "Acts." Pages 513–606 in *Commentary on the New Testament Use of the Old Testament*. Edited by G. K. Beale and D. A. Carson. Nottingham: Apollos; Grand Rapids, MI: Baker Academic, 2007.

Marshall, I. Howard. "Acts and the 'Former Treatise.'" Pages 163–82 in *The Book of Acts in its Ancient Literary Setting*. Edited by Bruce W. Winter and Andrew D. Clarke. BAFCS 1. Carlisle: Paternoster; Grand Rapids, MI: Eerdmans, 1993.

Marshall, I. Howard. "Church and Temple in the New Testament." *TynBul* 40 (1989): 203–22.

Marshall, I. Howard. "How Far Did the Early Christians *Worship* God?" *Chm* 99 (1985): 216–29.

Marshall, I. Howard. "New Wine in Old Wineskins: V. The Biblical Use of the Word Ekklēsia." *ExpTim* 84 (1973): 359–64.
Marshall, I. Howard. *Last Supper and Lord's Supper*. Exeter: Paternoster, 1980.
Marshall, I. Howard. *Luke: Historian and Theologian*. Exeter: Paternoster, 1970.
Marshall, I. Howard. *The Acts of the Apostles*. NT Guides. Sheffield: JSOT, 1992.
Marshall, I. Howard. *The Acts of the Apostles: An Introduction and Commentary*. TNTC. Leicester: IVP, 1980.
Marshall, I. Howard. *The Gospel of Luke: A Commentary on the Greek Text*. NIGTC. Exeter: Paternoster; Grand Rapids, MI: Eerdmans, 1978.
Marshall, I. Howard, and David Peterson, eds. *Witness to the Gospel: The Theology of Acts*. Grand Rapids, MI/Cambridge: Eerdmans, 1998.
Matthews, Shelly. *The Acts of the Apostles: Taming the Tongues of Fire*. PGNT 5. Sheffield: Sheffield Phoenix, 2013.
McConville, Gordon. "Jerusalem in the Old Testament." Pages 21–51 in *Jerusalem Past and Present in the Purposes of God*. Edited by P. W. L. Walker. Cambridge: Tyndale House, 1992.
McGee, Daniel B. "Sharing Possessions: A Study in Biblical Ethics. Selected Interpretations of Acts 2:43-47 and 4:32-37, Patristic Times to Present." Pages 163–78 in *With Steadfast Purpose: Essays on Acts in Honor of Henry Jackson Flanders, Jr*. Edited by Naymond H. Keathley. Waco, TX: Baylor University Press, 1990.
McKelvey, R. J. *The New Temple: The Church in the New Testament*. Oxford Theological Monographs. London: Oxford University Press, 1969.
Meek, James A. *The Gentile Mission in Old Testament Citations in Acts: Text, Hermeneutic, and Purpose*. LNTS 385. London: T&T Clark, 2008.
Meeks, Wayne A. *The First Urban Christians: The Social World of the Apostle Paul*. New Haven, CT: Yale University Press, 1983.
Menzies, Robert P. *Empowered for Witness: The Spirit in Luke-Acts*. JPTSup 6. Sheffield: Sheffield Academic, 1994.
Metzger, Bruce M. *A Textual Commentary on the Greek New Testament*. 2nd ed. Stuttgart: Deutsche Bibelgesellschaft/United Bible Societies, 1994.
Millar, Fergus. *The Roman Empire and Its Neighbours*. 2nd ed. London: Duckworth, 1981.
Miller, John B. F. *Convinced That God Had Called Us: Dreams, Visions, and the Perception of God's Will in Luke-Acts*. BibInt 85. Leiden: Brill, 2007.
Minear, Paul S. *Images of the Church in the New Testament*. London: Lutterworth, 1961.
Moberly, Walter. "Proclaiming Christ Crucified: Some Reflections on the Use and Abuse of the Gospels." *Anvil* 5 (1988): 31–52.
Moore, Thomas S. "'To the End of the Earth': The Geographic and Ethnic Universalism of Acts 1:8 in Light of Isaianic Influence on Luke." *JETS* 40 (1997): 389–99.
Morris, Leon L. "The Theme of Romans." Pages 249–63 in *Apostolic History and the Gospel*. Edited by W. W. Gasque and Ralph P. Martin. Exeter: Paternoster, 1970.
Moule, C. F. D. *An Idiom-Book of New Testament Greek*. 2nd ed. Cambridge: Cambridge University Press, 1959.
Moule, C. F. D. *The Birth of the New Testament*. 3rd ed. BNTC. London: A. & C. Black, 1981.
Moule, C. F. D. "The Christology of Acts." Pages 159–85 in *Studies in Luke-Acts*. Edited by Leander E. Keck and J. L. Martyn. London: SPCK, 1968.
Moule, C. F. D. *The Origin of Christology*. Cambridge: Cambridge University Press, 1977.
Moule, H. C. G. *Charles Simeon*. London: IVF, 1948.
Moulton, James H., Wilbert F. Howard and Nigel Turner. *A Grammar of New Testament Greek*. 4 vols. Edinburgh: T&T Clark, 1906–76.

Murphy-O'Connor, Jerome. *St Paul's Corinth: Texts and Archaeology*. 3rd ed. Collegeville, MN: Liturgical, 2002.

Nave, Guy D. *The Role and Function of Repentance in Luke-Acts*. SBLAcBib 4. Leiden: Brill, 2002.

Newbigin, Lesslie. "Witness in a Biblical Perspective." *MisSt* 3 (1986): 80–4.

Nolland, John. *Luke*. 3 vols. WBC 35A-C. Dallas. TX: Word, 1989–93.

O'Neill, J. C. *The Theology of Acts in Its Historical Setting*. 2nd ed. London: SPCK, 1970.

O'Reilly, Leo. *Word and Sign in the Acts of the Apostles: A Study in Lucan Theology*. AnGr 243. Rome: Editrice Pontificia Università Gregoriana, 1987.

O'Toole, Robert F., SJ. "Activity of the Risen Jesus in Luke-Acts." *Bib* 62 (1981): 471–98.

O'Toole, Robert F., SJ. "Luke's Understanding of Jesus' Resurrection-Ascension-Exaltation." *BTB* 9 (1979): 106–14.

O'Toole, Robert F., SJ. "Parallels between Jesus and His Disciples in Luke-Acts: A Further Study." *BZ* 27 (1983): 195–212.

O'Toole, Robert F., SJ. *The Unity of Luke's Theology*. GNS 9. Wilmington, DE: Michael Glazier, 1984.

Oakes, Peter. *Philippians: From People to Letter*. SNTSMS 110. Cambridge: Cambridge University Press, 2000.

Padilla, Osvaldo. *The Speeches of Outsiders in Acts: Poetics, Theology and Historiography*. SNTSMS 145. Cambridge: Cambridge University Press, 2008.

Pao, David W. *Acts and the Isaianic New Exodus*. BibStL. Grand Rapids, MI: Baker Academic, 2002.

Park, Hyung Dae. "Finding חרם? A Study of Luke-Acts in the Light of חרם." PhD diss., London School of Theology/Brunel University, 2005.

Park, Hyung Dae. *Finding Herem? A Study of Luke-Acts in the Light of Herem*. LNTS 357. London: T&T Clark, 2007.

Parsons, Mikeal C. *Body and Character in Luke and Acts: The Subversion of Physiognomy in Early Christianity*. Grand Rapids, MI: Baker Academic, 2006.

Parsons, Mikeal C. *The Departure of Jesus in Luke-Acts: The Ascension Narratives in Context*. JSNTSup 21. Sheffield: JSOT, 1987.

Parsons, Mikeal C., and Richard I. Pervo. *Rethinking the Unity of Luke and Acts*. Minneapolis, MN: Fortress, 1993.

Pelikan, Jaroslav. *Acts*. BTCB. Grand Rapids, MI: Brazos, 2005.

Pennington, Jonathan T. "Dualism in Old Testament Cosmology: *Weltbild* and *Weltanschauung*." *SJOT* 18 (2004): 260–77.

Pervo, Richard I. *Acts*. Hermeneia. Minneapolis, MN: Fortress, 2009.

Pervo, Richard I. *Profit with Delight*. Philadelphia, PA: Fortress, 1987.

Pesch, Rudolf. *Die Apostelgeschichte*. 2 vols. EKKNT. Zürich: Benzinger-Verlag, 1986.

Peterson, David. *Engaging with God: A Biblical Theology of Worship*. Leicester: Apollos, 1992.

Peterson, David. "The Motif of Fulfilment and the Purpose of Luke-Acts." Pages 83–104 in *The Book of Acts in its Ancient Literary Setting*. Edited by Bruce W. Winter and Andrew D. Clarke. BAFCS 1. Carlisle: Paternoster; Grand Rapids, MI: Eerdmans, 1993.

Phillips, Thomas E. "Reading Recent Readings of Issues of Wealth and Poverty in Luke and Acts." *CurBR* 1 (2003): 231–69.

Porter, Stanley E. *Idioms of the Greek New Testament*. 2nd ed. Biblical Languages: Greek 2. Sheffield: JSOT, 1994.

Porter, Stanley E. "The 'We' Passages." Pages 545–74 in *The Book of Acts in Its Graeco-Roman Setting*. Edited by David W. J. Gill and Conrad H. Gempf. BAFCS 2. Carlisle: Paternoster; Grand Rapids, MI: Eerdmans, 1994.

Powell, Mark Allan. *What Is Narrative Criticism?* London: SPCK, 1993.
Praeder, Susan M. "Jesus-Paul, Peter-Paul, and Jesus-Peter Parallelisms in Luke-Acts: A History of Reader Response." Pages 23–39 in *Society of Biblical Literature 1984 Seminar Papers*. SBLSPS 23. Atlanta, GA: SBL, 1984.
Rajak, Tessa. "Was There a Roman Charter for the Jews?" *JRS* 74 (1984): 107–23.
Ramsay, William M. *St Paul the Traveller and Roman Citizen*. London: Hodder & Stoughton, 1895.
Rapske, Brian M. "Roman Governors of Palestine." Pages 979–84 in *Dictionary of the Later New Testament and Its Developments*. Edited by Ralph P. Martin and Peter H. Davids. Leicester: Inter-Varsity Press; Downers Grove, IL: InterVarsity Press, 1997.
Rapske, Brian M. *The Book of Acts and Paul in Roman Custody*. BAFCS 3. Carlisle: Paternoster; Grand Rapids, MI: Eerdmans, 1994.
Ravens, David. *Luke and the Restoration of Israel*. JSNTSup 119. Sheffield: Sheffield Academic, 1995.
Read-Heimerdinger, Jenny. *The Bezan Text of Acts: A Contribution of Discourse Analysis to Textual Criticism*. JSNTSup 236. London: Sheffield Academic, 2002.
Reicke, Bo. "The Risen Lord and His Church: The Theology of Acts." *Int* 13 (1959): 157–69.
Resseguie, James L. *Narrative Criticism of the New Testament: An Introduction*. Grand Rapids, MI: Baker Academic, 2005.
Reynolds, Joyce. "Cities." Pages 15–51 in *The Administration of the Roman Empire 241 BC–AD 193*. Edited by David C. Braund. Exeter Studies in History 18. Exeter: University of Exeter, 1988.
Rhoads, David, David Esterline and Jae Won Lee, eds. *Luke-Acts and Empire: Essays in Honor of Robert L. Brawley*. Princeton Theological Monographs 151. Eugene, OR: Pickwick, 2011.
Riesner, Rainer. "Synagogues in Jerusalem." Pages 179–211 in *The Book of Acts in Its Palestinian Setting*. Edited by Richard Bauckham. BAFCS 4. Carlisle: Paternoster; Grand Rapids, MI: Eerdmans, 1995.
Rius-Camps, Josep, and Jenny Read-Heimerdinger. *The Message of Acts in Codex Bezae: A Comparison with the Alexandrian Tradition*. 4 vols. JSNTSup/LNTS 257, 302, 365, 415. London: T&T Clark, 2004–9.
Robb, Julie E. "The Prophet Like Moses: Its Jewish Context and Use in the Early Christian Tradition." PhD diss., King's College London, 2003.
Romm, James S. *The Edges of the Earth in Ancient Thought: Geography, Exploration, and Fiction*. Princeton, NJ: Princeton University Press, 1992.
Rowe, C. Kavin. "Acts 2.36 and the Continuity of Lukan Christology." *NTS* 53 (2007): 37–56.
Rowe, C. Kavin. *Early Narrative Christology: The Lord in the Gospel of Luke*. paperback ed. Grand Rapids, MI: Baker, 2009.
Rowe, C. Kavin. *World Upside Down: Reading Acts in the Graeco-Roman Age*. Oxford/New York: Oxford University Press, 2009.
Rowland, Christopher. *The Open Heaven: A Study of Apocalyptic in Judaism and Early Christianity*. London: SPCK, 1982.
Sachs, A. "Babylonian Observational Astronomy." *Philos. Trans. Royal Soc. A* 276 (1974): 43–50.
Safrai, Ze'ev. *The Economy of Roman Palestine*. London: Routledge, 1994.
Sanders, E. P. *Jesus and Judaism*. London: SCM, 1984.
Sanders, E. P. *Judaism: Practice and Belief 63 BCE–66 CE*. London: SCM, 1992.

Sanders, Jack T. *The Jews in Luke-Acts*. London: SCM, 1987.
Sandmel, Samuel. "Parallelomania." *JBL* 81 (1962): 1–13.
Scharlemann, Martin H. *Stephen: A Singular Saint*. AnBib 34. Rome: Pontifical Biblical Institute, 1968.
Schnabel, Eckhard J. *Acts*. Expanded digital ed. Grand Rapids, MI: Zondervan, 2012 (electronic book).
Schnabel, Eckhard J. *Acts*. ZECNT 5. Grand Rapids, MI: Zondervan, 2012.
Schnabel, Eckhard J. *Early Christian Mission*. 2 vols. Downers Grove, IL: InterVarsity Press, 2004.
Schneider, Gerhard. *Die Apostelgeschichte*. 2 vols. HTKNT. Freiburg: Herder, [1980] 1982.
Schürer, Emil, Geza Vermes, Fergus Millar, and Martin Goodman. *The History of the Jewish People in the Age of Jesus Christ (175 BC–AD 135)*. Rev. ed. 4 vols. Edinburgh: T&T Clark, 1973–86.
Schwartz, Daniel R. "Non-joining Sympathisers (Acts 5.13-14)." *Bib* 64 (1983): 550–5.
Scott, James M., ed. *Restoration: Old Testament, Jewish, and Christian Perspectives*. JSJSup 72. Leiden: Brill, 2001.
Seccombe, David P. "Luke's Vision for the Church." Pages 45–63 in *A Vision for the Church: Studies in Early Christian Ecclesiology in Honour of J. P. M. Sweet*. Edited by Markus Bockmuehl and Michael B. Thompson. Edinburgh: T&T Clark, 1997.
Seccombe, David P. "Was There Organised Charity in Jerusalem before the Christians?" *JTS* ns 29 (1978): 140–3.
Segal, Alan F. *Two Powers in Heaven: Early Rabbinic Reports about Christianity and Gnosticism*. SJLA 25. Leiden: Brill, 1977.
Seim, Turid Karlsen. *The Double Message: Patterns of Gender in Luke-Acts*. SNTW. Edinburgh: T&T Clark, 1994.
Shelton, Jo-Ann. *As the Romans Did: A Sourcebook in Roman Social History*. 2nd ed. Oxford: Oxford University Press, 1998.
Sherwin-White, A. N. *Roman Society and Roman Law in the New Testament*. Grand Rapids, MI: Baker, 1981 (reprint from: Oxford: Clarendon, 1963).
Simon, Marcel. *St Stephen and the Hellenists in the Primitive Church: The Haskell Lectures 1956*. London: Longmans, Green, 1958.
Skinner, Matthew L. *Locating Paul: Places of Custody as Narrative Settings in Acts 21–28*. AcBib 13. Atlanta, GA: SBL, 2003.
Skinner, Matthew L. *The Trial Narratives: Conflict, Power, and Identity in the New Testament*. Louisville, KY: Westminster John Knox, 2010.
Sleeman, Matthew. *Geography and the Ascension Narrative in Acts*. SNTSMS 146. Cambridge: Cambridge University Press, 2009.
Snowden, Frank M., Jr. *Before Color Prejudice: The Ancient View of Blacks*. Cambridge, MA: Harvard University Press, 1983.
Snowden, Frank M., Jr. *Blacks in Antiquity: Ethiopians in the Greco-Roman Experience*. Cambridge, MA: Harvard University Press, 1970.
Soards, Marion L. *The Speeches in Acts: Their Content, Context, and Concerns*. Louisville, KY: Westminster John Knox, 1994.
Spencer, F. Scott. *The Portrait of Philip in Acts: A Study of Roles and Relations*. JSNTSup 67. Sheffield: JSOT, 1992.
Squires, John T. *The Plan of God in Luke-Acts*. SNTSMS 76. Cambridge: Cambridge University Press, 1993.

Squires, John T. "The Plan of God in the Acts of the Apostles." Pages 19–39 in *Witness to the Gospel: The Theology of Acts*. Edited by I. Howard Marshall and David Peterson. Grand Rapids, MI: Eerdmans, 1998.

Stein, Robert H. *Luke*. NAC 24. Nashville, TN: Broadman, 1992.

Stenschke, Christoph W. *Luke's Portrait of Gentiles Prior to Their Coming to Faith*. WUNT II/108. Tübingen: Mohr Siebeck, 1999.

Stenschke, Christoph W. "The Need for Salvation." Pages 125–44 in *Witness to the Gospel: The Theology of Acts*. Edited by I. Howard Marshall and David Peterson. Grand Rapids, MI/Cambridge: Eerdmans, 1998.

Stier, Rudolf. *The Words of the Apostles*. 2nd ed. Edinburgh: T&T Clark, 1869.

Strange, William A. *The Problem of the Text of Acts*. SNTSMS 71. Cambridge: Cambridge University Press, 1992.

Strauss, David Friedrich. *The Life of Jesus Critically Examined*. Lives of Jesus. London: SCM, 1973.

Strauss, Mark L. *The Davidic Messiah in Luke-Acts: The Promise and Its Fulfillment in Lukan Christology*. JSNTSup 110. Sheffield: Sheffield Academic, 1995.

Strelan, Rick. *Strange Acts: Studies in the Cultural World of the Acts of the Apostles*. BZNW 126. Berlin: de Gruyter, 2004.

Strelan, Rick. "Strange Stares: ἀτενίζειν in Acts." *NovT* 41 (1999): 235–55.

Stronstad, Roger. *The Prophethood of All Believers: A Study in Luke's Charismatic Theology*. JPTSup 16. Sheffield: Sheffield Academic, 1999.

Swanson, Reuben J., ed. *New Testament Greek Manuscripts, Variant Readings Arranged in Horizontal Lines against Codex Vaticanus: The Acts of the Apostles*. Pasadena, CA: William Carey International University; Sheffield: Sheffield Academic, 1998.

Swidler, Leonard. *Biblical Affirmations of Woman*. Philadelphia, PA: Westminster, 1979.

Sylva, Dennis D. "The Meaning and Function of Acts 7:46-50." *JBL* 106 (1987): 261–75.

Tabb, Brian J. "Suffering and Worldview: A Comparative Study of Acts, Fourth Maccabees, and Seneca." PhD diss., London School of Theology/Middlesex University, 2013.

Tabb, Brian J. *Suffering in Ancient Worldview: Luke, Seneca and 4 Maccabees in Dialogue*. LNTS 569. London: Bloomsbury T&T Clark, 2017.

Taeger, Jens-Wilhelm. *Der Mensch und sein Heil: Studien zum Bild des Menschen und zur Sicht der Bekehrung bei Lukas*. SNT 14. Gütersloh: Mohn, 1982.

Tajra, Harry W. *The Trial of St Paul: A Juridical Exegesis of the Second Half of the Acts of the Apostles*. WUNT II/35. Tübingen: Mohr Siebeck, 1989.

Talbert, Charles H. *Reading Acts: A Literary and Theological Commentary on the Acts of the Apostles*. Revised ed. Macon, GA: Smyth & Helwys, 2005.

Tannehill, Robert C. *Luke*. ANTC. Nashville, TN: Abingdon, 1996.

Tannehill, Robert C. *The Narrative Unity of Luke-Acts: A Literary Interpretation*. 2 vols. Minneapolis, MN: Fortress, 1986, 1990.

Taylor, Justin, SM. "The Community of Goods among the First Christians and among the Essenes." Pages 147–61 in *Historical Perspectives: From the Hasmoneans to Bar Kokhba in Light of the Dead Sea Scrolls*. Edited by David Goodblatt, Avital Pinnick and Daniel R. Schwartz. Studies on the Texts of the Desert of Judah 37. Leiden: Brill, 2001.

Taylor, Nicholas H. "Luke-Acts and the Temple." Pages 709–21 in *The Unity of Luke-Acts*. Edited by J. Verheyden. BETL 142. Leuven: Peeters/Leuven University, 1999.

Theissen, Gerd. "Urchristlicher Liebeskommunismus: Zum 'Sitz im Leben' des Topos ἅπαντα κοινά." Pages 689–712 in *Texts and Contexts: Biblical Texts in Their Textual and Situational Contexts: Essays in Honor of Lars Hartman*. Edited by Tord Fornberg and David Hellholm. Oslo: Scandinavian University Press, 1995.

Thiselton, Anthony C. *New Horizons in Hermeneutics*. London: HarperCollins, 1992.
Thomas, John Christopher. *The Devil, Disease and Deliverance: Origins of Illness in New Testament Thought*. JPTSup 13. Sheffield: Sheffield Academic, 1998.
Thompson, Alan J. *One Lord, One People: The Unity of the Church in Acts in Its Literary Setting*. LNTS 359. London: T&T Clark, 2008.
Thompson, Alan J. *The Acts of the Risen Lord Jesus: Luke's Account of God's Unfolding Plan*. NSBT 27. Nottingham: Apollos; Downers Grove, IL: InterVarsity Press, 2011.
Thompson, Marianne Meye. "'God's Voice You Have Never Heard, God's Form You Have Never Seen': The Characterization of God in the Gospel of John." *Semeia* 63 (1993): 177–204.
Thompson, Richard P. *Keeping the Church in Its Place: The Church as Narrative Character in Acts*. London: T&T Clark, 2006.
Thornton, T. C. G. "Stephen's Use of Isaiah LXVI,1." *JTS* ns 25 (1974): 432–4.
Torrance, Thomas F. *Space, Time, and Resurrection*. Edinburgh: Handsel, 1976.
Towey, Anthony. *An Introduction to Christian Theology*. London: Bloomsbury, 2013.
Trebilco, Paul R. "Asia." Pages 291–362 in *The Book of Acts in Its Graeco-Roman Setting*. Edited by David W. J. Gill and Conrad H. Gempf. BAFCS 2. Carlisle: Paternoster; Grand Rapids, MI: Eerdmans, 1994.
Trebilco, Paul R. *Self-designations and Group Identity in the New Testament*. Cambridge: Cambridge University Press, 2012.
Treier, Daniel J. *Introducing Theological Interpretation of Scripture*. Nottingham: Apollos; Grand Rapids, MI: Baker Academic, 2008.
Trites, Allison A. "The Importance of Legal Scenes and Language in the Book of Acts." *NovT* 16 (1974): 278–84.
Trites, Allison A. *The New Testament Concept of Witness*. SNTSMS 31. Cambridge: Cambridge University Press, 1977.
Turner, C. H. "Chronology of the New Testament." Pages 403–25 in vol. 1 of *A Dictionary of the Bible*. Edited by James Hastings. 5 vols. Edinburgh: T&T Clark, 1898.
Turner, Harold W. *From Temple to Meeting House: The Phenomenology and Theology of Places of Worship*. Religion and Society 16. The Hague/New York: Mouton, 1979.
Turner, Max. "Interpreting the Samaritans of Acts 8: The Waterloo of Pentecostal Soteriology and Pneumatology?" *Pneuma* 23 (2001): 265–86.
Turner, Max. *Power from on High: The Spirit in Israel's Restoration and Witness in Luke-Acts*. JPTSup 9. Sheffield: Sheffield Academic, 1996.
Turner, Max. "The Spirit of Christ and 'Divine' Christology." Pages 413–36 in *Jesus of Nazareth: Lord and Christ. Essays on the Historical Jesus and New Testament Christology*. Edited by Joel B. Green and Max Turner. Carlisle: Paternoster; Grand Rapids, MI: Eerdmans, 1994.
Turner, Max. "The Spirit of Christ and Christology." Pages 168–90 in *Christ the Lord: Studies in Christology Presented to Donald Guthrie*. Edited by Harold H. Rowdon. Leicester: Inter-Varsity Press, 1982.
Turner, Max. "'Trinitarian' Pneumatology in the New Testament? – Towards an Explanation of the Worship of Jesus." *AsTJ* 57 (2003): 167–86.
Twelftree, Graham H. *People of the Spirit: Exploring Luke's View of the Church*. London: SPCK; Grand Rapids, MI: Baker Academic, 2009.
Twelftree, Graham H. "Sanhedrin." Pages 1061–65 in *Dictionary of New Testament Background*. Edited by Craig A. Evans and Stanley E. Porter. Downers Grove, IL: InterVarsity Press, 2000.
Tyson, Joseph B. "The Gentile Mission and the Authority of Scripture in Acts." *NTS* 33 (1987): 619–31.

van Kooten, George H. "'Ἐκκλησία τοῦ θεοῦ: The 'Church of God' and the Civic Assemblies (ἐκκλησίαι) of the Greek Cities in the Roman Empire: A Response to Paul Trebilco and Richard A. Horsley." *NTS* 58 (2012): 522–48.

van Stempvoort, P. A. "The Interpretation of the Ascension in Luke and Acts." *NTS* 5 (1958–9): 30–42.

Vanhoozer, Kevin J. *First Theology: God, Scripture and Hermeneutics*. Leicester: Apollos, 2002.

Vielhauer, Phillip. "On the Paulinism of Acts." Pages 33–50 in *Studies in Luke-Acts*. Edited by Leander E. Keck and J. L. Martyn. London: SPCK, 1968.

Volf, Miroslav. *Free of Charge: Giving and Forgiving in a Culture Stripped of Grace*. Grand Rapids, MI: Zondervan, 2006.

von Balthasar, Hans Urs. *Explorations in Theology*. 4 vols. San Francisco, CA: Ignatius, 1989.

Walaskay, Paul W. *And So We Came to Rome*. SNTSMS 49. Cambridge: Cambridge University Press, 1983.

Walker, Peter W. L. *Jesus and the Holy City: New Testament Perspectives on Jerusalem*. Grand Rapids, MI/Cambridge: Eerdmans, 1996.

Wallace, Daniel B. *Greek Grammar beyond the Basics: An Exegetical Syntax of the New Testament*. Grand Rapids, MI: Zondervan, 1996.

Walton, Steve. *A Call to Live: Vocation for Everyone*. London: Triangle, 1994.

Walton, Steve. "A Tale of Two Perspectives? The Temple in Acts." Pages 135–49 in *Heaven on Earth: The Temple in Biblical Theology*. Edited by T. Desmond Alexander and Simon J. Gathercole. Carlisle: Paternoster, 2004.

Walton, Steve. "Acts, Book of." Pages 27–31 in *Dictionary for Theological Interpretation of the Bible*. Edited by Kevin J. Vanhoozer, Craig G. Bartholomew, Daniel J. Treier and N. T. Wright. London: SPCK; Grand Rapids, MI: Baker Academic, 2005.

Walton, Steve. "Acts: Many Questions, Many Answers." Pages 229–50 in *The Face of New Testament Studies*. Edited by Scot McKnight and Grant R. Osborne. Leicester: Apollos; Grand Rapids, MI: Baker Academic, 2004.

Walton, Steve. "Evil in Ephesus: Acts 19:8–40." Pages 224–34 in *Evil in Second Temple Judaism and Early Christianity*. Edited by Chris Keith and Loren T. Stuckenbruck. WUNT 2/417. Tübingen: Mohr Siebeck, 2016.

Walton, Steve. "Jesus, Present and/or Absent? The Presence and Presentation of Jesus as a Character in the Book of Acts." Pages 123–40 in *Characters and Characterization in Luke-Acts*. Edited by Frank Dicken and Julia A. Snyder. LNTS 548. London: Bloomsbury T&T Clark, 2016.

Walton, Steve. *Leadership and Lifestyle: The Portrait of Paul in the Miletus Speech and 1 Thessalonians*. SNTSMS 108. Cambridge: Cambridge University Press, 2000.

Walton, Steve. "Primitive Communism in Acts? Does Acts Present the Community of Goods (2:44-45; 4:32-35) as Mistaken?" *EvQ* 80 (2008): 99–111.

Walton, Steve. "The Acts – of God? What is the 'Acts of the Apostles' All About?" *EvQ* 80 (2008): 291–306.

Walton, Steve. "The State They Were In: Luke's View of the Roman Empire." Pages 1–41 in *Rome in the Bible and the Early Church*. Edited by Peter Oakes. Carlisle: Paternoster; Grand Rapids, MI: Baker Academic, 2002.

Walton, Steve. "The State They Were In: Luke's View of the Roman Empire." Pages 75–106 in *Reading Acts in the Discourses of Masculinity and Politics*. Edited by Eric D. Barreto, Matthew L. Skinner and Steve Walton. LNTS 559. London: Bloomsbury T&T Clark, 2017.

Walton, Steve. "Trying Paul or Trying Rome? Judges and Accused in the Roman Trials of Paul in Acts." Pages 122–41 in *Luke-Acts and Empire: Essays in Honor of Robert*

L. Brawley. Edited by David Rhoads, David Esterline and Jae Won Lee. Princeton Theological Monographs 151. Eugene, OR: Pickwick, 2011.

Walton, Steve. "What Does 'Mission' in Acts Mean in Relation to the 'Powers that Be'?" *JETS* 55 (2012): 537–56.

Walton, Steve. "Where Does the Beginning of Acts End?" Pages 448–67 in *The Unity of Luke-Acts*. Edited by J. Verheyden. BETL 142. Leuven: Peeters, 1999.

Walton, Steve. "Whose Spirit? The Promise and the Promiser in Luke 12:12." Pages 35–51 in *The Spirit and Christ in the New Testament in Christian Theology*. Edited by I. Howard Marshall, Volker Rabens, and Cornelis Bennema. Grand Rapids, MI: Eerdmans, 2012.

Walton, Steve. "Ὁμοθυμαδόν in Acts: Co-location, Common Action or 'Of One Heart and Mind'?" Pages 89–105 in *The New Testament in Its First Century Setting: Essays on Context and Background in Honour of B. W. Winter on His 65th Birthday*. Edited by P. J. Williams, Andrew D. Clarke, Peter M. Head and David Instone-Brewer. Grand Rapids, MI/Cambridge: Eerdmans, 2004.

Weatherly, Jon A. *Jewish Responsibility for the Death of Jesus in Luke-Acts*. JSNTSup 106. Sheffield: Sheffield Academic, 1994.

Weinert, Francis D. "Luke, Stephen and the Temple in Luke-Acts." *BTB* 17 (1987): 88–90.

Weiser, Artur. *The Psalms: A Commentary*. OTL. London: SCM, 1962.

Wendel, Ulrich. *Gemeinde in Kraft: Das Gemeindeverständnis in den Summarien der Apostelgeschichte*. NTDH 20. Neukirchen-Vluyn: Neukirchener, 1998.

Wenham, David and Steve Walton. *Exploring the New Testament, vol. 1: A Guide to the Gospels and Acts*. 3rd ed. London: SPCK; Downers Grove, IL: InterVarsity Press, 2021.

Wenk, Matthias. *Community-forming Power: The Socio-ethical Role of the Spirit in Luke-Acts*. JPTSup 19. Sheffield: Sheffield Academic, 2000.

Wilcox, Max. *The Semitisms of Acts*. Oxford: Clarendon, 1965.

Wilson, Brittany E. "Contextualizing Masculinity in the Book of Acts: Peter and Paul as Test Cases." Pages 28–48 in *Reading Acts in the Discourses of Masculinity and Politics*. Edited by Eric D. Barreto, Matthew L. Skinner and Steve Walton. LNTS 559. London: Bloomsbury T&T Clark, 2016.

Wilson, Brittany E. *Unmanly Men: Refigurations of Masculinity in Luke-Acts*. New York: Oxford University Press, 2015.

Winter, Bruce W. *After Paul Left Corinth: The Influence of Secular Ethics and Social Change*. Cambridge/Grand Rapids, MI: Eerdmans, 2001.

Winter, Bruce W. *Divine Honours for the Caesars: The First Christians' Challenge*. Grand Rapids, MI: Eerdmans, 2015.

Winter, Bruce W. "Gallio's Ruling on the Legal Status of Early Christianity (Acts 18:14-15)." *TynBul* 50 (1999): 213–24.

Winter, Bruce W. "Introducing the Athenians to God: Paul's Failed Apologetic in Acts 17?" *Them* 31 (2005): 38–59.

Winter, Bruce W. "Official Proceedings and the Forensic Speeches in Acts 24–26." Pages 305–36 in *The Book of Acts in Its Ancient Literary Setting*. Edited by Bruce W. Winter and Andrew D. Clarke. BAFCS 1. Carlisle: Paternoster; Grand Rapids, MI: Eerdmans, 1993.

Winter, Bruce W. "On Introducing Gods to Athens: An Alternative Reading of Acts 17:18-20." *TynBul* 47 (1996): 71–90.

Winter, Bruce W. "Rehabilitating Gallio and His Judgement in Acts 18:14-15." *TynBul* 57 (2006): 291–308.

Winter, Bruce W. *Seek the Welfare of the City: Christians as Benefactors and Citizens*. Carlisle: Paternoster; Grand Rapids, MI: Eerdmans, 1994.

Winter, Bruce W. "The Importance of the *Captatio Benevolentiae* in the Speeches of Tertullus and Paul in Acts 24:1-21." *JTS* ns 42 (1991): 505-31.

Wire, Antoinette Clark. "Pauline Theology as an Understanding of God: The Explicit and the Implicit." PhD diss., Claremont Graduate School, 1974.

Witherington, Ben, III. *The Acts of the Apostles: A Socio-Rhetorical Commentary*. Carlisle: Paternoster/Grand Rapids, MI: Eerdmans, 1998.

Witherup, Ronald D., SS. "Cornelius Over and Over and Over Again: 'Functional Redundancy' in the Acts of the Apostles." *JSNT* 49 (1993): 45-66.

Wright, David F. "Theology." Pages 680-1 in *New Dictionary of Theology*. Edited by Sinclair B. Ferguson, David F. Wright and J. I. Packer. Leicester: Inter-Varsity Press, 1988.

Wright, N. T. *Jesus and the Victory of God*. Christian Origins & the Question of God 2. London: SPCK, 1996.

Wright, N. T. *The New Testament and the People of God*. Christian Origins & the Question of God 1. London: SPCK, 1992.

Wynn, Kerry H. "Disability in Biblical Translation." *BT* 52 (2001): 402-14.

Yamazaki-Ransom, Kazuhiko. *The Roman Empire in Luke's Narrative*. LNTS 404. London: T&T Clark, 2010.

York, John O. *The Last Shall Be First: The Rhetoric of Reversal in Luke*. JSNTSup 46. Sheffield: JSOT, 1991.

Ziesler, John A. "The Name of Jesus in the Acts of the Apostles." *JSNT* 2 (1979): 28-41.

Zwiep, A. W. *The Ascension of the Messiah in Lukan Christology*. NovTSup 87. Leiden: Brill, 1997.

Index of Biblical and Other Ancient Sources

OLD TESTAMENT

Genesis
1–3	165
1:1–2:3	180
1:26–28	69
12:1–3	104
12:3	34, 180
15:13–14	76

Exodus
2:11	47
4:18	47
6:14	151
13:21–22	167
15:11	60
20:11 (LXX)	180
24:12	172
28:33–35	36
32	80
35:1	52
40:35	167

Leviticus
4:13	52
4:14	52
4:21	52
8:3	51, 52
8:4	52
16:17	52
16:33	52
23:29	151
24:13–16	149
26:1	79
26:30	79

Numbers
6:13–20	77
6:14	77
6:16	77
9:8	172
10:4	151
11:29	95
13:2 (LXX)	151
13:3	151
13:3 (LXX)	151
13:4	151
14:4 (LXX)	151
20:3	47
20:8	51
24:17	151

Deuteronomy
4:10	51
6:13	168
9:10	51
15:4	68, 208
15:4–5	91
17:2–7	149
18:15	151
18:16	51
23:1	51, 85, 99, 205
23:2	51, 52
23:3	51, 52
23:4	52
23:8	51
23:9	51
31:30	51
32:4	151
32:15 (LXX)	170
32:21	151

Joshua
7:1	70

Judges
3:9	170
3:15	170
20:2	51, 52
20:28	47
21:5	51
21:8	51

1 Samuel
2:2	151
10:19	170

2 Samuel
6:17	79
7	80
7:1–2	80
7:3	80
7:4–10	80
7:11–16	80
7:13	80

1 Kings
2:28	79
8:4	79
8:14	51
8:14–30	81
8:15–53	80, 187
8:17	81
8:17–21	81
8:22	51
8:27	80, 187
8:27a	81
8:27b	81
8:55	51
8:65	51

1 Chronicles
5:24	151
13:2	51
13:4	51
25:8	49
28:2	51
28:8	51, 52
29:1	51
29:10	51
29:20	51

2 Chronicles
6:41–42	79
12:6	151

Ezra
2:64	52
9:15	151
10:1	51, 52
10:8	51, 52
10:12	51, 52
10:14	51, 52

Nehemiah
2:9	151
7:70	151
8:2	52
8:17	52
9:6	180
9:27	170
9:33	151
13:1	52

Esther
4:16	51

Job
22:12	

Psalms
1:1–2	59
2:1–2	94, 104
2:2	149
2:7	20, 153, 167, 185
2:12	59
2:33	20
7:11	151
7:12 (LXX)	151
8	182
10:7 (LXX)	151
11:7	151
14:1 (LXX)	79
15:8–11a (LXX)	20
15:10 (LXX)	20, 179
16	153
16:8–11a	20
16:10	20, 153, 179
16:35	20
23:5 (LXX)	170
24:1	69
24:5 (LXX)	170
26:1 (LXX)	170
27:1	170
34:9 (EVV)	60
34:10	60
34:17 (LXX)	94
35:17	94
37:16	180
38:15	172
42:1	185
45:5 (LXX)	79
46	182

46:5	79	30:1	56
61:3 (LXX)	170		
62:2	170	**Isaiah**	
66:1	179	1:4	151
68:26 (LXX)	93	1:18	120
69:25	93	2:1–13	197
70:22 (LXX)	151	2:18	79
71:22	151	3:6	151
73:1–2a (LXX)	54	3:7	151
73:3 (LXX)	60	5:19	151
73:7 (LXX)	79	8:9	85
74:1–2a	54	10:11	79
74:7	79	12:2	170
77:41 (LXX)	151	12:4	158, 171
78:41	151	12:16	151
80:18	158	14	185
80:19	171	14:11	185
82:4 (LXX)	60	14:13–15	185
88:19 (LXX)	151	14:22	85
89:18	151	16:12	79
94:1 (LXX)	170	17:10	170
95:1	170	17:45	170
106:13	172	19:1	79
108 (LXX)	93	21:9	79
108:8 (LXX)	93	28:16	56
109:1 (LXX)	20	30:4	151
109:8	93	31:7	79
110	153	32:15	85, 125
110:1	20, 169	37:16	180
112:6	94	37:35	150
114.5 (LXX)	151	40–55	60, 174
116:5	151	40:3	58, 59
117:21 (LXX)	136	40:3–4	157
118:22	34, 136, 153	40:3–5	60
119	59	40:28	156, 174
128.4	151	41:6	8
129.4	151	42:1	150
131:5 (LXX)	79	43:1	125
132	79	43:10–12	125
132:5	79	44:1–2	150
132:8–10	79	44:6	156, 174
132:13–17	79	44:8	125
137:6 (LXX)	94	44:9–20	156, 174
138:6	94	44:21	150
145:6 (LXX)	180	45:1	114
146:6	180	45:4	150
		45:15	170
Proverbs		45:21	151, 170
16:33	94	46:6	79

48:20	85	3:14	22
49:6	85, 125, 129, 159, 180, 197	10	186
		11	22
52:13	150	11:19	68
52:13– 3:12	150	37:1	22
53	153	43:5	22
53:7–8	159		
53:8 (LXX)	180	**Daniel**	
53:12	34	4:34	174
55:2	20	4:34–35	156
55:3 (LXX)	20, 153	5:4	79
55:6–8 197		5:23	79
55:10–11	185	7	61
55:34	20	7:13	61, 85, 161, 165, 171, 182, 183
56:3–8	205		
57:19 (LXX)	197	7:13–14	61, 157, 167
58:6	185	7:18	60, 61
59:20–21	86	7:21	60
61:1	202	7:22	60, 61
61:1–2	129, 185	7:25	60, 61
62:11	85, 170	7:27	60
64:1	185	8:24	60
66:1–2	80, 81	9:21	76
66:2	180		
66:6	81	**Joel**	
		2:28	22
Jeremiah		2:28–29	169, 208
7	80	2:28–32	20, 169, 197
7:1–15	82	2:30	152
10:13	85	2:32	158
26	80	3:1–2 (LXX)	169, 208
27:29 (LXX)	151	3:1–5 (LXX)	197
28:16	85	3:3 (LXX)	152
29:8	111	3:5 (LXX)	158, 197
31:8	52		
32:29	68	**Amos**	
32:32	85	9:11	87
35:16 (LXX)	85	9:11–12	25, 87, 103, 104, 198
36:8 (LXX)	111		
38:8	85	**Micah**	
39:32 (LXX)	85	1:13	151
44:14	52	2:5	52
45:8 (LXX)	85	4:7	84
50:9	52		
50:29	151	**Habakkuk**	
		1:5	20
Ezekiel		1:41	20
1:1	185		
3:12	22	**Zephaniah**	
		3:9	158, 171

Index of Biblical and Other Ancient Sources

Zechariah
8:20–23	86, 197
13:9	158, 171

Malachi
3:1	129, 158

NEW TESTAMENT

Matthew
1:20–21	207
5:17–48	49
8:21–22	48
9:14	49
10	135
10:19–20	135
10:24–25	49
11:2	49
16:18	53
18:17	53
19:28	61
22:15–22	34
22:16	49
22:34	66
23:15	109
23:21	82
24:9–13	135
24:29	182
24:30	161
26:64	161
27:34	93
27:48	93
28:18–20	125

Mark
2:18	49
2:23	49
3:31–35	48
4:15	57
4:16–	17
6:29	49
9:18	49
12:13–17	34
12:30	32
13	135
13:11	135
13:26	182
14:14	49
14:57–8	78
14:62	161
15:6	109
15:23	93
15:29	78
15:36	93

Luke
1–2	187
1:1	33
1:1–4	33, 42, 87, 127
1:2	33
1:3	33, 121
1:4	33
1:6	37
1:9	75
1:11	97
1:11–20	185
1:19	129
1:20	57, 172, 206, 207
1:21–22	75
1:26	129
1:26–38	185, 207
1:32	109
1:35	109, 152, 185
1:38	207
1:39–45	207
1:41–45	185
1:43	146
1:45	57
1:54	150
1:67	24
1:67–79	185
1:69	150
1:76	146
1:77	196, 199
1:79	186
2:8–14	185
2:11	109
2:14	180
2:15	178, 179
2:25–32	185
2:32	34, 159
2:36–38	207
2:46	37
3:2–5	60
3:3	195
3:3–5	59
3:4–6	146
3:8	195

3:16	186	9:1–19	24
3:21	179, 185	9:2	129
3:21–22	192	9:14	49
3:22	109, 152, 167, 178	9:16	49, 178
4:1	185, 192	9:20–21	109
4:1–11	110	9:23	36
4:5–6	199	9:31	34, 202
4:7–8	168	9:34	167
4:14	185, 192	9:34–35	167, 182
4:18	192	9:35	109, 152
4:18–19	185	9:40	38
4:25	179	9:48	129
4:26	129	9:52	129
4:31–37	202	9:54	179
4:34	151	10:1–3	129
4:41	109	10:3	129
4:43	129	10:13	195
5:12–14	186	10:15	179, 185
5:18	202	10:16	129
5:20	196	10:17	202
5:21	196	10:18	179, 185
5:24	180, 202	10:20	179
5:32	195	10:22	109
6:12–16	38	10:23	38
6:16	38	10:38	207
6:17	49	10:42	207
6:23	179	11:1	38, 49
6:40	49	11:4	196
7:1–11	202	11:13	179
7:11	49	11:20	185
7:18	49	11:40	37
7:18–23	109	11:42	37
7:22	202	11:50	180
7:27	129	11:52	37
7:30	37	12	135, 136
7:36–50	38	12:1a	134
7:40–47	37	121b	135
7:44–50	38	12:8–10	134
7:47–48	196	12:9–12	127
7:48–50	80	12:11	135
7:49	196	12:11–12	203, 204
8:1–3	207, 208	12:11a	134
8:12	57	12:12	12, 134, 135
8:13	57	12:22	49
8:22	49	12:23	179
8:25	38	12:24–28	180
8:28	109	12:29–30	199
8:39	105	12:49	180
8:43–48	186	12:50	34

12:51	180	20:20–26	34
13:1–3	24	20:21–26	34
13:2	24	20:25	108
13:3	195	20:42–43	169
13:5	195	21	135, 136
13:10–17	186	21:1–4	37
13:11–17	205	21:5–6	78
13:14–17	37	21:6	187
13:16	186	21:7	126
13:34	129	21:11	178
13:32–33	34	21:12	135
13:33–35	108	21:12–15	127, 135
14:26	49	21:12–19	204
14:27	36, 49	21:14	135
14:33	49	21:14–15	12, 135
15:7	179, 195	21:15	134
15:8–10	208	21:23	180
15:10	179, 195	21:24	199
15:18	178	21:25	180
15:21	178	21:27	161, 167, 182
16:14	37	21:33	180
16:17	180	21:35	180
16:19–31	193	22:3	38
16:22	131	22:3–21	24
16:23	179	22:14	24
16:30	195	22:14–38	39
17:3	195	22:15	40, 135
17:4	195	22:19	24, 39, 40
17:24	178	22:19–20	40
17:25	34	22:23	40
17:29	179	22:24	40
17:35	66	22:26	39
18:1–8	117, 141, 208	22:27	39
18:9–14	193	22:28	40
18:13	178	22:28–30	61
18:14	193	22:33–35	40
18:19	37	22:35–38	40
18:22	179	22:37	34
18:31–33	34, 108	22:40	38
18:37	151	22:42	108
19:1–10	205	22:43–44	186
19:11	126	22:45–46	38
19:37–38	109	22:47–48	38
19:38	179	22:50–51	108
19:45–46	35, 109	22:53	186
20:4	179	22:63–65	203
20:9–19	129	22:67–69	109
20:17	34	22:70	109
20:19b–20	40	22:71	109

23	10, 12, 34–7, 108–10, 206	24:31	165
		24:32	38
23:1–2	109	24:34	146
23:2	34, 108	24:36	127, 165
23:3	108, 109	24:44	127
23:3–4	109	24:44–49	38, 127
23:4	34, 109, 152	24:44–53	38
23:5	109	24:45	38
23:6–7	109	24:47	129, 195, 196
23:7–12	119	24:47–49	125
23:9	108	24:48–49	129
23:10	109	24:49	135, 169, 181, 183, 202
23:13–18	109	24:50	181
23:13–25	203	24:50–53	181
23:14	34, 109, 152, 204	24:51	161, 178, 181, 182
23:15	152, 204	24:52	168, 182
23:16	109	26:2–23	24
23:17	109	26:6	24
23:18	109	26:19	24
23:18–19	35	26:20	24
23:19	109	26:44	34, 108
23:21	109	26:46	34
23:22	34, 109, 152, 204		
23:23	109	**John**	
23:24	109	1:3	175
23:25	35, 109, 152	1:18	18
23:27	109	1:35	49
23:28–31	108	1:37	49
23:34	108	1:51	185
23:36	93	2:17	93
23:39	35	3:13	161
23:39–43	35	3:25	49
23:40–41	35	4:1	49
23:41	34, 109, 152, 204	4:31	49
23:42	35	7:39	161
23:43	108	8:54	161
23:44–45	35	9:2	49
23:45	76	11:8	49
23:45b	35	12:16	161
23:46	36	13:1–3	161
23:47	34, 109, 152, 204	13:29	73
23:48	34, 109	14:6	59
23:51	34	14:13	161
24	177	15:25	93
24:4–5	187	16:5	161
24:23	187	16:28	161
24:25	57	17:5	161
24:26–27	34	18:31	132
24:27	38, 108	19:15	108

19:19–20	36	1:24–25	94
19:29	93	1:24–26	20
20:21–23	125	1:26	94
		2	87, 168
Acts		2–7	13, 161, 169–72
1	17, 128, 177	2:1–4	38, 169, 184, 203
1–7	128	2:2	76, 169, 178, 183
1:1	159, 174	2:4	22, 85, 126, 207
1:1–11	147	2:4–11	22
1:1–29	17	2:4b	169
1:1–5:42	85	2:5	178, 183
1:2	159, 162	2:5–11	85
1:3	181	2:9–11	91
1:4	20	2:11	170
1:4–5	202	2:13	195
1:5	101, 183, 186	2:14	126, 195
1:6	125, 127, 128	2:14–36	20, 203
1:6–8	94, 127	2:16–18	203
1:6–11	181	2:16–20	153
1:7	167	2:16–21	20, 84, 85
1:7–8	125	2:16–27	22
1:8	8, 84, 85, 94, 120, 125–8, 159, 168, 180, 183, 187	2:17	95, 169
		2:17–18	208
		2:17–21	169
1:9	18, 84, 145, 157, 166, 174, 182	2:19	152
		2:21	147, 150, 158, 170, 174, 196
1:9–10	182		
1:9–11	13, 145, 161, 162–8, 178	2:22	20, 147, 151, 152, 185, 192, 201, 202, 203
1:10	166, 168, 182	2:22–24	128
1:10–11	178, 181, 184	2:23	195
1:10b	163, 166	2:23–24	20, 147, 152, 159, 175
1:11	126, 145, 157, 163, 166, 167, 168, 170, 174, 182, 183	2:24	17, 152
		2:25–28	20, 153
		2:27	179
1:12–26	12	2:28–32	197
1:13–14	84	2:29	48, 126
1:14	48, 66, 93, 127	2:31	20, 152, 153, 179
1:15	94	2:32	17, 90, 127, 152
1:15–26	93–4	2:33	8, 20, 149, 155, 157, 159, 168, 169, 170, 174, 183, 184, 203
1:16	19		
1:16–20	38		
1:16–26	20	2:33–35	170
1:18–19	93	2:33–36	166, 169–70, 183
1:20	20, 93	2:34	169, 178
1:21	127, 148	2:34–35	20, 153
1:21–22	94, 97, 127, 128	2:36	20, 109, 149, 170, 174, 182, 183
1:22	127, 152, 162		
1:23	97	2:37	13, 47, 195

2:38	68, 84, 85, 95, 116, 128, 141, 147, 150, 153, 158, 170, 174, 184, 195, 203	3:20–21	21, 126, 145, 169, 170, 183
		3:20a	21
		3:20b	21
2:38–40	203	3:21	94, 126, 168, 170, 178
2:39	20, 195, 197	3:21–22	202
2:41	18, 22	3:21b	21
2:42	11, 37, 40, 91, 203	3:22	178
2:42–47	48, 66, 203	3:22–23	128, 151
2:43	41, 168, 185, 202, 203	3:22–24	21
2:43–47	40	3:23	151
2:44	56, 57	3:25	22, 180
2:44–45	11, 48, 63–73, 91, 208	3:26	17, 22, 129, 150, 153
2:44a	41	4:1	202
2:44b–45	41	4:1–22	9, 204
2:46	37, 41, 75, 76, 85	4:2	152
2:46a	41	4:4	9, 22, 56, 95
2:47	41, 66	4:5–6	136
2:47a	41	4:5–22	12, 127, 132, 136–7
3–4	20, 21	4:7	147, 154, 172, 184
3:1	76	4:8	38, 85, 135, 136, 184, 203, 204, 207
3:1–10	9, 21, 22, 77, 86, 99, 136, 170, 205	4:8–12	22, 135
3:2	73, 77, 202	4:9	150
3:3–6	157	4:9–10	126
3:6	147, 149, 151, 154, 172, 184	4:10	17, 22, 84, 147, 149, 151, 152, 154, 168
3:6–7	168	4:10–11	142
3:8	21, 193, 205	4:11	22, 153
3:8–9	99, 205	4:12	19, 84, 147, 150, 153, 178, 184
3:9	21, 193, 205		
3:11	22, 205	4:13	127, 137
3:12	22	4:14–15	202, 203
3:11–16	21	4:15	203
3:11–26	9, 77	4:15–17	22
3:12–26	203	4:17	172, 184
3:13	21, 150	4:17–18	153, 170
3:13–15	61, 141, 152, 159, 175	4:18	22, 94, 129, 137, 202
3:13b–15	151	4:19	137, 170
3:14	128, 150, 151	4:19–20	8
3:15	17, 21, 127, 151, 152	4:20	137
3:16	21, 147, 168, 172, 184	4:21	137
3:16–17	157	4:23	76, 94
3:17	47, 48	4:23–30	22, 38
3:18	21, 149	4:23–31	12, 94–5
3:19	21, 84, 116, 141, 195, 196	4:24	9, 22, 94, 179, 180
		4:24–30	84, 104
3:19–21	125	4:25	24, 150
3:20	21, 84, 129, 145, 149	4:25–26	22

4:25–27	199	6:1–2	50
4:25–28	94, 153	6:1–6	64, 65, 71–2, 92
4:26	66, 149	6:1–7	12, 95
4:27	94, 110, 149, 150, 152	6:1–11:18	85
4:28	110	6:2	18, 25, 95, 97, 203
4:29	95, 137	6:3	84, 85, 97, 127, 207
4:29–30	9, 22	6:4	25, 95, 203
4:29–31	22	6:5	38, 84, 85, 95, 97, 203, 207
4:30	150, 172, 184, 185		
4:30–31	96, 147	6:6	97
4:31	9, 18, 22, 25, 38, 68, 85, 95, 137, 184, 203, 207	6:7	18, 22, 25, 50, 185, 203
		6:8	84, 168, 185, 202
4:32	9, 56, 57, 68	6:8–10	95, 203
4:32–35	11, 48, 63–73, 91, 92, 208	6:9–10	135
		6:10	38, 84, 135, 184, 203, 204
4:33	9, 127, 148, 152		
4:34	91, 208	6:11	78
4:34–37	9	6:12–7:60	127, 132
4:35	68	6:13	78, 127
4:36–37	64, 92	6:13–14	76, 78
5:1–11	64, 65, 92, 185	6:14	151
5:3	70	6:15	84
5:4	64, 70	7	36, 183, 186, 187
5:11	53, 55	7:2	48, 81, 187
5:12	77, 91, 168, 185, 202, 205	7:2–8	183
		7:2–53	80
5:12–14a	65	7:6	81
5:12–16	48, 67, 92	7:6–7	76
5:12b	92	7:7	81, 199
5:14	56, 155, 208	7:9	81, 187
5:15	86	7:13	48
5:16	184, 202	7:13–14	148
5:17–41	132, 204	7:17	20, 47, 81
5:19	84, 168, 184	7:20	81
5:20	77	7:25	81
5:21	77	7:27	158
5:21–41	127	7:29–34	187
5:28	151, 153, 170, 192, 198	7:32	81
5:29	170	7:34	129
5:30	17, 152, 170	7:35	78, 81, 129
5:31	116, 141, 150, 151, 153, 169, 170–1, 195, 196	7:37	78, 81, 151
		7:38	53, 55
5:32	127, 203, 204	7:41	80
5:34–39	39	7:42	81
5:40	153	7:44	127, 187
5:41	153	7:45	81
5:42	77, 149	7:46	78, 79, 81
6	17	7:46–50	78, 81, 82
6:1	102	7:47	76, 78, 79, 81

7:47–48a	79	8:26	22, 84, 99, 129, 168, 172, 184
7:48	79, 81, 82, 186		
7:48–50	77, 79, 87	8:26–39	85
7:49	179	8:26–40	99, 172, 186
7:49–50	79, 80, 81	8:27	85, 99, 205, 206
7:50	80, 180	8:29	22, 38, 85, 126, 129, 135, 172, 203
7:51	135		
7:51–54	187	8:30–34	99
7:52	151	8:32–33	150
7:54–60	133	8:32–35	159, 175
7:55	135, 149, 155, 171, 178, 184, 203, 204, 207	8:33	180
		8:34	153, 206
7:55–56	84, 85, 135, 148, 183, 187	8:35	153, 155
		8:36	99, 205, 206
7:56	81, 159, 178, 179, 183	8:38	99, 206
7:56–60	169, 171	8:39	22, 38, 85, 203, 206
7:57–58	183	9	13, 17, 61, 128, 171, 172
7:58	17, 127		
7:59	9, 84, 148, 153, 158, 171, 174, 187	9:1	50, 155
		9:1–2	9, 133, 204
7:59–60	84	9:1–9	159
8	128	9:1–19	85
8–9	17	9:2	59, 208
8:1	17, 53, 55, 99, 102	9:3	147, 178
8:3	17, 53, 204, 208	9:3–4	180
8:3–8	147	9:4	159, 175
8:4	99	9:4–5	135
8:4–25	85	9:5	149, 155, 172, 184
8:5	149, 155	9:6	172, 174
8:5–25	99	9:8	184
8:6	22	9:8–9	172, 206
8:6a	22	9:9	147
8:7	22, 184, 202	9:10	50, 148, 172
8:9–11	199	9:10–16	135, 172, 184
8:12	56, 147, 153, 155, 156, 208	9:10–18	96
		9:11	149, 159, 172, 174
8:13	56	9:13	60, 148, 149, 172
8:14	18, 25	9:14	153, 171, 184
8:15	85, 157	9:15	9, 149, 153, 172, 184, 204
8:16	84, 147, 153, 155, 156, 197, 203		
		9:15–16	159, 174, 207
8:17	38, 85, 184	9:16	9, 19
8:20	22, 157, 174	9:17	9, 38, 129, 148, 149, 155, 172, 184, 203, 207
8:22	195		
8:22–23	199	9:19	50
8:24	199	9:19–21	96
8:25	18, 25	9:19b–21	96
8:25–40	205	9:19b–22	203
		9:20	9, 155

9:21	153, 171, 184	10:25	198
9:22	9, 149, 155	10:28	100
9:24	17	10:29	129
9:26	50, 96	10:30–33	100, 172
9:26–30	96, 102, 128	10:31	18, 198
9:27	96, 184	10:31–32	22
9:28	96, 155	10:32	129
9:28–29a	96	10:33	129
9:28	96, 184	10:34	20, 205
9:29a	96	10:34–35	100
9:29b–30	96	10:34–43	20
9:31	22, 53–5	10:35	20
9:32	60	10:35–43	100
9:33	202	10:36	129, 146, 149, 157, 170, 174
9:34	84, 147, 154, 159, 168, 172, 184, 202	10:36–42	128
9:36	50, 65, 72, 92	10:38	20, 84, 128, 147, 149, 202
9:36–43	202	10:39	127
9:38	50	10:39–42	56
9:39	72, 92	10:39b–41	147
9:39–41	86	10:40	17, 20
9:41	60	10:41	20, 127
9:42	56, 155, 156	10:42	20, 152
10–15	12	10:43	20, 56, 57, 127, 128, 147, 150, 153, 184, 196
10:1–2	199	10:44	86, 184
10:1–8	99	10:44–47	22
10:1–48	85, 99–100, 128, 186	10:45–46	101
10:1–11:18	22, 128, 172	10:46	100
10:3	97, 168, 184	10:47	100
10:3–6	22, 99	10:48	147, 153, 155, 156
10:3–7	172	11:1	18, 25, 47, 103
10:5–6	97	11:1–18	99, 100
10:7	84	11:2	22, 24
10:8	99, 129	11:2–18	128
10:9–16	22	11:3	100
10:9–23	99	11:5	178
10:11	179, 180, 185	11:9	178
10:13	100	11:10	178
10:14	100	11:11–12	172
10:16	178	11:12	22, 85, 101, 126, 203
10:17	129	11:13	84, 129
10:19	85, 126, 135, 203	11:13–14	22
10:19–20	22, 100, 172	11:14	101, 150
10:20	129	11:15	22
10:22	84, 127, 129	11:16	101
10:23	100	11:17	56, 101, 148, 149, 159
10:23b	100	11:17–18	172
10:23b–24	198		
10:24–48	98		

11:18	101, 105, 116, 141, 195	13:7–12	102
11:18a	22	13:9	184, 203, 207
11:18b	22	13:12	56, 156
11:19	102	13:14–52	102
11:19–26	101	13:15	48
11:19–28:31	85	13:16–41	19
11:20	101, 102, 148, 155	13:17–22	19
11:21	56, 102	13:22	127
11:22	53, 102	13:23	19, 20, 150
11:23	152	13:26	129, 150
11:24	203, 207	13:27	19, 153
11:25	17	13:27–29	142, 195
11:25–26	96, 102	13:27–31	147
11:26	47, 50, 53	13:28	110
11:27–30	64, 92, 102, 208	13:29	19, 153
11:28	85, 184	13:30	17, 110, 127, 152
11:28–29	199	13:31	127
11:28–30	65, 72	13:32	20
11:29	50	13:33	19, 152, 153
12	17	13:34	152, 153
12:1	53	13:35	153
12:2	48, 66	13:37	17, 152
12:3–11	97, 204	13:38	150, 153
12:5	38, 53	13:38–39	196, 199
12:6–11	38	13:39	56, 57
12:7	168	13:42–49	199
12:7–11	84, 184	13:43	152, 200
12:11	129	13:44	18, 25
12:12	64, 66, 86	13:44–45	102
12:13	64	13:46	18, 102
12:15	38	13:47	26, 85, 102, 125, 127, 150, 180
12:16	38		
12:20–23	199	13:48	18, 56
12:23	184	13:48–49	185
12:24	18, 22, 25, 185	13:49	25
12:25	65	13:50	200
12:49	180	13:50–51	111, 204
12:51	180	13:52	48, 184, 207
13–14	48	14:1	56, 102
13:1	24, 48, 53, 93, 96	14:2	111
13:1–3	12, 86, 93, 96–7, 102	14:2–5	102
13:2	85, 92, 96, 97, 126, 184, 203	14:3	127, 185, 202
		14:5–6	204
13:2–4	135	14:8	202
13:4	85, 126, 129, 203	14:8–18	9
13:4–12	132	14:9	150
13:5	18, 25, 93, 103	14:11	192
13:6–12	172	14:11–18	187
13:7	18, 25	14:15	179, 180

14:15–17	26, 188	15:36–40	93
14:19	111, 204	15:38	93
14:19–20	51	15:40	47
14:20	48, 50	15:41	53, 54
14:20–22	50	16	97
14:21	50	16:1	50
14:22	9, 48, 50, 51	16:1–4	93
14:23	48, 53	16:2	127
14:24	180	16:5	22, 53, 54
14:26	152	16:6	24, 97
14:26–27	93	16:6–7	85, 126
14:27	48, 53, 102, 105	16:6–8	93
14:28	48, 50	16:6–10	12, 24, 97–8
15:1	47, 48, 103, 150	16:7	24, 97
15:1–2	93	16:9	24, 86, 97
15:1–35	102	16:10	24, 97
15:2–3	24	16:10–18	93
15:2b–4	103	16:13	86
15:3	47	16:13–15	97, 199, 208
15:4	53, 103, 105	16:14	195, 200
15:4–29	128	16:15	57, 196, 208
15:5	24, 56, 57	16:16–18	97, 168, 184, 202
15:6–29	198	16:16–19	137
15:7	25, 56, 103, 104	16:16–24	199
15:7–11	25, 99, 105	16:16–40	13, 127, 132, 137
15:7–9	22	16:17	150
15:8	25, 127	16:17–28	196
15:9	25	16:18	137, 138, 149, 154, 173, 184
15:10	25, 50		
15:11	84, 148, 150, 152	16:19–21	204
15:12	25, 105, 185, 202	16:19–24	97
15:13–18	104	16:20–21	137, 138, 199
15:14	24, 47, 103, 153	16:21	148
15:15–18	24	16:22–23	204
15:16–17	87	16:22a	137
15:16–18	198	16:23	204
15:17	103	16:24	137
15:19	25, 104	16:25	137
15:20	104, 199	16:28	198
15:22	53, 104	16:29a	198
15:23	48	16:29b	198
15:25	104	16:30	13, 195, 198
15:26	148, 153	16:30–31	150, 194
15:28	104, 199	16:31	56, 84, 159
15:30	93	16:32	18, 26
15:32	47, 48	16:33	196
15:33	47	16:35	138
15:35	18, 26	16:36	138
15:36	18, 36, 47	16:37–39	132

Index of Biblical and Other Ancient Sources

16:38–39	138	18:4	111
17	200	18:6	111, 159
17:1	93	18:6–7	199
17:1–15	132	18:7	200
17:3	152	18:8	56, 110
17:4	93, 199, 200	18:9	129
17:5	93, 111, 204	18:9–10	97, 114, 115, 135, 159
17:6	194	18:10	47
17:6–9	127	18:11	18, 26
17:7	111, 150, 154, 188	18:12	110, 114, 118, 204
17:10	93	18:12–17	114, 127, 132
17:12	56, 199, 208	18:12–27	12, 110–14
17:13	8, 26	18:13	111, 200
17:16	198, 200	18:14	112, 114
17:16–31	188, 200	18:14b	112
17:16–34	9, 13, 132, 138–9	18:14–15	110, 111, 112, 114
17:17	77, 200	18:15	13
17:18	20, 138, 147, 152, 188	18:15a	112
17:19	138	18:16	113
17:19–20	200	18:17	113, 200
17:20	138	18:22	53
17:22	200	18:23	50
17:22–23	200	18:25–26	59
17:22–25	199	18:25	59
17:22–31	20, 26	18:26	59
17:23	20, 139	18:27	50, 56
17:24	11, 75, 77, 82, 87, 174, 179, 180, 188, 189, 200	19:1	48, 49
		19:1–10	197
17:24–25	20, 188	19:2	56, 203
17:24a	139	19:2–7	154
17:24b	139	19:3	48, 49
17:25	139, 180, 189, 200	19:4	159
17:26	188	19:5	84, 147
17:27	188, 189, 201	19:8	126
17:27–28	20	19:9	50, 59, 111
17:27b–28	201	19:10	18, 26, 194
17:28	180, 188	19:11–12	202
17:28–29	200	19:12	184
17:29	20, 139, 200	19:13	154, 184
17:29–30	199	19:13–17	173
17:30	116, 141, 195	19:17	153, 173, 184
17:30–31	21, 139, 189, 199, 200	19:18	56
17:31	147, 151, 152, 183, 188, 189, 192, 201	19:18–19	199
		19	51
17:32a	188	19:20	22
17:34	56, 131, 208	19:21	85, 128
18	17	19:23	59
18:2	113	19:23–34	204
18:3	73, 92	19:23–37	199

19:23–41	132	21:11	24, 96, 203
19:24	75, 82	21:13	10, 148, 153
19:24–28	199	21:15–23:24	128
19:27	75, 200	21:16	50
19:30	50	21:20	56, 57
19:31	131	21:20–24	198
19:32	52, 53	21:20–25	57
19:33	135	21:23–24	73, 92
19:35	131, 199	21:24	77
19:35–40	39	21:25	56, 57
19:38	131	21:26	73, 92
19:39	52, 53	21:27–36	204
19:40	52, 53	21:27–26:32	127
20	17	21:28	76, 77, 116, 140
20:1	50	21:31–33	114
20:3	204	21:38	115, 140
20:6	41	22	13, 171, 172
20:7	37, 41, 42	22:1	48
20:7–8	86	22:3	85
20:7–12	41, 199, 202	22:4	59, 208
20:9	41	22:5	127
20:9–12	86	22:6	178
20:10	42	22:7	159, 174
20:11	37, 42	22:7–10	135
20:11b	41	22:8	151, 172
20:17	53	22:8b	155
20:18–35	39	22:10	129
20:19	40, 204	22:10–11	172
20:21	77, 116, 141, 148, 195	22:12	127
20:22	84, 85, 203, 207	22:14	151
20:22–24	10	22:15	127
20:23	203	22:16	84, 147, 153, 154, 158, 171, 174, 184, 196
20:23–24	204		
20:24	148, 152, 159, 174	22:17	76, 172
20:26	127	22:17–18	159
20:28	53–5	22:17–21	77, 136
20:29–30	204	22:18	127
20:30	50	22:19	56
20:32	60, 61, 152, 185	22:20	127
20:33	73, 92	22:21	129, 159
20:33–35	65	22:22	180
20:34	73, 92	22:22–23	204
20:35	18, 73, 92, 148	22:24–29	114, 204
20:36	42	22:26–30	132
20:36–38	86	22:29	114
21–28	204	22:30	115
21:4	50, 203	22:30–23:10	132
21:5–6	42	23–24	12, 13, 114–17
21:8–9	208	23:1	48

23:4	119	24:22	59, 116, 140
23:5	48	24:23	116, 140
23:6	152	24:24	141
23:10	204	24:24–26	116, 141
23:11	19, 115, 116, 118, 119, 127, 129, 136, 141	24:25	116, 141
		24:26	117, 141
23:12–15	204	24:27	117, 118
23:12–22	115	24:27b	115
23:13	119	24:27–25:12	132
23:16–30	132	25	17
23:21	20	25–26	12, 117–20
23:22	119	25:2–3	118
23:23–24	115	25:3	118
23:25	115	25:3b	118
23:25–30	115	25:6	118
23:26	115, 121, 140	25:7	118
23:26–30	139	25:8	76, 77, 118, 119, 135
23:29	115, 117, 119, 139, 141	25:9	118, 119
23:33–24:26	132	25:10	118, 119
23:34	115, 140	25:10–11	118
23:35	204	25:11a	118
23:35a	116, 140	25:11b	118
23:38	36	25:11c	118
23:44–45	186	25:12	119, 132
23:44–45a	186	25:13–26:32	132
23:45b	186	25:16	116, 119, 139
23:46	36	25:17	119
24–25	17	25:18–19	119
24:1	115, 139	25:19	152
24:1–2	204	25:20	119
24:1–21	116	25:21	119
24:2	115, 117, 140	25:23	119
24:2–8	39, 118	25:24	119
24:2b–3	139	25:25	119
24:3	115, 121, 140	25:26–27	119
24:6	77, 116, 140	26	13, 171, 172
24:6–9	115	26:1–2	135
24:10	115, 135	26:2–23	21
24:10–21	118, 140	26:4–5	21
24:12	76, 77	26:5	127
24:12–13	119, 140	26:6	20
24:14	59, 86, 140	26:6–8	20
24:14–18	136	26:9	151, 153
24:15	140, 152	26:9–11	21, 204
24:17	64	26:10	60
24:18	76, 77	26:14	159, 174
24:19	116, 140	26:15	21, 172
24:20	132	26:16	127, 129
24:21	152	26:16–18	172

26:16b	155	**1 Corinthians**	
26:17	47, 129	1:1	24, 86
26:18	21, 60, 150, 153, 199	1:2	61
26:19	21	5:4	155
26:19–21	77	6:2	61
26:20	21, 116, 141, 195	6:11	61
26:21	76	7:5	66
26:22	21, 127	7:14	61
26:22–23	21	10:1–5	172
26:22–23a	120	10:32	155
26:23	13, 152, 159, 173	11:3	53
26:23b	120	11:3–15	53
26:24	135	11:15	53
26:25	121	11:16	155
26:26	127	11:20	66
26:31	119	11:22	155
26:32	119	14:23	53, 66
27:3	199	14:26–33a	53
27:13–44	204	14:29	96
27:20	150	14:33b–35	53
27:23	84, 86	15:3–5	94
27:23–24	184	15:9	55, 155
27:31	150		
28	17	**2 Corinthians**	
28:2	199	8–9	92
28:4–6	199	8:13–14	92
28:7	131, 132	8:13–15	73
28:14–15	86	12:19	135
28:17	47, 48		
28:20	121	**Galatians**	
28:21	48	1:1	17
28:23	128	1:3	155
28:28	150	1:13	55
28:30–31	22	2:10	64
28:31	127, 148	5:13	48
Romans		**Ephesians**	
1:1	24, 86	1:30	161
1:18–32	200	4:7–13	161
2:15	135	5:26	61
5:12–21	192		
8:34	161	**Philippians**	
11:26–27	86	2:1–11	192
13	121	2:5–11	159
13:1–7	114	2:9	161
14:15	48	3:6	55
15:3	93	4:21	61
15:16	61		
16:13	36		

Colossians
1:15–17	175
2:12	17
3:1	161

1 Thessalonians
1:1	93, 155
1:10	161
2:14	155
4:16	161
4:17	183
5:20–21	96
5:23	61

2 Thessalonians
1:1	155
1:4	155

1 Timothy
3:16	161
4:5	61

2 Timothy
2:21	61

Hebrews
1:2	175
1:3	161
10:20	186

1 John
2:10	48
3:10	48
3:16–17	48
4:20–21	48

Revelation
1:7	183
1:10–11	167
1:19	167
3:21	161
4:1	185
5:6–14	161
7:17	161
13	121
14:14–16	183
18:11	185
21:25	35

APOCRYPHA

1 Maccabees
1:11	111
2:58	162
3:9	85
4:30	170
9:61	151

2 Maccabees
1:24	151
4:47	109

4 Kingdoms
2:9	162
2:10	162
2:11	162

Baruch
4:22	170

Judith
6:16	51
6:21	51
8:18	79
9:1	76
9:11	170
14:2	151

Psalms of Solomon
17:34–35	197

Sirach
24:2	52
32:24	56
36:18–19	82
48:9	162
49:14	162

Tobit
3:2	151

Wisdom of Solomon
14:8	79
18:9	60

Index of Biblical and Other Ancient Sources

PSEUDEPIGRAPHA

1 Enoch
17–36	165, 167
37–71	60
39.1	60
39.4–5	60
41.2	60
43.4	60
47.2	60
47.4	60
48.7	60, 171
48.9	60
50.1	60
51.2	60
51.5a	171
58.3	60
58.5	60
61.8	60
61.10	60
61.12	60
62.8	60
65.12	60
69.13	60
71.4	60
100.5	60
92–105	60

2 Baruch
6.7	186
8.2	186
22.1	185

2 Enoch
3–66	165

3 Maccabees
2.3	151
4.22	109
6.29	170
6.32	170
7.16	170

4 Maccabees
15:23	206
15:30	206
16:14	206

Sibylline Oracles
3.616–17	197
3.772–73	197

Testament of Dan
5.13	56

Testament of Levi
2.6	185

QUMRAN LITERATURE

CD (Damascus Document)
1.8–13	58
2.6	58
1.13	58
7.17	52
11.2	52
12.6	52
14.13	71
20.18	58

1QH (Hodayot)
10.30	52

1QM (War Scroll)
1.16	60
10.9–11	60
11.16	52
12.1	60
12.7–8	60
14.5	52

1QS (Community Rule)
5.2	66
5.4–7	80
6:20	70
6.21–22	69
6.19–20	69
6.24–25	69
8.4–7	80
8.12–15	58
9.3–6	0
9.8–9	69
9.11	151
9.17	58
9.17–21	58

9.18	58
10.21	58
11.13	58

1QSa (Rule of the Congregation)
2.4	52
2.8–9	60

4Q174 (4QFlor) (4QFlorilegium)
1.12	87

4Q175 (4QTest) (4QTestimonia)
5–7	151

OTHER ANCIENT SOURCES

Aristotle
Metaphysics
12.7.2 (1073a)	165

Nicomachean Ethics
9.8.2	68

Poetics
21–22	165

Rhetoric
3.2.6–4.4	165
3.2.7–11.15	165

pseudo-Aristotle
810a25–29	205

Augustine
City of God
6:11	114
8.1	32

Augustus
The Deeds of the Divine Augustus (Res Gestae Divi Augusti)
Preface	130

Babylonian Talmud
Sanhedrin
41a	133

Cicero
Letters to Atticus (Epistulae ad Atticum)
VI.1.15	131

On behalf of Gaius Raibirius on a charge of Treason (Pro Rabirio Perduellionis Reo)
4:12	114

Diogenes Laertius
Lives
5.20	68

Herodotus
3.148.2	111

Jerusalem Talmud
Sanhedrin
18a	132
24b	132

Josephus
Against Apion (C. Ap.)
2.160	56

Jewish Antiquities (Ant.)
3.5.3	72
3.8.9 (§§3.215–218)	82
8.3.2	76
13.10.15	49
14.2.2	72
14.4.3	76
14.12.3 (§309)	186
19.5.2–3 (§§278–91)	111
20.2.5	72
20.7.1 (§§141–44)	116, 141
20.8.5 (§162)	115, 139
20.8.7 (§§173–78)	115, 139
20.48	56

Jewish War (J. W.)
1:59	206
2.8.1 (§117)	132
2.13.3 (§§254–57)	115, 139
2.13.5 (261–63)	115, 140
2.13.7 (§§266–70)	115, 139
2.14.1 (§§272–73)	117, 141
2.17.1 (§405)	132
2.187	56
5.5.2 (§§193–94)	133
15.11.4 (§406)	115

Ovid
Fasti
2.684   130

Metamorphoses
8.621–96   192

Philo
Hypothetica
1.10–11   72, 91

Moses
2.115   32

On Abraham
135–36   206

On the Contemplative Life
59–61   206

On Rewards and Punishments
28   56
53   32

On the Special Laws
1.60.325   206
3.1–6   167

Who is the Heir of Divine Things?
90   56
101   56

Polemo
5.15–19   205

Polybius
12.25   39

Plutarch
Dialogue on Love
21.9   68

Moralia
767 E   68

Thucydides
3.37–40   39
3.42–48   39
3.49   39

Index of Subjects

accused 107–21, 140, 188
Aeneas 147, 154, 159, 172, 184, 202
Agrippa 21, 38, 117, 119, 120, 127, 132
alms, almsgiving 18, 65, 72
Ananias and Sapphira 64, 65, 69, 70, 92
angels 18, 23, 28, 38, 60, 77, 97, 99, 100, 101, 109, 121, 129, 135, 141, 145, 158, 163, 167, 168, 169, 177, 178, 184, 185, 186, 187, 204
anthropology 191–209
　See 'human, humanity'
Antioch 19, 24, 25, 26, 48, 50, 53, 72, 73, 86, 92, 93, 96–7, 98, 101–2, 103, 127, 131, 142, 153, 199, 203
apocalyptic 165, 166, 179, 185
Apollos 59
apostles 7, 10, 15–27, 40, 41, 49, 70, 76, 77, 78, 83, 85, 86, 90, 91, 92, 94, 95, 96, 98, 102, 103, 104, 105, 127, 128, 137, 152, 154, 159, 169, 170, 173, 192, 193, 201, 202, 203, 204
　See 'twelve'
Artemis 32, 75, 82, 188
ascension 10, 13, 145, 149, 155, 161–76, 178, 179, 181–5, 189, 194
　See 'exaltation'
assembly 7, 11, 47, 48, 51–6, 104, 131, 138
　See 'ecclesia', 'church'
Athens 9, 26, 75, 77, 82–3, 131, 132, 138–9, 142, 152, 180, 188, 192, 200
　- Areopagus 13, 131, 132, 134, 138–9, 188, 200, 201
atonement 34, 36, 55, 83
authority 12, 22, 70, 84, 85, 98, 118, 124, 130, 132, 133, 134, 135, 136–7, 138, 148, 152, 161, 167, 168, 169, 171, 173, 180, 196, 200, 202, 204, 207

baptism, baptize 23, 34, 37, 84, 96, 99, 100, 137, 147, 153, 154, 156, 158, 167, 179, 184, 185, 186, 195–6, 197, 201, 202, 203, 206

Barabbas 35, 109, 152, 203
Barnabas 12, 24, 25, 28, 64, 65, 69, 86, 92, 93, 96, 98, 101–2, 103, 104, 105, 127, 129, 188, 203
believers 4, 8, 9, 11, 12, 20, 21, 22, 23, 24, 32, 36, 37, 38, 39, 41, 42, 45–142, 145, 148, 149, 150, 151, 152, 153, 154, 155, 157, 158, 159, 160, 161, 171, 173, 174, 180, 183, 184, 186, 189, 191, 196, 197, 198, 199, 200, 202, 203, 204, 206, 207, 209
　See 'believing communities'
believing communities 3, 7, 8, 9, 10, 11, 12, 22, 24, 26, 32, 40, 41, 45–142, 148, 153, 155, 184, 197, 198, 202, 203, 205, 206, 207, 208, 209
　See 'believers'
blood 40, 54
body 7, 40, 72, 89, 204, 206
brothers and sisters 11, 47–8, 50, 51, 91, 92, 195

Caesar 34, 35, 108, 111, 113, 118, 119, 149, 150, 177, 186, 187, 188
　- emperor 13, 27, 32, 69, 112, 118, 119, 130, 131, 133
　- imperial cult 107, 111, 112, 133
　- imperial order 52, 118, 130, 132, 134, 150
Caesarea 12, 50, 100, 107, 114–17, 118, 132, 139–41, 142
calling 21, 24, 77, 96–7, 142, 154, 158, 183, 184, 186, 187, 201
character, characterization 10, 12, 13, 16, 18, 24, 26, 32, 33, 37–8, 39, 42, 50, 76, 83, 87, 89, 97, 120, 123, 128, 142, 145–60, 162, 164, 171, 172, 180, 192, 196, 199, 202, 204, 205, 206, 207

Christ 7, 21, 33, 38, 55, 92, 137, 158, 164, 175, 194, 198, 201, 202
  See 'Jesus'
Christian 3, 4, 6, 7, 9, 11, 12, 13, 16, 18, 20, 24, 27, 31, 33, 36, 40, 41, 42, 45–62, 68, 70, 71, 72, 75–7, 82, 83, 84, 86, 87, 89, 93, 121, 123, 124, 128, 132, 137, 142, 146, 148, 173, 177, 187, 188, 197, 198, 204, 206, 207, 208
Christianity 31, 45, 61, 149
Christology 7, 13, 18, 61, 145–60, 161–75, 184
church 3, 4, 11, 12, 16, 31, 40, 42, 45–62, 64, 65, 71, 84, 85, 87, 90, 93, 98, 102, 104, 155, 173, 187, 193, 203, 208
  See 'believers', 'believing communities', 'brothers and sisters', 'disciples', 'assembly', 'the way', 'the holy ones'
Cilicia 48, 53, 115, 116, 140
circumcision 23, 24, 27, 48, 93, 100, 103, 104, 198
city 11, 25, 52, 53, 73, 85, 86, 102, 103, 110, 113, 131, 134, 138, 153, 159, 199, 200
  - citizens 52, 53, 114, 115, 117, 118, 131, 132, 138, 142
Claudius Lysias 64, 111, 114, 115, 119, 132, 139, 140, 187
communism 11, 63–74
community 3, 8, 9, 11, 12, 13, 22, 24, 25, 26, 27, 32, 40, 41, 46, 47, 51–8, 59–62, 63–73, 80, 85, 87, 90, 99–104, 110, 112, 113, 119, 126, 127, 131, 136, 153, 154, 184, 191, 192, 194, 197–8, 201, 202, 203, 205, 206–8, 209
  - fellowship 40, 41, 90, 91
conversion, converts 23, 65, 85, 100, 102, 187, 196
Corinth 12, 26, 53, 107, 110–14, 115, 120, 121, 131, 132, 159
Cornelius 23, 24, 25, 97, 99–100, 101, 102, 103, 105, 129, 172, 199
cosmology 10, 13, 31, 177–89
creation, creator 4, 20, 22, 55, 87, 94, 139, 156, 147, 165, 166, 168, 173, 174, 175, 177, 179, 180–1, 183, 186, 187, 188, 189, 192, 200, 201
cross, crucifixion 10, 34, 36, 42, 109, 152, 186, 203

crowd 21, 28, 37, 49, 134, 137, 183, 188, 195
Cyprus 25, 72, 102, 132, 155

Damascus 21, 50, 57, 59, 71, 96, 129, 133, 159, 172, 184
David 78, 79, 80, 81, 87, 103, 150, 169, 178, 185, 198
defile See 'unclean'
demons 38, 149, 151, 173, 177, 192, 202
  See 'Satan'
  - deliverance, exorcism 9, 13, 23, 39, 86, 137, 138, 149, 154, 168, 170, 171, 172–3, 174, 184, 185, 192, 202
disability 9, 21, 73, 77, 99, 147, 149, 154, 193, 204, 205, 209
disciples, followers 11, 12, 27, 32, 38, 39, 40, 42, 47, 48–51, 65, 76, 87, 91, 103, 108, 120, 125–29, 134–36, 154, 155, 157, 159, 164, 167, 168, 172, 174, 177, 179, 182, 183, 187, 196, 202, 203, 204, 207, 208
divine 9, 10, 13, 16, 18, 19–20, 21, 22, 23, 34, 37, 48, 56, 68, 69, 78, 79, 94, 95, 97, 98, 99, 100, 110, 126, 129, 136, 137, 138, 146, 148, 152–3, 156, 157, 158, 161, 162, 165, 166, 167, 168, 169, 170, 172, 173–5, 178, 179, 185, 199, 202

earth 8, 13, 69, 78, 81, 82, 83, 84, 85, 104, 120, 121, 125, 126, 128, 129, 136, 145, 146, 156, 157, 160, 161, 164, 165, 167, 168, 169, 173, 174, 175, 177, 178, 179–80, 181, 184, 185–7, 189
  See 'world'
ecclesia 54, 55
  See 'assembly', 'church'
elders 39, 40, 54, 61, 73, 92, 103, 104, 105, 136, 204
empire 12, 69, 107, 108, 110, 111, 114, 117, 120, 121, 124, 130, 131, 132, 133, 141, 185, 187
Ephesus 26, 39, 50, 51, 52, 53, 54, 59, 61, 73, 92, 127, 131, 132, 154, 173, 188, 197, 199, 204
Epicureans 20, 26, 188, 189
eschatology 60, 61, 62, 84, 103, 125, 146, 182, 197
Essenes 63, 69, 71, 72, 91, 104
  See 'Qumran'

Index of Subjects

ethnicity 6, 27, 67, 85, 96, 191
eunuch (Ethiopian) 23, 85, 99, 129, 153, 155, 159, 172, 186, 205, 206
Eutychus 41, 42
evangelism 4, 23, 24, 27, 48, 53, 97, 100, 109, 116, 141, 146, 153, 177, 189, 191
evil 112, 154, 168, 173, 177, 184, 186, 199
exaltation 13, 21, 32, 50, 60, 86, 87, 96, 103, 104, 120, 129, 136, 145, 146, 147, 149, 150, 152, 157, 158, 161, 163, 164, 166, 167, 168, 169–71, 173, 174, 175, 178, 179, 181, 182, 183, 184, 185, 187, 188, 189, 193, 194, 202, 204, 206
  See 'ascension'
exile 52, 60, 69, 132
eyewitness 33, 127, 129

faith 3, 4, 7–8, 9, 21, 31, 33, 38, 39, 51, 56, 57, 77, 83, 84, 87, 96, 98, 102, 103, 105, 111, 121, 128, 137, 140, 141, 156, 198, 199, 201, 203, 204, 206
family, blood-relations 26, 47, 48, 49, 50, 89, 90, 98, 133, 180, 197
famine 64, 72, 92, 102, 179
fasting 24, 96, 98
Father, father 9, 18, 28, 32, 35, 42, 49, 108, 109, 113, 126, 133, 135, 157, 161, 163, 169, 173, 179, 181, 184, 196
Felix 12, 107, 117–21, 132
fellowship *See* 'community'
Festus 12, 107, 117–21, 132
followers *See* 'disciples, followers'
food 40, 42, 49, 71, 91, 100
  - bread 40, 41, 42, 90, 91, 133, 134
  - meat 101
forgiveness 35, 37, 38, 84, 108, 125, 147, 150, 151, 153, 170, 171, 195, 196, 199, 201
friendship 67, 68, 126, 134
fulfilment 11, 19, 20, 22, 24, 26, 27, 33, 34, 39, 49, 59, 68, 84, 87, 91, 103, 116, 118, 141, 153, 183, 186, 204, 208

Galatia 50, 102, 103
Galilee 54, 65, 91, 109
Gallio 12, 107, 110–14, 118, 120, 121, 132
gentile, gentiles 12, 21, 24, 25, 27, 34, 35, 47–8, 61, 77, 84, 85, 98, 99–105, 110, 125, 128, 129, 159, 173, 180, 187, 194, 197, 198, 199, 201, 205
gift, generosity 9, 11, 23, 38, 64, 65, 68, 72, 73, 84, 92, 95, 126, 137, 146, 152, 157, 183, 195, 196, 197
glory 36, 167, 179, 182
God *See* YHWH
godfearers 20, 21, 27, 199
gods 9, 13, 27, 31, 32, 83, 133, 134, 139, 149, 157, 174, 188, 189, 198
goods, possessions 9, 11, 40, 41, 49, 57, 63–73, 91, 92, 117, 136, 141, 146, 149, 154, 157, 180, 200, 208
gospel 5, 9, 10, 11, 22, 23, 24, 25, 26, 32, 38, 73, 86, 92, 95, 99, 100, 116, 117, 119, 120, 121, 126, 129, 141, 142, 195, 206, 208
Gospels 16, 17, 18, 19, 25, 27, 31, 32, 33, 37, 46, 48, 49, 50, 51, 57, 71, 75, 78, 84, 107, 127, 128, 129, 134–6, 145, 147, 148, 157, 161, 167, 171, 174, 177, 181, 183, 185, 187, 191, 194, 202, 208
governors 12, 107, 115, 116, 118, 119, 120, 130, 131, 132, 139–41
grace 38, 66, 67, 84, 102, 150, 152
Graeco-Roman 9, 11, 16, 17, 26, 27, 39, 47, 49, 51, 52, 57, 60, 67, 68, 72, 91, 94, 178, 192, 193, 204, 206, 207
  See 'world'
guilt 12, 35, 120, 152, 186, 203

healing 9, 13, 21, 22, 23, 37, 77, 84, 86, 96, 99, 128, 136, 147, 149, 150, 154, 168, 169, 170, 171, 172, 174, 184, 185, 192, 193, 202, 205
heart 25, 32, 41, 49, 57, 58, 66, 67, 68, 91, 126, 195
heaven 13, 21, 82, 84, 136, 145, 146, 148, 149, 156, 157, 159, 160, 161, 162–73, 174, 177–89
Hellenism, Hellenists 32, 56, 64, 65, 92, 95, 113, 157
Herod 34, 38, 73, 80, 108, 109, 110, 119, 184, 204
holy ones 11, 47, 60–2, 71
homes, house 36, 40, 41, 53, 57, 64, 66, 67, 75, 76, 77, 79, 80, 81, 86, 90, 91, 99, 101, 110, 112, 137, 196, 207
  See 'household'

honour and shame 37, 134, 139, 153, 156, 160, 171, 173, 187
hospitality 9, 66, 100
household 25, 56, 85, 99, 100, 101, 105, 137, 186, 196, 197, 206
human, humanity 4, 5, 10, 11, 13, 23, 32, 33, 35, 36, 37, 55, 60. 68–9, 72, 75, 80, 81, 82, 83–4, 90, 94, 96, 97, 98–9, 110, 120, 124, 129, 137, 139, 145, 151–2, 155, 159, 167, 169, 170, 177, 180, 182–3, 184, 185, 188, 189, 191–209

identity 89, 90, 177, 191, 197
identity (divine) 10, 13, 42, 139, 146, 151, 156, 158, 161–175, 202
identity (Christian) 11, 42–62
idolatry 20, 79, 82, 101, 157, 174, 179, 188, 199, 200, 201
ignorance 198, 199, 200, 201
inclusion 47, 59, 85, 98, 99–105, 198, 205
innocence 34, 35, 109, 110, 117, 119, 120, 121, 152, 153, 203, 204
instruction 33, 41, 49, 52, 53, 59, 97, 99, 100, 135, 159, 172, 174, 202
Israel 8, 11, 13, 19, 26, 27, 34, 35, 47, 48, 51, 52, 53, 55, 59, 60, 61, 68, 80, 85, 87, 91, 94, 101, 103, 125, 126, 128, 139, 150, 151, 157, 158, 159, 160, 166, 167, 170, 171, 173, 175, 177, 179, 183, 198, 208
- Israelites 9, 47, 51, 167

James 25, 87, 103, 104, 105
Jerusalem 8, 11, 12, 19, 22, 24, 34, 35, 40, 41, 46, 48, 50, 53, 54, 59, 64, 65, 66, 68, 71, 72, 73, 75, 77, 79, 82, 83, 85, 87, 91, 92, 93, 95, 96, 98, 99, 100–1, 102, 103, 105, 108, 110, 114, 118, 126, 129, 132, 133, 136, 137, 139, 142, 151, 159, 161, 177, 187, 195, 196, 197, 198, 199, 202, 203, 205
Jesus 9–14, 16–18, 19–28, 31–42, 47–51, 56–7, 69–70, 62, 68, 77, 78, 83–7, 91, 93–6, 98, 101–10, 119–20, 121, 126–29, 134–41, 142, 145–60, 161–75, 178–89, 191–208
John (the Baptist) 37, 49, 59, 60, 129, 146, 154, 157, 158, 185, 186, 196
Jonathan 115, 140

Joppa 50, 85, 99, 100, 156, 186
Joseph of Arimathea 34
Judaea 8, 54, 72, 85, 103, 116, 117, 119, 128, 130, 132–3, 141
- Judeans 12, 48
Judaism, Jews 4, 8, 9, 11, 12, 16, 19, 21, 22, 27, 32, 34, 35, 36, 37, 39, 47, 48, 50, 51, 55, 56, 57, 62, 69, 70, 76, 77, 82, 84, 86. 87, 90, 91, 92, 94, 95, 96, 99, 102–3, 104, 105, 107, 108–10, 111, 112, 113, 114–15, 116, 117–20, 129, 130, 132, 133, 134, 140, 149, 156, 170, 173, 174, 183, 187, 194, 195, 196, 197, 198, 199, 201, 204, 206, 209
- antisemitism 110, 113, 114, 120, 129
- Jewish perspectives 4, 7, 9, 11, 13, 20, 21, 24, 26, 27, 34, 37, 47, 48, 57, 58, 60, 61, 64, 65, 70, 72, 73, 76, 77, 80, 81, 83, 87, 99, 100–1, 126, 132, 137, 139, 140, 151, 156, 157, 158, 165, 167, 168, 169, 171, 174, 179, 181, 182, 206, 207
- kosher 101
Judas 19, 20, 38, 48, 93, 95, 127
justice, judgement 12, 21, 35, 37, 107, 108, 109, 110, 114, 116, 117, 118, 120, 131, 132, 135, 137, 138, 139, 141, 142, 150, 152, 155, 178, 183, 184, 189, 199
- judges 71, 107–21, 141
- judicial 116, 117, 127, 133, 135, 140, 141
- jurisdiction 34, 115, 118, 131, 132, 138, 140, 183, 187

king, kingdom, kingship 35, 36, 51, 80, 108, 114, 125, 128, 153, 156, 157, 132, 149, 150, 161, 163, 182, 184, 185, 188, 192, 208

land 11, 64, 68, 76, 85, 86, 91, 128, 130, 139, 178, 186, 187, 188, 200
law 24, 34, 47, 56, 58, 59, 67, 68, 77, 78, 100, 103, 104, 111, 112, 119, 131, 137, 138, 140, 180
leaders, leadership 12, 19, 22, 34, 35, 37, 39, 40, 42, 65, 93, 94, 95, 96, 98, 103, 105, 107, 109, 113, 117, 118, 119, 120, 133, 136, 151, 159, 202, 207, 208
letters 59, 133
light 35, 125, 126, 173, 180, 186, 195, 209

Lord 9, 10, 12, 16, 17, 18, 19–20, 21, 25–6, 28, 32, 37, 38, 39, 40. 41, 56, 57, 58, 59, 60, 62, 65, 66, 68, 69, 80, 82, 84, 91, 96, 97, 100, 103, 114, 115, 116, 117, 118, 119, 129, 137, 141, 145, 148, 149, 150, 152, 153, 155, 156, 157, 158, 159, 168, 169, 170, 171, 172, 174, 179, 180, 183, 184, 185, 197, 198, 202, 204
love 32, 33, 37, 48, 49, 68, 72, 127
loyalty 49, 57, 134, 150, 198
Luke 4, 8–9, 10–11, 12, 13, 15–16, 19–20, 22–24, 25–7, 29, 31–42, 46–7, 48, 49–51, 54–7, 59–60, 61, 62, 64, 65, 67, 68, 73, 75,-6, 77, 78–9, 82–3, 86–7, 91–4, 97, 99, 101, 104, 107, 108–10, 111, 112, 114–21, 124, 125–9, 132, 133, 134–6, 137, 139, 140–1, 145–61, 162–73, 177–82, 191–209
 - Lukewise 10, 13, 31–42, 191
Lydia 97, 199, 208
Lystra 9, 26, 50, 51, 53, 93, 180, 188

Macedonia 12, 24, 86, 97–8
magistrates 13, 131, 132, 133, 137–8, 142
martyr 85, 171, 183, 206, 207
Mary 145, 185, 207
Matthias 12, 93–4, 95, 98
meals 37, 40, 41, 42, 66, 69, 91, 100, 134
men, masculinity 7, 35, 51, 53, 59, 71, 73, 94, 100, 103, 124, 138, 162, 163, 187, 191, 194, 198, 205, 206, 207, 208
Messiah, messianic 8, 9, 10, 12, 20, 21, 27, 28, 35, 56, 57, 61, 62, 66, 68, 87, 109, 111, 120, 125, 126, 138, 141, 147, 148, 149, 152, 154, 155, 156, 159, 169, 170, 172, 173, 179, 182, 185, 186, 187, 196, 204
mind 32, 38, 72, 97, 100, 105, 135, 195, 196, 207
ministry 9, 20, 21, 23, 24, 25, 26, 39, 42, 49, 77, 84, 86, 93, 102, 114, 125, 128, 151, 159, 180, 184, 185, 186, 187, 192, 196, 202, 203, 208
miracle 21, 35, 85, 97, 163
 See 'signs and wonders'
mission 4, 8–10, 12–13, 16, 21, 22–6, 77, 83, 85–6, 92, 93, 97, 98, 102, 114, 116, 123–42, 159, 180, 181, 185, 187, 197
money See 'wealth'

monotheism 26, 27, 139, 157
Moses 32, 34, 78, 129, 135, 151, 167

name, names 11, 17, 19, 21, 22, 23, 25, 35, 38, 45–62, 96, 101, 104, 112, 136, 137, 138, 146–56, 157, 158, 159, 168, 170, 171–3, 174, 179, 184, 194, 196, 197, 202
narrative 4, 10, 12, 13, 15, 16, 20, 22, 32, 33, 34, 36, 37, 38, 39, 40, 42, 45, 46, 53, 78, 107, 109, 146, 147, 159, 161, 163, 164, 168, 171–3, 175, 191, 192–3, 204, 207
nations 86, 94, 125, 126, 129, 130, 158, 174, 196
nature 35, 67, 198

offerings 64, 77, 133, 150, 189
outsiders 33, 47, 57, 59, 60, 69, 99, 206
ownership 11, 64, 65, 67, 69, 72, 73, 184

pagan 13, 20, 21, 26, 27, 32, 82, 94, 100, 108, 114, 177, 180, 183, 187, 188, 199, 200
parable 37, 57, 117, 129, 141, 179, 193, 208
parousia 62, 65, 183
Paul, Pauline 4, 8, 9, 10, 11, 12–13, 16, 18, 19, 20–61, 24, 25–6, 31, 35, 39–40, 41–2, 50, 51–6, 57, 59, 60–1, 64, 65, 73, 75–6, 77, 82, 84, 85–6, 87, 92–3, 94, 96, 97–8, 102–5, 107–21, 125, 129, 132, 134, 136, 137, 138, 139–41, 142, 152, 153, 154, 155, 157, 159, 161, 173, 174, 180, 186, 188–9, 192, 194, 198, 200, 201–4, 206–7, 208
 See 'Saul'
peace 84, 115, 117, 131, 139, 140, 179, 180, 197
Pentecost 13, 22, 23, 56, 68, 76, 84, 85, 91, 94, 95, 98, 99, 101, 152, 153, 155, 158, 159, 166, 168, 169, 183, 186, 192, 195–8, 202, 203, 208
persecution 9, 51, 99, 101, 128, 172, 204, 208
Peter 9, 12, 13, 16, 20, 21–3, 24–5, 28, 38, 61, 64, 69, 70, 76, 77, 93, 94, 97, 98, 99–101, 103, 105, 126, 129, 134, 135, 136–7, 142, 149, 150, 151, 152, 153, 154, 155, 157, 158, 159, 162, 166, 168,

169, 170, 172, 178, 179, 180, 191, 192, 195, 196, 197, 201–4, 208
Pharisees 21, 37, 49, 57, 104, 115, 193, 196
Philip 23, 85, 99, 129, 153, 155, 159, 172, 202, 203, 208
Philippi 12, 13, 26, 56, 98, 131, 132, 133, 134, 137–8, 142, 154, 173, 194, 195, 198, 208
Phrygia 50, 102
physical 13, 73, 92, 146, 147, 165, 166, 191, 192, 193, 194, 201, 204–5
politics 12, 22, 34, 52, 110, 112, 117, 120, 123, 124, 130, 133–4, 139
Pontius Pilate 34, 107, 108–10, 117, 119, 120
poor, poverty 6, 63, 64, 65, 68, 71, 72, 73, 91, 175, 194, 209
power, empowerment (divine) 20, 21, 23, 66, 69, 70, 85, 114, 123–42, 147, 152, 153–4, 155, 161, 167, 168, 169, 173, 174, 178, 180, 183, 184, 185, 186, 187, 196, 197, 199, 201, 202, 203, 204, 205, 206, 208, 209
powers 12, 32, 116, 123–42
praise 22, 23, 41, 156, 205, 207
prayer 9, 11, 18, 20, 22, 23, 35, 38, 40, 41, 42, 50, 53, 66, 68, 75, 76, 77, 79, 80, 82, 84, 85, 86, 87, 90, 93, 94, 95, 96, 98, 99, 100, 104, 112, 134, 148, 149, 153, 157, 158, 171, 174, 178, 180, 184, 187, 196
preaching 17, 20, 21, 24, 26, 77, 82, 84, 96, 97, 137, 159
priests 35, 36, 83, 95, 108, 109, 115, 133, 139
prison 35, 36, 38, 77, 97, 109, 116, 117, 118, 120, 137, 138, 141, 198, 204
proconsul 25, 102, 107, 110, 111, 112, 113, 114, 118, 120, 132, 155
procurator 115, 117, 120, 130, 139, 140
promise 12, 20, 21, 24, 35, 38, 60, 68, 76, 84, 94, 101, 114, 118, 126, 134–6, 145, 151, 167, 168, 169, 183, 186, 197, 203, 204, 207
property 9, 64, 67, 68, 69, 70, 72
prophet, prophecy 19, 20, 21, 24, 31, 34, 49, 53, 57, 60, 68, 78, 96, 97, 129, 135, 146, 151, 152, 153, 179, 182, 187, 196, 208

Qumran 11, 52, 58, 59, 60, 69, 70, 71, 72, 80, 92
See 'Essenes'

redemption 55, 175
religion 12, 33, 52, 57, 73, 133–4, 148, 194, 199, 200
repentance 35, 101, 116, 121, 128, 141, 151, 170, 171, 179, 195, 196, 197, 199, 200, 201, 206
See 'turning'
restoration 21, 60, 62, 87, 94, 103, 125, 126, 128, 129, 145, 167, 168, 170, 183, 192, 193, 198
resurrection 19, 20, 21, 26, 38, 42, 49, 50, 51, 57, 60, 61, 66, 68, 86, 87, 94, 103, 104, 109, 120, 125, 139, 140, 142, 146, 147, 148, 149, 151, 152, 153, 161, 165, 166, 181, 182, 186, 187, 188, 189, 194
revelation 77, 199
righteousness 49, 116, 128, 141, 150
ritual 77, 103, 154
Rome 8, 12, 19, 86, 107–121, 127, 129, 130
rule, rulers 3, 7–8, 39, 69, 108, 110, 113, 126, 136, 142, 148, 149, 150, 156, 161, 167, 168, 171, 174, 175, 177, 178, 192, 199

sacred 3, 11, 19, 82, 83, 86, 87, 128
sacrifice 35, 36, 76, 77, 83, 84, 87, 133, 139, 150, 188, 189, 200
salvation, saviour 7, 13, 19, 24, 26, 35, 41, 55, 56, 59, 84, 87, 91, 101, 119, 125, 137, 146, 147, 149, 150, 151, 152, 153, 158, 184, 194, 195, 196, 197, 198, 199, 201
Samaria, Samaritans 8, 23, 25, 54, 85, 99, 128, 197
Sanhedrin 12, 22, 23, 38, 94–5, 104, 115, 126, 132, 133, 134, 135, 136–7, 148, 149, 153, 154, 169, 170, 187, 192
Satan 177, 179, 185, 199
Saul 9, 12, 13, 17, 19, 24, 26, 28, 50, 57, 59, 85, 86, 93, 96, 98, 102, 128, 129, 133, 147, 149, 153, 155, 158, 159, 161, 171, 172, 180, 184
See 'Paul'
Scripture 3–8, 19–20, 21–2, 25–7, 34, 35, 38, 49, 68, 91, 94, 95, 98, 102, 103,

104–5, 108, 126, 133, 140, 150, 151, 153, 158, 166, 171, 172, 174, 183, 198
  See 'words'
seeing 5, 6, 13, 17, 38, 80, 83, 84, 113, 162, 164, 173, 178, 191–209
sending 17, 21, 23, 42, 81, 93, 96, 97, 99, 100, 101–2, 103, 104, 115, 116, 125, 128, 129, 138, 141, 151, 158, 159, 169, 183, 185
  See 'mission'
Seneca 67, 68, 72, 114
Sergius Paulus 25, 102, 132, 155
servants 25, 33, 61, 99, 110, 114, 120, 121, 125, 129, 150, 159, 175
  See 'slave'
sexual behaviour 116, 141, 192, 206
sharing 9, 11, 40, 41, 42, 63, 64, 65, 70, 71, 72, 73, 91, 92, 208
signs and wonders 9, 23, 25, 40, 41, 90, 92, 127, 147, 152, 168, 178, 184, 202, 203, 205
Silas 12, 26, 48, 56, 93, 97, 98, 137, 138, 194, 198
Simon 36, 37, 79, 80, 157, 196, 199
  See 'Peter'
sin 35, 36, 77, 83, 142, 151, 153, 179, 198, 199, 201
slave 22, 137, 138, 154, 173
  See 'servants'
soldiers 36, 99, 131
Solomon 77, 78, 79, 80, 81, 91, 205
son 28, 35, 80, 109, 129, 146, 151, 161, 167, 175, 178, 185
Son of Man 61, 85, 146, 148, 157, 167, 171, 182, 183, 187
space 13, 87, 91, 128, 163, 165, 166, 178–81, 185–7
speech, speeches 10, 11, 12, 13, 16, 19, 20–2, 23, 25, 26, 31, 33, 35, 39–40, 42, 75, 77, 81, 82, 98, 100, 101, 103, 115, 118, 126, 135, 136, 138, 139, 140, 146, 147, 149, 150, 151, 152, 155, 158, 161, 166, 168, 169–71, 180, 185, 186, 187–9, 191, 192, 195, 200, 201, 203, 204
Spirit, Holy Spirit 7, 8, 9, 10, 12, 13, 17, 18, 20, 22, 23, 24, 26, 28, 33, 37, 38, 42, 68, 76, 83, 85, 86, 87, 93, 94, 95, 96, 97, 98, 99, 100, 101, 102, 103, 104, 125, 126, 127, 128, 129, 134, 135, 136, 137, 149, 154, 155, 157, 159, 168, 169, 171, 173, 174, 177, 183, 184, 185, 186, 187, 192, 194, 195, 196, 197, 201, 202–3, 204, 207, 208
spiritual 32, 47, 84, 199
Stephen 11, 36, 55, 75, 76, 77, 79, 80, 81, 82, 84, 85, 86, 95, 99, 127, 133, 135, 148, 149, 151, 153, 155, 158, 159, 169, 171, 174, 178, 179, 180, 183, 186, 187, 202, 203
stewardship 69
Stoics 20, 26, 188, 189
stoning 51, 102, 148, 149, 179, 183
story, storytelling 10, 15, 16, 19, 21, 22, 23, 24, 26, 27, 31–42, 48, 49, 55, 80, 84, 89, 93, 98, 99, 100, 101, 114, 115, 119, 120, 121, 129, 137, 138, 139, 142, 145, 147, 154, 161, 163, 164, 166, 172, 177, 180, 181, 182, 191, 192, 197, 198, 205, 206, 208
  See 'narrative', 'speeches'
suffering 9, 19, 34, 36, 39, 40, 49, 50, 51, 84, 93, 108, 125, 150, 153, 158, 159, 172, 175, 179, 180, 183, 184, 185, 203, 204, 206, 207, 208
synagogue 25, 37, 51, 59, 66, 71, 78, 95, 102, 111, 113, 127, 153, 155, 199, 202
Syria, Syrian 48, 50, 53, 96, 101, 102, 115, 117, 140, 182

Tarsus 9, 12, 85, 96, 102, 155, 159, 171, 172, 184
taxes 108, 130, 131, 178, 193
teaching, teach, teacher 4, 7, 16, 26, 32, 39, 40, 41, 42, 49, 50, 51, 58, 77, 78, 83, 90, 91, 92, 102, 134, 135, 145, 155, 156, 159, 174, 180, 192–3, 199, 200, 202, 203, 204
Temple (Jewish) 9, 11–12, 13, 22, 35–6, 40–1, 48, 64, 66, 67, 73, 75–87, 91–2, 95, 99, 101, 103, 114, 116, 128, 133, 140, 149, 154, 159, 169, 170, 177, 186, 187, 188, 193, 198, 200, 205
temples (pagan) 138–9
temptation 58, 82, 110, 185
tent 78, 79, 80, 81, 87, 103, 167, 198
Tertullus 39, 115, 116, 117, 118, 139, 140

testimony, witness, witnesses 7, 8, 9, 20, 21, 33, 41, 66, 78, 96, 98, 100, 101, 103, 105, 116, 121, 126, 127, 128, 129, 130, 138, 140, 141, 142, 148, 152–3, 154, 155
  See 'Scripture'
Theophilus 33, 42, 121
thief 35, 108, 109
throne 170, 179
Tiberius 34
time 7, 12, 21, 35, 46, 52, 64, 65, 68, 76, 91, 92, 93, 96, 103, 104, 115, 116, 125, 126, 135, 140, 153, 163, 166, 168, 170, 174, 179, 181, 183, 185, 186, 194, 202, 207
Titius Justus 112, 199
tomb 134, 187
tongues 23, 53, 100, 135, 169
Torah See 'law'
towns, town 39, 52, 73, 131, 132, 134
tradition 4, 32, 45, 46, 49, 54, 55, 114, 133, 164, 182, 191, 193, 194, 201, 204, 205, 207
transcendence 78, 80, 81, 82, 83, 84, 86, 87, 169
transfiguration 167, 182
transformation 9, 10, 12, 13, 38, 84, 96, 100, 101, 153, 177–89, 191, 194–201, 204, 209
travels, travelling 12, 24, 49, 50, 51, 61, 63, 92, 93, 100, 102, 129, 132, 157, 163, 167, 186, 203
trials, trial, tribunal 12, 21, 39, 40, 107–21, 130, 132, 134, 135, 136, 137, 138, 139, 140, 141, 153
trust 6, 9, 11, 37, 38, 56, 57, 69, 72, 98, 99, 102, 128, 149, 156, 207
truth 33, 41, 42, 107, 115, 120, 123, 124, 137, 138, 139, 141, 142, 163, 182
turning 25, 61, 98, 99, 107, 116, 121, 125, 141, 186
  See 'repentance'
twelve 25, 49, 51, 94, 95, 129, 154, 197, 202 See 'apostles'

unclean 85, 100, 140, 177, 186, 202, 206
unite 68, 204

universe 9, 13, 155, 156, 163, 164, 165, 166, 168, 170, 175, 177, 178, 179, 180, 181, 184, 185, 188
urban 91, 131

vindication 102, 110, 114, 138, 142, 152, 187, 194, 198
vision, visions 21, 23, 24, 77, 97, 98, 99, 100, 101, 148, 149, 162, 174, 178, 179, 182, 185, 187
voice, voices 3, 4, 8, 16, 19, 27, 50, 58, 94, 96, 98, 99, 105, 118, 145, 153, 156, 162, 166, 167, 185, 208
vow 92, 198

water 84, 186, 196, 203
Way (the) 11, 58–60
wealth, money 35, 37, 39, 40, 63, 69, 70, 71, 73, 91, 131, 193, 200, 207
white 120, 162, 167, 168, 183
widow, widows 37, 64, 65, 71, 72, 92, 95, 208
wife 73, 134
wilderness 52, 58, 202, 203
wisdom 94, 158
witness See 'testimony, witness, witnesses'
woman, women 6, 35, 28, 37, 38, 47, 53, 59, 84, 103, 109, 124, 133, 186, 187, 191, 194, 196, 205, 206, 207, 208
wonders See 'signs and wonders'
words (divine) 7, 16, 23, 25–6, 31, 33, 37, 95, 116, 119, 128, 127, 135, 141, 151, 154, 155, 162, 167–8, 169, 180, 185, 202, 204
  See 'Scripture'
work, working 9, 11, 23, 25, 26, 31, 38, 39, 40, 50, 59, 73, 83, 84, 86, 91, 93, 94, 95, 96, 101, 102, 126, 159, 173, 185, 195, 203
world 4, 5, 7, 11–13, 20, 24, 34, 35, 36, 39, 42, 49, 53, 54, 55, 61, 72, 77, 83, 85, 86, 87, 89, 107, 124, 125, 126, 128, 130, 133, 139, 142, 145, 149, 152, 156, 158, 159, 162, 163, 164, 165, 173, 178, 179–80, 183, 187, 188, 192, 194, 197, 206, 208
  See 'Graeco-Roman', 'earth'

worship 20, 24, 27, 41, 50, 83, 84, 85, 86, 87, 96, 99, 111, 112, 139, 140, 149, 157, 158, 168, 171, 174, 182, 187, 188, 189, 193, 199, 200, 205

writers, writings 33, 38, 50, 60, 68, 72, 86, 87, 157, 164, 165, 177, 193, 195, 204

YHWH 8, 9, 35, 52, 59, 68, 69, 80, 81, 82, 83, 136, 148, 150, 151, 152, 156, 157, 158, 168, 169, 170, 171, 172, 174, 175, 182, 196

Index of Names

Aarflot, Christine H. 8
Adams, Edward 53, 164
Adams, Sean A. 148
del Agua, Augustín 128
Aitkenhead, Decca 89
Alexander, T. Desmond 36, 46, 75, 186
Alexander, Loveday 15, 33, 115, 124, 140, 152, 191
Allen, Leslie C. 79
Alter, Robert 146, 147
Anderson, Kevin L. 145, 151, 152, 181

Ball, David M. 59
von Balthasar, Hans Urs 32
Bammel, Ernst 34, 204
Barreto, Eric D. 12, 206
Barrett, C. K. 17, 20, 46, 53, 54, 55, 58, 59, 65, 66, 76, 77, 78, 79, 80, 81, 86, 111, 112, 113, 115, 117, 121, 141, 146, 149, 151, 162, 163, 170, 180, 182, 183, 198, 201
Bartholomew, Craig G. 114, 129
Bartsch, Hans-Werner 164
Bauckham, Richard 9, 13, 27, 58, 60, 62, 66, 71, 94, 103, 104, 115, 126, 139, 156, 157, 158, 161, 170, 173, 174, 175, 198, 204
Bayer, Hans F. 170
Beale, G. K. 153
Beard, Mary 133
Beasley-Murray, George R. 132
Becking, Bob 60
Belle, Gilbert Van 207
Bennema, Cornelis 37, 134, 169, 203
Betz, Hans Dieter 154
Bieringer, Reimund 207
Biggar, Nigel 95
Biguzzi, Giancarlo 128
Bird, Michael F. 197
Blickenstaff, Marianne 206, 207
Bock, Darrell L. 135, 150, 153,, 207
Bockmuehl, Markus 47, 54, 179

Boismard, M.-É. 17
Bolt, Peter 127, 128
Bond, Helen K. 109, 110, 117, 120
Booth, Wayne C. 147
Bourquin, Yves 147, 154
Bovon, François 181
Branigan, Edward 33
Braund, David C. 130
Brawley, Robert L. 16, 17, 25, 108, 110, 124, 132, 149
Brent, Allen 32, 124
Brooke, George J. 58
Brown, Raymond E. 36, 76, 108, 186
Bruce, F. F. 54, 66, 76, 140, 146, 148
Bryan, Christopher 124
Buckwalter, Douglas 136, 169, 183, 184, 194
Bultmann, Rudolph 6, 163, 164
Burke, Sean D. 206
Burridge, Richard A. 16, 17
Burton, G. P. 132
Busch, Eberhard 6
Buswell, Geoffrey 34, 62, 145, 167, 184, 199
Buzzard, Anthony 126

Cadbury, Henry J. 45, 61
Calvin, John 84
Capper, Brian J. 63, 64, 65, 66, 69, 70, 71, 72
Carroll John T. 126
Carson, D. A. 132, 153
Carter, Tim 196
Carter, Warren 110, 124, 196
Casey, Maurice 61
Cassidy, Richard J. 110, 111, 112, 113, 116, 117, 118, 119, 121, 124, 141
Chance, J. Bradley 80, 83
Chen, Diane G. 181
Cheng, Ling 8, 16, 160
Churchill, Timothy W. R. 24, 172

Clark, Andrew C. 192
Clarke, Andrew D. 17, 19, 39, 46, 67, 93, 118, 153, 191, 196
Collins, John J. 60, 61
Conzelmann, Hans 13, 34, 62, 76, 128, 145, 146, 147, 152, 159, 167, 170, 14, 199
Cosgrove, Charles H. 19, 170
Cotter, Wendy 112
Cunningham, Scott 204

Dahl, Nils Alstrup 16, 47
D'Angelo, Mary Rose 206, 207
Danker, Frederick W. 193
Davies, Douglas 68
Davila, James 58, 66
Dibelius, Martin 82, 192, 200
Dicken, Frank 37, 166
Dodd, C. H. 104, 105
Downs, David D. 64
Dunn, James D. G. 82, 128, 148, 163, 164, 166, 184, 185, 197, 202
Dupont, Jacques 47, 61, 162
Dyas, Dee 85

Ellington, Scott A. 203
Ellis, E. E. 92
Esterline, David 124, 132, 149
Estrada, Nelson P. 127, 128

Farrow, Douglas 161, 181
Fee, Gordon D. 5, 87
Ferguson, Sinclair B. 31
Fishwick, Duncan 133
Fitzmyer, Joseph A. 20, 45, 47, 49, 50, 54, 55, 58, 59, 76, 111, 113, 116, 135, 140, 150, 166, 181, 186
Flessen, Bonnie J. 206
Fletcher-Louis, Crispin H. T. 84
Fornberg, Tord 63
Fowl, Stephen E. 3
France, R. T. 4
Franklin, Eric 80, 84, 121, 146, 157, 181, 182
Frizell, Sam 89
Fuller, Michael E. 62, 103
Fuller Reginald H. 164

Gaebelein, Frank E. 22
Garland, Robert 138, 200

Garrett, Susan R. 185
Gärtner, Bertil 80, 82
Gasque, W. W. 15
Gathercole, Simon J. 36, 46, 75, 186
Gaventa, Beverley R. 16, 24, 117, 118, 119, 120, 141, 159, 173, 184, 207, 208
Gempf, Conrad H. 20, 39, 82, 93, 130, 131, 199, 200, 201
Giles, Kevin N. 45, 53, 54, 55
Gill, David W. J. 93, 111, 115, 117, 130, 131, 139
Goldingay, John 61, 184
Goodblatt, David 66
Gooding, David W. 163
Gorman, Michael J. 5, 6, 159
Green, Joel B. 3, 6, 7, 15, 108, 109, 136, 155, 170, 186, 187, 191, 194
Gregson, Fiona J. Robertson 11, 41, 92, 208
Grudem, Wayne A. 97
Guthrie, Donald 157

Haenchen, Ernst 23, 76, 78, 113, 114, 117, 126, 127, 137, 152, 158, 166, 181, 200
Hardin, Justin K. 188
Harris, Murray J. 54
Harrison, Everett F. 64
Hart, H. StJ. 34
Hartman, Lars 63, 154, 184, 196
Harvey, A. E. 107
Hastings, James 22
Hawthorne, Gerald F. 82
Haya-Prats, Gonzalo 203
Hays, Richard B. 157, 158, 168, 174, 202
Head, Peter M. 17, 46, 67, 69, 75, 93
Heath, Thomas 165
Heitmüller, Wilhelm 154
Hellholm, David 63
Hemer, Colin J. 131, 199
Hengel, Martin 47
Hill, Craig C. 80, 81
Hills, Julian V. 67
Holtzmann, J. J. 64
Horbury, William 47, 53, 55, 62, 76, 80
Horsley, Richard A. 52
van der Horst, Pieter Willem 60
Houlden, Leslie 179
Hultgren, Arland J. 146
Humphreys, W. Lee 16

Hurtado, Larry W. 8, 9, 50, 148, 158, 171, 174, 182

Instone-Brewer, David 67, 93

Jackson, F. J. Foakes 45
Jacobs, Alan 8
Jeremias, Joachim 41, 71, 72, 73, 99, 151
Jervell, Jacob 16, 17, 20, 21, 24, 26, 47, 76, 84, 121, 187
Jewett, Robert 36
Jipp, Joshua, W. 4
Johnson, Andy 183
Johnson, D. E. 125, 127
Johnson, Luke T. 19, 20, 78, 108, 109, 114, 116, 117, 119, 140, 141, 145, 148, 183, 185, 203
Jones, A. H. M. 130
Jones, David L. 151
Judge, E. A. 115
Juel, Donald H. 16, 76, 152

Käsemann, Ernst 46
Keathley, Naymond H. 63
Keck, Leander E. 31, 145, 200
Keener, Craig S. 158, 199
Keith, Chris 154, 173
Kilgallen, John J. 78, 79, 80
Klijn, A. F. J. 80
van Kooten, George H. 52, 53
Koperski, Veronica 207
Kraabel, A. Thomas 176, 152
Krodel, Gerhard 64, 65, 151
Kümmel, W. G. 194, 200

Lacey, W. K. 130
Lake, K. 45
Lawrence, Louise J. 63, 68
Lee, Jae Won 124, 132, 149
Lennartsson, Gören 62
Levine, Amy-Jill 206, 207
Levinsohn, Stephen H. 181
Lewis, D. M. 47
Lichtenberger, Hermann 114, 163
Limburg, James 76, 152
Lincoln, Andrew T. 107
Lindemann, Andreas 67
Lintott, Andrew 130
Lohfink, Gerhard 181

Longenecker, Richard N. 22, 103, 109
Lucas, Ernest 61
Lüdemann, Gerd 4
Lyman, Eric J. 90

Macro, Anthony D. 130, 132
Maddox, Robert 8, 15
Malbon, Elizabeth S. 147
Malherbe, Abraham J. 67
Malina, Bruce J. 197
Mallen, Peter 26, 42, 60, 125, 128, 193
Marcus, Joel 161
Marguerat, Daniel 16, 19, 147, 152, 154
Marshall, I. Howard 19, 40, 41, 56, 81, 86, 87, 127, 134, 149, 150, 153, 163, 169, 179, 185, 186, 191, 194, 202, 203
Martin, Ralph P. 15, 82, 115
Martyn, J. L. 31, 145, 200
Matthews, Shelly 207
Mattill, Andrew B., Jr. 15
Mattill, M. B. 15
McConville, Gordon 80
McDonough, Sean M. 164
McGee, Daniel B. 63
McKelvey, R. J. 85, 87
McKnight, Scot 15
Meek, James A. 198
Meeks, Wayne A. 52
Menken, Maarten J. J. 193
Menzies, Robert P. 126, 185, 197, 202, 203
Metzger, Bruce M. 17, 54, 79, 108, 109, 113, 149, 162, 182, 186, 202
Millar, Fergus 130, 131, 132
Miller, John B. F. 96, 97, 162
Mills, W. E. 15
Minear, Paul S. 45
Moberly, Walter 108
Moore, Thomas S. 125
Morris, Leon 15, 18
Mosendz, Polly 89
Moule, C. F. D. 27, 34, 47, 113, 145, 146, 148, 149, 171, 183
Moyise, Steve 193
Murphy-O'Conner, Jerome 110

Nave, Guy D. 195
Newbigin, Lesslie 127
Nolland, John 26, 127, 179, 186, 194
North, John A. 133

Oakes, Peter 12, 112, 130, 133, 134, 149, 187
Ogden, Schubert M. 6
O'Neill, J. C. 171
O'Reilly, Leo 202
Osborne, Grant R. 15
O'Toole, Robert F. 146, 181, 201

Packer, J. I. 31
Padilla, Osvaldo 39
Pahl, Michael W. 148
Pao, David W. 125, 185
Park, Hyung Dae 70
Parsons, Mikeal C. 15, 146, 181, 193, 204, 205
Pelikan, Jaroslav 8
Penner, Todd 15, 206
Pennington, Jonathan T. 164, 165
Pervo, Richard I. 15, 33, 54, 158
Pesch, Rudolph 23, 111, 200
Peterson, David 19, 77, 81, 127, 153, 194
Phillips, Thomas E. 63, 152, 191
Pietersen, Lloyd K. 152, 191
Pinnick, Avital 66
Pite, Sheila 42
Porter, Stanley E. 23, 93, 130
Powell, Mark Allan 37, 108, 147
Praeder, Susan M. 192, 201
Price, Simon R. F. 133

Rabens, Volker 134, 169, 203
Rajak, Tessa 111
Ramsay, William M. 110
Rapske, Brian M. 114, 115, 116, 117, 139, 140, 141, 204
Ravens, David 62
Read-Heimerdinger, Jenny 17, 46, 113, 148
Reicke, Bo 146
Reid, Daniel G. 82
Reynolds, Joyce 130, 131
Rhoads, David 124, 132, 149
Riesner, Rainer 71
Rius-Camps, Josep 17, 46, 113, 148
Robb, Julie E. 151
Romm, James S. 130
Rowdon, Harold H. 147
Rowe, C. Kavin 124, 146, 149, 150, 200, 201
Rowland, Christopher 179

Sachs, A. 164
Safrai, Ze'ev 72
Sanders, E. P. 82, 197
Sanders, Jack T. 110, 136, 198
Sandmel, Samuel 58
Scharlemann, Martin H. 80
Scharper, Philip J. 124
Schnabel, Eckhard J. 59, 72, 111, 126, 129, 148, 166, 188
Schneider, Gerhard 116, 141
Schürer, Emil 130, 132
Schwartz, Daniel R. 65, 66
Scott, James M. 62, 94, 126, 167, 170
Scullion, John J. 172
Seccombe, David P. 54, 55, 71
Segal, Alan F. 148
Seim, Turid Karlsen 207
Shelton, Jo-Ann 130
Sherwin-White, A. N. 109, 111, 116, 140
Silk, Michael S. 165
Simon, Marcel 78, 79, 80
Skinner, Matthew L. 12, 116, 130, 136, 141, 204, 206
Sleeman, Matthew 128, 146, 160, 171
Snowden, Frank M. 205
Snyder, Jula A. 37, 67, 166
Soards, Marion L. 10, 82, 136, 192
Spencer, F. Scott 23, 152, 191
Squires, John T. 16, 19, 20, 153
Stein, Robert H. 136
van Stempvoort, A. 162, 181
Stenschke, Christoph W. 191, 194, 198, 199, 200
Stier, Rudolf 94
Strange, William A. 46
Strauss, David F. 163
Strelan, Rick 162, 168, 178, 181, 182
Strauss, Mark L. 87, 153
Stronstad, Roger 76
Stuart, Douglas K. 5, 87
Stuckenbruck, Loren 154, 173
Swidler, Leonard 207
Sylva, Dennis D. 78, 79, 80, 81

Tabb, Brian J. 51, 203, 204
Tabor, James D. 167
Taeger, Jens-Wilhelm 199, 201
Tajra, Harry W. 110, 111, 115, 116, 117, 121, 140, 141

Index of Names

Talbert, Charles H. 67
Tannehill Robert C. 4, 109, 113, 114, 117
Taylor, Justin 66, 67, 70
Taylor, Nicholas H. 86
Theissen, Gerd 63
Thiselton, Anthony, C. 6
Thomas, John Christopher 172
Thompson, Alan J. 46, 62, 204
Thompson, Marianne Meye 16, 18
Thompson, Michael B. 47, 54
Thompson, Richard P. 45
Thornton, T. C. G. 81
van der Toorn 60
Torrance, Thomas F. 181, 183
Towey, Anthony 32
Trebilco, Paul R. 45, 47, 48, 49, 50, 52, 53, 54, 56, 57, 58, 59, 60, 61, 131
Treier, Daniel J. 3, 114, 129
Trites, Allison A. 107, 126, 127, 128
Turner, C. H. 22
Turner, Harold, W. 11, 78, 83
Turner, Max 9, 84, 85, 125, 126, 134, 153, 155, 157, 167, 169, 170, 183, 184, 185, 192, 197, 198, 202, 203
Twelftree, Graham H. 45, 132, 133, 201, 202
Tyson, Joseph B. 198

VanderStichele, Caroline 206
Vanhoozer, Kevin J. 8, 114, 129
Verheyden, J. 19, 84, 86, 128, 207
Vermes, Geza 130, 132
Vielhauer, Philip 31, 200
Vincent, John J. 194
Volf, Miroslav 196

Walaskay, Paul W. 109
Walker, Peter W. L. 80, 82
Wallace, Daniel B. 23, 25, 56, 57, 77, 113

Walton, Steve 12, 15, 19, 24, 16, 37, 39, 40, 46, 48, 54, 67, 73, 84, 85, 86, 91, 92, 93, 107, 112, 114, 120, 121, 129, 130, 132, 134, 139, 149, 152, 154, 166, 169, 172, 173, 174, 175, 186, 187, 191, 192, 201, 203, 204, 206, 208
Ward, W. R. 47
Weatherly, Jon A. 110, 136, 195
Weinert, Francis D. 78, 79, 80
Weinrich, William C. 46
Weiser, Artur 79
Wendel, Ulrich 37, 72
Wenham, David 40, 85
Wenk, Matthias 203
Wilcox, Max 66
Williams, P. J. 67, 93
Wilson, Brittany E. 193, 206, 207
Wilson, B. W. J. G. 130
Wilson, R. McL. 76, 113, 152
Wilson, S. G. 112
Winter, Bruce W. 17, 19, 39, 46, 67, 93, 101, 110, 111, 112, 113, 115, 118, 119, 132, 133, 138, 139, 140, 153, 188, 191, 200
Wire, Antoinette Clark 16
Witherington, Ben, III 15, 26, 78, 79, 80, 81, 103, 115, 194, 198
Witherup, Ronald D., SS 99
Wright, David F. 31
Wright, N. T. 69, 114, 129, 149, 161, 183
Wynn, Kerry H. 77

Yamazaki-Ransom, Kazuhiko 124
York, John O. 193, 194

Ziesler, John A. 84, 147, 184
Zwiep, A. W. 181

www.ingramcontent.com/pod-product-compliance
Lightning Source LLC
Chambersburg PA
CBHW062122300426
44115CB00012BA/1777